Praise for *Evocative Coaching*

"Brilliantly illuminates the precious space that can exist between a teacher and a coach. As is clearly delineated in *Evocative Coaching*, that remarkable space holds the power to truly transform schools, one person and one relationship at a time."

—**Jim Loehr**, Ed.D.,
best-selling author and co-founder,
Human Performance Institute

"This practical and sophisticated book is worth reading. *Evocative Coaching* regards teachers as wanting to learn and coaching as skillfully getting out of the way of learning. To enhance trust, liberate creativity, and build autonomy, coaches choreograph story, empathy, inquiry, and design, providing value to any professional learning community."

—**Arthur L. Costa**, Ed. D. and **Robert J. Garmston**,
Ed. D., Professors Emeriti, California State University,
Sacramento and co-authors of *Cognitive Coaching*

"Coaching is as much about the heart as about the head. *Evocative Coaching* brings together head and heart in ways that unleash the transformational potential of coaching in schools. It makes an extremely valuable contribution to the field."

—**Jim Knight**, author,
Instructional Coaching

"I have long subscribed to the belief that there is no such thing as teaching, only learning. *Evocative Coaching* turns that belief into a way of working with teachers that inspires their cooperation and engagement in the process of performance improvement. *Evocative Coaching* is horse sense for teachers, to paraphrase my recent book title, and it promises to make a real difference in the schools and school leaders who put its principles into practice."

—**Monty Roberts**, author of
The Man Who Listens to Horses,
www.MontyRoberts.com

"Do you care deeply about empowering teachers, schools, and students to enjoy and benefit from the light of learning? *Evocative Coaching* provides a wise, practical, and content-rich guide for those of us who believe in the necessity-and the dream-of a future enlivened by successful education. I encourage you to get it, use it, and share it with others; it will make a huge difference!"

—**Marilee Adams**, Ph.D., author of,
Change Your Questions, Change Your Life,
adjunct professor, American University,
School of Public Affairs

"*Evocative Coaching* makes a gift to our schools and the administrators, faculty, and staff. The authors' diverse experiences and gifts combine to present a clear and coherent model and process for transforming schools. Their model will serve in many other relationships and situations as well. It really is about transformation 'one conversation at a time.'"

—**Ralph Kelly** and **Jane Magruder Watkins**,
authors of *Appreciative Inquiry: Change at the Speed of the Imagination*, www.AppreciativeInquiryUnlimited.com

"*Evocative Coaching* is a lovely and ambitious volume that offers a far-reaching synthesis of leading edge thinking when it comes to coaching in schools. Teachers, school counselors, and administrators will find both inspiration and practical tools for creating bold new conversations of discovery and learning. Read this!"

—**Doug Silsbee,** author,
The Mindful Coach and *Presence-Based Coaching*

Evocative Coaching is a generous gift for all of us who work to support teachers to do the vitally important job of teaching, in the most skillful and enriching way possible. As well as providing a thorough and well-documented compendium of coaching practices, *Evocative Coaching* presents a unique blend of two proven practices—Nonviolent Communication and Appreciative Inquiry—along with some new moves that clearly demonstrate how to engage teachers in a positive, effective, no-fault approach to continual growth and improvement.

—**Sura Hart**, certified trainer with the
International Center for Nonviolent Communication,
co-author of *The No-Fault Classroom*, *The Compassionate Classroom*,
and *Respectful Parents, Respectful Kids*

"*Evocative Coaching* is the best book about how to assist individuals through coaching that I have ever read. A realistic and easy to use process that everyone can learn and use."

—**Cynthia Lemmerman**, Ed.D.,
Ohio Department of Education,
Associate Superintendent for School Improvement

EVOCATIVE COACHING

EVOCATIVE COACHING

Transforming Schools One Conversation at a Time

Bob and Megan
Tschannen-Moran

JOSSEY-BASS
A Wiley Imprint
www.josseybass.com

Published by Jossey-Bass
A Wiley Imprint
989 Market Street, San Francisco, CA 94103-1741—www.josseybass.com

Jossey-Bass books and products are available through most bookstores. To contact Jossey-Bass directly call our
Customer Care Department within the U.S. at 800-956-7739, outside the U.S. at 317-572-3986, or
fax 317-572-4002.

Jossey-Bass also publishes its books in a variety of electronic formats. Some content that appears in print may
not be available in electronic books.

Library of Congress Cataloging-in-Publication Data

Tschannen-Moran, Bob.
 Evocative coaching : transforming schools one conversation at a time / Bob & Megan Tschannen-Moran.
  p. cm.
 Includes bibliographical references and index.
 ISBN 978-0-470-54759-5 (pbk.)
 1. Teachers—In-service training. 2. Communication in education. 3. School improvement programs.
I. Tschannen-Moran, Megan, 1956- II. Title.
 LB1731.T73 2010
 370.71'55—dc22

                                                                           2010003900

Printed in the United States of America

FIRST EDITION
PB Printing 10 9 8 7 6 5 4 3 2

CONTENTS

LIST OF FIGURES AND TABLES

Figures

Tables

For Margaret Moore and Wellcoaches

Your support and collaboration have meant so much to me in developing my ideas and approach.

Thanks for giving me the opportunity to play with you, and for stretching me to be my very best self.
— Bob Tschannen-Moran

For Wayne Hoy and Anita Woolfolk Hoy

Here is how I've invested the conceptual capital that you invested in me. It continues to appreciate through "the miracle of compound interest"!

I will always be grateful for your invitation to explore the world of Big Ideas and the simple yet profound notion that there is nothing so practical as a good theory.
— Megan Tschannen-Moran

GRATITUDES

This book, perhaps like most books, has taken on a life of its own. In the final month of writing, there were so many serendipities and surprises, so many discoveries and developments, that we came to speak of it as "the book that wanted to be written" and "the book that was writing itself." It felt like we were working an enormous jigsaw puzzle. As one thing fell into place, something else had to move or be created. Just when we thought we had it all figured out, a new book, resource, or conversation would come along that would give us new ideas on how or where to put something better. It was a classic case of design thinking: inspiration, ideation, and implementation. And it could not have been more stimulating. Ideas were bursting in such rapid succession that we could hardly keep up with them ourselves. So we start by expressing gratitude for the creative process itself and for the encouragement of our editor at Jossey-Bass, Kate Gagnon. The entire Jossey-Bass team, including our copyeditor, Pam Suwinsky—whose work launched a whole new round of helpful and significant revisions—our production editor, Justin Frahm, and our editorial assistants, Julia Parmer, and Tracy Gallagher, were a delight to work with.

We also express gratitude for what the process of writing this book has taught us about coaching, adult learning, and growth-fostering relationships. As professionals, we both coach individuals and teach classes that have benefited and are benefiting greatly from the insights and understandings that have emerged through the process of writing this book. You, the reader, will be introduced to those concepts, as best we were able to articulate them, through the words, quotes, and pictures on these pages. For us, however, it was the process of writing and completing the book that taught us so much. Having written it, we are better coaches and teachers today.

There is such a wide range of factors that made this book what it is today that it is hard to know where to start. We each, of course, have formal background and training in our respective disciplines with mentors and teachers along the way. Both of us have been changed profoundly, however, both in our practice and in our understanding, by the exposure and training we have received in appreciative inquiry (http://appreciativeinquiry.case.edu) and Nonviolent Communication (NVC; www.cnvc.org). These two disciplines, as you will learn, are integral parts of evocative coaching. We thank David Cooperrider and Marshall Rosenberg, who launched the disciplines of appreciative inquiry and Nonviolent Communication many decades ago, for introducing them into the world. We thank Jane Magruder Watkins and Ralph Kelley for teaching us appreciative inquiry and a cadre of certified NVC trainers, including Robert Gonzales, Sura Hart, Gregg Kendrick, Wes Taylor, and Jeff Brown, for teaching us Nonviolent Communication.

We have, however, been taught by our students perhaps more than by any of our trainers. There may be nothing more practical than a good theory, but there is nothing like having the opportunity to teach a good theory to people who really want to learn. That has been our experience with our students in the Wellcoaches training program and in the educational leadership program at the College of William & Mary. We thank them for the continuing ways in which they call us into greatness. In so many ways, they have become our teachers. We especially express our gratitude to the graduates of the William & Mary Educational Leadership program who contributed their stories to this book. Without their stories of coaching in schools, the principles of evocative coaching would not have been developed as fully and would not have come alive on the pages of this book.

We feel deep gratitude for the work of our colleagues and friends, Erika Jackson, Christina Lombardo Ray, Kate Kriynovich, Cynthia Lemmerman, and Janet Chahrour, who reviewed an earlier draft of this book and offered helpful suggestions, questions, and comments that served to deepen and enrich our thinking and to improve the quality of the final product. Erika also collaborated with us in designing the evocative coaching training program. She has always been willing to give tirelessly and generously of her energy and ideas. We are grateful for who she is and what she does.

We would be remiss if we did not thank our immediate families for their indefatigable interest in and concern for how this book was coming along. Our children, Bryn Moran and Evan and Michelle Tschannen, have grown up to be great friends and thinking partners. Megan's sister, Maura Moran, has been steadfast in her support and in urging us over many years to get these ideas out into the world. Most of all, Bob's parents, Bob and June Tschannen, deserve special recognition for their boundless support throughout our lives and for their unfailing enthusiasm for this project. We would not be where we are today without them.

Finally, we express gratitude to each other. When we first told our colleagues and friends our aspiration of writing a book together, some looked askance at the thought of collaborating with a spouse or partner. "Are you sure your relationship can survive that?" was the underlying question. Our relationship not only survived, it thrived. We have worked together since the beginning of our courtship and marriage more than thirty-five years ago. Although we each have our own individual, professional pursuits, we enjoy greatly the opportunities we have to stimulate each other's thinking and energy around areas of mutual interest and concern. We love working together, and people tell us it shows. The book you hold in your hand is just one more expression of our shared interests in life and work. How can we be anything but grateful for that?

Bob and Megan Tschannen-Moran
www.EvocativeCoaching.com
July 2010

PREFACE

Individuals have within themselves vast resources for self-understanding and for altering their self-concepts, basic attitudes, and self-directed behavior; these resources can be tapped if a definable, growth-promoting climate can be provided.

—CARL ROGERS (1980, P. 115)

This book is written for students, but it is not about students. *Evocative Coaching* was born of a desire to see students everywhere learning in vibrant, life-giving environments. It is designed to assist teachers to reinvigorate their teaching practices so that students can flourish. When teachers and schools come alive, the work of student learning is sure to follow. This book is about creating relationships that foster and support the ongoing learning of the women and men who show up every day to share their curiosity, knowledge, and spirits with students. Teachers know all too well the pressure of the bottom line of student achievement and success; in this book we describe a method through which instructional leaders—coaches, mentors, peer coaches, department chairs, supervisors, and others—can assist teachers to more fully meet that bottom line, not by increasing the pressure on teachers but by increasing their trust, self-efficacy, motivation, appreciation, resourcefulness, and engagement.

When one educational leader heard the title of our book, she responded with instant enthusiasm. "I like the word *evocative*," she exclaimed. "I want to see if my people are willing to have 'evocative conversations,' to have different conversations than we are used to having. The word communicates that I want them to come up with stuff, to be active learners, to not just sit there and listen to me talk." Her response captured what we hope this book will accomplish: we hope it will infuse those responsible for the work of schools with energy and mutuality in the search for transformation. Old models of telling and selling teachers on how to do things better in their classrooms have not proven to be effective. New models are replacing the old. This book represents new-model wisdom and practice, combining our two areas of expertise in adult learning and educational leadership.

After graduating from Yale Divinity School in 1979, Bob served churches in the inner city of Chicago and in downtown Columbus, Ohio, before becoming a professional business and life coach in 1998. Since becoming a coach, he has participated in four coach training programs, worked with hundreds of individuals and organizations, and become an active member of the faculty of Wellcoaches Coach Training School. Wellcoaches graduates are health, fitness, and wellness professionals who assist people to master the challenges of health and well-being, including nutrition, weight management, exercise, life satisfaction, stress management, and medical conditions. The Wellcoaches model enables people to discover a better way to change and Bob has had a significant hand in developing the curriculum for teaching that model, recently published in book form as a *Coaching Psychology Manual* (Moore & Tschannen-Moran, 2010). We have learned that it is tough to get people to change when you are trying to change them. We have also learned that people can change themselves, often profoundly, when they are trusted and empowered to do so. *Evocative Coaching* promotes working with teachers in just that way.

Megan's work as a school leader began during the fourteen years we lived and worked in the inner city of Chicago. There she started and led a K–8 school for a multicultural and multiracial population of primarily low-income students. She did this on a shoestring budget with young teachers who were willing to work for very little money because they were inspired by the vision of "unleashing the power of education early in the lives of disadvantaged children." They also valued the quality of the relationships among the staff, students, parents, and community. In the face of oftentimes daunting challenges, two ingredients—self-efficacy and trust—made the difference between success and failure. When we moved to Columbus, Ohio, in 1993, Megan earned her doctorate at The Ohio State University and took on an active research agenda documenting the importance of those two ingredients for successful schools. She has published numerous scholarly articles on teacher self-efficacy and the role of trust in schools, as well as her book, *Trust Matters: Leadership for Successful Schools* (2004, Jossey-Bass).

Evocative Coaching represents a synergistic combining of our two careers. Increasingly, as school leaders have read *Trust Matters*, they have asked us to assist them in evaluating their culture of trust, to foster high-trust environments, and to repair trust once it has been broken. Our efforts in response to these requests have, in their own way, led to this book. We have seen how existing models of supervision, professional development, and accountability work against cultures of trust. We have seen how they demotivate rather than motivate change. And we have seen how those models interfere with the performance and joy of teachers. It has been heartbreaking to see so many well-intentioned people dig themselves into ever-deeper holes.

Many educators have attempted to diagnose what's wrong with current practice and to recommend solutions. Their efforts have not always met with success. Megan recently heard a well-known educational scholar speak about his attempts to bring about constructive change among a group of teachers he was working with. He was apparently encountering a great deal of resistance and was clearly frustrated. He suggested that if educators ever wanted to be considered professionals, they would need to begin to collaborate like professionals. "And that is not always nice," he asserted. "When doctors collaborate, they don't worry about being polite. Lives are at stake!" He then built on his medical analogy by saying, "The practice of medicine is not gentle. When doctors do open heart surgery, they slice open the chest wall and break the ribs in order to get to the heart." Megan began to see why he might be encountering resistance with the teachers he was working with. If the energy and analogy he had in mind was to break open ribs in order to repair defective hearts, teachers might well be wary of his efforts!

Fortunately there are ways to broker change that people warm up to and that we have had the privilege of facilitating through a combination of our one-on-one coaching and group work. By using the principles and practices described in this book, paying careful attention to the process we call "Story–Empathy–Inquiry–Design" (S-E-I-D), and working in evocative ways with individuals and their environments, we have had the privilege of sharing in the joy of discovery, the passion born of self-efficacy, the cultivation of trust, and the invigoration that comes from shifting energy and direction. We believe in the ability of schools and school leaders not only to do better but to fulfill their destiny as agents of transformation and citizenship in society. If this book makes a contribution to that fulfillment, if it helps coaches and principals to assist teachers to reignite their passion and to discover better means to serve their purposes, if it assists coaches and other instructional leaders to have more evocative conversations with both struggling and spectacular teachers, then we will have accomplished our goal.

The quality of the coaching relationship must come before all else. Ours is not a "tough love" approach to coaching. We do not push and prod teachers to change behavior, let alone shame them into changing, as though they are children who cannot be trusted. We begin with the premise that teachers are capable adults who can be trusted to figure out a great many things for themselves; we inspire teachers to change and we partner with them in the change process. "First things first" means that coaches put people before projects; if we fail to get the people part right, we may as well forget about the project. Once we get the people part right, we can work the project hard, and teachers often respond in ways that far exceed our expectations. Even teachers who have not shown life for many years can be reawakened to the joy of teaching. When teachers are entrusted with personal responsibility, deep thinking, self-discovery, and self-efficacy, they find better answers and create better possibilities than any that could be handed to them by others. Teacher-driven visions, plans, and behaviors are the ones that stick.

When we turn people into projects, we lose connection to their humanity.

We are not the first ones to recognize and work with the relational context of learning partnerships. Many others have gone before us, including Costa and Garmston (*Cognitive Coaching*, 2002), Knight (*Instructional Coaching*, 2007), Kise (*Differentiated Coaching*, 2006), Barkley (*Quality Teaching in a Culture of Coaching*, 2005), and Lipton and Wellman (*Mentoring Matters*, 2003). There is overlap between evocative coaching and these other systems, but differences emerge through our application of principles gleaned from positive psychology, appreciative inquiry, Nonviolent Communication, social cognitive theory, and design thinking. As Kurt Lewin famously said, "There is nothing so practical as a good theory." This book is chockfull of well-grounded, well-researched theories that support the work of coaching in schools. We believe that, with the help of these bodies of knowledge, our work evokes fresh insights and new approaches for improving schools one conversation at a time.

Although this book is written for instructional leaders tasked with improving the quality of teaching, *Evocative Coaching* is not about teacher evaluation. Evaluation is an important function, and schools need sound evaluation systems to fulfill their obligation to parents and taxpayers and ensure that teachers are performing adequately to warrant their continued employment. We appreciate the efforts of those who have worked to make those systems both fair and reliable in distinguishing between teachers who are meeting acceptable standards and those who are falling below those standards. We also know, however, that the action plans generated by evaluation processes often do not result in significant performance improvement. Teachers may be warned and written up, but that does not make them ready, willing, and able to change. Indeed, it can make them even more intransigent and resistant than before. Making evocative coaching an integral part of school communities can assist more teachers to do better more of the time. When evocative coaching comes into play, the bar is raised, complacency goes down, motivation goes up, and teachers live into the full measure of their calling. We have seen it happen, and we would like to see it happen more often.

This book is about how the evocative coaching process works and how to bring it into schools to support the professional development of teachers in individualized and small group settings. It is our hope that this book will advance the training and practice of coaches in all manner of educational settings. It is also our hope that the principles and practices of evocative coaching will become institutionalized in the cultures of learning that make up school environments. As a few individuals begin to make use of this method, a new energy may begin to infuse entire school communities, transforming schools one conversation at a time.

About the Book

To assist readers to gain facility in using the evocative coaching process, we have organized this book around the flow of coaching conversations themselves. In Part One, we focus primarily on the concept of coaching presence. How coaches show up for coaching is the single most important factor in the course and outcomes of the coaching relationship. How do we hold and carry our image of teachers and their potential? What are our intentions, orientation, energy, attitudes, focus, perspectives, and way of being with teachers? How do we understand our role and function? We explore the concept of coaching presence—our awareness in the moment of who we are, what is going on, and how to engage—and encourage its development through specific, teacher-centered practices.

Part Two describes the flow of coaching conversations using a Möbius strip model involving two turns, or loops, and four steps. The first turn, "the No-Fault Turn," works with Story and Empathy to set the stage for the second turn, "the Strengths-Building Turn," which forwards the action through Inquiry and Design. Each turn or loop of the Möbius strip is introduced with a brief interlude, before the steps of Story–Empathy–Inquiry–Design are described in detail. By the end of Part Two, readers will understand not only how these steps work in practice but also the large and growing research base that undergirds the use of these steps in our work with teachers. If we hope to promote teacher learning and growth, then the artful use of S-E-I-D is a requisite coaching and leadership skill.

Part Three seeks to make the artful use of Story–Empathy–Inquiry–Design more likely, natural, and compelling. In Chapter Seven we introduce the concept of aligning environments to bring systems thinking into the mix. Coaching never happens in a vacuum, and evocative coaches assist teachers to create the conditions that support their success. In Chapter Eight we compare the artful use of S-E-I-D to a dynamic dance, replete with choreography—the "Great 8 Movements" and "16 Style Points" of evocative coaching—for navigating our way through the two turns and four steps. Here we also highlight important considerations for coaches to attend to before coaching sessions begin and after they end.

Finally, in Chapter Nine, we encourage coaches to become life-giving and self-renewing role models through daily mindfulness, self-care, and reflective-learning practices.

Additional Resources

The four appendixes support further learning, teaching, and mastery of the evocative coaching model. Appendix A lists the principles and sample questions that appear and are discussed more fully throughout this book. There, in one convenient place, we have brought them all together. We see Appendix A as a kind of ready reference guide for mastering the evocative coaching process in schools.

For those readers who would like to incorporate the ideas in this book into a formal training or university course, there are resources in Appendixes B and C that you might find useful. Appendix B includes practice exercises that invite students to practice and reflect on the skills introduced in this book. Instructors who are using this book for a class may want to use these exercises as classroom experiences and homework assignments to enhance student learning. The exercises are designed to bring alive the principles of evocative coaching. Appendix C provides content review questions that can assist instructors to assess student comprehension of key concepts. Individuals who would like to engage in a deeper level of self-study may also find these resources useful.

Finally, for those readers interested in seeking coach certification through an independent, international coach-certifying body and for those interested in comparing the evocative coaching model to an independent definition of coaching mastery, we reprint in Appendix D the nine Coaching Masteries™ of the International Association of Coaching (IAC), www.CertifiedCoach.org. It is our sense and hope that learning the evocative coaching process will equip people to pass the IAC certification exam.

As you begin to implement the ideas in this book, we invite you to visit our companion Web site, www.EvocativeCoaching.com, where you will find templates, related articles, and additional resources to support the evocative coaching process. There you will also find announcements and opportunities for coach training, utilizing convenient telephone and Internet technologies, so that you can better apply and engage the transformational principles and practices of evocative coaching in your own life and work. We look forward to hearing from you, staying in touch, and participating in your journey.

EVOCATIVE COACHING

PART ONE

INTRODUCTION TO
EVOCATIVE COACHING

CHAPTER 1

WHAT IS EVOCATIVE COACHING?

You cannot teach a person anything. You can only help him find it within himself.

GALILEO

The Promise and Practice of Coaching

Teachers are capable adults who, with the right mix of understanding and engagement, are well equipped to improve the quality and outcomes of their instruction. Take, for example, Renee, a third-grade teacher who took her teaching to a new level through an evocative coaching process that appreciated her efforts, focused her attention, brainstormed ideas, and celebrated her progress.

> When I met with Renee before my first observation, I was very clear that this process was not about evaluation and that it was solely my desire to be of assistance to her to improve her instruction. She said that she welcomed visitors to her room and thought the observation would be helpful, but she seemed anxious, e-mailing me twice to explain what I would be seeing during my visit. I assured her that she was not going to hear any judgments, either positive or negative, from me; that this was an opportunity for learning and that we were going to let the data do the talking from the observation tool she'd selected.
>
> I observed two lessons: a reading lesson and a math lesson. Despite my assurances and calm demeanor, Renee began our conversation afterward saying, "I'm sure you've written, 'What a horrible lesson.'" I reflected back her concern
>
> *(Continued)*

and frustration, but not her conclusion. Inviting her to review the completed observation tools, she immediately started comparing the two lessons. She was shocked to see the differences. In reading, she engaged with all of the students, and there was a lot of praise and encouragement, while in math, she neglected whole groups of students and there was much more scolding. After a few minutes, hunched over the data, she sat back and said with a sigh, "This is right. I do teach math differently."

Renee confided that she enjoyed reading instruction and that she was much more confident in this area. Concerning math, she noted, "I just think of math as something to get through." The instruction in her math lesson reflected this discomfort; she was more rigid in her delivery and impatient when students made errors. Initially, she seemed overwhelmed, so I suggested we focus on just two things: planning for math instruction and the introduction of new math concepts. Then we talked about what she knew about herself as a learner and how she wanted to learn about these two things. She was very clear that workshops were not helpful to her. She said, "I go to these workshops and I get my head full of ideas, but when I get back to my classroom, I still don't know what to do differently." So we brainstormed and designed a different learning strategy for her. We made plans for her to observe in the classrooms of two colleagues on her grade level and to meet with them to discuss what she'd seen. Out of that grew more joint planning. The next time I observed, using the same observation tool, there were dramatic differences in the quality and tone of the math lesson. Now, this year, she has had several special education students placed in her room for the first time, which again caused great anxiety for her. I suggested that she use the same learning strategy, and she is having a very successful year and has developed so much more confidence as a result.

Beth, elementary resource teacher

Results like Renee's have made coaching a popular approach for fostering skills and performance improvement, whether in the context of schools or other organizational settings. Coaching facilitates learning that sticks. Like Renee, most people recognize the limitations of training, demonstrations, and professional development seminars. Regardless of how inspiring and memorable such experiences may be, they seldom translate into sustained attitude and behavior changes. Instead, they get relegated to the proverbial bookshelf as dispassionate reminders of what might have been.

Coaching has arisen, then, to fill the professional development gap. It does so not only by getting people to think about their own experiences and to practice new behaviors over time but, more importantly, by getting people excited about the prospect of learning new things and becoming masterful practitioners. At its best, coaching enables people not only to make incremental improvements in technique but also, on occasion, to make quantum leaps forward in their ways of working and being in the world. And it does so through the age-old art of conversation. Simply put, coaching is a conversational process that brings out the greatness in people. It raises the bar of the possible, so that people reinvent themselves and their organizations in the service of transformational learning.

If ever there was a setting ripe for the new possibilities and energy that such conversations have to offer, it is the twenty-first-century schoolhouse. Teachers and students alike are adrift in a sea of expanding requirements and dwindling resources. The toll of such pressures is evident in both the process and outcomes of education: people are neither having fun nor doing well. People are discouraged, frustrated, and spiraling downward. It is time for the change coaching can bring. That promise can be realized, however, only when coaches develop strong learning partnerships with teachers and only when coaching conversations move beyond the two most common and rudimentary of educational practices: "show and tell" as well as "review and comment." Familiar with these practices since childhood, people often return to them when they have the opportunity to coach someone else. But such practices, especially in adult learning, undermine the quality of relationship, limit the scope of conversation, and diminish the effectiveness of coaching. With adult learning, a different coach approach—the evocative approach—is required. That approach is what this book is all about.

The evocative approach aims to inspire motivation and movement without provoking resistance or power struggles. Evocative coaching honors both the autonomy needs of teachers and the educational standards of the schools in which they teach. It is challenging but not impossible to address both at the same time. As one person once remarked, my coach "held my feet to the fire and made it feel like a foot massage." That is the tightrope evocative coaches seek to walk, and it only happens when teachers are viewed as having the inherent creativity, intelligence, and tacit knowledge to figure out for themselves how to be successful. Rather than taking an instructional approach, evocative coaching emphasizes listening more than talking, asking more than telling, and reflecting more than commenting. Such coaching is not about giving advice, demonstrating techniques, solving problems, or offering constructive criticism (Crane & Patrick, 2007). Although these approaches occasionally become part of the process, they are neither the starting point nor the primary method we employ. We prefer empathy and inquiry as approaches because of how they open up teachers to the prospect of change and because of how they engage teachers in their own, unique performance-improvement processes.

Mastery in any profession, including teaching, is a lifelong journey. People must believe that they have what it takes to learn and grow. Evocative coaching is rooted in that framework. It delivers a growth-fostering relationship that challenges and supports people along the journey. Instead of taking over and directing traffic, as though one could mandate how to get from Point A to Point B, evocative coaches assist teachers to clarify and define their own paths of development. What works for one teacher may not work for another. Evocative coaches respect the individuality of teachers and collaborate with them by exploring their stories, understanding their feelings, appreciating their strengths, and enhancing their strategies. The process of evocative coaching can be viewed as a dance that builds self-efficacy through awareness, trust, and experimentation.

Yet this is neither a common understanding nor common parlance of coaching in schools. Indeed, the expression, "Can I give you some coaching about that?" usually means, "Can I tell you what I think you should do differently?" But the "tell you what I think" approach to coaching, often coupled with explicit or implicit rewards and punishments, tends to generate resistance and impede change. That is because it undermines teacher autonomy and provokes enemy images, both internal and external. Such interference makes it harder rather than easier for teachers to find motivation and movement (Pink, 2009). It may be commonplace for supervisors, consultants, and trainers to diagnose problems, give instructions, and provide incentives for performance improvement, but these approaches contradict what we know about adult learning. "Change or die" is not an effective threat (Deutschman, 2007). At best "facts, fear, and force" generate temporary compliance; at worst they generate resistance and outright rebellion. No wonder we face so many power struggles and political battles in schools. The collection and analysis of student-performance data highlights problems, identifies gaps, quantifies deficiencies, and creates a widespread sense of urgency and threat. In such an environment, it is easier to point fingers and throw stones than to open up and change. Coaches can end up guilty by association when we are brought in to "fix" low-performing teachers or departments. We become part of the problem when teacher energies are diminished and diverted by criticism, defensiveness, and self-protection. Such dynamics tend to immobilize teachers and make things worse, even when they are offered with the best of intentions.

Personally, I'm always ready to learn, although I do not always like being taught.

Winston Churchill

Fortunately, there is a way for coaches to cut this Gordian knot: we have to stop trying so hard to make teachers do better. Teachers do not resist making changes; they resist people who try to make them change. Once coaches abandon the role of change agent, we can build trust and rapport and engage teachers in nonjudgmental conversations about their experiences, feelings, needs, ambitions, and goals. We can assist teachers to outgrow negative data by working with positive data regarding their strengths, vitalities, aspirations, and possibilities. We can see teachers come alive, right before our eyes, as they brainstorm new ideas and experiment with new approaches. When learning becomes a self-directed task, it becomes an enjoyable task, as teachers come to appreciate and live into their "destiny, cause, and calling" (Secretan, 2004). That is what we have witnessed and hope for from evocative coaching: it connects teachers to the best of what is and moves teachers to the best of what might be. In even the worst of circumstances, with even the most problematic of data, evocative coaches can use the process of Story–Empathy–Inquiry–Design to shake loose something new. These four steps make up the dynamic dance of evocative coaching conversations, conversations that enable teachers to loosen their sense of constriction, to reconnect with their passion, and move to ever-higher levels of personal and professional mastery.

Evocative Coaching Defined

To understand why we have come to call this approach "evocative coaching," it helps to consider the root meanings of each word:

- *Evocative*: Calling to mind, bringing into existence, eliciting emotions, causing to appear, summoning into action, finding one's voice (from Latin *ēvocāre*, to call, akin to *vōx*, voice)
- *Coaching*: Transporting to a desired destination in a comfortable carriage (from Hungarian *kocsi*, after Kocs, a town in northwest Hungary where such carriages were first made)

Putting those two words together captures both the power and the promise of a coaching process that respects and fully applies the insights of adult learning theory and growth-fostering psychologies. Building on their root meanings, we define evocative coaching in this way:

- *Evocative coaching*: Calling forth motivation and movement in people, through conversation and a way of being, so they achieve desired outcomes and enhance their quality of life

This definition differs significantly from what might be called "provocative coaching." When we "provoke" someone, we do something *to* them in ways that provoke a reaction. To "evoke" means that we do something *with* someone that unleashes or calls forth their full potential. When that happens, when coaching evokes the very best from people en route to ever-higher levels of personal and professional mastery, coaching generates transformational shifts rather than mere incremental improvements. Instead of generating resistance, such coaching metaphorically transports people to where they want to go by unleashing their innate cognitive, emotive, aspirational, and experiential processes. It enables people to find their voice, to answer their call, and to affect the systems in which they live and work.

> It is one of the most rewarding things I've ever done, to reconnect a person with their passion and then to see the difference that makes for all of their students as a result.
>
> *Matt, social studies department chair*

Why Evocative Coaching Works

Evocative coaching works because it applies the principles of both adult learning theories and growth-fostering psychologies. It not only supports self-directed learning, it also draws upon the increasing evidence base regarding the impact of positive relationships, images, energy, and emotions in fostering positive actions (Cooperrider & Sekerka, 2003; Fredrickson, 2003, 2009). Evocative coaching is definitely a feel-good process. By respecting the underlying interests and abilities of teachers, by empathizing with and appreciating their experiences, and by building on their strengths, evocative coaching enables teachers to achieve better results than they would on their own or through the use of more traditional methods.

As children, most of us were taught through a combination of two processes: instruction and incentives. Parents and teachers told us what to do and how to do it correctly. They may then have offered incentives, such as rewards, compliments, punishments, and reprimands, to get us to do the work and master the domain. Although it is not uncommon for these same processes to be used with adults, especially in training and knowledge transfer, research by both educators and psychologists documents the limitations of this approach. Adults seek to figure things out for themselves, for their own reasons, in their own ways, on their own schedules, and with their own resources. For coaching with adults to be effective, it needs to take these and other adult-specific factors into consideration. It needs to be evocative.

Timothy Gallwey's (2008) book *The Inner Game of Tennis*, first published in 1974, was a call to limit the use of instructions and incentives in coaching because of their oftentimes debilitating impact on the internal dynamics that make for optimum skill development and performance improvement. Ironically, he noted, the more important the stakes of the external requirements and reinforcements, the more instruction distracts people from their own "natural learning" styles (p. 22). Gallwey's book marked a turning point for athletic coaching and is frequently hailed as a milestone in the modern coaching movement, particularly since the publication of his companion book, *The Inner Game of Work* (Gallwey, 2000). Gallwey's inner-game principles, however, are inextricably tied to the research and practice of adult education and learning theories dating back throughout the past century (Cox, 2006; Knowles, 1950, 1990; Knowles, Holton, & Swanson, 2005; Lindeman, 1926). Through this rich body of knowledge, the following characteristics of adult learners have come into focus:

- Adults are autonomous and self-directed.
- Adult learning builds on a wide variety of previous experiences, knowledge, mental models, self-direction, interests, resources, and competencies.
- Adults are relevancy oriented. They must see a reason for learning something, often connected to the developmental tasks of their social roles.
- Adults are solution focused. Instead of being interested in knowledge for its own sake, adult learning seeks immediate application and problem solving.
- Adult learning needs to be facilitated rather than directed. Adults want to be treated as equals and shown respect both for what they know and how they prefer to learn.
- Adults need specific behavioral feedback that is free of evaluative or judgmental opinions.
- Adults need follow-up support to continue and advance their learning over time.

These characteristics of adult learners help to explain why instructions and incentives so often interfere with high performance. Although it is tempting to tell people how to do things better, to make them practice, and to reward their progress, such "tell-and-sell" approaches fail to inspire and leverage the best of human learning and functioning. Indeed, they can just as easily undermine motivation, provoke resistance, usurp responsibility, rupture relationships, ignore reality, discourage risk taking, limit imagination, and restrict results (Pink, 2009; Kohn, 1999). They may "work" in the short run (if *work* is understood as compliance), but they seldom work in the long run (if *work* is understood as mastery), and they rarely generate significant improvement, at least not until they are abandoned in favor of self-directed learning. Instructions come with an implicit *should* as to what is to be done, implying that there is a right way to do something. That *should* undermines autonomy and self-direction. Instructions also build more on the experience base of the coach than of the teacher, which may or may not be viewed as relevant and workable in the eyes of the teacher. Incentives only make this worse, setting up a dynamic of enforcement rather than support. In short, the use of instructions and incentives violates much of what has been learned about adult education and learning theory. They generate the resistance with which many teachers and schools are all too familiar. Gallwey (2000, 2008) was right when he asserted there must be a better way to learn.

> Todd left the business world to become a teacher because he wanted to do work that was more meaningful to him. But he had just two months of training in the summer and he was assigned to teach freshman English in an urban high school to a class who were reading between a second- and a sixth-grade reading level. He was scared and unsure. He didn't understand the students' behavior. He felt defeated and ineffective. He wasn't sure he could make a difference. The students sensed his fear and took advantage of it. He knew I wanted him to be successful. He was open to suggestions, and we worked on setting up routines and procedures. We worked by brainstorming, planning, and problem solving. As time went on, he began to come up with more and more of the ideas on his own. I did a lot of scaffolding, with a kind of gradual release model. Now he's using that same philosophy with his students. He's becoming an effective teacher and he plans to continue teaching!
>
> *Cheryl, high school literacy coach*

At the same time that educators were studying and developing adult learning theories, psychologists were seeking to understand and improve the dynamics of growth-fostering relationships. These psychologies include many schools of thought and a wide variety of therapeutic orientations. Traditions that most directly inform evocative coaching include humanistic psychology, positive psychology, appreciative inquiry, social cognitive theory and neuroscience, motivational interviewing, and Nonviolent Communication. Drawing upon these traditions, we can say that the following recognitions undergird evocative coaching (Tschannen-Moran, B., 2010, p. 213):

- People are inherently creative and capable.
- The human brain is hardwired to enjoy novelty and growth, which leads to an inherent joy of learning.

- Learning takes place when people actively take responsibility for constructing meaning from their experience (either confirming or changing what they already know).
- The meanings people construct determine the actions they take.
- Every person is unique, and yet all people have the same universal needs.
- Empathy, mutuality, and connection make people more cooperative and open to change.
- "People don't resist change; they resist being changed" (Borwick, 1969, p. 20).
- The more people know about their values, strengths, resources, and abilities, the stronger their motivation and the more effective their changes will be.

These recognitions explain why evocative coaching represents such a promising model for generating performance improvements in teachers and other educators. By assisting teachers to explore their experience with empathy and inquiry, rather than with evaluation and interrogation, evocative coaching produces freedom, increases positivity, stimulates curiosity, elevates self-efficacy, and leverages latent competencies in the service of desired outcomes. Such coaching does not try to change teachers and does not try to persuade them to do things the "right" way; rather, evocative coaching dances with teachers as they consider their options and invites them to become fully engaged in the process of discovering their own unique strategies for doing better.

> When I first started as a coach, there were not many people doing this, so we pretty much had to make it up. They said, "Here's the school you're assigned to. Go to it." The principal didn't seem to know what I was supposed to do either. So I embraced that. I knew how to teach, so I adapted what I knew about teaching kids to teaching adults. I differentiated according to their differing needs.
>
> *Nancy, technology integration coach*

What Makes Coaching Evocative?

The consistent awareness and application of the aforementioned principles from adult learning theories and growth-fostering psychologies is what makes coaching evocative. Teachers open up and find their voice when coaching taps into five salient, animating factors: consciousness, connection, competence, contribution, and creativity. If coaches do not properly attend to these five concerns, the promise of transformational change is unlikely to be realized. When coaches do properly attend to them, educators often rise to new heights of ambition and ability, discovering, in the process, powerful new solutions to even the most persistent and complex of challenges.

Concern for Consciousness

Coaching becomes evocative when the coach's concern for *consciousness* generates increased self-awareness, self-knowledge, and self-monitoring on the part of the teacher. This lays the groundwork for all experiential learning. *Mindfulness,* defined as the nonjudgmental awareness of what is happening in the present moment, represents both the consciousness that makes conversations evocative as well as the consciousness generated by such conversations. There is no way to foster learning and growth apart from mindfulness. What happens in coaching conversations, both positive and negative, gets transferred to the learning laboratory of life experience. When coaching conversations are full of pressure, demands, and instructional "how-to's," teachers take that consciousness into their efforts to improve performance. They want to do things right, and they bring back reports of what they did wrong. When coaching conversations are full of empathy, requests, and curious "what-if's," however, teachers become more willing and able to play with different variables and to make appropriate, just-in-time innovations. They want to try new things, and they bring back reports of what went well.

Understanding this, evocative coaches enjoy listening to stories, expressing empathy, asking questions, and co-creating experiments that increase mindfulness. By demonstrating an appreciative interest in the whole person, including the fullness of their experience, evocative coaches expand awareness to include what is happening in the moment, what needs are being stimulated, and what strategies or approaches are working better than others. Assisting teachers to attend to such matters facilitates "natural learning." Paulo Freire (2000) called such facilitation the raising of a "critical consciousness" that engages learners in "reading their world." The goal of critical consciousness, according to Freire, is for people to become active agents in the creation of their own lives and of the democratic ideal in society.

A clear and accurate appreciation of the present moment, without generalizations, exaggerations, or evaluative judgments, is critical to continuous skill and performance improvements. One must recognize what is really going on. Evocative coaches learn to listen for the observational core behind stories and then, through empathy and inquiry, to make those dynamics known to the teacher. It is not a matter of pointing them out; it is rather a matter of helping teachers to recognize and understand those dynamics for themselves. As Zeus and Skiffington (2000) write, "Coaching involves helping individuals access what they know. They may never have asked themselves the questions, but they have the answers. A coach assists, supports, and encourages individuals to find these answers" (p. 3).

As part of the self-awareness that grows from evocative coaching relationships, teachers may come to a greater awareness of their readiness to change. When teachers are feeling ambivalent about how best to meet instructional challenges, for example, evocative coaching can assist teachers to appreciate what that ambivalence is about and what they can learn from it. When teachers express resistance or defeat, communicating either an "I won't" or "I can't" attitude, the adroit use of empathy and inquiry, rather than analysis and pressure, soon translates into attitudes of "I might," "I will," "I am," and "I still am" (Prochaska, Norcross, & DiClemente, 1994). Building motivation and mobility is the key work of evocative coaching.

Concern for Connection

Coaching also becomes evocative when coaches establish a life-giving *connection* with teachers. As with consciousness, this connection spills over in the ways teachers connect with themselves and with others in the school environment. The carrot and the stick may goad and prod people into action, but only life-giving, high-trust connections have the ability to inspire greatness. They free up teachers to venture out and take on new challenges by virtue of the safety net they represent. When the connection between teacher and coach is strong, the adventure of learning and performance improvement becomes an enjoyable game rather than a punishing task. Without such connections, coaches and teachers inevitably fall short of accomplishing their mission to promote student learning and success (Bryk & Schneider, 2002; Tschannen-Moran, 2004). With such connections, a zone of possibility opens for teachers and schools to accomplish that mission in new and satisfying ways.

Attachment theory holds that incentives are not required for people to want to connect in productive ways with themselves and with others, because human beings are hardwired for connection. Connection is a universal human need that people seek to meet throughout the course of our lifetimes. Evocative coaching accepts and applies that view to the conversational process. It recognizes the power of listening, empathy, and inquiry to establish connection and foster growth. Freire (1970) attributed this power to "dialogue" and the action-reflection model of praxis learning. He noted that "dialogue cannot be reduced to the act of one person's 'depositing' ideas in another, nor can it become a simple exchange of ideas to be 'consumed' by the discussants." It is rather an act of co-creation that comes from the connection itself. "Dialogue cannot exist," Freire observed, "in the absence of a profound love for the world and for people" (p. 89). It is an act of courage and a sign of commitment to others.

Evocative coaching is dialogue coaching in Freire's sense of the word. It is neither depositing ideas nor consuming information. It is rather engaging, energizing, and challenging people to discover the best in themselves and in their methods through the "miracle of dialogue" (Howe, 1993). That only happens when nobody is trying to win (Bohm, 1996). When coaches are trying to win over teachers to our point of view, dialogue does not happen, and no real connection is possible. Evocative coaching sets aside the desire to be right. It is love in action. It seeks to establish the quality of connection that makes learning and growth possible.

That quality of connection in schools has been heralded as the key for transforming schools into professional learning communities that have a shared focus on student learning (Lieberman, 2005; Stoll & Seashore Louis, 2007). When they are functioning as they should, professional learning communities evidence productive collaboration, deprivatized teaching practice, and reflective dialogue (Seashore Louis, Kruse, & Marks, 1996). Members of the community continually research best practices to better serve students. Ongoing, rigorous professional inquiry supports joint deliberation as participants pursue data to bolster decision making (Elmore, Peterson, & McCarthey, 1996; Fullan, 2003). Because of the complexity of the decisions to be made by teachers, the quality of those decisions is enhanced by structures and time that foster connection and allow for collective deliberation. These processes, in turn, create the conditions that support educational excellence and student learning (Tschannen-Moran, M., 2009). Evocative coaching is one such process.

> *Good teachers possess a capacity for connectedness. They are able to weave a complex web of connections among themselves, their subjects, and their students so that their students can learn to weave a world for themselves.*
>
> *Parker Palmer (1998, p. 11)*

Concern for Competence

Evocative coaches believe that teachers are whole (not broken and needing to be fixed), creative, resourceful, resilient, and able to master the art and science of teaching, even when teachers are out of touch with these abilities (Stober, 2006). The concern for *competence*, then, is not to "make" teachers competent. That approach gives priority to the expert knowledge of the coach. The concern is rather to discover, recognize, and celebrate the competence teachers already have. By appreciating that competence, both obvious and latent, evocative coaches give priority to the learning process of teachers. Assisting teachers to clarify what they want and need, to identify and build upon their strengths, and to conduct no-fault learning experiments in the service of mutually agreed-upon goals are the keys to assisting teachers to make quantum leaps forward in the identification of designs and strategies that work for them.

The challenge for coaches, as already noted, is to suspend the desire to be right and to demonstrate our expertise. As well intentioned and as evidence-based as that demonstration may be, the expert approach communicates judgment and undermines confidence in the abilities of teachers to figure out their own best ways to meet both personal and professional requirements. Professional competence is not just a matter of knowing the right way to do something; it includes adaptively applying skills to masterfully meet the changing needs of emerging situations.

All professions deal with this dynamic. Professionals work within systemic constraints. Professional athletes, for example, compete within the rules of the game. The work of architects is governed by a set of codes and standards. So, too, with teachers, whose competence is increasingly being judged by the documented, standards-based learning of their students. The challenge of evocative coaching is to inspire teachers to meet those standards for their own good reasons and in their own unique ways. There is no one universal path to competence in any profession, unless that path is the love of learning and a commitment to continuous performance improvement. Until and unless that passion is evoked, the process of coaching will revert to instructions and incentives, and the competence of teachers will go both unrecognized and unfulfilled. Once that passion is evoked, however, coaching enables teachers to engage their competence for performance improvement. By paying attention to strengths, opportunities, aspirations, and results, teachers find the motivation and self-efficacy for taking their competence to another level. Instead of a remediation of problems, evocative coaching generates an appreciation of possibilities. This shift from incompetence to competence changes both the tone and the outcomes of coaching.

Concern for Contribution

Most teachers enter the field of education for more than just a paycheck; they want to make a *contribution* to the learning and well-being of students, families, and communities. Unfortunately, that interest too often gets buried under the stresses and strains of life and work. The pressures of schooling, exacerbated in the era of data-driven, standards-based accountability, can cause teachers to lose sight of the reason they became educators in the first place. Evocative coaches never fail to remember and always manage to communicate respect for that original inspiration.

Contribution, like all the other life-giving concerns of evocative coaching, is a universal human need. When it is recognized, honored, and met, people gain not only a sense of their destiny, cause, and calling (Secretan, 2004), they also gain the satisfaction that comes from connecting the dots between everyday realities and transcendent activities. When teachers believe that they are making a difference—a contribution—then they yearn to express and improve that contribution on every front.

That is the powerful gift evocative coaches give to discouraged and burned-out teachers. By honoring teachers' contributions, evocative coaches awaken teachers' passions. That alone is enough to trigger a quantum leap forward for some teachers. When the need for contribution is dismissed, minimized, ridiculed, or caught in the crossfire of conflicting interests, teaching becomes a chore, and surviving to retirement becomes the goal. No wonder such teachers fail to experiment with new methods and inspire student success! They no longer believe in even the possibility, let alone the certainty, of contribution. Evocative coaches turn the tables on this dynamic by our own certainty that a contribution can always be made. "My certainty is greater than your doubt" is a key framework of evocative coaching (Buck, 2006). Evocative coaches never fail to acknowledge contribution, regardless of how small or seemingly insignificant, in the experiences teachers share. By framing manageable goals and celebrating successful moments, by sharing in what is all too often the private glory of a teachable moment seized, evocative coaches build teacher self-efficacy.

Self-efficacy is the belief that one has the capability to initiate or sustain desired performance improvements (Bandura, 1994, 1997). This belief has been linked to effort, persistence, and resilience in the face of setbacks. It is the coach's job, then, to communicate a contagious confidence in the teacher's capability. When coaches have a "can-do" attitude, teachers develop a "can-learn" attitude. That is the subtle shift we hope to stimulate through the evocative coaching process. Evocative coaches support the development of self-efficacy beliefs through four sources: encouragement from others (verbal persuasion), modeling (vicarious experiences), awareness of emotions (somatic awareness), and experiences of success with the target skill (mastery experiences) (Bandura, 1997). This becomes easier and more effective when people shift from aversive motivators, such as fear and disgust, to attractive motivators, such as hope and contribution.

Concern for Creativity

In addition to paying attention to consciousness, connection, competence, and contribution, coaching must also unleash *creativity* if it is to be evocative. That happens naturally when coaches approach the coaching space as a no-fault playground in which teachers can follow their intrinsic motivation and adopt a beginner's mind as to what exactly will be the best steps for them to take in order achieve desired outcomes and enhance their quality of life. Creativity cannot be coerced; it can only be invited. The more attached coaches become to a particular strategy, and the harder we press for teachers to adopt that strategy, the more we will generate constriction and conformity rather than expansion and creativity. Instead of entertaining new interpretations and possibilities, brainstorming and exploring a wide variety of hypotheses, coaches can have the opposite effect on teachers when we push or incentivize them to do things the "right way." Although evidence-based methodologies are worth watching and practicing to see how they go and how they feel, true performance mastery emerges only when teachers have the freedom and desire to creatively adapt and appropriate these methodologies for themselves.

Creativity starts with curiosity, an intrinsic part of human nature that needs only to be unleashed and encouraged. Just as little children leverage curiosity to learn through the process of trial and correction, falling down and picking themselves up again to get where they want to go (much to the delight of adoring parents and significant others), so do mature adults have a natural inclination to explore new frontiers, to test their limits, and to make just-in-time adjustments in the service of desired outcomes. Unfortunately, this natural inclination is thwarted by the adult tendency to frame experience in terms of "trial and error" rather than "trial and correction," "win-lose" instead of "win-learn." Nothing blocks the creative impulse more than judgments of failure, both internal and external.

> *The problem with judgment is that it makes people feel shamed. They are humiliated by being judged, and this lessens their ability to listen actively, recognize what they might do differently, and learn from the experience.*
>
> Terry Bacon (2006, pp. 86–87)

Understanding this, evocative coaches use empathy and inquiry to turn the coaching dynamic into a safe and engaging opportunity for give and take in which coaches and teachers alike can explore freely what they want on the way to performance improvement. There is no performance anxiety when it comes to evocative coaching. There is only positive energy, as the conversational space is filled with laughter, humor, delight, and wonder. Whether things work well or not, evocative coaches respond with fascination and joy. No experience is so terrible as to have no redeeming aspects; nor is any experience so perfect as to have no improvable aspects. All experience is cherished for what it has to teach and give us. Creativity frames everything through the lens of appreciation. In a word, evocative coaching is fun.

The Dynamic Dance of Evocative Coaching

As we shall see throughout the rest of this book, and as we have alluded to in our introductory remarks, evocative coaching is a dynamic dance that can be choreographed with four steps: Story–Empathy–Inquiry–Design. The first two steps, Story–Empathy, constitute what we call "the No-Fault Turn." They are designed to help teachers relax, to establish trust, to introduce new perspectives on experience, and to appreciate the intrinsic value of whatever is going on. They set the stage, then, for the second two steps, Inquiry–Design, which represent "the Strengths-Building Turn" of evocative coaching. Instead of trying to identify and fix weaknesses, evocative coaches invite teachers to identify and build on their strengths. Once designs are field tested, the process then loops back for additional iterations. Simply put, evocative coaching uses *empathy* and *inquiry* to appreciate *story* and create *design*. It is a teacher-centered, no-fault, strengths-based coaching model that departs in significant ways from what often goes on under the guise of coaching or supervision. Rather than focusing on how coaches can improve teacher performance, often through constructive criticism and advice giving, we focus on how coaches can improve our relationships with teachers, so that teachers get motivated and empowered to improve their own performance and quality of life. This happens when coaches:

- Give teachers our full, undivided attention
- Accept and meet teachers where they are right now, without making them wrong
- Ask and trust teachers to take charge of their own learning and growth
- Make sure teachers are talking more (ideally much more) than we are
- Enable teachers to appreciate the positive value of their own experiences
- Harness the strengths teachers have to meet challenges and overcome obstacles
- Reframe difficulties and challenges as opportunities to learn and grow
- Invite teachers to discover possibilities and find answers for themselves
- Dialogue with teachers regarding their higher purposes for teaching
- Uncover teachers' natural impulses to engage with colleagues and students
- Assist teachers to draw up personal blueprints for professional mastery
- Support teachers in brainstorming and trying new ways of doing things
- Maintain an upbeat, energetic, and positive attitude at all times
- Collaborate with teachers to design and conduct appropriate learning experiments
- Enable teachers to build supportive environments and teams
- Use humor to lighten the load, and
- Inspire and challenge teachers to go beyond what they would do alone

FIGURE 1.1 THE MÖBIUS MODEL OF EVOCATIVE COACHING

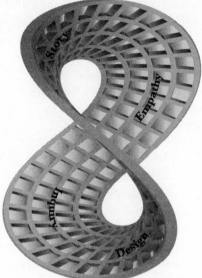

The No-Fault Turn

The Strengths-Building Turn

All this constitutes the distinctive elements of evocative coaching. Story–Empathy–Inquiry–Design represents the dance steps that evocative coaches follow. The four steps are portrayed on a Möbius strip, where each loop of the strip represents one of the turns (see Figure 1.1), to reflect the dynamic and expansive interplay of these elements in the service of continual learning and growth. The steps are easy to remember, albeit challenging to practice. Coaches are so accustomed to traditional "tell-and-sell" methods that we find it hard to trust more evocative, teacher-centered approaches. Yet traditional methods have not reliably produced desired results in a desired fashion. They too often lead to power struggles, disillusionment, and declining performance rather than to power sharing, encouragement, and improving performance. To turn that around, it is time for a new vision, model, and framework for improving instruction, one conversation at a time.

We portray the dynamic dance of evocative coaching on a Möbius strip for good reason: Möbius strips are fascinating, expansive, and iterative creations. Although named after the German mathematician and theoretical astronomer August Ferdinand Möbius (1790–1868), who was one of two people to "discover" its unique characteristics in 1858 (the other was Johann Listing, another German mathematician), variations on the Möbius design can be dated back more than 4,000 years ago to the early alchemists of Alexandria, Egypt. The mysterious qualities of the design, as a two-dimensional object in three-dimensional space, reflect the human quest for continuity and novelty within the bounds of space and time. To see how a Möbius strip works, take a strip of paper, give it a half-twist, and attach the ends. Now trace along the surface with a pencil, and without ever lifting the point you will end up back where you started, having traversed both sides of the paper. Cut along that line and the Möbius strip doubles in size rather than splitting in half. Amazing! It is not unlike how we experience the evocative coaching process: we find ourselves engaged by its intriguing complexity and invited to explore its endless possibility.

Story

Coaching begins when teachers share their stories. These stories reflect the sense teachers are making of their experiences. Stories are never the experiences themselves (i.e., the map is not the territory); they are rather attempts to understand, value, and shape experiences in ways that fit together and guide future actions.

Because stories—both the stories teachers tell to themselves and those they tell to others—represent the raw materials of coaching, it is possible for everything to change in the twinkling of an eye. Tell a new story (draw a new map), and we get a new experience. That is especially true when we begin to work with the attributions of cause and effect that are explicit and/or implicit in most stories (Loehr, 2007, p. 4). Coaches listen for those attributions because they illuminate a teacher's path of development. For example:

- What is the overarching theme? Does it lie more with danger or opportunity?
- Where is the locus of control? Does it lie more with the teacher or with others?
- How is the problem defined? Does it use more enemy or ally images?
- What is the language of capacity? Does it lie more with skills or resources?
- How is the objective defined? Does it lie more with metrics or morale?
- What is happening with energy? Is it emptying out or filling up?
- What is happening with values? Are they being honored or compromised?
- What is happening with needs? Are they being met, denied, or sacrificed?

There is a multitude of attributions we can listen for, because there is a multitude of stories teachers tell in explaining the way things are. Explanatory style theory makes clear the wide range of differences we may encounter, including optimistic and pessimistic attributions (Seligman, 2006). The secret is to listen mindfully, creating a safe, no-fault zone without a hint of judgment or haste, and then to ask new questions that invite teachers to explore story variants and takeaways. How else can the story be told? What might have happened if different decisions had been made? How does the experience advance our understandings of and aspirations for professional praxis? Reframing stories in this way, approaching and expanding on teacher stories through curiosity, is a technique we call "imaginative listening." Developed further in Chapter Three, such listening is an attempt to flesh out the details and enlarge the meanings of stories in the service of teacher learning, growth, and change. It may be tempting for coaches to rush through stories to get to strategies, but that often generates unhappy results. Quick fixes rarely work, and if they work they rarely stick. Unappreciated stories tend to undermine behavioral change efforts. That is why evocative coaching views story listening as an essential first step in the dynamic dance.

Empathy

The stories teachers tell are filled with attributions as to what is going on, what works and what doesn't work, who deserves credit or blame, and how things might improve. Most of the time, those attributions include a mix of empirical observations and subjective evaluations, both positive and negative. When things are going well, the story has a more upbeat and happy energy. When things are not going well, the story has a more downbeat and unhappy energy. Either way, teachers need to feel emotionally secure, understood, appreciated, and accepted in order to release their energy and channel it in creative directions. Until and unless this happens, not much will come from coaching. The confusion between observations and evaluations will escalate into a distracting din, making it harder rather than easier for teachers to find a way forward. That is why empathy represents such a critical part of evocative coaching. Empathy, an essential aspect of story listening, clears the palette so that new interpretations and ideas can emerge. It soothes the inner voice and facilitates the inner game.

Although expressing empathy has long been recognized as a critical part of therapy, it is not often talked or written about in the context of coaching. That may be due, in part, to confusion among pity, sympathy, and authentic empathy. Pity is feeling sorry for someone, which does not foster change. Sympathy, also known as "emotional contagion," is sharing someone's feelings, which can provide valuable clues as to what is going on but which can also lead to advising, rescuing, and defending behaviors. Authentic empathy is a respectful, no-fault understanding and appreciation of someone's experience; as such, it is an orientation and practice that fosters radically new change possibilities.

Empathy does this by shifting the focus from particular strategies to universal needs. As we have noted, people tell stories to make meaning of experiences; we attempt to describe and account for things that happen through our narratives. When good things happen, we celebrate with stories; when bad things happen, we mourn with stories. Human beings are nothing if we are not sense-making and storytelling beings. Often, however, we misattribute our feelings to the particular strategies of who did what to whom when, rather than to what is happening with the underlying needs in a much broader and more life-affirming sense. As a result of this misattribution, people get caught up in self-defeating cycles of interpretations, judgments, criticisms, and diagnoses (Rosenberg, 2005, pp. 52–54). This cycle is counterproductive to both the coaching dynamic and to performance improvement.

Being ashamed of our mistakes turns them into crimes.

Confucius

Evocative coaches guide teachers to sort out strategies and needs in order to facilitate the movement and flow of both the coaching conversation and the developmental progress of teachers. To do that, as we will see in Chapter Four, coaches can learn to effectively use the Nonviolent Communication model developed by Rosenberg (2005) and others over the past fifty years. Upon hearing a story, coaches can notice and reflect the teacher's feelings and needs in ways that release tension, facilitate calm, and expand awareness. Doing this effectively requires fluency in the language of authentic feelings and universal human needs (d'Ansembourg, 2007). Although expressing empathy and connecting with teachers in this way is choreographed as the second step in the dynamic dance of evocative coaching, it is, in fact, a step coaches return to over and over again. Empathy not only feels good, it expands a teacher's range of options and prepares her or him to move forward in new ways.

Inquiry

As teachers tell and explore the richness of their stories, receiving empathy for the feelings and needs that are most alive for them, the flow of evocative coaching turns naturally to the steps of Inquiry and Design. Through Story–Empathy, teachers come to understand themselves in new ways and become open to the consideration and observation of new possibilities. As a result, they eagerly want to notice what works and to learn how to make things work better. The first two steps of evocative coaching, "the No-Fault Turn," are designed to broker that eagerness. Once it is there, the next two steps, "the Strengths-Building Turn," translate that eagerness into action. And that happens best when coaches inquire into teacher strengths, vitalities, aspirations, and possibilities rather than into weaknesses, deficiencies, requirements, and avoidances.

As we have seen, coaching does not become evocative when coaching conversations revolve around how teachers can fix the problems they are having. This is not to say that teachers have no problems; this is rather to say that it is easier to outgrow problems when teachers focus on their strengths, vitalities, and aspirations. Both adult learning theories and growth-fostering psychologies support this approach. Research indicates that appreciative, strengths-based inquiries are more effective and empowering than analytic, deficits-based inquiries (Buckingham, 2007; Cooperrider, 2000; Fredrickson, 2002, 2003, 2009). They also represent a much more enjoyable way to learn. Building on assets facilitates change. It also represents yet another way to reframe stories and engage in story listening. It is wonderfully reorienting and empowering to ask open-ended, strengths-based questions such as:

- What is working with your approach? What else is working? What else?
- What talents and abilities are serving you well? What else?
- What's the best thing that's happening now? What else?
- What fills you with energy and hope? What else?
- What enables you to do as well as you are doing? What else?
- What is the positive intent of your actions? What else?
- What resources do you have available? What else?
- What would success look like? What else would it look like?

The point of such inquiries, which can easily be used in all kinds of conversations, is to elevate the focus, self-efficacy, resourcefulness, and wherewithal of teachers. The more aware teachers are of their problems, deficits, and limitations, the less likely they are to imagine and pursue new possibilities. In Chapter Five we explain how appreciative, strengths-based inquiries and observations turn that around (Cooperrider, 2000). They remind teachers that they have what it takes to learn what they want to learn and to go where they want to go.

Asking teachers what and how they want to learn, rather than telling them what to do, enables teachers to discover and design that learning for themselves through observation and exploration. Strengths-based questions also remind teachers that stories of hardship, difficulty, frustration, and failure do not represent the whole story. The point of asking "What else?" on multiple occasions is to raise awareness as to other ways of telling the story. Knowing that in every situation something is always working, no matter how bleak or discouraging things may appear, coaches can be courageous in our inquiries about the high points and life-enriching moments that are worth celebrating.

Along with appreciating teacher strengths and vitalities, evocative coaches inquire into the aspirations teachers carry for themselves, their students, and their schools. Aspirations power change. Where do teachers want to go with their own best practices? Who would they like to observe and how would they like to learn from the practices of others? Assisting teachers to visualize their answers to and feelings about such questions increases both motivation and self-efficacy. The more concrete and tangible the images, the more teachers anticipate, appropriate, and assimilate their energy. Through focusing exercises and other creative modalities, teachers become engaged with their visions, open to new possibilities, and eager to try new approaches. Coaches can ask both direct questions ("If you could make any three wishes come true, wishes that would infuse you and this situation with energy and life, what would they be?") and indirect questions ("If a miracle happened tonight such that these problems were gone and everything was wonderful, what would be the first thing you would notice when you got to school in the morning?") to get the juices flowing. Such questions mount aspirations and invite possibilities that beckon teachers forward.

Design

When teacher stories are received and reframed properly, through story listening, expressing empathy, and appreciative inquiry, ideas bubble up and teachers become inspired to design ways to turn their aspirations into actions and their possibilities into realities. Little to no instructions or incentives are required to get this going. Instead, once teachers become detached from both the fear of failure and the illusions as to how bad and impossible things are, they become fearless in the self-directed pursuit of that which will enable them to learn and grow.

The key in the design phase of evocative coaching, then, is for coaches to avoid reintroducing judgmental frames as to how things are to be done "right" or even "better." Coaches are not the experts telling teachers what to do. We are the co-creators with teachers of experimental designs that may or may not work out as expected. Either outcome represents success, as long as the experiments are conducted, the data are collected, and the results are incorporated into future experiments. Skills and performance improvements are continuous, iterative, personalized, and evolutionary. What works for one person, in one place, at one time may not work for another. Coaches and teachers therefore design strategies that teachers find intrinsically interesting, imminently doable, and inherently relevant to the challenges they face. That is why we refer to Inquiry–Design as constituting "the Strengths-Building Turn": it builds on the best of what is to generate the best of what might be.

Brainstorming, a topic we explore more fully along with field testing in Chapter Six, is an essential part of design thinking that forwards the action. Brainstorming evokes many new ideas about how to do things better without regard to their value, feasibility, or desirability. Asking teachers "What else?" engages their creativity. Sharing in the process of generating new ideas, taking turns with teachers as one idea cascades and morphs into another, can open up the process even further. Basic protocols for brainstorming include:

• Setting a minimum number of possibilities to generate
• Setting a time limit to keep things moving rapidly
• Withholding judgment or evaluation of possibilities
• Encouraging wild and exaggerated possibilities
• Letting no possibility go unsaid
• Building on the possibilities put forth by others
• Combining and expanding possibilities
• Going for quantity rather than quality

An excellent question for teachers and coaches to brainstorm around is, "What could I pay attention to that most directly impacts on how things are working in this situation?" Another question is, "Where could I go and who could I watch to learn techniques I may not yet have tried or mastered myself?" A third question is, "How could I handle this situation differently than I have ever tried before?" Such questions expand awareness and make learning both self-directed and enjoyable. When teachers are helped to identify and focus their attention on what's important, without being told what to do, they are nudged to make new choices and to try out new behaviors with a minimum of resistance. The fully engaged mind, freed from judgments and prescriptions, quiets negative self-talk and frees up energy for change.

Whatever gets generated through brainstorming, evocative coaches assist teachers to review the options and field test their ideas through learning experiments that are challenging and yet not overwhelming. There is no way to predict what any particular teacher will come up with, but we can dance with teachers to play with different possibilities, to pick the ones that appear intrinsically interesting and valuable, to design experiments to see what they have to offer, and to align environments so as to make those experiments more fruitful. By assisting teachers to become confident and optimistic about their ability to conduct learning experiments, coaches become catalysts for growth and change. The old maxim, "Where there is a will there is a way," holds even more power the other way around: "Where there is a way there is a will." As teachers see a way forward for improving their skills and performance in the classroom, motivation and movement are sure to follow—at which point the dynamic dance of evocative coaching starts all over again.

Summary

Evocative coaching is a dynamic dance between story and design set to the music of empathy and inquiry. Although the dance always contains elements of improvisation, the flow of Story–Empathy–Inquiry–Design serves as an excellent starting point for new coaches as well as a challenging counterpoint for veteran coaches who may be used to more traditional "tell-and-sell" approaches. Given its foundation in adult-learning theory and growth-fostering psychologies, as well as its demonstrated success in skills and performance improvement, evocative coaching holds great promise as it becomes an integral part of professional learning communities.

Questions for Reflection and Discussion

1. What did Galileo mean when he said, "You cannot teach a person anything. You can only help him find it within himself"?
2. How does evocative coaching differ from your experience of traditional supervision and mentoring?
3. What is the best learning experience you have ever had as an adult? What made that experience so wonderful? How has that affected the ways you work with others?
4. What principles of adult learning theory are most relevant to your own experience of learning as an adult? How are those principles different, if at all, from the pedagogy of children?
5. What makes learning enjoyable for you? Why is it valuable to incorporate fun into the coaching process?
6. How can you suspend judgment in coaching when you disagree with something someone has said or done? Why is this important to the coaching process?
7. What happens to the coaching conversation when coaches get attached to an outcome? How can you release attachment and engage curiosity?
8. Call to mind a particular teacher you know or have worked with. How might evocative coaching enable that teacher to achieve instructional improvement in ways that other approaches have not?

CHAPTER 2

COACHING PRESENCE

Relational authenticity in coaching is about a quality of presence that contributes power-fully to flourishing in connection. The coach's emotional presence is an important source of information for teachers and a resource for growth in the coaching relationship.

ADAPTED FROM JUDITH JORDAN (2004b, P. 67)

A New Metaphor for Coaching

Evocative coaching cannot be reduced to a tool or technique. Without the right intention and the right way of being, coaches fail to be evocative, and teachers fail to realize their full potential, no matter what approaches are used or strategies tried. Those of us who seek to improve the performance and fulfillment of teachers and other educators would do well to examine our own motivation and manner. Ironically, the more coaches *want* to help, the less effective we may be. That is because the coach-as-helper metaphor shifts the dynamic of coaching away from its evocative core. It places responsibility for change primarily with the coach rather than with the teacher, where it belongs. What is needed is a new metaphor for coaching presence that reflects a life-giving understanding of our awareness in the moment regarding who we are, what is going on, and how to engage: the coach as whisperer.

Whisperers have a long history of working effectively with animals, people, and spirits through the power of their evocative presence. Take, for example, the following description of a horse whisperer as a "horse trainer who adopts a sym-pathetic view of the motives, needs, and desires of the horse, based on natural horsemanship and modern equine psychology" ("Horse whisperer," 2009). Horse whisperers do not understand themselves as helping the horse. They rather un-derstand themselves as connecting and communicating with the horse on such deep levels as to evoke transformation. And they do not have much time to establish that connection. From the moment of first contact, whisperers interact with horses in a way that communicates respect, understanding, acceptance, freedom, willingness, cooperation, and engagement. It is both calming and riveting to be embraced with such attention and trust.

In many work settings, people are far more likely to be jostled into compliance with requirements and incentives than to be motivated into cooperation through understanding and respect. That is not the way of evocative coaching, however, which always seeks to convey a benevolent presence. If coaches approach teachers caring more about correction than connection, if we do not authentically value the teachers we are coaching, if we think of them as "defective," "uncooperative," or "uncoachable," and if we do not like them, then we are likely to stir up resentment and resistance rather than willingness and engagement (Pink, 2009). Apart from a teacher-centered presence, none of the tools and techniques in this book or any other coaching book will do much good. Coaching becomes evocative only when our connection with teachers communicates respect, acceptance, appreciation, freedom, willingness, cooperation, and shared destiny. Benevolence is a hallmark of trust and a central tenet of evocative coaching.

Teachers don't care how much we know until they know how much we care.

Whisperers seek to create that bond of caring in their work with animals, people, or spirits. Whispering is not an inborn trait, aptitude, or capacity with which some people are uniquely endowed. Whispering is rather a method and a mindset that some people choose to learn and to take in relation to others. That is what makes it a powerful metaphor for coaching presence. Anyone can develop that way of being if they choose to do so and if they carry themselves accordingly. When coaches take on the mindset of listening deeply for the needs of teachers, without judgment or intimidation, and when they show up with a mindful awareness of all that is possible in the coaching moment, coaches—like whisperers—can generate amazing transformations in relatively short periods of time. Horse whisperers understand the dangers of losing their presence and connection with wild horses who have never trusted human beings before. It can literally be life threatening. Coaches would do well to approach the coaching moment with equal wisdom and care. Our physical lives might not be at stake, but our life-giving abilities to stimulate learning and growth are certainly at risk.

Evocative Coaching as a Way of Being

Tim Gallwey (2000) defined *coaching* as "the art of creating an environment, through conversation and a way of being, that facilitates the process by which a person can move toward desired goals in a fulfilling manner" (p. 177). This definition highlights two key dimensions of coaching: coaching supports growth and change by what coaches do (having conversations) and by who coaches are (a way of being with people). We include that in our definition, too. Coaches, like whisperers, are concerned not only with results but also with the spirit of the person who seeks to achieve those results. The two always go hand in hand. Failure to exhibit full coaching presence with people undermines the potential of coaching conversations. If teachers are failing to engage and progress, it often has less to with the application of specific coaching techniques than with the nature of coaching presence. Evocative coaches master the art of both.

One universal trait of coaching presence is the dance between intention and attention in the present moment (Silsbee, 2008). Although coaching presence may appear graceful, and even effortless, in the hands of a masterful coach, it never happens by accident. It takes clear intention and plenty of practice. Evocative coaches prepare ourselves mentally and emotionally to be fully present and attentive before each and every coaching conversation. We do not multitask or rush through the coaching conversation. We do not show up with an agenda, such as to dispense expert advice, to teach a new technique, to explain a better way, to correct mistakes, or to commiserate with a struggling teacher. All such intentions interfere with the work of evocative coaching. It is only through life-giving connection and presence that adult learning gets stimulated and encouraged. Evocative coaches therefore pay close attention during coaching conversations to the energetic dynamics of the coaching space. When things begin to spiral downward, when the negatives come to preoccupy the conversation, and when agitation and anxiety threaten to overpower the moment, evocative coaches whisper a different tune. Without a shred of judgment or fear, evocative coaches calm things down and call things out. We receive such challenges as gifts to unwrap and explore without trepidation. We find positive ways to be with teachers and to generate new possibilities. All this comes from the heart of coaching presence.

> *Presence is a state of awareness, in the moment, characterized by the felt experience of timelessness, connectedness, and a larger truth.*
>
> *Doug Silsbee (2008, p. 21)*

The International Coach Federation (ICF), a leading association dedicated to the advancement of professional coaching, identifies coaching presence as a core coaching competency. The ICF defines coaching presence as the "ability to be fully conscious and create a spontaneous relationship with the client, employing a style that is open, flexible, and confident" (International Coach Federation, 2008b, p. 2). To this end, the ICF indicates that a professional coach:

1. Is present and flexible during the coaching process, dancing in the moment
2. Accesses one's own intuition and trusts one's inner knowing—"goes with the gut"

3. Is open to not knowing and takes risks
4. Sees many ways to work with the client, and chooses in the moment what is most effective
5. Uses humor effectively to create lightness and energy
6. Confidently shifts perspectives and experiments with new possibilities for own action
7. Demonstrates confidence in working with strong emotions, and can self-manage and not be overpowered by or enmeshed in client's emotions

Such qualities describe a way of being in the world as human beings, not just a way of going about our work as coaches. Whether coaching or not, evocative coaches radiate a steady, confident energy outward to others. Evocative coaches also embody a full-trust relationship to life itself. "Don't just do something, stand there!" is a Buddhist saying that expresses this understanding. It is not up to us to solve every problem and put out every fire; it is up to us to trust that life has a way of working things out. From this vantage point, we become available to participate in the process of transformation rather than consumed with making things happen. Coaches combine urgency on behalf of students with patience on behalf of teachers by "leading from the future as it emerges" (Scharmer, 2007; Senge, Scharmer, Jaworski, & Flowers, 2004). Modeling this presence and trust not only in the coaching moment but in our way of being in the world, evocative coaches generate the self-efficacy needed for teachers to move forward successfully with their vision and goals.

Teachers grow not only because of what coaches do with them, but also (and perhaps even more so) because of who coaches are in relationship to them. The disposition of the coach matters greatly to teacher outcomes.

Lessons from a Horse Whisperer

Evocative coaches have much to learn from those who whisper to animals in the service of understanding and gentle direction. Monty Roberts (2002, 2009) is probably the best-known horse whisperer of our day. The popularity of his autobiography, *The Man Who Listens to Horses* (2009), a *New York Times* bestseller, suggests that the book speaks to far more than horse lovers; it speaks to the human condition itself with stories of triumph and tragedy, as well as to the hope that there is a better way to promote learning and growth than the tired old strategies of punishments and rewards. People are apparently hungry for the presence that Roberts embodies. Evocative coaches have much in common with Monty Roberts in both our presence and our practices. Evocative coaches are humble, curious, and strong advocates for teachers. Instead of subjecting them to interference, we want to understand and appreciate them fully in their own right.

Roberts makes clear that the presence he conveys as a horse whisperer is neither a genetic nor a magical endowment. He developed it through a combination of curiosity, mindfulness, empathy, practice, and dogged determination. Where did that desire come from? Roberts was around horses from birth, and he witnessed the suffering they endured while they were being "broken" by cowboys and other trainers to accept their first saddle and rider. It was a process that could take six weeks, using humiliating and hurtful techniques, as the spirits of horses were slowly extinguished at the hands of their more powerful and often cruel masters. Monty decided that he wanted no part of that, either for humans or horses. So he set about the task of learning how horses communicated and behaved in the wild. Through many seasons of careful observations and experimentation, Roberts ultimately became able to understand and connect with horses in what he called their "own silent language."

> It occurred to me that I could (perhaps) use the same silent system of communication myself. If I understood how to do it, I could effectively cross over the boundary between human (the ultimate fight animal) and horse (the flight animal). Using their language, their system of communication, I could create a strong bond of trust. (Roberts, 2009, p. 24)

As a result of learning their language, Roberts gained the ability to "start" (rather than to "break") horses in thirty minutes or less. The speed of this method allowed him to start thousands of horses in the course of his career and to shift the way the entire world approaches the process. These dynamics parallel what happens through coaching presence. We seek to create strong bonds of trust and to speak in language with which teachers can identify and relate. Instead of making teachers come to us, evocative coaches step over the divide. Understanding the vulnerability of people in coaching, evocative coaches seek to calm and soothe the flight response.

Roberts achieved his remarkable results through a process he called "Join-Up®," or the establishment of trust and rapport. With the right attitude and approach, Join-Up could be accomplished in a matter of minutes rather than the days and weeks generally required for breaking a horse. The starting point of Join-Up was the intention Roberts brought to the relationship.

> My goal is not to make the horse submit. I want to gain his confidence and make him happy to follow the bit and bridle—as he'll be doing for the rest of his working life. (Roberts, 2009, p. 33)

Evocative coaches similarly want every coaching encounter, as well as the entire coaching relationship, to be positive and life-giving ones. Our presence is not that of a demanding taskmaster but of a compassionate friend.

> I don't want horses to work out of fear, but out of willingness. To destroy the willingness in a horse is a crazy, unforgiveable act. Inherent generosity is among the dominant characteristics of the horse, and if nurtured can grow into the most rewarding aspect of their working lives. Of the horses I have been close to in my life, I have marveled most at their willingness to try for me, over and over again. (Roberts, 2009, p. 40)

Evocative coaches understand that horses are not the only beings who naturally want to do their best and to succeed. We do not have to motivate or tell teachers to strive for that. We just have to encourage them to believe it is possible and invite them to pursue their full potential in self-directed ways. In the absence of fear and intimidation, and in the presence of trust and connection, coaches can leverage a teacher's desire to its full advantage. Evocative coaches believe in the inherent ambition of teachers and other educators. Most teachers want to make a difference in the lives of students and society. Understanding this, evocative coaches encourage the willingness of teachers to try new things and to do their best. This does not have to be taught, only encouraged.

> Join-Up is always the most thrilling part of the process. Not because I ever doubt it will happen, but simply because it proves the possibility of communication between human and horse. A flight animal giving her trust to a fight animal, human and horse spanning the gap between them, always strikes me as miraculous. The moment it occurs is always fresh, always satisfying. . . . (Roberts, 2009, p. 169)

Evocative coaches come alongside teachers, matching their energy, emotion, pacing, and style, until such a strong bond of trust is created that all suspicion and resistance is eliminated. Without this deep level of connection, without such trust and rapport, no real transformations will ever grow out of the coaching relationship. Such presence and connection are essential prerequisites to everything else.

> [When joining up with a mustang in the wild,] it was necessary for all of us to keep uppermost in our minds a sense of calmness, an utter lack of urgency. These horses need patience. If you act like you've only got fifteen minutes, it'll take all day. If you act like you've got all day, it'll take fifteen minutes. (Roberts, 2009, p. 240)

Evocative coaches take our time. The press for results does not trick evocative coaches into hurrying through the coaching process; such movements are always counterproductive. It may appear to save time to just tell people what to do and how to do it, with a great deal of urgency and impatience in our voice and body language, but it actually takes more time. And the solutions seldom work. Evocative coaches get results more quickly than directive coaches precisely because of how we connect with teachers using a calm, compatible, and confident energy that generates engagement, willingness, cooperation, openness, and excitement.

Evocative coaches respect the learning process that is unique to each and every teacher. There is no one universal path, let alone rate, of development. Some teachers immediately seize new opportunities, while others play with the possibilities over much longer periods of time. Either way, evocative coaches respect the learning process of teachers. We convey patience rather than urgency for change. It comes down to attending to and awakening what teachers want, need, and feel comfortable with.

> My way of thinking about horses was enriched by this critical idea: a rider or trainer should never say to a horse, "You must." Instead, the horse should be invited to perform because, "I would like to." Taking that a step further— to ask a horse to perform is not as clever as causing him to want to perform. Horses naturally want to run, and if they are trained correctly we can harness their willingness to do just that, to race to their potential. . . . There is no need for [whips] if training procedures take advantage of a well-bred horse's overpowering desire to run. (Roberts, 2009, p. 65)

Evocative coaches communicate certainty in the ability of teachers to learn and grow. We never write someone off as intractable or impossible. Instead we understand that when things are not going well, it says more about our approach and presence than about the capacity of the teacher we are coaching. When teachers fail to progress, it is either time to change who we are being in relationship to them or it is time to find them a new coach. Carl Rogers, a founder of humanistic psychology, noted how this dynamic works in human beings:

> If I want to help [someone to] reduce his defensiveness and become more adaptive, I must try to remove the threat of myself as his potential changer. As long as the atmosphere is threatening, there can be no effective communication. So I must create a climate which is neither critical, evaluative, nor moralizing. It must be an atmosphere of equality and freedom, permissiveness and understanding, acceptance and warmth. It is in this climate and this climate

only that the individual feels safe enough to incorporate new experiences and new values into his concept of himself. (Rogers & Farson, 1957, p. 3)

Evocative coaches know when to let up from the work of learning and trying new things. There is a time and place for people to push themselves; there is also a time and place for people to relax and have fun. Evocative coaches know how to do this dance. We understand the choreography. We keep just the right amount of tension on the line so as to neither snap it nor lose the catch.

Roberts's thinking and approach was shaped not only by his relationships with horses but also by a teacher, a Catholic nun, who made a claim that captured young Monty's imagination.

Sister Agnes Patricia was the most influential teacher I ever knew. What I will always remember about her is her statement that there is no such thing as teaching—only learning. She believed that no teacher could ever teach anyone anything. Her task as a teacher was to create an environment in which the student can learn. Knowledge, she told us, . . . needs to be pulled into the brain by the student, not pushed into it by the teacher. Knowledge is not to be forced on anyone. The brain has to be receptive, malleable, and most important, hungry for that knowledge. (Roberts, 2009, pp. 87–88)

Evocative coaches are emotionally aware and intelligent in our pursuit of performance gains. We know how to recognize, manage, and leverage emotions both for their intrinsic value and for their functional utility. We seek an emotional connection with teachers that is both fulfilling and generative. Through honesty and empathy we make our presence known. Evocative coaches take teachers' feelings into account. We listen not only to what is being said, but to what is not being said, to what wants to be said, and to what must be said. It can all happen in a whispering voice. Evocative coaches pay attention to what is happening in the moment. We do not accept gossip, triangulation, or secondhand reports. We rather respond directly to the teacher's actions and reactions.

Monty Roberts's presence and process as a horse whisperer hinges upon empathy. It is his *intention*: to connect with and understand horses rather than to correct and control them. It is his *presence*: to be a compassionate and fun-loving friend rather than a fearsome and hard-driving master. It is his *orientation*: to give every horse the benefit of the doubt and the opportunity to realize his or her full potential. And it is his *technique*: to communicate in the horses' language, on their terms, at their pace, with their sensitivities, and in their environment so as to foster learning and growth. Evocative coaches share these intentions, presence, orientation, and techniques with horse whisperers. They are the keys to our success, learning, and enjoyment as coaches. Without this way of being with teachers, few possibilities take off and soar. With this way of being, all kinds of possibilities emerge and are realized.

Fostering Trust and Rapport

Trust opens our work and dreams to each other, and makes possible continuous improvement of how we teach and what our students learn.

Carl Glickman (2002, p. xii)

Trust is a word that runs throughout Roberts's book. It is, indeed, the foundation of his entire work with horses: he seeks to develop trust above all else, and he refuses to move forward until that trust is solid. The same can be said for evocative coaches. Without a solid foundation of trust and respect, no coaching alliance can generate a productive and fulfilling change process. Unfortunately, the establishment of such an alliance is made even more difficult when educators and school environments find themselves under the gun. Teachers start to worry that coaching may be seen as a remedial punishment rather than as an exciting opportunity. As a result, they avoid seeking help because they fear the judgment of others. When they are told to seek help, their defenses go up and their openness to change goes down. In such settings, the trustworthy presence of an evocative coach becomes all the more important. It is the key not only to the success of individual teachers but also to the potential transformation of entire school environments. Just as Roberts became a catalyst for transformation in the entire horse-training industry, so, too, can evocative coaches affect the schools and settings in which we work. The dynamic of one generative coaching relationship can be contagious. It can make everyone more sensitive to the many ways in which trust matters, and it can transform schools, one conversation at a time.

For more than a decade, Megan has studied the ways in which trust affects and lubricates the work of schools. Her educational scholarship supports the practical wisdom of Monty Roberts and gives us yet another framework for understanding how and why his approach works. She defines *trust* as the "willingness to be vulnerable to another based on the confidence that the other is benevolent, honest, open, reliable, and competent" (Tschannen-Moran, 2004, p. 17). Understanding the importance of these five facets of trust, evocative coaches keep them in mind and seek to model them in our every interaction with teachers. Each facet will be considered in turn.

> You have to create the context for meaningful dialogue to occur. I think you
> have to get to them early. You have to develop that relationship and that trust;
> otherwise you are really not going to get anywhere.
>
> *Luke, high school department chair*

Benevolence

Perhaps the most essential ingredient in establishing trust and rapport in a coaching relationship is a sense of caring or *benevolence*. Coaches who hope to earn the trust of teachers need to demonstrate goodwill and genuine concern for the well-being of teachers. Coaches can promote trust by showing consideration and sensitivity for teachers' feelings and needs and by acting in ways that protect teachers' rights (Baier, 1994; Zand, 1997). In a coaching relationship characterized by benevolence, there is a sense of caring not just about the immediate outcome of the coaching project but also about the teacher as a person and about the coaching relationship itself. Benevolence enlivens the coaching relationship with a sense of warmth, which generates full engagement. It is a contagious quality of being that invigorates conversations, relationships, and circumstances. When people warm up to each other, their energy elevates, ideas come, light bulbs go off, and new possibilities are created.

As we have seen, evocative coaching requires a judgment-free environment. Safety and a strong sense of support, preconditions for success in all coaching sessions, are especially important when teachers are challenged to stretch to the edge of their abilities. Establishing such an environment enables teachers to be open and authentic so that the important things can get said and considered. The caring or benevolence required in trust has also been described as "unconditional positive regard" (Rogers, 1989, p. 62) or as being completely accepting toward another person, without reservations. Without such empathic support and understanding, the coaching alliance will be weak and unsuccessful. Judgment, criticism, and contempt—spoken or unspoken—do not motivate or support behavior change. It is not our place as coaches to point out teachers' shortcomings and show them a better way. Rather, we are called to champion their strengths and invite them to figure out a better way. When we believe in teachers and hold positive regard for them—regardless of what they do or do not accomplish—we establish a relationship that can bolster self-efficacy and confidence. Unfailing positive regard is the key to establishing rapport and trust and is foundational for the work of evocative coaching.

I'm working with Kathryn, a fourth-grade teacher, on teaching reading. The principal made the decision to put all of the strategic and intensive readers in fourth grade in her one classroom. Although she's a seasoned teacher, Kathryn has poor classroom management skills. On the first day I was introduced to Kathryn, the principal and I observed in her classroom together, and I went back after school to talk with her about how she thought it went. As I was trying to talk with her, she was sitting at her desk and she started humming. She was humming a song and rearranging the papers on her desk and not making any eye contact with me. I was like, "This is not good." I realized that she was really uncomfortable so I excused myself and left. The next day I went back and shared with her my sense that our conversation the day before had been creating a lot of stress for her. I said, "I don't want it to be that way. What can I do to make it better?" It turned out that when the principal and I had observed in her classroom, he wasn't happy with the instruction. This principal is a very gruff man, and he went in afterward and basically told Kathryn that she was making the school look like a bunch of idiots and that she needed to get her act together. There was a lot of tension as she shared this. The good thing was that she was able to share her experience. I listened to her and was very sympathetic. I shared an experience I'd had when I'd felt similarly. I think the one thing that saved me in that situation was that I had worked with other teachers in that building and they told her that I was a good person. We were able to kind of laugh about it, so I think that was good. But I definitely wasn't set up for a successful situation. I'm glad that it's now proving to be a very successful relationship.

Danielle, elementary literacy coach

Honesty

Honesty is not only the best policy; it is the *only* policy in coaching. *Honesty* concerns a person's integrity and authenticity. *Integrity* is the perceived match between words and deeds. People with integrity walk their talk. When people fail to do that, by saying one thing and doing another, trust is compromised. In an effort to please, coaches may be tempted to promise things we cannot fully deliver in a timely fashion. To avoid conflict, we may also be tempted to be less than completely honest and upfront with teachers. The revelation of such apparent dishonesties may be more damaging to trust than lapses in other facets, because it is read as an indictment of the coach's character. Once a coach has been caught in even a "little lie," and teachers have lost faith in a coach's word, trust can be difficult to reestablish because the communication process itself is now suspect.

Authenticity is the perceived match between words and experience. People with authenticity share what is there. Perhaps the most challenging way of being for many coaches involves the courage to do just that. The word *courage* may conjure up images of conflict and tough talk. But being courageous is about honestly sharing our sense of what is happening and what is alive in order to increase teacher awareness, create connection, and generate movement (Scott, 2004). Such is the key to courageous and authentic conversations in coaching as well as life in general. It is not about evaluating people or telling them what we think they are doing wrong. It is rather about courageously sharing with people what we observe, feel, need, and request. It often takes time and effort to explore this deeper level of connection, but the dividends can be significant. Respectful and genuine interactions with teachers can evoke new understandings and readiness to change.

Evocative coaches understand the difference between being nice and being authentic (d'Ansembourg, 2007). We boldly and yet gently express our heartfelt understanding of what is going on in the service of teacher outcomes and vitality. Evocative coaches have a fearless, conversational prowess that shakes things loose and stirs things up without offending, violating, blaming, shaming, or demeaning people. We have a genuine and humble way of stepping up to the plate and making conversations real. "Sharing what is there" becomes the mark and measure of such conversations, since honest communication leads to learning and growth. Evocative coaches can do this without sounding critical or judgmental because we do not harbor these attitudes in our hearts and minds and because we have learned other ways to communicate about difficult subjects. Steeped in compassion, empathy, and appreciation, equipped with life-enriching understandings, inquiries, and reflections, evocative coaches know how to build authentic, meaningful, and growth-fostering relationships with teachers.

Approaching teachers in this way may be difficult and intimidating at first. As long as we stay with accurate observations, however, free from evaluations, and as long as we reflect a judgment-free understanding of what we are experiencing and seeing, evocative coaches enable teachers to gain new awareness and understanding of who they are and what they are facing. As a result, teachers can muster the courage to more fully meet their needs. By shining a light on what "wants to be said," by noticing carefully what is happening, coaches can move teachers forward in dynamic and powerful ways.

We were pleased to hire Ruth, an experienced third-grade teacher, to fill a last-minute opening because she seemed very strong in the interview. Within the first couple of weeks of school, though, we started getting calls from parents with

concerns about disorganized instruction, lack of communication, and kids having no idea what was expected on their homework. I was not responsible for
evaluating her, but I took her under my wing to try to assist her. She liked kids
but she was more of a camp counselor, spontaneous and playful. She wasn't getting the instruction across. The first time I observed her, I didn't sugarcoat it.
I was honest with her and said, "Look, we're getting a lot of complaints here."
It always comes down to relationships, and she knew I was not out to get her—
that I was trying to help her be successful. We spent hours together observing,
planning, finding resources, getting and giving feedback. In the end, she was
not angry when her contract was not renewed. She didn't feel betrayed because
she could see the enormous effort that we'd all been making on her behalf.
She resigned and made plans to go back to school to become a media spe-
cialist, which is probably a better fit for her.

Lydia, elementary assistant principal

Openness

Openness is a process by which people make themselves vulnerable to others by
sharing information, influence, and control (Zand, 1997). In taking the initiative
to extend trust by engaging in acts of openness, evocative coaches induce the
same dynamic in teachers (Kramer, Brewer, & Hanna, 1996). That works because
openness is reciprocal. When coaches exchange thoughts and ideas freely with
teachers, it increases the likelihood that teachers will become more open and willing to share their thoughts, feelings, and ideas with their coaches (Butler, 1991;
Zand, 1997). This initiates an upward spiral of trust in the coaching relationship.
Information shared is always a giving of self, whether it is strictly about professional matters or whether it includes obviously personal information (Butler &
Cantrell, 1984).

It is important to start off the coaching relationship on the right foot. That
certainly includes an open yet brief disclosure of our backgrounds, our intentions,
how we work with people, as well as our passion for coaching, learning, and the
teaching profession. "What more do you want to know about me?" is a great way
to end an introduction and to invite questions that build rapport. How much personal disclosure is helpful? People come to coaching not only to learn techniques,
but also for inspiration. Most people already know, or at least have a sense of, what
they "should" be doing to improve teaching. They just do not know *how* to do it
consistently, and they may not even be sure that they *want* to do it. By drawing
close to someone who believes not only in the value of education but also in the

possibility of mastering educational challenges, teachers gain insight and inspiration for the journey. Personal disclosure on the part of the coach is appropriate and valuable when it serves the best interests of the teacher and the coaching program. It becomes counterproductive, however, when the conversation revolves around the feelings and needs of the coach rather than the teacher. As coaches, we must carefully discern if and when to share who we are, why we care about teaching, how we live, what our victories and struggles are, and what we know and do not know about teaching.

Openly sharing stories, feelings, needs, and ideas is essential for the coaching relationship to be successful. Some, if not most, teachers may initially be intimidated or uncomfortable about personal disclosure. To allay those fears, evocative coaches establish from the very beginning the safety of the coaching space as well as the parameters of coaching confidentiality. Appropriate, professional confidentiality is an essential part of evocative coaching. Evocative coaches cannot be spies for the administration; we work hard to reassure teachers that no information will be either intentionally or inadvertently shared with others without the prior permission or knowledge of the teacher. The coach should make this clear both orally and in writing to everyone concerned (including the administration). There may be instances when a teacher wants to share something personal but does not want it to be recorded in a coach's files or coaching log. They may explicitly say something like, "I want to tell you something, but not if you have to make it part of my record." After making the appropriate disclaimer to do one's duty to report child abuse or other illegal activities, it is important to make clear one's willingness to suspend record keeping and note taking. Documentation is not helpful if it undermines the openness of the coaching conversation.

> When I start working with a collaborative team, I say, "It's like Vegas. What happens in collaboration stays in collaboration." I share that I've told their administrators that I will not tell them anything that the teacher is doing good or bad unless the teacher asks me to do that. And I give them some examples and kind of role play for them how I would respond to an inquiry from the administrator. So I think that kind of helps them see that I'm really serious about that. And I tell them, I'm a person of my word so you can hold me to that. I'm here to help you and I don't have any agenda except identifying with you the things that you need to learn more about and helping you do that.
>
> *Julie, elementary literacy coach*

Reliability

For coaches to garner trust, we must demonstrate consistency in our behaviors so as to inspire the confidence that teachers can count on us in their time of need. In a situation of interdependence, when something is required from another person or group, a reliable individual can be consistently counted upon to supply it (Butler & Cantrell, 1984; Mishra, 1996). *Reliability* implies that you can rest assured that you can depend on a person to do what is expected on a regular, consistent basis. One need not invest energy worrying whether the person will come through or making mental provisions as to how to manage the situation in case of failure. It is not enough for coaches to show support from time to time or to demonstrate benevolence occasionally. The sense that one is able to depend on another consistently is an important element of trust. Teachers may conclude that their coach is a nice person and means well, and even that he or she is very capable and helpful, but trust will be broken if the coach fails to follow through on promises, has trouble managing his or her time, gets distracted easily, or otherwise demonstrates a lack of reliability. Such tendencies do not make for evocative coaching.

There is a maxim in coaching to "underpromise and overdeliver." Trust and rapport is compromised by broken promises. That is why evocative coaches are extremely careful to monitor and select our words carefully, both during coaching sessions and in communications between sessions. Be sure to deliver or overdeliver on every promise. Some promises, such as being on time, ready, and available for observations and coaching appointments, are unspoken parts of the coaching agreement. Other promises, such as sending teachers information, are offered in the course of conversation. Delivering on promises is crucial to the coaching relationship. Delivering even more than promised creates an even stronger bond. Going beyond the expected minimum is a great way to build trust and rapport. For example, coaches may contact teachers by e-mail between coaching sessions to congratulate them or to remind them of something important. When teachers e-mail or get in touch with their coaches, evocative coaches respond within twenty-four hours, if only to acknowledge the contact and to promise a date and time for a more thoughtful response. Be careful to not fall into the trap of overpromising and underdelivering. This may be common in society, as people seek to make themselves look good, but it quickly leads to failed relationships in coaching with poor outcomes. When coaches model such thoughtful self-monitoring and self-management, teachers may adopt underpromising and overdelivering for themselves.

Competence

When building trust, evocative coaches demonstrate two forms of *competence*. On the one hand, we may demonstrate subject matter expertise. Few teachers will trust the instructional advice of coaches, for example, who have never effectively taught students in classroom settings. On the other hand, we cannot just use our subject-matter expertise to show off what we know to others. No one likes to be shown up, embarrassed, or otherwise dominated, even by a master practitioner. So evocative coaches also demonstrate change-management expertise, which means we set aside our subject-matter expertise in order to facilitate the natural, discovery-learning process of teachers.

In this sense, coaching competence means giving less advice, or even no advice, so teachers can figure out their own ways of working more effectively. It means slowing down, paying full attention, and asking good questions. It means establishing trust and rapport in each and every coaching conversation. Trust is not earned once and for all. It is earned, or lost, during every moment of every coaching conversation. If coaches are in a hurry to "get down to business" or to tell teachers what they ought to do, trust and rapport will be compromised or lost. As a result, progress will be impeded or blocked altogether. Evocative coaches set aside enough time to have a relaxed—and relaxing—presence with teachers. Even when appointments, observations, or conversations happen back to back, we need to slow down and savor every minute.

Good listening and discovery learning require that we slow down. It is not possible to do these things in a hurry. They take time and patience. We have to be quiet to hear what people are saying and, perhaps, to hear what they cannot hear themselves and do not know how to express. As a listening presence, evocative coaches empower people to become more deeply aware of and connected to what they are trying to say. That is the very point at which learning becomes accelerated. When we act like we have all day, learning can seem to take hardly any time at all. That is because deep listening is a powerful magnet for moving people in the direction they want to go. Unfortunately, most of us think we have no time for such powerful listening. And when we think that way, it becomes a self-fulfilling prophecy. When we act like we have hardly any time at all, learning can seem to take all day. We cannot be good listeners when we feel impatient and rushed. We cannot pay attention and enjoy the conversation when we have other things on our mind. We cannot discover new wisdom and truth when our agenda takes us through life at warp speed. Understanding this, evocative coaches demonstrate competence by slowing down to listen well.

In addition to slowing down, evocative coaches also pay full attention. Teachers can tell when coaches are not 100 percent present: our energy becomes less focused and engaging. Teachers will often accept this low level of focus and engagement, since it is the norm in modern culture. It is up to the coach, therefore, to take the conversation to a higher level by paying full attention. Trust and rapport are not built through multitasking. When coaches are distracted, whether physically, intellectually, emotionally, or spiritually, the coaching relationship suffers. Trying to do two things at once may cause us to lose strands of the conversation and may degrade the quality of our inquiries and reflections.

To facilitate ease and full attention, evocative coaches extend our presence to the coaching space. We notice what is going on in our many environments and take action to minimize distractions (e.g., foot traffic, noise, bystanders, or phone and computer alerts). We use relaxation and reminder techniques to assist us to leave our own thoughts and concerns "at the door," in order to focus our attention entirely on the teacher. This is especially helpful during times of emotional strain and may be worth doing with teachers at the start of conversations when there is clearly tension or disruption in the air.

Changing subjects prematurely reflects the problem many of us have not only with listening but also with time management and being in the present moment. We are one step ahead of ourselves, or one step behind, but seldom truly attentive to the here and now. We are quick to come up with answers, to tell people what is on our mind, and to voice our opinions rather than to patiently ask questions that will draw out the speaker. It is, of course, impossible to not have our own ideas especially when we do have subject matter expertise. Someone tells us something and connections are made, solutions are seen, and alternatives are explored. That is a normal part of conversation. But when we share what we know too soon or change the subject too quickly, we send the message: "I'm more interested in what I know than in what you can figure out."

In conclusion, trust and rapport are essential elements of the coaching relationship. Without trust, the teacher's energy will be invested in self-protection or in assessing the available recourse in case of disappointment or betrayal. To free these energies for the coaching process, the coach needs to embody benevolence, honestly, openness, reliability, and competence.

I make a firm commitment not to share any evaluative feedback with principals about any of the teachers I am coaching. If they ask me, I'll say, "Why don't we go and observe together and you can let me know what you see that you are concerned about or that you'd like us to work on?"

Danielle, elementary literacy coach

Holding the Coaching Space

As we have seen, to be successful, evocative coaches pay special attention to the quality of the dynamics between the coach and the teacher. Teachers resonate in response to the way coaches come across. Ideally, a coach's presence promotes mutuality and involvement. It is the coach's job to hold open the interpersonal space or relational field in which the work of coaching takes place (Silsbee, 2008). A key element coaches attend to in that space or field is the flow of energy and emotion between coach and teacher. Evocative coaches can tell when we are connected in life-giving ways, since the dynamics become those of calm assurance, playfulness, and openness to new possibilities.

> *One of the tasks of the coach is to create a safe and creative* change space. *This involves a place that invites [teachers] to feel safe enough to explore and disclose, and a creative place for brainstorming, playing around with ideas and options, experimenting, and taking risks.*
>
> L. *Michael Hall and Michelle Duval (2004, p. 255)*

Calm Assurance

Evocative coaches extend calm assurance both to ourselves and to others, because we come from a framework of deep appreciation for the present moment. The present moment is the only moment we have in which to do our work. There is no way to arrive at any future moment other than through the present moment. There is also no way for the present moment to be any different than it is, given all the past moments. If we see every situation as perfectly designed for our own learning and growth, then we can embrace every situation for where it comes from and where it leads us. Extending calm assurance, regardless of the situation, is about assisting teachers to respond to life's experiences without catastrophizing.

That is the posture evocative coaches generally take in life, and especially with teachers. We neither disparage ourselves nor others. The notion that things are not okay is dissipated by recognizing that all life-alienating thoughts, words, and actions are expressions of unmet needs. By hearing the needs that underlie those thoughts, words, and actions, evocative coaches can maintain a calm and compassionate presence in relationship both to ourselves and to others. Evocative coaches understand the impossibility of learning in high-strung and overstimulated emotional states. We take a calm, single-minded approach to even the most frenzied, multifaceted of situations.

Calm assurance is about steadfastly acknowledging a person's capacities, characteristics, and strengths for change. Over time, this positive tone affects both self-esteem and self-efficacy. The mantra, "My certainty is greater than your doubt," expresses the framework that evocative coaches come from in holding the coaching space (Buck, 2006). When teachers know that coaches believe in their capacity to change and achieve desired outcomes, they are more likely to get out of their own way and try new strategies. Such an endorsement enables teachers not only to get excited about the possibilities generated through the coaching conversations but also to move forward with one or more of them.

Playfulness

Although coaching is serious business with serious goals in which people are seriously invested—performance improvement—the coaching conversation itself need not have a serious tone. In fact, a consistently serious tone may cause teachers to dread their coaching sessions and consequently fail to thrive. The more often we can get teachers to laugh and see the lighter side of their challenges and opportunities, the more they will open themselves up to change. A playful approach can make teachers more open to experimentation with trial and correction.

Playfulness ignites our energy for and engagement with life. Both humor and curiosity underlie playfulness. Without the ability to laugh, especially in the face of life's ironies, incongruities, and adversities, one would seldom find the energy to play. Young children laugh hundreds of times per day; older adults average about seventeen times per day. Perhaps that is why laughter clubs, which started in India, have turned into a global movement. These groups run through a series of laughter patterns that eventually give way (after an initial warm-up) to an epidemic of spontaneous giggles, chuckles, and guffaws. Participants report feeling refreshed, relaxed, revitalized, and rejuvenated by the experience. Evocative coaches, and other healthy adults, know how to laugh and have fun (Wooten, 1996; Balick & Lee, 2003).

In the service of playfulness, evocative coaches avoid joking about things that may make a teacher feel vulnerable. We use empathy to distinguish between those areas that are ripe for humor and those that may make teachers feel worse if treated too lightly. We make sure that teachers never think we are laughing *at* them. It is fair game, though, to laugh at ourselves. Using humor, laughter, and playfulness in coaching energizes the behavior change process so that solutions expand in scope, sustainability, and effectiveness.

You can't take yourself too seriously in this position. You need to have a sense of humor and have fun. I've learned to laugh at myself. I'm a technology coach, so my principal teased me, saying, "You know, every time you do a technology demonstration, it seems like the technology breaks down!" We had a good laugh at the absurdity of it. She went on to say, "You always hang in there and stay positive and that is great modeling."

Nancy, technology integration coach

Openness to Possibility

Part of the coach's response-ability comes from a presence of mind that always maintains an optimistic stance toward what is possible. By anticipating the best, evocative coaches create conditions that bring out the best in people. In spite of life's obvious challenges, evocative coaches radiate openness to possibility in ways that generate conversations for change. It is almost impossible for coaches who are filled with optimism and hope not to infuse that energy into coaching conversations. Teachers catch wind of and come to share our emotional state (De Waal, 2006, 2009). When that state demonstrates positivity and openness to possibility, motivation and movement are sure to follow.

In their book, *The Art of Possibility*, Rosamund and Ben Zander (2000) draw attention to "shining eyes" as evidence of people dwelling in the realm of possibility. The opposite of openness to possibility is residing in what the Zanders call "the downward spiral," where it seems that we are facing insurmountable odds, and options for the future look bleak. Many teachers have experienced the accountability movement this way. It is the coach's job to shore up teachers who are experiencing the downward spiral and to train their attention on the positive options that are present. Wonderful vitalities can always be observed, if you are willing to look for them.

It may not be possible to radiate this energy every minute of every day, but evocative coaches maintain that presence of mind more often than not. That is what makes coaching successful. Demonstrating openness to possibility is an incredibly attractive energy that people want to get close to and build on. It is a self-reinforcing and radiating spiral dynamic. It supports resilience and self-efficacy in the service of coaching outcomes.

One simple strategy for bringing positive energy and emotions into the coaching conversation is to cultivate gratitude. Noticing, remembering, and celebrating good things that happen are powerful antidotes to the well-worn litany of bad things that tend to build up over time. Mandates, restrictions, lack of appreciation, and pressure for results may be part of teachers' daily experience, but they are not the sum total of that experience. Turning attention to what is working and building on those successes can renew and refresh even the most discouraged of teachers. Understanding this, evocative coaches stoke our own attitude of gratitude through daily positive practices that build happiness, balance, and self-esteem (Csikszentmihalyi, 1997; Fredrickson, 2009; Lyubomirsky, 2007; Seligman, 2006).

When we live and experience life as a delightful adventure, it is easy to approach our work with teachers in much the same way. There is no telling what teachers will come up with!

Conveying Coaching Presence

Coaching presence is conveyed in many ways, including body language, facial expressions, eye contact, intonation, word choice, phrasing, and pacing. When coaching presence is conveyed artfully, coaches and teachers lean into each other with full engagement. This leaning in can be seen in the eyes and heard in the voice as one thing leads spontaneously to another. If one or the other is leaning out or pulling away, then something isn't working. It is time for the coach to try a different approach. Evocative coaches use all modalities at our disposal, including somatic and vocal shifts. Sometimes we move our bodies or use our voices to build excitement with stimulating optimism and energy. At other times, we move our bodies and use our voices to calm things down with soothing energy. Either way, coaching presence is conveyed not only by what we say and do in the moment but also by how we say and do it.

> *People feel more at ease with others who match their body language and voice tone and rhythm. Match as in a dance, not copy exactly, which is very annoying.*
>
> *Joseph O'Connor and Andrea Lages (2007, p. 92)*

Although our metaphors and descriptions of coaching presence may sound superhuman, everyone understands that coaches are, in fact, humans who sometimes experience impatience at the rate of change or irritation at some of the attitudes or behaviors of the teachers we are coaching. This may be especially true if we focus on the educational experience and outcomes of the students placed in the teachers' care. In these instances, the coach can step back from the coaching encounter, take a deep breath, grieve these unmet needs, and then reengage in ways that are "charge neutral." *Charge neutral* means that our body language, words, and voice tone carry neither a negative nor an inauthentic positive tone. It is to communicate in a manner that is both even and direct.

Silence, too, is an important part of coaching presence. It conveys comfort, respect, and spaciousness for the teacher's experience. Feelings, needs, and desires can take a while to surface and become clear. When coaches are comfortable with silence, our presence becomes more evocative (Silsbee, 2008).

In the beginning, I invested a lot of time in building relationships. There were teachers who didn't want to have anything to do with me at first. I would start by maybe stopping by classrooms and asking how things were going—just

(Continued)

---

being interested in them. I'd say, "I noticed a great lesson you were doing, tell me about that." I'd be their friends first. And I'd listen. That is the key, you have to really listen. Sometimes I'd overhear a teacher talking about a student she was frustrated with, and so I would ask about that and we'd start to brainstorm. We'd talk a while, and pretty soon we had a lesson!

Nancy, technology integration coach

Coaching Presence in the Context of Hierarchy

It is easier and more natural to take a nonjudgmental, low-threat, and collaborative stance when coaching in the absence of the power dynamics created by hierarchy. When coaches are not in the position to "make" teachers do things, let alone to terminate their employment, our presence as learning partners can flower fully. Issues of trust and rapport become easier to negotiate and manage. Conversations about what is going well and what teachers would like to improve become more open and forthcoming. The spirit of calm assurance, playfulness, and openness to possibility comes more naturally. That was why many of the coaches interviewed for this book explicitly sought to assure teachers of their distance from the evaluative role, with clear principles and practices regarding confidentiality. By setting boundaries in this way, they were better able to establish trusting connections with teachers.

Professionals working at different levels within school hierarchies, however, are also tasked with improving the quality of instruction and solving the problems of practice. Indeed, few people in charge of running schools and school districts, departments, or grade levels would not see that as being part of their responsibility. It is their job to make sure that students are well served, in every sense of the word. They yearn to make their schools successful, which is increasingly judged in terms of student performance on standardized learning tests and other quantifiable measures. Whatever one may think about that form of evaluation, no one can argue that the pressures and stakes are high to meet those standards. As a result, schools are continually rolling out new initiatives to assist teachers to do better, and coaching is increasingly included in the job descriptions of those with positional authority over teachers.

Fortunately, the fact that supervision, evaluation, and coaching are often intertwined in the real world does not mean that the principles and practices of evocative coaching cannot be adapted and used in such settings. The key is to develop an evocative coaching presence. That is just as important, if not more important, when coaching in the context of hierarchy. If we fail to establish trust and rapport, our coaching will come up short even if we technically have the ability to "make" teachers do things or "incentivize" them to change their behavior. The limits of behaviorism have been well documented. If we fail to make the coaching space inviting and evocative, with calm assurance, playfulness, and openness to possibility, and if we fail to connect with teachers on an emotional level, there is little likelihood that they will respond positively to our presence or go beyond minimum contractual obligations in improving their own performance. Evocative coaching is more challenging when coaches occupy boxes that are higher in the organizational chart than teachers, but it is not impossible to modify the form such that our coaching opportunities become more enjoyable and effective.

One of the biggest challenges supervisors and evaluators face in evocative coaching is bracketing our own power in the relationship. We may think we are just voicing an opinion or brainstorming an idea, but teachers may hear those words as mandates. We may think we are just making an observation as to something that is happening in the present moment, but teachers may hear those remarks as judgments or criticisms to which they will be held accountable. The more those dynamics get personalized, the more teachers may come to view supervisors and evaluators as adversaries or enemies rather than as collaborators and allies. There is no way for coaching to be evocative if teachers are intimidated or afraid in the relationship. Supervisors and evaluators must therefore bend over backwards to establish trust and rapport and to watch what we say in the context of coaching conversations. The more we use our authority, the less teachers will warm up to the process, and the less successful they will be in imagining and implementing new behaviors. That is especially challenging when we are accountable for evaluating teacher performance on an official document that reports on target behaviors to those who are even higher up the organizational chart. Layers upon layers of bureaucracy and hierarchy can undermine coaching presence and make us prone to go back to those old "tell-and-sell" approaches.

To avoid these dynamics and to foster coaching presence while also holding a supervisory or evaluative role, it is important to be transparent about our responsibilities to the school system, to the taxpayers or other funders, and to the parents in monitoring whether teachers are doing what they are paid to do. It is also important to be open about the criteria on which teachers will be judged, the evaluation tool to be used, as well as when and how the evaluation will take place. Such transparency and openness facilitate trust. Once these dynamics are out on the table, it helps to check in as to how teachers are feeling. It is helpful to check in on feelings periodically, to empathize with teacher needs, and to acknowledge the challenges of being "under the microscope." Once such a human connection is made, more things become possible.

People do better when they are not governed, constricted, and tightened up by fear.
Rosamund Stone Zander (Harvard Coaching Conference, 2009)

A serious problem with many official evaluation tools is that they do not include a clear rubric of what various performance levels would look like or entail, leaving things up to the subjective judgment of the evaluator. If such a rubric does not exist, it may be worthwhile to spend some time with the teachers you will be evaluating to develop common understandings of what is meant by the descriptors used on the tool. It may also be valuable to ask teachers to offer their own self-evaluation on each of the criteria before we share our ratings. If rapport is maintained throughout the conversation, with honest observations as to school requirements and occasional empathy check-ins, it will support teacher engagement in the development of a set of professional learning goals that can be integrated into the coaching conversations to come.

It is also extremely important when coaching in the context of hierarchy to keep the conversation focused on the strengths, vitalities, and aspirations that teachers can leverage for learning rather than on the weaknesses they have to fix and problems they have to solve. This appreciative approach is a fundamental part of the evocative coaching model as discussed in Chapters Five and Six and can be successfully integrated into both professional development and evaluation processes (Preskill & Catsambas, 2006). Such an orientation lowers the threat level, opens up teachers to the coaching process, and elevates their readiness to change. When supervisors and evaluators maintain a strengths-based, can-do framework in coaching, our presence becomes evocative of change. It enables teachers to have the energy, creativity, and confidence to develop successful designs for skills and performance improvement over time.

Mentoring relationships may share some of the same challenges as that of school leaders and evaluation officers in that they can introduce a power differential into the coaching relationship. There is an expectation that mentors hold and will share their greater professional knowledge with the novice. Their advice may be welcomed by the novice, but it can also interfere with the developing self-efficacy of new teachers and may limit the ideas they come up with themselves. Comparisons can be debilitating, and once an idea is put on the table by a designated mentor, that idea quickly becomes the focus of conversation. Mentors can use the evocative coaching model to avoid these dynamics and to engage teachers more fully in designing their own learning and development plans.

Peer coaching and collaborative teams minimize or even eliminate the power differential but may suffer from problems with confidentiality and a lack of coach training if care is not taken as they are established. Studying and reviewing the evocative coaching model together is one way to stimulate thinking and conversation about how to be with one another in coaching relationships that more effectively contribute to the professional growth of colleagues.

> Our county makes it easy for me to separate coaching from evaluation because they provide a specific evaluation form for use with all teachers with check boxes for "Met expectations," "Exceeded expectations," and "Has not met expectations." I am very explicit with teachers when I am doing evaluations that if I see areas where I think they have not met the basic standards, then they will be the first to know and we will develop a process to deal with it. But as long as they are meeting standards, or moving toward meeting standards, they are free to design their own learning goals as well.
>
> *Beth, elementary resource teacher*

Summary

There is a reason we have started this book by focusing on the way of being and presence that describes evocative coaches: apart from that authentic intention to connect and enrich life, no tool or technique will work. Evocative coaches do not see ourselves as helpers with answers and assistance; we rather see ourselves as whisperers who can call out the best from teachers in even the most difficult and challenging of situations. What constitutes the presence of a whisperer? Someone who connects deeply, laughs easily, accepts readily, trusts implicitly, and understands fully the larger truth of who people are and what they can do. Evocative coaches see teachers as whole human beings who can figure out for themselves how to be more successful once they find supportive environments and encouraging relationships. Evocative coaching is one such relationship.

Evocative coaching can be used by and can enhance the effectiveness of administrators, supervisors, department chairs, mentors, peer coaches, collaborative teams, and other professionals responsible for improving performance in schools. The basic insight of evocative coaching—that we have to "join up" with people rather than break them down if we want to facilitate their cooperation and growth—works across the board and in every setting. No leadership task can be effective without trust and rapport, sensitivity and engagement, as well as mutuality and respect. The evocative coaching model therefore encourages coaches and leaders to pay attention to the quality of our presence as a key dynamic in fostering growth and affecting change.

Questions for Reflection and Discussion

1. What dimensions of coaching presence resonate with your experience? How do these dimensions promote mutuality and involvement?
2. How do you convey coaching presence in your everyday interactions with others, even when you are not coaching?
3. What helps you to get into a coaching frame of mind? What practices assist you to make it so before a coaching session?
4. How do you nurture your sense of calm assurance during a coaching session, and how do you convey that to the teachers you are coaching?
5. What is the difference between being nice and being authentic? How can a coach share perceptions and hunches without blaming or shaming the teacher?
6. What does Monty Roberts mean when he writes, "If you act like you've only got fifteen minutes, it'll take all day. If you act like you've got all day, it'll take fifteen minutes"? How could you communicate less time urgency in coaching?
7. Who could you listen to today, with your undivided attention, for at least ten minutes?
8. What helps you to bracket the pressures of your position in order to attend to the quality of your presence?
9. How open are you to possibility? What would support you in cultivating greater optimism and gratitude?

PART TWO

THE FOUR STEPS OF EVOCATIVE COACHING

LOOP I: THE NO-FAULT TURN

As coach, my first responsibility [is] to maintain a nonjudgmental focus, provide appropriate opportunity for natural learning, and stay out of the way.

TIM GALLWEY (2000, P. 11)

The first two steps in the dynamic dance of evocative coaching are story listening and expressing empathy. Together, Story–Empathy represents the opening turn or loop of our Möbius strip (see Figure LI.1). Although they are presented individually as distinct steps of evocative coaching, in reality they are inextricably intertwined and continually co-created. They represent the initial give and take, the opening rhythm, of evocative coaching conversations. Teachers share their stories in conversation with coaches, revealing their understandings, energies, and emotions in the process. Coaches respond, then, with listening and empathy. Back and forth those two steps go, in iterative fashion, entwining until they become generative. When teachers feel heard in this way, and when coaches hear in this way, it opens up both the potential and movement of the conversation. When Story–Empathy is done right, it naturally turns the conversation in the direction of Inquiry–Design.

Unlike some approaches to coaching, which move quickly into skill building and training, evocative coaching starts and lingers in Story–Empathy because of how these steps change the tone and texture of the coaching process. There is no way to rush through the building of trust, rapport, and positivity that expands awareness and facilitates readiness to change. Coaches just have to let it happen, in its own good time. We take this approach because skill building means little, and may even be counterproductive, unless teachers are first open and receptive to what training has to offer. We also take this approach because we

FIGURE LI.1 LOOP I: THE NO-FAULT TURN

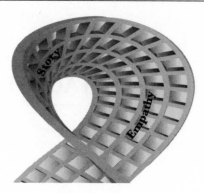

know that teachers, in the end, must always figure things out for themselves, even when they are implementing directives. They are the ones who have to make things work, and no one can do it for them. By communicating our trust in teachers' abilities to do this, evocative coaches bolster teacher motivation and increase the probability that the answers teachers come up with will actually work.

Story–Empathy pivots, as we have seen, around the benevolent presence of the coach and the quality of the coaching relationship. Although evocative coaches make use of many interesting and creative conversational techniques, facilitating the heart of dialogue, how we show up and engage with teachers in the coaching moment make all the difference in the world. When our presence and connection are vital and life giving, when our energy and orientation are respectful and caring, then teachers will turn in a positive direction in response to just about any approach. In the absence of such vitality and respect, however, no technique can be expected to generate desired results. By setting and sustaining the intention to understand and respond to the experiences and emotions of teachers without judgment, blame, or coercion, evocative coaches set teachers on the path to self-discovery and self-directed learning. Our presence invites a bond that proves to be transformational.

> *Research points to four ways to build high-quality connections. The first is respectful engagement. Be present, attentive, and affirming. The second is to support what the other person is doing. Do what you can to help her succeed. The third is trust. Believe you can depend on this person to meet your expectations, and let it show. The fourth way is play. Allow time simply to goof off, with no particular outcomes in mind.*
>
> *Barbara Fredrickson (2009, p. 201)*

That is why we understand Story–Empathy, taken together, as the No-Fault Turn. The work of coaching is not to evaluate teacher performance, and the more teachers feel evaluated by coaches the less inclined they are to dance with us. If we want teachers to do the work of designing new strategies for performance improvement, then we must eliminate the fear of failure from the equation. There are no failures in evocative coaching. There are only fascinating experiences that teachers can learn from and build on once they feel safe enough to try. If we want teachers to risk considering new perspectives and trying new things, then coaches must listen to their stories and respond with empathy regardless of how things work out. We never communicate a sense of impatience, ridicule, or judgment. We rather communicate a sense of ease, understanding, clarity, and discernment. In every instance, with every decision, teachers have authentic feelings and legitimate needs. Story–Empathy brings those into the foreground so they can be worked and played with in the crucible of coaching.

The power lies in the no-fault zone created by coaching presence and the effective use of Story–Empathy. The typical ways most people process experiences and emotions include all manner of assumptions, evaluations, judgments, attributions, conclusions, and demands. After having experiences or feeling emotions, we look for their cause and decide what they mean. In the process, we generally ascribe credit or blame to people and events, pigeonholing their significance in familiar terms. We function, in other words, in a fault zone that can rock our foundations with the destructive force of an earthquake.

The No-Fault Turn changes all that. By creating a no-fault zone, a safe place where teachers and coaches can work and play together with impunity, the first loop of evocative coaching puts both the relationship and the conversation on trustworthy ground. Teachers become willing to talk candidly about their experiences and emotions. They become less self-conscious and more able to share what is there. Instead of hiding their mistakes, pretending to know more than they know, stretching the truth, and jockeying for position, they let down their defenses and engage their curiosity. Instead of framing their experiences and emotions as problems to be solved, they come to see them as possibilities to be explored and mysteries to be embraced. Who else? How else? What else? Story–Empathy pivots around such questions in ways that propel teachers forward in the direction of the second turn: Inquiry–Design.

A no-fault zone is a possibility zone. Once teachers feel heard, accepted, and understood, they turn away from their attachment to what is wrong—a defensive crouch that does not facilitate change—and turn toward the possibility of discovering what is right. That is the energy coaches seek to facilitate through the first turn of evocative coaching: the awakening hope of transforming schools, one conversation at a time.

CHAPTER 3

STORY LISTENING

Great works of fiction and humble everyday stories both can open our imaginative eye. When good stories are shared, evocative images arise in the interaction between teller and listener. Such poetic language stirs and stretches our imagination of what might be true.

DANIELLE ZANDEE (2008, KL. 1712)

Once upon a time, a first-year special educator named Naomi, fresh from finishing her master's degree, joined the faculty of an elementary school. Her assistant principal, Lydia, shared the story of that first year:

Naomi was quickly overwhelmed by the stress of the job. She complained that she had not been prepared for the multiple demands on her time—the amount of paperwork, the need to collaborate with general education teachers, the meetings with parents. It's a tough job. One afternoon she shared her story with me. She had lost her mother when she was young and she was thrust into the role of mothering her younger brothers. I could see where her sense of overwhelm and of being unprepared for the demands placed on her were playing on old themes. Knowing her story helped me to understand where she was coming from, and that she needed more hand-holding and support. I could also see why she didn't always have a good sense of what was appropriate. Sometimes she needed to be told, "You can't say that, but here's what you could say instead." She hung in there, and now in her second year she is an enthusiastic mentor to a first-year special educator who joined our staff.

Stories are like that. They make sense of experience in ways that integrate emotion and meaning, facilitating movement, direction, and purpose. Stories have evocative power. Recently we were driving in a car on a highway when an aggressive driver sped up from behind and started to weave his way erratically through traffic at a very high speed. It was at once frightening and aggravating to be endangered and cut off in this way. As Bob started to berate this driver as a crazy idiot, Megan asked, "And how would you be driving right now if I was in the back seat, in labor, and about to have a baby any minute?" That question, which attached a possible story to an observable behavior, changed everything in the twinkling of an eye. Instead of fusing and fuming about this person's aggressive driving, Bob instantly calmed down with a new sense of perspective. It *was* possible, at least in theory, that there was a story that would explain and make sense of this person's behavior. That reminder reframed and relieved the emotion of the situation so that we could get back to the business at hand: driving safely down the highway to our destination.

The Power of Story

In Chapter Two we described how coaching presence includes careful attention to the dynamics of the coaching relationship. Evocative coaches are more concerned about the person than about the project being coached. In this we are taking our lead from a key insight of twentieth-century physics: "Relationships are more fundamental than things" (Senge, Scharmer, Jaworski, & Flowers, 2004, p. 193). If we fail to get the relationship right, then few things are possible. If we do get the relationship right, then all sorts of things become possible.

But what does it take to get the relationship right? First and foremost, it requires coaches to practice what might be called "story listening." People need to be heard before they can be helped, and stories carry the heart of what they want others to know. If that driver were to have been pulled over by the police, and if there was a story like the one we imagined to tell, it is likely that the driver would have continued to travel at high speed to the hospital, only now escorted with flashing lights and sirens. Stories have that kind of power because stories are among the most ancient forms of human communication. People get stories. Long before humans had developed written or even oral languages, people were telling stories with the use of gestures, facial expressions, pictures, music, and dance. After the sun would set, the long hours of darkness with their occasional perils encouraged families and tribal groups to gather around fires where they would naturally review, rehearse, and recreate the days of their lives. Over time, our brains evolved to pay attention to the structure and meaning of stories in special ways (Haven, 2007). Stories are our first and still our most memorable and meaningful of mental constructions. So, for example, people use mnemonic devices to remember lists. Once a list becomes attached to a story—"Every Good Boy Does Fine" (for the lines of the treble clef) or "My Very Earnest Mother Just Served Us Nine Pizzas" (for the planets in our solar system, before Pluto was demoted)—it becomes indelibly locked in our brains.

> *The default activity of our brains and minds seems to be telling stories, especially ones to do with people. The great advantage of this is the human capacity to "live" in the past and future as well as in the present.*
>
> David Rock and Linda Page (2009, p. 107)

As cognitive neuroscientists unlock the mystery of the human brain, we have come to see just how and where stories function in the brain as people make sense of experience. Our brains are literally hardwired to attend to and glean meaning from stories. For all its analytic powers, the left side of the brain is too small a canvas on which to paint a compelling picture. The right side of the brain must be engaged to create the stories that explain our past, explore our present, and envision our future. Stories are a specific type of narrative that features characters who face challenges, strive to overcome obstacles, and work toward important and meaningful goals. Although stories have plots, the primary focus and reason for telling stories are the characters. Haven (2007) highlights five core elements of stories:

1. *Character.* You need a viewpoint character to see who is doing the action and to gauge relevancy by assessing this character. To do that, you need perspective, viewpoint, and sufficient detail about the character to interpret emotional state, beliefs, attitudes, and to activate our "character" banks of prior knowledge and experience as well as your neural story maps to create meaning and relevance.
2. *Intent.* You need to know what story characters are after and why. As discussed, intent is composed of two key elements: goal—what the character is after (goal defines story outcome or *resolution*)—and motive—why that goal is important to the character. Goal and motive reveal the point and purpose of a story as well as of every scene and event in it.
3. *Actions.* You need to see what characters *do* to achieve their goals. You will assess characters' beliefs, attitudes, and values by comparing their actions to banks of expected or "normal" behavior. The definition for *actions* corresponds to the dictionary definition for a story ("a narrative account of a real or imagined event or events"). Actions are the plot. In a story, you want to see those events—and only those events—that relate to a character's efforts to reach a goal. Stories exist to explain and illuminate characters.
4. *Struggles.* Struggles are never easy or trivial. Struggles break with expected, normal behavior. Struggles are actions characters take in the face of risk

and danger. Actions make no sense and elicit no interest unless we see that these actions represent an attempt to reach an important goal. However, there can be no struggle unless there is something to struggle against: obstacles that block a character from reaching a goal. Obstacles may either be conflicts (blockages created by other characters—or entities—in the story) or problems (blockages not created by a character). Obstacles may either be internal (the best fighting is against yourself) or external (created by something outside the character). The risk and danger they create need not be physical. Emotional, mental, social—any kind will do as long as it is real to the character. To establish context and relevance, we need to know that something is at stake. We need to be aware of the risk and danger a character will have to face, and we need to see the character act and make decisions in the face of those obstacles and that risk and danger.

5. *Details*. Details about the character, settings, actions and events, and objects that drift through a story create the mental imagery that you use to envision and evaluate the story. Details facilitate blending and memory. (pp. 75–76)

When coaches do story listening, we listen carefully to teachers and we assist them to explore these five core elements. Stories represent the raw materials that coaches and teachers have to work with together. They reveal what teachers are dealing with, how they are feeling, where they want to go, and how they might get there. In his book, *A Whole New Mind*, Daniel Pink (2005) concluded that "we are our stories. We compress years of experience, thought, and emotion into a few compact narratives that we convey to others and tell to ourselves" (p. 113). Jim Loehr (2007) adds that stories help us "navigate our way through life because they provide structure and direction" (p. 4). Although teachers often express opinions or conclusions as to how they understand experience, their stories may reveal other layers of dimensionality and possibility. By noticing what stories are being told, and by getting people to work through the core elements of their stories, coaches have the opportunity to generate those insightful "Aha!" moments that expand awareness and alter behavior.

> *[Stories are] the creative conversion of life itself to a more powerful, clearer, more meaningful experience. . . . [They] are the currency of human contact.*
>
> Robert McKee (1997, p. 27)

David Drake (2008) describes the process of tapping into the generative power of stories as "narrative coaching." He frames stories as having three levels: the situation, the search, and the shift. Each level, the beginning, middle, and end of the story, presents an opportunity for coaches to engage in story listening.

The situation gives us the context for the story and a reason for caring about what happens to the primary character(s). The search gives us the quest of the character(s) to deal with the situation, to put life back in balance, as well as the underlying assumptions, mental models, and cultural forces that come into play. The shift gives us what happens to the primary character(s), both internally and externally, as things get understood, resolved, and appropriated. As teachers tell their stories, all three levels inevitably come into play. Drake summarized the role of story in coaching as follows:

> The stories that [teachers] share in coaching conversations shed light on their efforts to reclaim, retain and/or reframe their larger narratives about who they are and who they want to be in the world. These stories generally reflect the inherent tensions between their drive for continuity (and stability) and their yearning for discontinuity (and change). At the same time, these same stories contain clues for what will resolve this tension and, thereby, lead to a new story about themselves, their lives and/or others who matter to them. It is incumbent on coaches to have the pedagogical and practical tools to work with these stories in ways that are both honouring and transformative. (Drake, 2008, p. 67)

This chapter is about understanding and developing those tools. Telling stories is a powerful way for people to make sense of experience. When those stories are received by an attentive and caring coach with the wisdom to see their potential for personal and professional transformation, those stories shift and become evocative catalysts for change. When people tell a new story, they experience a new reality. Through telling and exploring their stories, people feel heard and discover new alternatives. By holding this invitation in the coaching space, coaches create the conditions for teachers to draw connections among the various elements of their stories and to entertain the possibility of telling a new story. In this way, through deep story listening, coaches facilitate motivation, movement, and change.

Evoking Coachable Stories

Since human beings have a natural propensity for telling stories, it is not hard to evoke stories from teachers at the start of a coaching session. Indeed, stories typically pour forth once we create a safe space and ask the right questions. Stories are not put on the table in hostile environments. It takes an absence of judgment and fear for people to open up and speak freely. That is especially true when telling stories about our own experiences. Such stories make us feel vulnerable because they expose what is happening in our world from our point of view. Whether they be trivial or transcendent, tragic or triumphant, such stories paint a picture of what our experience looks, sounds, and feels like from the inside out. They reveal much about our understandings, feelings, needs, and commitments. No one is going to risk sharing such stories if they fear being disparaged, analyzed, or violated. Evocative coaches allay such fears by being genuinely interested, expressing acceptance, and honoring confidentiality. Our coaching presence communicates that we will listen respectfully and carefully to teacher stories, no matter how difficult or disappointing, because they represent the raw materials that coaches and teachers have to work with together. Such stories are gifts to be received with care.

Although a safe environment is necessary for evoking stories, it is not sufficient for evoking coachable stories. Apart from asking the right questions, a safe environment alone will often induce teachers to do little more than to ramble, grumble, and/or gossip. Although telling such unfocused, disassociated, and idle tales may release steam and feel good, it does not typically generate the kind of stories and energy we are looking for in coaching. That is why evocative coaches pay attention not only to setting the stage but also to crafting the script. We seek to ask questions that trigger stories related to teacher learning and growth. We want teachers to tell stories that focus, empower, and engage their efforts to be the best teachers they can be, and that takes a script that invites both connection and exploration.

> *At the heart of any good story is a central narrative about the way an idea satisfies a need in some powerful way.*
>
> Tim Brown (2009, p. 137)

We wrote in Chapter Two about the importance of coaching presence, comparing it to the way of being of a horse whisperer. Nowhere is that metaphor more apt than at the outset of a coaching conversation. To invite teachers to open up and tell their stories, coaches have to "Join-Up" and come alongside them in terms of energy, emotion, pacing, and understanding. Before we connect as coaches, we first have to connect as human beings. If we get down to business too quickly, or if we get out in front or behind them, teachers will feel pulled or pushed to do what we want. When that happens, especially when that happens at the outset of a coaching conversation, we fail to establish rapport and risk losing effectiveness. In order to minimize this risk, the best way to start a coaching conversation is to check in briefly with how teachers are feeling in the moment. When these feelings are expressed, acknowledged, and accepted, rather than analyzed or argued with, coaches will have laid a good foundation for evoking coachable stories.

To get a sense of a teacher's feelings at the outset of a coaching conversation, coaches can ask a wide variety of preliminary and yet evocative questions. After setting things up by saying something like, "Before we get started, I'd like to ask . . . ," coaches can, for example, say:

- How would you describe your energy right now, on a scale of 0 to 10?
- What three adjectives might describe how you're feeling right now?
- What's especially present for you in this moment?
- How would you describe your mood right now?
- What color might capture how you feel right now?
- What's on your mind right now?
- How are you showing up for this coaching session?
- What is stirring inside you?
- What song could be the theme song for your day?
- What object can you see that reflects how you are right now?
- What physical sensations are you most aware of right now?
- What is alive for you right now?

The reason for setting up the initial check-in by saying, "Before we get started, I'd like to ask . . . ," is to give teachers permission to talk about whatever is most present and pertinent in the moment, whether personal or professional. It expresses caring for the personhood of the teacher even as it recognizes the work of coaching that is yet to come in the conversation. By inquiring as to how teachers are feeling in the moment, rather than by immediately asking about or commenting on how things are going in their classroom or with their "homework" from the last coaching session, coaches gain insight into the teacher's presenting emotional energy. Are they discouraged and depressed? Are they excited and optimistic? Are they frustrated and overwhelmed? Are they exhilarated and confident? There are endless possibilities as to how teachers may show up for coaching; and there is certainly no guarantee that teachers will pick up where they left off in the last coaching session. By doing a brief, initial check-in, coaches can come up alongside whatever energy teachers bring to the conversation through empathy and inquiry.

This is a recurrent theme in evocative coaching. We pay attention to feelings to navigate our way and to successfully move through the coaching conversation. When emotions are ignored, neglected, or demeaned, they confine and constrict the realm of the possible. When they are noticed, recognized, and respected, they unleash that realm. Evocative coaches appreciate how emotions generate motion, both in the coaching conversation itself, as teachers open themselves up to new possibilities, and in the classroom, as teachers experiment with those possibilities in real-world applications. Coachable stories will not be evoked until emotions are acknowledged and accepted.

> *Stories serve as windows into the architecture of [our] psyches and the longing of [our] souls as well as the platform from which to build and express new ways of being in the world.*
>
> *David Drake (2008, p. 52)*

One way for coaches to do that is through the lost art of attentive listening. After asking an evocative question, coaches can stop talking, lean into the space, and wait silently for teachers to respond fully. Honoring our natural proportions in that we have two ears and one mouth, evocative coaches seek to listen at least twice as much as we talk during a coaching session. That receptivity is what validates emotions and invites stories. It may be difficult to do, especially when coaches are in a hurry or think of some value-added comment we want to make, but listening carefully, attentively, patiently, and deeply is the first work of coaching. Talking too much or too soon short-circuits the transformational power of teachers opening up, sharing coachable stories, and feeling heard.

On occasion, the initial check-in will lead immediately to a coachable story. That is especially true when teachers show up for coaching with a lot of emotional energy around an experiment they conducted or an ongoing coaching project. Most of the time, however, the initial check-in simply establishes an emotional bond between the teacher and the coach. It serves as the gateway to one or more follow-up questions that ask specifically for developmental stories. There is no telling exactly which questions will be the most productive, since that depends upon many variables, including the emotional state of the teacher and the intuitive inklings of the coach. One thing is clear, however: coaches can do better than simply asking teachers, "How did it go?" That question invites an outpouring of complaints, evaluations, analyses, opinions, thoughts, assertions, and anecdotes. It typically generates one or more variants of the seven archetypal stories that tend to be told in organizations (Martin, Feldman, Hatch, & Sitkin, 1983):

1. The rule-breaking story
2. Is the big boss human? story
3. Can the little person rise to the top? story
4. Will I get fired? story
5. Will the organization help me? story
6. How will the boss react to mistakes? story
7. How will the organization deal with obstacles? story

Although filled with energy that coaches can respond to with empathy if and when such stories come out, those are not often the best stories for fostering personal and professional development. "How did you grow?" questions are more likely to evoke coachable stories. Assuming that trust and rapport have been established during the initial check-in, "How did you grow?" questions invite teachers to tell stories about themselves in relation to their goals, actions, struggles, and accomplishments through a different lens. They invite teachers to share their challenges and excitements with stories that express the learning orientation of coaching. "How did you grow?" is an intrinsically positive frame through which teachers can view even the toughest of experiences. Such stories set the mood and form the groundwork for all that will follow in the steps of Empathy–Inquiry–Design.

One way to evoke these fruitful stories is for coaches to invite teachers to tell stories about times when they felt engaged in, excited about, or challenged by the work of teaching. Examples of such invitations include the following:

- Tell me the story of how you came to be a teacher.
- Tell me the story of how you came to take on this particular teaching assignment.
- Tell me a story that illustrates what has been working well for you.
- Tell me a story about a time when you handled a tough situation well.
- Tell me a story about a time when you made a real contribution.
- Tell me a story that illustrates what you love most about your work.
- Tell me a story about a time when you had a lot of fun in the classroom.
- Tell me a story about a time when you felt strongly connected to one of your students.
- Tell me a story that illustrates how your values come through in your teaching.
- Tell me a story about an experience in the classroom that taught you a valuable lesson.
- Tell me a story about a time when you felt respected and honored as a teacher.
- Tell me a story about a time when you tried something new.
- Tell me a story of a time when your lesson plan went surprisingly well.
- Tell me a story that illustrates what helps you to do your very best.
- Tell me a story from your first year of teaching and an insight that emerged from that.

Such invitations sparkle with evocative energy. They transport people to a very different place than rambling, grumbling, or gossiping. They shape the stories that get told and the possibilities that get considered. They elevate motivation and prepare people for a productive conversation regarding methods. By inviting teachers to remember and to reveal the growth-fostering dimensions of their experience, they communicate respect for a teacher's experience as well as confidence in a teacher's abilities to handle new experiences. Such respect and confidence are crucial to the learning dynamic. These are the coachable stories that promote openness to change. When they enter the ecosystem of the school, they have the power to shift the entire system.

Notice that all of the sample "Tell me . . ." invitations are in the form of open-ended inquiries. It is hard to generate a story when an inquiry can be answered with "Yes" or "No." The two best question words, when it comes to generating stories in coaching sessions, are *what* and *how*. These words seek descriptions rather than reasons. They beg for longer, narrative answers. Ideally, more than 50 percent of all questions in a coaching session will be open-ended questions or "tell me . . . " invitations. Such questions and invitations allow teachers to take an active role in the coaching conversation as they explore the fullness of their experience. Too many closed-ended questions, that invite short "sound bite" answers, tend to shut down this dynamic. Examples of closed-ended questions include:

- How many days did you remember to write your objectives on the board last week?
- Do you know about balanced literacy?
- When was the last time you used cooperative groups?
- Did you learn anything from trying the new approach we discussed?

Such questions can be reframed as open-ended questions by using "What" and "How":

- How did the students respond when you wrote your objectives on the board?
- What have you heard about or tried when it comes to balanced literacy?
- What has been one of your better experiences with using cooperative groups?
- What has become clearer to you since last we met?

Although *why* is also an open-ended question word, it does not tend to evoke coachable stories because it invites analysis and can easily provoke resistance by communicating judgment. For example, asking, "Why did you approach the lesson in that way?," may cause a teacher to shut down and/or to respond defensively. "Why" questions can nevertheless be powerful when asked at the right time and in the right way. *Why* is best used after stories are told, to explore motivation. For example, after hearing a story, coaches can connect teachers to the meaning and measure of their stories by asking, "Why did you care so deeply about reaching that particular student?" or "Why did you reach out to that student in that way?"

If teachers are failing to open up and tell their stories at the start of a coaching session, it means that we have either set the wrong stage or asked the wrong questions. The stage is wrong, as we have noted, if it is perceived to be a hostile environment—a perception that can arise in many ways. It is obviously hostile if teachers sense they will be evaluated or judged on the basis of the stories they tell. It is also hostile, however, if teachers sense that coaches have a hidden agenda or do not have the time or interest to listen to their stories. Evocative coaches do not ask leading questions, with an implied right answer, and do not rush teachers through the telling of their stories. We communicate a sense of spaciousness and a genuine desire to unearth and savor whatever the stories have to teach us.

Instead of asking teachers to cut to the chase, getting to whatever business is ostensibly at hand, evocative coaches therefore invite teachers to tell their stories fully, teasing out the nuances, meanings, and treasures that seem to be important to them. The wisdom is in the details. For all our interest in stories, however, evocative coaches do not force teachers to share what they do not want to share and to reveal details they do not want to reveal. If teachers appear reluctant to open up, if they cannot come up with anything right away, if they appear to be avoiding a question, or if we do not think they are being totally honest, that usually says more about the stage we have set, the questions we have asked, and the level of trust we have established than about the teachers' coachability. It is best, then, to reset the stage, to ask new questions, and to connect with the heart. Check in on how the teacher is feeling. Find a different path of development to explore. Hammering away in the same vein for an extended period of time is counterproductive when it generates resistance rather than curiosity and openness to change. One can always circle back later, reframing questions to evoke coachable stories in a particular area of interest, once trust and rapport have been reestablished. At their best, "How did you grow?" questions trigger a wealth of material that teachers and coaches alike learn from and enjoy sharing together. That is the promise of evocative coaching.

Great questions elicit what is on the teacher's mind rather than what is on the coach's mind.

Mindful Listening

The most powerful way to evoke coachable stories is to ask story questions and then to listen mindfully. Mindful listening is one of the most important of all coaching skills. It requires "calmness, an open mind, and focused attention" (Shafir, 2000, p. 75). It requires calmness because it is not in a hurry to get anywhere. It values listening in its own right, not as a stepping stone to something else. Mindful listening requires an open mind because we are listening to understand the experience of another. We make no assumptions and no judgments regarding that experience as we seek to appreciate a different point of view. It requires focused attention because distractions interfere with our ability to listen to what teachers have to say. Whatever may be going on with us as coaches, both personally and professionally, is consciously set aside in order to pay singular attention to the agendas of those we are coaching. It is a rare privilege to be listened to in this way. To be listened to calmly, with an open mind, and with focused attention in the "age of distraction" is so atypical and satisfying that it proves to be transformational for both the teacher and the coach. If coaches do nothing other than to listen mindfully to a teacher's stories, we will have done a lot.

The first key to mindful listening, then, is to stop whatever else is going on, including the internal chatter and opinions about what "should" happen in a coaching session or classroom situation, and just listen. It is the coach's job to dance with teachers, not to drag them to a destination. Multitasking is so rampant in the modern world that we often fail to pay attention with both ears. We tend to listen with one ear, as we frame what we want to say and mentally consider other things. Whenever this happens, whenever we listen halfheartedly, we fail to hear, experience, respond to, and grow from all that the other person has to share. There is evocative power in being and paying full attention in the present moment; such presence imbues ordinary and familiar details with new energy and radiance. Although we know this to be true, it can be quite difficult to give someone our undivided attention.

Understanding this dynamic, evocative coaches get ourselves ready for mindful listening in the minutes prior to the start of every coaching session. A coach's ritual of preparation is just as important to the course of a coaching session as whatever we say or do during the session itself. No horse whisperer would dare to get into the ring with a wild horse if he or she was not in the right frame of mind; so, too, do coaches make sure that we are in the right mindset for coaching. No tool or technique will prove effective if we are not fully present, in the moment, with the teachers we coach. In the minutes just before the start of a coaching session, it can be helpful to mentally rehearse what we know of the teacher's experience (reviewing notes, memories, and communications) and to engage in practices that get us in the mood for listening. One such practice is taking a few, deep centering breaths. Breathe in to the count of four, hold to the count of seven, and exhale slowly to the count of eight. Breathing in and out through the nose is more relaxing, calming, and centering than mouth breathing because it stimulates and soothes the vagus nerve, the main pathway of the rest-and-recover nervous system. We can take three or four such breaths to prepare ourselves for mindful listening. Another such practice is to set aside our papers, turn aside from our computers and mobile devices, look out the window, and/or go for a short walk, noticing whatever physical or emotional sensations come up in response. Whatever rituals work, the key is to practice these activities routinely in advance of coaching sessions and at other times throughout the day. The more familiar we become with practices that contribute to mindfulness, the more impact they will have on our coaching presence.

> *Listening is only powerful and effective if it is authentic. Authenticity means that you are listening because you are curious and you care, not just because you are supposed to. The issue, then, is this: Are you curious? Do you care?*
>
> *Douglas Stone, Bruce Patton, and Sheila Heen (1999, p. 168)*

Listen Calmly

Although mindful listening is based on a foundation of calmness, this may be the most challenging of all dimensions to bring into educational settings. When time is divided into periods with ringing bells, and when demands come at us from many directions in staccato, rapid-fire bursts, it is hard to approach someone as if we had all the time in the world to listen. That explains the value of those preparatory rituals. They may take only sixty seconds, but we will not even do that, slowing down and collecting ourselves before a coaching session, unless we understand how important such rituals are to the coaching process. The more rushed we are to get down to business, the more anxious we are to grill teachers on what happened and to tell them how to do it better, the more resistance we provoke. A Swahili proverb, "*Haraka, Haraka, haina Baraka,*" reminds us that "hurry, hurry has no blessings." That is especially true in evocative coaching. If we do not have the time to listen mindfully to teachers, then it is not the right time to try to coach them at all.

One reason for this is that we become agitated and reactive when we feel a sense of time pressure or time poverty. Little things irritate us that we might otherwise find fascinating. We overrespond with an emotional charge in our voice that is counterproductive to the learning frame of evocative coaching. And we end up talking too much. All this happens just by coaching in the absence of calm energy. To listen well, or even to listen at all, we have to listen calmly.

> *The most important moments in a coaching session are often the moments just before it begins, when the coach takes the time to become fully present to what is about to happen.*

Listen Openly

We also have to listen openly. There may be no greater gift than listening to someone with genuine curiosity and an open mind. Such listening acknowledges the value of their experiences as human beings, regardless of whether or not we would choose to handle things in a similar way. Listening openly has the power to transform situations and people because it builds trust and fosters the possibility of discovering new ideas, new energy, and new life. In order to listen openly, evocative coaches suspend the judgments and bracket the opinions that surface in ordinary listening. Our job is not to filter and categorize what we are hearing as "good" or "bad," "right" or "wrong." Our job is rather to understand the fullness and to appreciate the deep dimensions of the stories teachers share with us. Evocative coaches seek to enter into the world being created by those stories. Such engagement facilitates lines of communication that foster an openness to change.

Evocative coaches can always find something to respect in teachers' stories, even when we disagree with their approaches, disapprove of their attitudes, or doubt the effort they invest in teaching. When we listen openly, especially to those we disagree with, disapprove of, or doubt, we establish the relationship on a very different basis. We grant that whatever the other person is trying to share, no matter how dissonant it may sound to our ears, is worthy of a respectful hearing and a considerate response. Legitimate needs are always at play in teacher stories. By suspending judgment and listening openly, we enable teachers to tell their stories fully, to hold them lightly, and to reveal details they might otherwise choose to leave out.

The posture of suspending judgment and listening openly is very different from harboring judgmental attitudes about teachers and biting our tongues. Listening openly takes place only when we authentically trust that wonderful things can be found, when we choose to listen and look for them. This can be especially difficult, as Melissa found out, when we perceive that teachers are doing objectionable things that do not facilitate student learning and success.

I found it a challenge to suspend judgment of Suzanne, a veteran teacher I'm coaching. Suzanne volunteered to implement this new balanced literacy program in her ninth-grade English class, but seemed to assume that my role as coach would be akin to that of a teacher's aide. She has steadfastly rebuffed my offers to plan lessons together, and it has emerged as the year has gone on that Suzanne keeps no written plans. (This has not been addressed by the department chair because she *is* the department chair!) She asserted that an hour to plan a week's lessons was too much time. Her lack of planning shows in her instruction. Her lessons generally follow a set pattern of reading aloud to her students, having them complete a worksheet, and then giving them the remainder of the ninety-minute block to chat or work on homework from other classes. I have been dismayed to hear Suzanne regularly refer to her students as criminals, sometimes even within their hearing. My concern for the students has made maintaining a nonjudgmental posture really difficult. Yet, if I were to communicate negative judgments, either verbally or nonverbally, it would likely squelch any openness to the coaching relationship as a place to explore new ways of teaching.

Melissa, high school literacy coach

When coaches find ourselves in such situations, it is up to us to turn our attitudes around, to engage our curiosity, to avoid condemnation and ridicule, and to sincerely go on a treasure hunt for a teacher's best qualities. That quest, in and of itself, regardless of what we find, can help to create a productive interpersonal space. Teachers notice when we fail to take the bait of blaming and shaming them for doing things poorly. By holding teachers in respect, the space between us becomes trustworthy space in which teachers relax and learning can take place. This appreciative attitude and approach eliminates "the endless defensive crouch, which is, of course, the worst possible posture from which to learn" (Harry Spence, as quoted in Kegan & Lahey, 2009, p. 72). If coaches fail to listen openly, dialogue breaks down. And without dialogue, we are not likely to be of assistance to teachers as they consider making changes to their teaching practices. When we extend openness, we change the conversational climate and the possibilities teachers are willing to consider.

Listen Attentively

To listen attentively as teachers tell their stories means more than just clearing our minds, setting aside distractions, suspending judgment, and giving teachers our undivided attention. That is a good start, but we also have to pay attention to what those stories are generating in the coaching space. Sometimes tears will flow, laughter will erupt, palms will sweat, feelings will surface, and inklings will emerge. Once we understand that coaching is not about getting teachers to do what we want them to do, but about enabling teachers to figure out how they can do what they want to do to serve their students better, coaches can attend to these and other such reactions without attachment to an outcome. The lack of outcome attachment combined with careful attention to what is happening in the coaching space transforms physiological and affective reactions into valuable grist for the coaching mill, giving us insights and intuitions that can assist us then to better respond with Empathy–Inquiry–Design. Listening attentively in this way is what makes coaching evocative.

Stories generate reactions that are different from logical deductions or rational inferences. They are more like feelings or impressions that something might be the case. Paying attention to and using those impressions in coaching therefore means that we are listening simultaneously to the story and to what the story is surfacing. The things that come up for coaches while listening to teacher stories, including physical sensations, visual images, charged feelings, spontaneous connections, and intuitive hunches, offer guidance as to what may be going on for the teacher. We dare not assume a one-to-one correspondence between what is coming up for us and what is going on with them, but we also dare not ignore what our intuition is saying. Evocative coaches are not afraid to tune into the intuition channel, bringing imagination, inspiration, and integration into the coaching process (Peirce, 1997). Those hallmarks of intuition assist coaches to better follow and guide what is going on in the service of desired developmental outcomes.

Gallwey (2000) views the ability to get an intuitive sense of what lies behind someone else's experience as "perhaps the fundamental skill of the coach." He calls it "transposing." Put yourself in the shoes of the person you are coaching, he writes, "and ask yourself the following questions: 'What am I thinking? What am I feeling? What do I want?'" (p. 183). Coaches can do this in preparation for coaching, but it can also be done in the moment, while coaches are listening attentively to teacher stories or observing teacher behaviors. When we get this right, when we transpose someone accurately, fully, and compassionately, learning happens more quickly, easily, and enjoyably. Gallwey (2000) writes:

> [Transposing] allows the coach to have a richer picture of the three primary levels of the other person: thinking, feeling, and will. It is important, however, to remember that at best you are making educated guesses about how the other person thinks and feels. It is important to keep yourself open to feedback and new information, and to be willing to adjust your picture of the other person's reality. The purpose of transposing is not just to gain insight, but to be more effective in your communication. I find it helps me to anticipate how my message might be misinterpreted and to say it in a way that has a better chance of getting through. (p. 185)

Quiet Listening

In a certain sense, coaches are always in listening mode, even when we are talking; however, we listen most fully when we are quiet. Listening requires coaches to shift into a relaxed and receptive stance. For that to happen effectively, it is vital that coaches become comfortable with silence. Rearrange the letters in *listen* and you get *silent*. Silence is an important part of every coaching conversation. As teachers tell their stories, and as coaches respond with empathy and inquiry, teachers often pause to think, feel, or connect with their truth. It is essential for coaches to honor this silence, to be comfortable with pauses, to avoid interrupting, and to not intrude prematurely. Once the ball is in the teacher's court, it is usually best to wait until the teacher hits it back. After asking a question, give the teacher time to answer. Speaking again too quickly or rescuing teachers from the discomfort of silence prevents teachers from making new connections, discoveries, and sense of their stories. Silence communicates both the coach's desire to hear what the teacher has to say and the coach's trust in the teacher's ability to handle the situation.

> *If the coach waits for a longer period, teachers tend to respond in whole sentences and complete thoughts. There is a perceptible increase in the creativity of the response as shown by greater use of descriptive and modifying words and an increase in speculative thinking. There is also an increased feeling of being valued and respected by the coach.*
>
> *Arthur Costa and Robert Garmston (2002, p. 79)*

It is a special gift to be with teachers in silence, especially those who are introverted, since silence gives them time to organize their thoughts, feelings, and desires before translating them into words. Be prepared for the surprises of silence. Teachers will often come up with additional details, new perspectives, alternative possibilities, and unexpected turns when given a chance to fully express themselves. That is because silence has a way of evoking greatness from people. It sends the empowering message: "I believe that you can figure this out by going deeper." Often, silence will lead to insights and directional shifts that coaches may never have anticipated.

A big piece of what I do is listening. You have to listen more than you talk. Some of the coaches that I have talked with, when they describe what's going on, you can tell they really didn't listen to the teacher. They had their own preconceived notions about what was going on instead of listening and starting with that. I'm big on listening to my teachers. In turn, when I'm talking they're all ears and paying attention because they know that I give them that respect too. It is a two-way street for everybody.

Robin, elementary mathematics coach

To be comfortable with silence during coaching sessions, it helps for coaches to become comfortable with silence outside of coaching sessions. Slow, rhythmic breathing is not only a way to increase mindfulness before a coaching session (or during a coaching session, for that matter), it is also a way to introduce silence into the rhythms of daily life. Starting and ending each day with rituals of silent reflection, meditation, appreciation, and/or respiration are great patterns for coaches to adopt and follow. Simple actions throughout the day, like turning aside from electronics and taking intentional breaks from what must be done are also helpful habits to develop and practice on a routine basis. Regardless of their duration, such breaks give coaches time to connect with silence. As every teacher knows, even small timeouts can make a big difference. The key is for coaches not only to understand the value of silence, but also to experience that value through daily visits to the eye of the storm. The richer our experience with silence, the easier it is for coaches to practice quiet listening with teachers.

Reflective Listening

In typical conversations, we often fail to listen mindfully or quietly. Once we hear something that we have an opinion about, we stop listening and start talking at a natural break or whenever we can work our way into the conversation. Most talking involves sharing our ideas, opinions, stories, evaluations, comparisons, recommendations, and assertions as to what we think should be happening. As we strive to get our point across, the focus of the conversation shifts to our agenda and may never get back to the agenda of the original speaker. Depending upon the assertiveness of the parties involved, conversations can become a competition for air time rather than an opportunity for deep listening, discovery, and growth.

Evocative coaching conversations do not follow this pattern. They are not typical or ordinary conversations. They are unusual conversations in that they are one sided and teacher focused. The whole point of such conversations is to attend so well to a teacher's experience as to generate acceptance, appreciation, and authenticity. When coaches approach teachers from this stance, a stance of receptivity and possibility, teachers will often figure out for themselves what they want to do differently and how best to move forward. They become change interested rather than change resistant. That is why evocative coaches spend so much time listening to the developmental stories of teachers. Such time is quality time. It is the seedbed out of which new shoots rise. It primes the pump for future plans and actions.

So what do evocative coaches think about while teachers are telling their stories and what do evocative coaches say when teachers are done telling their stories? We think about and then verbalize our best guess as to what we hear them saying, feeling, needing, and wanting. Instead of trying to make a point or push an agenda, we seek to be a mirror that will assist teachers to clarify, understand, accept, appreciate, and enhance their own experience. As reflective listeners who are comfortable with silence, evocative coaches are able to listen all the way to the last word and then, after pausing for an appropriate length of time, to reflect whatever topics or themes would be most helpful for the teacher to hear again and ponder anew. Such reflections are very different from taking the conversation in new directions (although shifting the focus is occasionally helpful and appropriate, as we shall see at the end of the next chapter). Such reflections are more about going deeper in the same direction, so that teachers can extract the full value of their experiences before moving forward.

This stands in stark contrast from what might be called "deflective listening." Here, instead of reflecting what we understand someone else to be saying, we deflect the conversation to what we want to be saying. Instead of listening to understand, we listen to evaluate, educate, and explain. We may even jump on bits and pieces of story logic with which we can argue and dispute. Such listening is agenda driven. It does not listen to the last word. Like a debater waiting to give a rebuttal speech, such listening stops once it hears something that can occasion a response. The wheels start turning as soon as we notice an opportunity to add value and make a point. Once we get into the mode of commenting on what someone has said, whether to acknowledge the things that we think they are doing well or to correct the things that we think they are doing poorly, we deflect the conversation to the things we want to say, the stories we want to tell, the lessons we want to teach, and the sense we want to make of what is going on.

Understanding the importance of listening fully to teacher stories, evocative coaches do not approach coaching conversations in this way. Our job is not to comment on teacher stories but to develop them as if the coaching space or relational field was the reagent in a photographer's darkroom. The story goes in the chemical bath and develops over time into a positive image. For that to happen, the bath—how coaches listen and respond—has to include the right mix of understanding, appreciation, and reflection. As teachers are telling their stories, coaches periodically check in with reflective summaries and paraphrases in order to confirm that we have heard correctly and fully what teachers are trying to say. Such reflections enable teachers to better understand, explore, and develop their own experience. By capturing not only the content of what teachers are saying, but also the energy, commitments, and desires that lie behind that content, coaches invite teachers to go deeper in the search for meaning and movement in their story dynamics.

In evocative coaching sessions, teachers talk more than the coach. To facilitate this, coaches take a WAIT and SEE attitude: W.A.I.T.—Why Am I Talking? and S.E.E.—Stop Explaining Everything (Stevens, 2005, p. 161).

Imaginative Listening

Perhaps you have heard the story of the three baseball umpires trying to impress each other with how they call the pitches from behind home plate. To demonstrate his accuracy, the first umpire proclaims boldly, "I call them the way they are." Questioning whether anyone can ever know for sure whether a pitch is a ball or a strike, the second umpire proclaims sincerely, "I call them the way I see them." Without disputing the importance of either accuracy or sincerity, the third umpire proclaims, with a wink and grin, "They ain't nothin' until I call them." That is as true with instant replay as it is with an umpire's snap decision. In the end, according to the rules of the game, someone still has to call them.

When teachers tell their stories they are, in effect, calling the balls and strikes of their experience. The things that hit and miss the mark are filled with emotional energy, both positive and negative, and teachers want to process those feelings by telling their stories. Teachers do not always realize, however, that the stories they tell are not reports of the world as it is; they are rather recreations of the world as it might be. They are not the experience in itself; they are rather hypotheses we are testing out regarding the experience as we understand it. No story is ever "the truth, the whole truth, and nothing but the truth." It is rather a slice of the truth told from a certain vantage point, and the story that gets told is always a game-changing call. It creates impressions, parameters, boundaries, and possibilities for coaches to work with through story listening. Joseph Jaworski (1998) captured the game-changing power of stories when he wrote:

> As I considered the importance of language and how human beings interact with the world, it struck me that in many ways the development of language was like the discovery of fire—it was such an incredible primordial force. I had always thought that we used language to *describe* the world—now I was seeing that this is not the case. To the contrary, it is through language that we *create* the world, because it is nothing until we describe it. And when we describe it, we create distinctions that govern our actions. To put it another way, we do not describe the world we see, but we see the world we describe. (p. 178)

Ann Hartman (1991) has put this premise even more simply and memorably: "Words create worlds." Both the stories we tell ourselves, and the stories we tell others, not only determine the sense we make of the past but also create the way we experience the future. The now famous "Pygmalion effect" study, named after a Cypriot sculptor in an ancient Greek myth and first published in 1968, demonstrated the impact of telling stories to teachers regarding which students were significantly brighter than others in their classrooms (Rosenthal & Jacobson, 2003).

Although the students were selected at random and although there were, in fact, no significant differences between the so-called bright students and the other students at the outset of the experiment, things quickly began to shift, and by the end of the experiment the students designated as gifted had conformed to teacher expectations. Story created reality. Over the past forty years there have been literally hundreds of other studies confirming this effect, attesting to both its continuing theoretical and practical importance.

Experience does not construct stories; people construct stories, and, in turn, stories construct experience. How we describe a situation, how we characterize the actors, intents, actions, struggles, and outcomes, both reflects and affects how that situation is for us (Johnson, 1999). We should therefore be careful and intentional regarding the stories we tell (Loehr, 2007). If we tell a story as a "just-so story," explaining how a situation just is, then our experience—as in the Pygmalion effect—is circumscribed accordingly. Such stories may explain how the leopard got its spots, for example, but they do not invite the leopard to change its spots. If we tell the story as a "maybe-so story," portraying how a situation might be, then our experience opens up accordingly. Even as we tell one story about leopards and their spots, we recognize that other stories can be told. The work of coaching, then, is to listen to stories as "maybe-so" constructions and to invite the teachers who tell those stories to do the same. We are looking for new angles from which to appreciate stories and design reality. The more vividly we do so, the more reality takes off.

> *The facts are always less than what really happens. I mean the facts are just on the surface. . . . To me, [the facts don't] tell you nearly as much as the story of one individual who lived through [them].*
>
> *Nadine Gordimer (1976)*

Listening to stories in this way is transformational. Instead of being viewed as givens, to be accepted with resignation, they are viewed as propositions, to be explored with anticipation, imagination, and curiosity. Evocative coaches yearn to understand how else stories can be told; the act of reworking and retelling stories from different perspectives opens the door to new frameworks, understandings, and possibilities. It is a form of empathy to imagine and play with stories as sources of inspiration and possibility rather than to use stories as occasions for criticism and humiliation.

The transformational power of reworking and retelling stories was amusingly and poignantly captured in the 1993 movie, *Groundhog Day*. In this movie, Bill Murray plays Phil Connors, an egocentric Pittsburgh TV meteorologist who goes to Punxsutawney, Pennsylvania, in order to cover the annual appearance of the legendary groundhog, "Punxsutawney Phil." Connors does so with great sarcasm and reluctance, since he sees this as a demeaning and stupid assignment. After covering the festivities of the day, Connors ends up spending the night in Punxsutawney when a blizzard that he had forecasted would miss the town makes the roads impassable. Upon waking up in his hotel room the next day, Connors discovers that the calendar has not advanced. It is still Groundhog Day and he still has to cover the same event, meeting the same people, in the same town, and going through the same motions—but he is the only one who is consciously aware of being stuck in a time warp.

This is understandably confusing, troubling, and disorienting for Connors, who at first assumes he must be having a dream. So he plays along and relives the day. After getting stuck in the blizzard again, and returning to his hotel room, Connors figures that he will wake up from his dream and all will be right with the world. But when he wakes up, the scenario plays itself out all over again. He is still in Punxsutawney and it is still Groundhog Day. Connors is consigned to relive the same day, over and over again, with no apparent way to get out of the seemingly endless loop.

Over time, Connors goes through many emotions. He is variously angry at, depressed about, stimulated by, and despairing over his predicament; exasperated and enamored with different characters; empowered, entertained, and amused by his knowledge of the future; engaged by opportunities for learning and growth; and alternately indifferent as well as compassionate about the things that happen to other people. He doesn't get out of the day until he loses his attachment to an outcome (getting out of the day) and gains an authentic relationship to both himself and others.

The entire plot of the movie hinges upon the discovery and exploration of story variants. Originally, Connors had one story, and only one story, as to how he saw the world and what went on that day. By the time his time warp was over, however, Connors had gained a multitude of new perspectives. He saw how other people experienced their day, how making different decisions changed the course of events, and how he could learn important life lessons from the experiences of one single day. Those same dynamics can be created in coaching sessions when coaches invite teachers to imagine new scenarios and interpretations of their experiences. Such invitations expand the repertoire of teachers' ability to respond. To paraphrase Wittgenstein and other philosophers, "The limits of our stories are the limits of our world." It is the work of story listening to expand the range of teacher stories.

> *Storytelling needs to be in the tool kit of the design thinker—in the sense not of a tidy beginning, middle, and end but of an ongoing, open-ended narrative that engages people and encourages them to carry it forward and write their own conclusions.*
>
> *Tim Brown (2009, p. 158)*

Imagine Vantage Points

The easiest way to get teachers involved in exploring different facets of their stories is to ask them to imagine what the experience might have been like for one or more of the characters in their stories. We all know that every person has a unique vantage point, but we often fail to do the work of transposing in order to understand, appreciate, and value those perspectives. Evocative coaches assist teachers to do this work as part of the coaching conversation. The first time teachers tell a story, it comes primarily from their points of view. That is like the first time Phil Connors went through his day. But most stories involve characters who are related to the teacher's path of development in both positive and negative ways. The more teachers can learn to see things from the vantage points of other characters, the more open teachers become to considering alternatives.

> *Stories are like flight simulators for the brain.*
>
> *Chip and Dan Heath (2007, p. 213)*

Asking teachers to describe their experience from the vantage point of one of their characters, perhaps even retelling the story from that point of view, is an effective, engaging, and fun way to try on different perspectives. So, for example, after a teacher finishes telling the story of a challenging classroom situation, he or she can be invited to transpose one of the characters in that story, perhaps a student or a colleague, and to retell the story as that character might have experienced the situation. Coaches can also interview teachers while they are playing different roles to take them more deeply into the character's experience. Such transposing, retelling, and recreating often generate new understandings and possibilities for moving forward because of how the process engages the brain. Neurons fire as if the story variants were actually happening. Such "perspective taking," creates attunement, resonance, and shared intention (Siegel, 2007). It changes the neural mechanisms of the brain (Ruby & Decety, 2004) in ways that facilitate the empathy and mindful awareness required to contemplate and construct new possibilities.

Imagine Pivot Points

A more creative and challenging approach when listening to teacher stories is to ask teachers to imagine how an experience might have turned out if they had handled a situation differently or if they had viewed it from a different perspective. Teachers may have resistance to doing this, since they probably did what they did for their own good reasons. The actions they took may be understood as defining parts of their identities. But when trust is high and judgment is low, teachers may be willing to explore those critical junctures where they could have gone in different directions. We see this in the evolution of Connors's endless day. At first, he was attached to his persona and to doing things his way. Indeed, he did it the same way, over and over again. As time went on, however, Connors started to experiment with different decisions, approaches, and techniques. He connected in new ways with different people and situations. As a result of such experimentation, he experienced a gradual yet tangible transformation.

That can happen for teachers when they are willing to explore the pivot points in their stories. What if they had chosen a different path or taken a different approach? What if they had understood the situation differently? Asking teachers to play with and retell their stories from such hypothetical stances, carrying the narrative forward as it might have gone rather than defending their position, opens up entirely new possibilities. After a teacher finishes telling the story of a disrupted lesson, for example, she can be asked, "What if instead of sending her to the principal's office, you had realized she was embarrassed and helped her to save face? Tell the story as it might have gone from there." "What if?" and "How might?" are invaluable openers when exploring such pivot points. When teachers are willing to play creatively with their experiences, they often shake loose attachment to decisions they made in the moment and generate engagement with alternatives they may want to try in the future. By so doing, teachers can discover new wisdom for improving instruction.

Imagine Lesson Points

As we have seen, teachers tell stories to make sense of their experiences and to glean lessons for moving forward. The "moral of the story" is, in a sense, the reason for telling the story, and usually they have but one. Teachers think they know what their stories mean. After playing with different vantage and pivot points, however, teachers may be ready, willing, and able to imagine new lessons or takeaways. Those lessons were always there, embedded in the folds of the story, as it were, but teachers may not have had the eyes to see them or the courage to look for them. All that can change in the context of a safe space and in the presence of evocative questions. Instead of intimidating teachers, "What else?" then becomes an occasion for extracting new material and even the occasional stroke of insight. Asking what teachers may have learned from imagining different vantage or pivot points invites teachers to go deeper and to see what else might be possible, just as Phil Connors discovered more and more about himself and the meaning of life by reflecting on and growing through the curious dynamics of his seemingly never-ending day. The more articulate teachers become about the many things they can learn from their experiences, especially the positive, growth-oriented things, the more open they will become to trying new things in the service of desired outcomes.

Whether or not teachers are willing to explicitly imagine and play with the vantage, pivot, or lesson points of their stories, coaches navigate through coaching conversations with good-natured curiosity. If teachers do not respond to the invitation to rework and retell stories, they should not be pushed. It is not a requirement of evocative coaching. It is important, however, for coaches to be genuinely curious about the stories teachers are telling. Upon first telling, stories are like diamonds in the rough. Curiosity assists teachers to polish them into gems of personal and professional mastery. There is a difference, however, between curiosity and interrogation. Curiosity is an enjoyable exploration that generates the "Aha!" of insight and innovation. Interrogation is just the opposite. It is a high-pressure grilling that generates defensiveness, suspicion, and resistance. Evocative coaches therefore avoid asking too many questions in a row. Question blitzes are off-putting and destabilizing of the coaching relationship.

Evocative coaches also avoid asking leading questions that have an implied right answer. Neither do we ask deep, probing, and challenging questions until after teachers tell their stories fully, feel heard, are in the flow of the coaching session, and have a receptive frame of mind. Even then there is a difference between authentic questions that connect with the heart and leading questions that surreptitiously deliver constructive criticism. Teachers can see through that in an instant. It is not helpful for coaches to make assumptions, give advice, or evaluate methods while teachers are sharing their stories. It is better for coaches to listen to what is being said, to what is not being said, and to what teachers may want to say, in order to gently guide them through the exploration of their stories.

The point of imaginative listening, then, is to evoke a robust engagement with storytelling, replete with story variants. The more teachers understand their stories as stories, rather than as settled facts over which they have no control, the more they are cultivating a willingness to change. It is dangerous to have only one story to tell regarding what happened and what could have happened. Such stories become self-fulfilling and self-limiting prophecies. They tend to confirm what teachers already know; they do not invite the consideration of what they might learn and how they might grow. Imaginative listening takes teachers in the opposite direction as they ponder the possibilities of what might have been and what might be.

Summary

Evocative coaching begins with a deep concern for teachers as human beings. By the quality of our presence, evocative coaches establish strong trust and rapport with teachers before turning to techniques. We care more about the person than the project we are coaching. Once a living connection is made, through vital check-ins, coaches evoke "How did you grow?" stories from teachers in order to begin the exploration of how teachers see themselves and the worlds in which they work.

By listening mindfully, quietly, and reflectively as teachers tell their stories, coaches disarm resistance and evoke openness to change. In the normal course of affairs, people seldom have the undivided attention of anyone, even for brief periods of time, let alone without judgment. That alone may account for why evocative coaching is powerful and refreshing enough to transform an entire school. To have someone listen to you for a good chunk of time, with no agenda other than your agenda, is a rare and beautiful thing. It can make a world of difference and a difference in the world.

Once teachers share their stories, evocative coaches confirm what we have heard and respond with curiosity in order to explore the rich learning nuances that are embedded in the stories. Teachers and coaches can do this by imagining and playing with at least three variables: the perspectives of other characters, the impacts of different decisions, and the takeaways of lessons learned. Through exploring these variables together, teachers and coaches become partners in opening up new opportunities and paths for lasting change.

Questions for Reflection and Discussion

1. Who is the best listener in your life? What makes that person so? How does that listening make a difference?
2. What are the components of mindful listening? How do we cultivate mindfulness in our everyday lives?
3. What helps you to be comfortable with silence? How can you best leverage silence for teacher learning and growth?
4. What are the benefits of reflecting what you hear them saying, feeling, and wanting? What are the costs of "deflective listening"?
5. What do you make of the statement, "Words create worlds"? How have you seen that playing out in your own life? How can you use that in coaching?
6. Tell one of your own stories in three different ways: change the vantage point, change the plot line, and change the moral of the story. What was that like? What did you learn?
7. How could you assist teachers to explore their stories in ways that generate new insights and innovations for moving forward? How can we make such explorations both fun and productive?

CHAPTER 4

EXPRESSING EMPATHY

When a coach empathetically listens to another person's ideas, thoughts, and concerns, the coach communicates that the other person's life is important and meaningful. This may be the most important service that a coach can provide.

JIM KNIGHT (2007, P. 43)

Understanding Empathy

The psychologist Carl Rogers, perhaps more than any other modern psychologist, brought to our attention the connection between empathy and growth-fostering relationships (Joseph, 2010). In 1964, he delivered a lecture titled "Experiences in Communication" at the California Institute of Technology in Pasadena. He decided to communicate at a feeling and experiential level rather than to give a traditional academic lecture in order to demonstrate what he had learned about growth-fostering communication through his therapeutic and intensive group experiences. His lecture included frequent references to the nature and power of empathy. For example, Rogers observed:

> When I truly hear a person and the meanings that are important to him at
> that moment, hearing not simply his words, but him, and when I let him know
> that I have heard his own private personal meanings, many things happen.
> There is first of all a grateful look. He feels released. He wants to tell me
> more about his world. He surges forth in a new sense of freedom. He becomes
> more open to the process of change. I have often noticed that the more deeply
> I hear the meanings of this person, the more there is that happens. Almost
> always, when a person realizes he has been deeply heard, his eyes moisten.
> I think in some real sense he is weeping for joy. It is as though he were saying,

"Thank God, somebody heard me. Someone knows what it's like to be me."
(p. 10)

    I can testify that when . . . someone really hears you without passing
judgment on you, without trying to take responsibility for you, without trying
to mold you, it feels damn good! At these times it has relaxed the tension in me.
It has permitted me to bring out the frightening feelings, the guilts, the despair,
the confusions that have been a part of my experience. When I have been
listened to and when I have been heard, I am able to re-perceive my world in
a new way and to go on. It is astonishing how elements that seem insoluble
become soluble when someone listens, how confusions that seem irremediable
turn into relatively clear flowing streams when one is heard. I have deeply
appreciated the times that I have experienced this sensitive, empathic,
concentrated listening. (Rogers, 1980, pp. 12–13)

If schools are to become more life-giving places, where not only students
but also teachers learn and grow, then it is time to more fully put into practice
Rogers's wisdom regarding empathy. Schools without empathy are schools without learning. There may be compliance and orderly conduct, there may even be
measurable signs of achievement, but power- and fear-based organizations do not
facilitate the connection, passion, openness, resilience, and initiative that real learning requires. Simply put, empathy facilitates communication that facilitates change.
In the absence of empathy, schools become places where people are watching their
backs, doing the minimum, defending their territory, digging in their heels, and
resisting change. That is true all the way down the line: from school boards to
superintendents to principals to teachers to parents and students. In the presence of empathy, the climate shifts to that of a learning orientation. People come
to trust each other, to open up, to explore new possibilities, to share frustrations,
and to embrace change. These qualities distinguish schools that learn (Rogers,
1968; Senge, Cambron-McCabe, Lucas, Smith, Dutton, & Kleiner, 2000) as
well as coaching that works. Until and unless people communicate authentically
with others, in ways that facilitate trust and understanding, schools will not realize their mission as learning organizations.

    We believe that the dynamics between coaches and teachers can be catalysts
for institutional change. When teachers feel frustrated, angry, disgusted, suspicious,
embarrassed, disheartened, or otherwise troubled by the way coaches and leaders listen to and explore their stories, it is not long before those hard feelings spill
over into the community at large. Such reactions make it less likely if not impossible for teachers to want to participate in and benefit from professional development. The opposite happens when teachers feel understood, respected, happy,
trusted, empowered, engaged, or otherwise supported by the ways their stories are

heard and handled. Empathy, like trust, is both a lubricant for change and a glue that binds people together. It behooves coaches, then, to make empathy our way of being with teachers, both as an orientation and as a process for receiving and working through the stories teachers share regarding their experiences. In evocative coaching, empathy does not come after story and before inquiry in a chronological sense. It is rather an integral component of the story-listening process. Opportunities for empathy crop up at every turn. Recognized and handled adroitly, such moments can solidify the coaching relationship and advance the coaching process. Handled poorly, or not handled at all, those moments can jeopardize everything.

So what is the orientation of empathy? In common ways of speaking, empathy is a sympathetic feeling toward another person based on compassion or friendship. We tend to feel empathy for people we view as victims or friends, while we may harbor animosity toward people we view as incompetent, unlikable, or mean. This conventional understanding of empathy, although commonplace, falls short of what Carl Rogers was talking about and fails to make coaching evocative. If we feel empathy only for teachers we feel sorry for or like, and if our coaching amounts to little more than agreeing with their approaches and commiserating with their predicaments, then we have not done much to shift either their internal frameworks or their behavioral dynamics. For teachers to learn and grow through the process of coaching, we need a much more robust and all-inclusive definition of what empathy is and of how it works. When teachers share stories regarding how things went and how they grew, they need more than the sympathy of a friend. They need the empathy of a coach who accepts them right where they are and just the way they are. A more helpful definition of empathy that meets those requirements is "a respectful understanding of what others are experiencing" (Rosenberg, 2005, p. 91). Since "experience" includes all of life, both positive and negative, both external circumstances and internal dynamics, this definition provides guidance as to how empathy shows up and gets expressed in coaching.

Teacher stories include explicit descriptions and implicit indications of how teachers are processing their experiences. Listening mindfully, quietly, and reflectively to those stories, as we have seen, is the first work of coaching. By receiving these stories with empathy—with respect, appreciation, and understanding— especially the hard stories when things do not go well and teachers do not feel good, we facilitate acceptance, expand awareness, create openness, and generate a readiness to change. Such empathy is more than a passive intention; it is an active stance and skill that takes energy and practice to master. Empathy uses both emotional and cognitive awareness to connect with and give voice to what teachers are feeling, needing, and desiring. It requires coaches to suspend judgment, analysis, comparisons, suggestions, and the motivation to fix things in favor of connecting with what is stirring in the present moment.

Approaching teachers with an orientation of empathy does not mean, however, that we pity or sympathize with them. Empathy differs from pity and sympathy in that it is a coach's reflection of the teacher's perceived experience rather than a full-fledged sharing in it. Understanding the distinctions among empathy, pity, and sympathy is important for the mastery of evocative coaching. *Pity* is grieving someone's experience, usually because of his or her circumstances. For example, we may pity an undernourished child or a person who has faced unfair discrimination. Such sorrow can lead to charitable actions, such as giving assistance or showing mercy. Although helpful, these actions, which often stem from viewing and relating to people as victims or casualties, do not serve to empower people within the context of a coaching relationship. A person who pities someone communicates, in effect, "I feel sorry for you." That attitude undermines self-efficacy. Few people like to be pitied, no matter how difficult their situations. Coaching comes from the framework of believing in the teacher's ability to learn from and grow in any situation. Pity runs counter to this framework, implying fateful resignation to an unfortunate set of circumstances. Empathy is not about feeling sorry for someone; it is about understanding and respecting where the person is coming from.

Sympathy is identifying with another person's experience primarily on an emotional level. We feel the pain of another as our pain and the joy of another as our joy. Sympathizing with someone who feels sad, for example, means that we, too, feel sad. The same holds true with the entire range of emotions. This happens naturally, because emotions are intrinsically contagious. "Emotional contagion" is, in fact, a dynamic shared by virtually all animals; it can be seen, for example, when one bird becomes startled and the entire flock flies away (De Waal, 2006, 2009). Empathy is quite different from sympathy. Whereas sympathy is typically not discretionary, welling up in us in ways that are sometimes helpful and sometimes not, *empathy* requires a conscious treasuring of emotions as the gateway to learning, growth, and change. Although sympathy utilizes some of the same faculties as empathy and can offer clues as to what the other person may be experiencing, it doesn't engage the deeper faculties of consciousness, reflection, and choice required for emotional processing and transformation. Indeed, sympathy can easily interfere with story listening because it can trigger reactive responses and turn our attention more to our own concerns than to those of the other. The result can be overlooking or even shying away from where teachers are coming from and what they are dealing with. Someone who is sympathetic identifies fully with the emotions of others, while an empathetic person steps back and seeks to understand and appreciate those emotions as an integral part of the sense people are making of their experiences.

While pity and sympathy can be helpful at times, they do not have the trans-formational power of empathy. When we are empathetic, we say, in effect, "I understand your pain," or "I celebrate your joy." Doing so recognizes the felt sense of the emotion and appreciates what it has to teach us—no matter how difficult, painful, or confusing that may be. Such engagement and facility requires coaches to cultivate and speak the language of empathy. Empathy is first and foremost a language of the heart. Although empathy proceeds from an intellectual framework—that respectful understanding of feelings and needs is the doorway to growth and change—it must be embodied as a felt sense to become effective and durable. People can tell when empathy is not authentic. Evocative coaches therefore adopt practices that cultivate empathy as a way of being. Empathy is not a professional mask that we put on for coaching sessions; empathy is a compassionate and heartfelt orientation that we consistently come from in life and work.

Embodying Empathy

The notion of empathy as a heartfelt orientation is not just a euphemism for sincerity. There are many references throughout history to the heart as the locus of a special form of intelligence rooted in the body. The mind does not consent to an idea until the heart internalizes that idea on a cellular level. Empathy is a case in point. It may sound like a good idea to accept people right where they are and just the way they are, but what happens when we encounter someone who doesn't work hard, doesn't follow directions, doesn't play nice, or gossips about other people? That is when empathy has to bubble up from the heart; otherwise the head is likely to find all kinds of reasons for abandoning empathy in favor of more judgmental or coercive approaches.

The philosopher Blaise Pascal famously asserted that "the heart has its reasons which reason does not know." The distinction between head and heart has long been a source of intrigue and inspiration for artists, poets, playwrights, and philosophers. It is understood that the two are not always in sync and that the heart has more to do with feelings while the head has more to do with thoughts. The heart is variously described as a source of compassion, integrity, courage, generosity, celebration, mourning, and love. It is also cast as the repository of meaning and purpose—the very stuff out of which stories grow. Such descriptions, it turns out, may be more than just metaphors. A growing body of scientific research suggests that the heart as an organ with its particularly rich locus of nerves and the body in general have their own distinct parts to play in memory, motivation, and mobility. One person who pursued this line of research was Paul Pearsall, a psychoneuroimmunologist and pioneer in the field of energy cardiology (Pearsall, 1998). Pearsall drew a distinction between the intelligence of the brain and the intelligence of the heart, suggesting that the heart has an orientation around empathy, ease, and egalitarianism, while the brain is more naturally self-protective, territorial, busy, pessimistic, restless, and phobic. The brain, Pearsall noted, "sticks compulsively to the task of trying to win 'the human race'" (p. 25). The heart, on the other hand, functions along an opposite axis. The heart yearns to make heartfelt connections. It naturally seeks and warms up to the satisfaction of needs.

Those who seek to cultivate empathy in their dealings with self and others would do well, then, to adopt practices that contribute to and flow from positive heart energy. As we saw in Chapter Two on coaching presence, we cannot be evocative coaches unless we cultivate a way of being with people that communicates trust, respect, choice, openness, engagement, and possibility. Evocative coaches cannot be one way in coaching sessions and a different way in other settings. In every situation we must seek to understand people's motives and methods. Practices that contribute to and flow from positive heart energy include breathwork, meditation, journal writing, focusing, physical exercise, and getting adequate rest and sleep. The key is to find those practices that assist us to cultivate empathy and then to do them on a regular basis until they become second nature. Such practices are not things we get paid to do as part of our work life; they are rather things we love to do as part of our whole life.

> *I often say we've got a budget deficit that's important, we've got a trade deficit that's critical, but what I worry about most is our empathy deficit. When I speak to students, I tell them that one of the most important things we can do is to look through somebody else's eyes.*
>
> *Barack Obama*

Access Points for Empathy

Evocative coaches set the stage for coaching by creating a calm, safe, and judgment-free relational space in which teachers are free to honestly share their stories without fear of ridicule, pressure, or reprisal. Without such a stage, teachers will not open up in and derive full benefit from coaching so as to move forward in their teaching practices. They will certainly not be willing or able to transpose their stories, imaginatively playing with coaches to explore different vantage, pivot, and lesson points. This is especially true when the stories they have to share are tales of woe about seemingly unsolvable problems or unbridgeable gaps between what they want and where they are currently situated. The more teachers feel "stuck" and unable to move, the more they may seem to be doing a "terrible" job, the more important it is for coaches to express empathy and to appreciate the discomfort of immobility and futility. When teachers are struggling, it is espe-cially important that we connect with their feelings, needs, and desires in positive, supportive, and life-giving ways. A coach who is empathetic is curious without being demanding, interested without being intrusive, compassionate without being con-descending, and persistent without being impatient. Empathy seeks solely to gain an appreciative "felt sense" of a person's experience (Campbell & McMahon, 1997). It is the intention to "join up" or to "get with" where someone is coming from, and nothing else (Jordan, Walker, & Hartling, 2004). When teachers trust that their feel-ings and needs matter, and that their stories are being heard and recognized respectfully by their coaches, a zone of new possibilities is created.

Presenting Energy

Coaching relationships include many access points for empathy as coaches listen, observe, and respond to the stories teachers tell and the work they do in the class-room. Before digging into the task at hand, the first access point for empathy has to do with how teachers are showing up for coaching in the moment. Their pre-senting energy and emotions, combined with how we respond as coaches, will affect the course and value of the entire session. Our goal as coaches is to com-municate that we care about teachers as human beings and respect them as per-sons, not just as teaching professionals. That is why evocative coaches start every coaching conversation and interaction with at least a brief check-in as to how teachers are doing now. Asking "How are you?" or "How are you doing?" is a common and appropriate way of doing that, but there are far more evocative and creative ways to communicate a genuine interest in and respect for whatever may be stirring inside a teacher as the conversation commences. It is wise to ask those "How did you grow?" questions, presented in Chapter Three, and to not rush through this initial access point for empathy so as to avoid stimulating perfunctory answers such as "Fine" or "Okay."

Story Elements

Once the check-in is complete and teachers begin to tell their experiential learn-ing stories, coaches will find many other access points for empathy. That is true whether teachers are telling their stories for the first time, in the first person, or whether they are retelling their stories from the vantage point of different char-acters, decisions, or lessons learned. There are many things to listen for that are tailor-made for empathy.

In Chapter Three, we noted the five core elements of stories: characters, intent, actions, struggles, and details (Haven, 2007). All five represent access points for empathy because all five can stimulate either positive or negative feelings. The stories, as we have seen, are mental and verbal constructions of the storyteller. They are not the event itself; they are rather commentary on the event as teachers try to process and make sense of their experiences. Our emotions and needs get intertwined with our perceptions and the way we construct our stories. That is especially true when people are struggling with interference and obstacles that are seemingly frustrating their ability to achieve desired outcomes.

Although people think that the interference and obstacles are the cause of their frustration and unhappiness, such internal dynamics are the product of a complex set of thinking and feeling patterns. Stories can be told in many ways, and the point of expressing empathy in coaching, along with story listening, is that it gives teachers a new lens through which to view how they are reporting the drama and details of their stories. Instead of looking at constraints, actions, words, and expressions as things that are making us feel the way we feel, empathy enables teachers to view these emotionally charged stimuli as opportunities for discovering and learning more about their thinking and feeling patterns. The more teachers come to see themselves as the creators of their stories, the more they will increase the range of options available to them for processing their emotions and taking action. Empathy therefore creates a heretofore unimagined possibility zone. It increases our sense of understanding and control regarding what is happening and why. It expands our response repertoire as we move beyond limitation, constriction, and victimization to a place of authorship, creativity, and empowerment. By shifting from fault finding to a no-fault interpretation of events, regarding both self and others, empathy opens the door to life-giving change.

Classroom Observations

Another access point for empathy is classroom observations. Unlike story elements reported by teachers that may not have been witnessed by the coach, classroom observations afford coaches and teachers the opportunity to share experiences and to craft their stories together. Traditional feedback models often lack empathy; their emphasis is on the coach showing up as an expert to watch what teachers are doing, to identify the things they are doing "wrong" and the areas that need improvement, so as to make recommendations as to how they can improve their teaching. Whatever value this approach may have for evaluation, it undermines the value of coaching as a tool for professional learning and growth. By turning classroom observations into threatening fault zones rather than engaging no-fault zones, coaches provoke anxiety, constriction, and stress rather than evoke composure, receptivity, and readiness (Gallwey, 2009).

Learning how to conduct classroom observations through an empathic and appreciative lens, what we call "observing vitality," is discussed in detail in Chapter Five. For now, it is important to recognize classroom observations as one of the most significant access points for empathy in the coaching process. When empathy becomes the hallmark of a coaching relationship, when teachers know that they will be understood and not judged regardless of what they say or do with their coaches, then teachers welcome classroom observations and look forward to the learning such observations can evoke. This learning happens both in the moment, as observations increase teacher awareness of what they are doing and why, and after the fact, as coaches and teachers debrief from the experience in a coaching conversation. Evocative coaches seek to make both parts of the experience safe, honest, empathic, and insightful opportunities for teachers to experience the "Aha!" of coaching. Empathy alone has that much potential. As coaches and teachers come into an ever more trusting and common understanding of their experiences and stories together, new possibilities emerge and new designs become possible.

Resistance to Change

A final access point for empathy arises when teachers express resistance to making a change or doing something new. Although it is tempting on such occasions to push teachers to "give it a try" or to "get going," such approaches usually serve to escalate resistance to change. Expressing empathy, on the other hand, serves to deescalate the resistance and renew both the coaching relationship and the work of coaching itself.

When teachers are resistant to change, it is often a sign that teachers are experiencing ambivalence, an uncomfortable state of indecision or uncertainty growing out of competing commitments or values. Everyone feels this way at times. Ambivalence is not pathological, and it is not a deficiency. It is a natural part of life. Although ambivalence is not a fun place to stay for extended periods of time, it can stimulate deep thinking, feeling, and soul searching about two or more possible courses of action. When teachers receive empathy for ambivalence instead of judgment, when coaches seek to respectfully and fully understand what teachers are experiencing as they anticipate the prospect of making a change, then teachers become more ready, willing, and able to move forward (Miller & Rollnick, 2002; Kegan & Lahey, 2009).

For coaches to express empathy when teachers are ambivalent, it helps to understand that readiness to change falls on a spectrum and that different approaches are called for depending upon where people are on that spectrum. The readiness-to-change spectrum can range from not thinking about changing a behavior, to thinking about it, to planning to change, to testing out ways to do it before we actually start trying and then doing it for good (Prochaska, Norcross, & DiClemente, 1994). This continuum can be thought of as stages ranging from "I won't," "I can't," or "I may" on one end to "I will" in the middle, to "I am" and "I still am" on the opposite end (Moore & Tschannen-Moran, 2010, pp. 34–39). Teachers are most likely to feel ambivalent about changing their teaching practices when they are in those initial three stages of change. Although expressing empathy always has value in coaching, it can be of great value in assisting teachers to open up and to release their resistance to change.

Distinctive Empathy Reflections

In Chapter Three, we wrote about the importance of reflective listening in evocative coaching conversations. Although there are many different types of reflections (Miller & Rollnick, 2002), the primary work of reflective listening is to express empathy. Instead of probing with questions, we clarify with reflections. Whether or not we agree with what a teacher is saying or doing, it is nevertheless possible and even required that evocative coaches communicate a respectful understanding of the teacher's perspective and experience. Teachers do things for their own good reasons; empathy reflections seek to understand and honor those reasons as having validity in the mind of the teacher. Until that validity is acknowledged and communicated, teachers become more rather than less resistant to the idea of changing their approaches or exploring new behaviors. Granting that validity to teachers facilitates clarity, insight, connection, and movement. This framework is foundational to the evocative coaching process and to moving the conversation forward into Inquiry–Design.

For coaches to express empathy, we must learn how to recognize and reflect the life-giving elements of teacher stories and experiences. Quiet and mindful listening are both ways to facilitate that recognition. Evocative coaches cannot express empathy in a reactive state. We must pay attention without judgment and allow silence to work its magic. The language of Nonviolent Communication (NVC)—developed since the 1960s by Marshall Rosenberg (2005), a student of Carl Rogers—is another way to distinguish and draw out those elements that infuse teachers with life. It can give coaches the awareness, vocabulary, and ability to connect respectfully with teacher feelings and needs in any situation, regardless of how seemingly positive or negative that situation may be. NVC makes and works with four important distinctions. To express empathy, coaches are encouraged to distinguish between *observations* and evaluations, *feelings* and thoughts, *needs* and strategies, and *requests* and demands. Gaining facility in the use of these distinctions can assist coaches to communicate in ways that foster empathy.

Although evocative coaches often make use of these distinctions in reflecting teacher experiences and reframing teacher stories, we do not use the distinctions to correct teachers or instruct them as to how *they* should talk. On the contrary, we simply use the distinctions to offer different reflections and to ask different questions than might otherwise be expected. In so doing, we awaken teachers to the possibilities latent within them and within their stories. We honor their process, respect their autonomy, and evoke their readiness to change. If coaches are asked about how we are communicating, we can certainly explain the process. But NVC is less a skill set than an orientation. Unless it is an authentic intention of the coach to truly understand and appreciate the experience of the teacher, no process for expressing empathy will work.

It might be said, then, that evocative coaches speak distinctly when expressing empathy with teachers. In common parlance, "speaking distinctly" has the connotation of speaking cleanly, clearly, understandably, and without muddying the waters with extraneous information. In light of the four NVC distinctions, "speaking distinctly" can also mean speaking with a conscious and mindful awareness of the NVC model. Figure 4.1 depicts that model. By reflecting our understanding of what teachers are saying with the use of observation, feeling, need, and request language, without reiterating or wrestling with their evaluations, thoughts, strategies, and demands, we assist teachers to process their emotions more cleanly, to see their situations more clearly, and to open their minds more fully. Each distinction is considered in turn.

Distinguish Observations

The first distinction made in the NVC model is that we communicate observations and not evaluations. We reflect those details that can be detected by the five senses (sight, hearing, taste, smell, and touch) without including any derogatory or laudatory remarks or overtones. When Sergeant Friday of the 1960s television program *Dragnet* used to say his famous line, "I want the facts, ma'am, just the facts," he was asking characters to sort out their interpretations, judgments, and feelings from what actually happened. This is far more difficult than it sounds. To monitor and suspend the tendency to praise, criticize, compliment, judge, exaggerate, interpret, moralize, generalize, catastrophize, or assume is not a normal way of conversing. Most of the time, when we see or hear something we like, for example, we respond with positive evaluations such as "That lesson was terrific!" or "You're such a wonderful teacher." While those assessments may be welcomed by teachers in the moment, they put us in the role of evaluator, and they turn the coaching space into a stage for winning the coach's approval. This is not the space of evocative coaching, since teachers may become motivated

FIGURE 4.1. NONVIOLENT COMMUNICATION MODEL

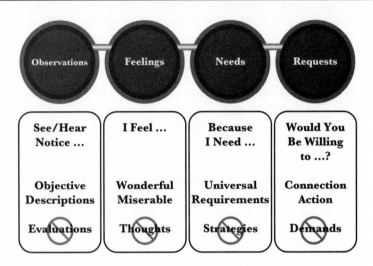

by self-protection to take fewer risks, to set smaller goals, and to pay attention to the coach's standards for quality rather than challenging themselves to ever-higher quality standards.

Stories, as we have seen, revolve around characters with goals (they want something) and motives (for a reason). As characters pursue their intents, they encounter systems, environments, resources, and connections that either help or hinder them as part of the plot. Teachers may assign roles—such as villains, victims, victors, or vindicators—to the people in their stories. In telling their stories, it is easy for teachers to identify characters as being naughty or nice, wrong or right, stupid or smart, lazy or diligent, enemy or ally. They may assess them as being disorganized, inept, ignorant, incompetent, ineffective, or inefficient. They may even diagnosis them as having clinical disorders such as ADHD, OCD, paranoia, or bipolar disorder. The problem with pigeonholing people in these ways is that we miss their full texture and depth as human beings. The characters in our stories become caricatures. We start thinking that we know who people are and how they are going to act without having to look any further. Labeling, name calling, and enemy images interfere with the ability of teachers to transpose the characters in their stories, to view those characters as fully capable human beings, and to imagine the possibility of real change. "What can I do? That's just the way it is" becomes the implied message of resignation.

Whenever coaches hear judgments and evaluations in teacher stories, whether pointed inward or outward, we have an opportunity to respond by making distinctive reflections. We can consciously choose to mirror back only what can be perceived by the five senses and to bypass any commentary and embellishments teachers may be making about the motives or moral fiber of the actors in their stories. By responding in this way, coaches neither communicate agreement nor disagreement with teachers' conclusions or judgments as to motive and agency; we simply attend to what was experienced in the sensible universe. If a teacher's story does not provide sufficient observational details, we may ask for clarification. We do not ask for this in a way that implies rightness or wrongness; instead, we ask in ways that communicate our heartfelt desire to capture and understand the story elements that could be recorded on a video camera.

In order to speak distinctly in this realm, when reflecting what we have heard teachers say, it is important for coaches to avoid introducing our own judgments into the conversation. Judging teachers does not facilitate their growth and change. To avoid implying rightness or wrongness in our reflections, we not only refuse to make outright compliments and criticisms, we may even want to be careful with euphemisms that can subtly trigger defensive reactions. For example, "When you arrived late" may imply wrongness, whereas "When you arrived after the meeting had begun" is a cleaner statement of fact. Likewise, "When you yelled at her" might be expressed more clearly as "When I heard you say, 'What a mess you've made.'" While coaching, our job is not to evaluate teacher effectiveness; our job is to value teacher experiences starting with a clean and supportive understanding of what teachers are saying and doing. Communicating this understanding reframes teacher stories and frees them up to make new choices if they are so inclined. By distinguishing between observations and evaluations, coaches engage in a form of story listening and lay the foundation for observing vitalities, to be discussed in Chapter Five.

At one point I noticed that Jessica seemed uncomfortable with the question I'd asked. I was concerned that she might be becoming defensive, thinking I was judging her. I leaned forward, keeping my eyes on her, as I sought to clarify what I meant. She relaxed then—her shoulders dipped and her face became less tense. I can see how keeping my attention focused on the other person's body language and stance is so important to keeping lines of communication open.

Matt, high school department chair

Distinguish Feelings

Another way to reframe teacher stories is to distinguish between the feelings teachers may be experiencing and the judgmental thoughts they may be harboring about themselves or others. Teachers' positive and negative feelings are integral to their experiences, even when they do not quite know how to describe these feelings. Feelings are important because they serve as indicators of what is going on in the realm of needs. Like a fuel gauge on the dashboard of a car, feelings provide information about whether this living system has all that it needs to thrive. Wonderful feelings provide a self-reinforcing feedback loop, saying "Whatever you're doing, keep doing it because my needs are being met." Teachers in these situations may communicate contentment, happiness, delight, satisfaction, gratitude, energy, or calm. Unpleasant feelings are also feedback loops that serve as warning signals from the limbic brain that needs are not being met. Teachers in this condition may communicate anger, resentment, disappointment, confusion, dissatisfaction, worry, embarrassment, or sadness. In either case, whether teachers are feeling wonderful or terrible, coaches can express empathy by using the NVC distinctions to communicate an appreciative and respectful understanding of teacher experience at the deep level of their core feelings and underlying needs.

Stephanie had a newborn at home, her first, and she was suffering from the postpartum blues. She had been a strong teacher but her heart was not in it after the baby was born. Her negativity about being at school was really affecting the morale of the whole staff. When we met before my first observation, the feeling from her was just flat—she didn't show any emotion at all. And when I showed up to observe, she was showing a video. She said defiantly, "You can stay if you want but you're not going to see anything but me sitting at my desk." She was disengaged, not stopping the video periodically to discuss important points with the students as I would have liked to see. She was marking papers at her desk. I had a choice to put on my evaluator hat or to stay in my coaching role. I said, "I'll come back another time." Later she was a little sheepish, but I just told her again that we'd find another time for me to observe. If I'd come down on her then, I feel certain I would have lost her to coaching for the whole year. When I showed her the observation data from my next visit, she came up with three goals to work on. I held back and didn't address the day when she was showing the video or her general lack of motivation and negativity. After I observed the second time using the same observation tool, I asked how things were coming on the experimental design strategies we'd discussed before. She said straight out, "I really haven't implemented any of them." That's when I said, "That's not like you. What's going on? You're a strong teacher but I'm not seeing the same engagement I've always seen before." She said, "Beth, I just want to be home with my baby," and she started to cry. That was the elephant in the room, and that's when the coaching really began. I said, "I know you do," and I just stayed with that and empathized with her sadness. After that, when she was having a bad day, I could connect with how she was feeling but then remind her that "you have twenty-three babies right here and they need you too." In addition to brainstorming strategies for her classroom, we brainstormed ways that she could spend more time home with her baby, and this year she is working four hours a day, three days a week as a reading teacher. She is motivated and happy. It's turned out to be a good solution all the way around.

Beth, elementary resource teacher

Sometimes it is easy to understand what teachers are feeling because they tell us directly. Other times teachers express their feelings indirectly, through body language, tone of voice, energy, moods, hesitation, and pacing. More often than not, as we have noted, feelings are mixed into teachers' stories and garbled with a variety of positive and negative judgments. Coaches can then either ask for clarification as to how teachers are feeling or venture a guess as to what might be alive in them. Guessing is often a better approach, because teachers may not be aware of their core feelings. Offering a guess with the intention to "join up" rather than to judge communicates the coach's desire to understand, appreciate, and value those feelings. If we guess correctly, the teacher is likely to appreciate the empathic connection created. Even if our guesses miss the mark, however, they represent attempts to understand what is going on, and they open pathways for teachers to clarify the feelings they are experiencing in the moment.

Empathy requires practitioners to maintain a stance of hypothesis, always checking with their clients to ascertain whether they have accurately understood the essence of the client's experience.

Dianne Stober (2006, p. 23)

Sharing our best guess as to what teachers may be feeling not only facilitates connection, it also awakens teachers to the distinction between their core feelings and the judgmental thoughts and stories that are wrapped around those feelings. Core feelings are what we feel first, at the primitive level of the limbic system, before the cerebral cortex—the extensive outer layer of folded "gray matter" responsible for higher brain functions in humans—starts to infuse those feelings with thoughts and stories as to what is right and wrong, who is to blame, and how things should be different (Siegel, 2007). Reflecting a teacher's judgmental thinking serves to codify and reinforce that thinking. It gives tacit consent to a teacher's conclusions and strategies. Expressing empathy does not seek to confirm or dispute such thinking; it rather seeks to shift the attention of teachers from their heads to their hearts. We invite teachers to momentarily set aside their judgmental thoughts and stories in order to explore the deeper realm of their feelings and needs. To do that, we may, for example, ask teachers to notice how emotions are showing up in their bodies, whether in a churning stomach, a tight throat, tension in the shoulders, a clenched jaw, or hands balled up in fists. We may also reflect how those things are showing up for us in the coaching space.

Teachers can experience great relief when they take a break from thinking about issues of right and wrong, who is to blame, and how things should be different. Such thinking often degenerates into a downward spiral that produces great suffering, taking the form of anger, guilt, shame, or depression. By reflecting the core feelings of teachers without reflecting their judgments, coaches can assist teachers to interrupt those destructive cycles and experience greater freedom, movement, and growth. To distinguish a teacher's underlying feelings is arresting in the most positive sense of the word. To be seen and heard on that level gets one's attention and evokes an emotional release that leads to clarity, trust, openness, choice, and change. Learning how to make such reflections is an essential part of expressing empathy in coaching. Table 4.1 includes a list of feeling words that coaches can use to help teachers become more aware of their feelings as distinct from their judgmental thoughts and stories.

When teachers give voice to strong feelings infused with passionately held judgments and beliefs, empathy reflections can be especially challenging. To avoid confirming teacher diagnoses and strategies, coaches must hone our ability to distinguish between the two in order to reflect the core feelings without reflecting the judgmental thoughts. The English language offers many convenient loopholes for conflating thoughts as feelings. Although grammatically correct, none of the following sentences directly expresses core feelings: "I hear that you feel like a failure," "You feel that the parents just don't care," or "You feel she is being manipulative." Following "You feel . . ." or "I feel . . ." with *that*, *like*, or a noun or pronoun that is not an emotion always introduces an evaluative overtone.

In addition, there is a set of feeling words associated with thinking of other people as foes that are sometimes called "faux feelings." These words are inextricably intertwined with judgmental thoughts that another person has *caused* our feelings by doing something that they should not have done. Verbs in the past tense that are followed by an explicit or implicit "by you"—such as *attacked, belittled,*

TABLE 4.1.   FEELING WORDS

When Needs *Are Not* Being Met	When Needs *Are* Being Met
Hostile animosity, antagonistic, appalled, aversion, cold, contempt, disgusted, dislike, distain, hate, horrified, repulsed, scorn, surly, vengeful, vindictive	**Exhilarated** ecstatic, elated, enthralled, exuberant, giddy, silly, slap-happy
Angry enraged, furious, incensed, indignant, irate, livid, mad, outraged, resentful, ticked off	**Excited** alive, amazed, animated, eager, energetic, enthusiastic, invigorated, lively, passionate
Annoyed aggravated, bitter, cranky, cross, dismayed, disgruntled, displeased, exasperated, frustrated, grouchy, impatient, irked, irritated, miffed, peeved, resentful, sullen, uptight	**Inspired** amazed, astonished, awed, dazzled, radiant, rapturous, surprised, thrilled, uplifted, wonder
Upset agitated, alarmed, discombobulated, disconcerted, disturbed, disquieted, perturbed, rattled, restless, troubled, turbulent, turmoil, uncomfortable, uneasy, unnerved, unsettled	**Joyful** amused, buoyant, delighted, elated, ecstatic, glad, gleeful, happy, jubilant, merry, mirthful, overjoyed, pleased, radiant, tickled
Tense antsy, anxious, bitter, distressed, distraught, edgy, fidgety, frazzled, irritable, jittery, nervous, overwhelmed, pressured, restless, stressed out, uneasy	**Relaxed** at ease, carefree, comfortable, open
Afraid apprehensive, concerned, dread, fearful, foreboding, frightened, hesitant, mistrustful, panicked, petrified, reserved, scared, sensitive, shaky, suspicious, terrified, timid, trepidation, unnerved, unsteady, wary, worried	**Curious** adventurous, alert, interested, intrigued, inquisitive, fascinated, spellbound, stimulated
Vulnerable cautious, fragile, guarded, helpless, insecure, leery, reluctant	**Confident** empowered, proud, safe, secure, self-assured
Confused ambivalent, baffled, bewildered, dazed, flustered, hesitant, lost, mystified, perplexed, puzzled, skeptical, torn	**Engaged** absorbed, alert, ardent, engrossed, enchanted, entranced, involved

(*Continued*)

TABLE 4.1. (*CONTINUED*)

When Needs *Are Not* Being Met	When Needs *Are* Being Met
Embarrassed ashamed, chagrined, contrite, guilty, disgraced, humiliated, mortified, remorse, regretful, self-conscious	**Hopeful** expectant, encouraged, optimistic
Longing envious, jealous, nostalgic, pining, wistful, yearning	**Grateful** appreciative, moved, thankful, touched
Tired beat, burned out, depleted, exhausted, fatigued, lethargic, listless, sleepy, weary, worn out	**Refreshed** energetic, enlivened, rejuvenated, renewed, rested, restored, revived
Disconnected alienated, aloof, apathetic, bored, cold, detached, disengaged, disinterested, distant, distracted, indifferent, lethargic, listless, lonely, numb, removed, uninterested, withdrawn	**Affectionate** closeness, compassionate, friendly, loving, openhearted, sympathetic, tender, trusting, warm
Sad blue, depressed, dejected, despair, despondent, disappointed, discouraged, disheartened, downcast, downhearted, forlorn, gloomy, grief, heavy hearted, hopeless, melancholy, sorrow, unhappy	**Peaceful** blissful, calm, centered, clear headed, mellow, quiet, serene, tranquil
Shocked appalled, disbelief, dismay, horrified, mystified, startled, surprised	**Relieved** complacent, composed, cool, trusting
Pain agony, anguished, bereaved, devastated, heartbroken, hurt, miserable, wretched	**Content** glad, cheerful, fulfilled, satisfied

criticized, intimidated, manipulated, pressured, provoked, put down, threatened, or *tricked*—communicate a judgmental thinking pattern of causal attribution. Such words imply that an external agent was the cause of our internal feelings. NVC maintains that it is our thinking that causes our feelings and not the actions of another person or events themselves. As Viktor Frankl famously noted after living through the bondage of a Nazi concentration camp, "Everything can be taken from a man but one thing: the last of the human freedoms—to choose one's attitude in any given set of circumstances, to choose one's own way" (Frankl, [1959]2006, p. 66).

The notion that we are always at choice as to our feelings, as to how we tell the stories that account for our feelings, and as to how we respond to our feelings means that our emotions are not at the mercy of others whom we do not control. Control is, after all, just another story (and an often tenuous and elusive one at that). Even when educators have a measure of authority over other people, we rely on consent for compliance. If a person's autonomy needs get stimulated, that consent may be withdrawn. When teachers use faux-feeling words to describe their feelings, it is likely that they have a solution or strategy in mind that involves a desire to control or require something from someone else (an implicit "should"). For example:

- "I feel disrespected (by someone)" may imply "I think that he should go to the principal's office to be punished."
- "I feel taken advantage of (by someone)" may imply "I think that she should do her share of the joint lesson planning."
- "I feel criticized (by someone)" may imply "I think that he should let you know that he appreciates your efforts."
- "I feel coerced (by someone)" may imply "I think that you should be allowed to teach the way you like."
- "I feel pressured (by someone)" may imply "I think that she should ease up on all that she is demanding of you."

Evocative coaches avoid reflecting a teacher's judgmental thoughts and faux-feeling words when we express empathy. Such communications do not expand understanding, bolster motivation, or facilitate movement. They tend to turn coaching conversations into gossip and gripe sessions. Distinctive reflections, on the other hand, point a teacher's attention to the feelings and needs that lie beneath these causal attributions, the realm where teachers have access to life-giving energy as opposed to the life-depleting and often futile attempts to force other people to conform to their wills.

When teachers give voice to judgments and evaluations it is important for coaches with an NVC consciousness not to criticize or correct such language. Judgments and evaluations are real thoughts underlaid with real feelings and needs. Coaches instead use the NVC distinctions to introduce new perspectives and openness into the coaching space around those thoughts. The emotional charge associated with evaluations and judgments must be recognized and honored. NVC enables coaches to do that by gaining an awareness of and a vocabulary for the core feelings that may lie behind those thoughts. When we find the right words, and use the right tone, teachers nod with understanding and expand their willingness to consider the underlying needs they are trying to meet. Reflecting the core feelings that may be alive in teachers rather than parroting the evaluative or judgmental thoughts that may come out of their mouths is an important skill for coaches to learn in order to speak distinctly. Table 4.2 includes a more complete list of causal judgments, or faux-feeling words, along with their associated core feelings and underlying needs.

As coaches, we want to be especially careful to avoid adding our own causal judgments and attributions into coaching conversations. Since emotions are

TABLE 4.2.   REFRAMING CAUSAL JUDGMENTS

Causal Judgments	Possible Underlying Feelings	Possible Underlying Needs
Attacked	Scared, angry	Safety, respect
Belittled	Indignant, distressed, tense, embarrassed, outraged	Respect, autonomy, to be seen, acknowledgment, appreciation
Blamed	Angry, scared, antagonistic, bewildered, hurt	Fairness, justice, understanding
Betrayed	Stunned, outraged, hurt, disappointed	Trust, dependability, honesty, commitment, clarity
Boxed In	Frustrated, scared, anxious	Autonomy, choice, freedom, self-efficacy
Coerced	Angry, frustrated, scared, anxious	Autonomy, choice, freedom, self-efficacy
Criticized	Humiliated, irritated, scared, anxious, embarrassed	Understanding, acknowledgment, recognition
Disrespected	Furious, hurt, embarrassed, frustrated	Respect, trust, acknowledgment
Distrusted	Hurt, sad, frustrated	Honesty, authenticity, integrity, trust
Harassed	Angry, aggravated, pressured, frightened, exasperated	Respect, consideration, ease
Hassled	Irritated, irked, distressed, frustrated	Autonomy, ease, calm, space
Insulted	Angry, embarrassed, incensed	Respect, consideration, acknowledgment, recognition
Interrupted	Irritated, hurt, resentful	Respect, consideration, to be heard
Intimidated	Frightened, scared, vulnerable	Safety, power, self-efficacy, independence

TABLE 4.2. (*CONTINUED*)

Causal Judgments	Possible Underlying Feelings	Possible Underlying Needs
Left Out	Sad, lonely, anxious	Belonging, community, connection, to be seen
Manipulated	Resentful, vulnerable, sad, angry	Autonomy, consideration, choice, power
Misunderstood	Upset, dismayed, frustrated	Understanding, to be heard, clarity
Overworked	Angry, tired, frustrated, resentful	Respect, consideration, rest, caring, ease
Pressured	Overwhelmed, anxious, resentful	Relaxation, ease, clarity, space, consideration
Rejected	Hurt, scared, angry, defiant	Belonging, connection, acknowledgment
Taken Advantage Of	Angry, powerless, frustrated	Autonomy, power, trust, choice, connection, acknowledgment
Taken For Granted	Hurt, disappointed, angry	Appreciation, acknowledgment, recognition, consideration
Tricked	Indignant, embarrassed, furious	Integrity, honesty, trust
Unappreciated	Sad, hurt, frustrated, irritated	Appreciation, respect, acknowledgement
Unsupported	Sad, hurt, resentful	Support, understanding
Violated	Outraged, agitated, anxious, sad	Safety, trust, space, respect

contagious, it is inevitable that coaches will experience a wide range of feelings and physical sensations as we listen to teacher stories. When that happens, we receive our reactions as gifts and we view them as signs that there is something worth paying attention to and processing in the moment. Awareness of the NVC distinctions can keep us from becoming either judgmental or sympathetic in response to what may be coming up for us as teachers tell their stories. To do that requires mindful awareness and cognitive processing so as to understand what is going on and then to language it using the NVC distinctions in ways that facilitate awareness, trust, understanding, and forward movement. The following forms of communication are incompatible with empathy and are to be avoided in evocative coaching regardless of what coaches may be feeling in the moment:

- Moralistic judgments: "What a terrible thing to do!"
- Diagnostic labels: "You must have ADHD."
- Enemy images: You'd better watch yourself; he's out to get you."
- Guilt trips: "You should have known better—look at the mess you've made!"
- Making demands: "You don't have a choice. Do it or else!"
- Denying choice or responsibility: "There was nothing you could have done."
- Rewards and punishments: "If you do this, you'll be in big trouble."
- Making comparisons: "If you were just more like _____."
- One-upping: "That's nothing; wait till you hear what happened to me."

Distinguish Needs

Intertwined with the practice of distinguishing thoughts from feelings is the ability to distinguish between strategies and needs. When coaches venture a guess not only about the core feelings a teacher may be experiencing, but also about the underlying needs that may be generating those feelings, teachers feel even more deeply heard and moved. What makes empathy possible in every situation is that human beings all share the same universal needs as well as the motivation to meet those needs. Since the time of Abraham Maslow (1943, 1954, 1968), psychologists, economists, and other students of human behavior have sought to classify those needs and have created a wide variety of taxonomies (e.g., Alderfer, 1972; Max-Neef, 1992; McClelland, 1987; Pervin, 2003). Although social scientists may not agree on the exact nature and number of human needs, they do largely agree that humans have needs, that needs must be met to sustain and enrich life, that needs motivate behavior, and that feelings are indicators as to whether or not needs are being met. When needs are being met, we feel good; when needs are not being met, we feel bad.

> *Needs serve the organism, and they do so by generating wants, desires, and strivings that motivate whatever behaviors are necessary for the maintenance of life and the promotion of well-being and growth.*
>
> Ping Zhang (2007, kl. 679)

The recognition that universal needs drive all human behaviors can assist coaches to extend empathy to teachers, even when we disagree with their methods or disapprove of their instruction, since everything they say and do can be understood as strivings to meet legitimate human needs. Regardless of how ineffective their words and actions may prove to be in getting their needs met, the needs themselves are bona fide and understandable. Noticing what needs are being stimulated, satisfied, and/or ignored is a helpful way for coaches to express empathy in difficult situations. Figure 4.2 presents ten universal needs on a wheel diagram. The needs across from each other on the wheel represent qualitatively different energies that may be in creative tension with one another, while the needs next to

FIGURE 4.2. WHEEL OF NEEDS
(KEY DISTINCTION: NEEDS VERSUS STRATEGIES)

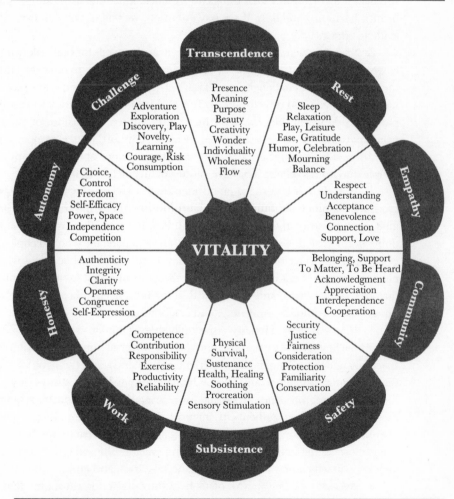

Source: Inspired by the work of Jim and Jori Manske (2005), Marshall Rosenberg (2005), and Manfred Max-Neef (1992).

each other represent more closely related energies. All of the needs are understood to be equally important and active throughout the human lifespan.

1. *Subsistence-Transcendence.* The realities and possibilities of existence require us to meet certain basic needs to support physical survival. These include such things as sustenance (including air, water, food, and shelter from the elements), sensory stimulation, and health. People fight long and hard over the strategies used to meet those needs, and no one denies their importance to life. The need for transcendence lies at the other end of the spectrum, but it is just as elemental as subsistence. It incorporates such things as presence, meaning, inspiration, evolution, beauty, harmony, and flow. If we pay attention, we will notice that even children evidence this need.

2. *Safety-Challenge.* Children also make clear the needs for both safety and challenge. They love to venture out, to risk, to learn new things, to discover, and to test their limits. These challenges are all part of the trial-and-correction process that leads to growth and development. But children are also quick to run to their parents' side when they feel fear, hurt, pain, anger, confusion, or rage. They need safety and protection. They need security, comfort, justice, respect, and consideration. These things are not strategies; they are not options relevant to some people and not to others. They are requirements of life itself.

3. *Work-Rest.* It is perhaps no accident that a Hebrew creation story portrays God as working for six days to create the universe and then resting on the seventh. The needs for work and rest are universal. People can neither work nor sit around doing nothing all the time. There is a rhythm to making life whole. People get into gear when they have reason to become active; they pull back and rest when they need to recover. Work incorporates such things as industry, exercise, competence, purpose, contribution, and creativity. Rest includes sleep, relaxation, play, leisure, humor, ease, gratitude, mourning, and celebration.

4. *Honesty-Empathy.* Honesty, respectfully sharing our life experiences with others, makes coaching evocative because honesty is a universal human need. Empathy, respectfully understanding the life experience of others, works the same way. Both of these dynamics are important, and both take courage. It is not always easy to speak the truth in love; the same can be said for hearing the truth. Honesty requires clarity, self-understanding, authenticity, integrity, and self-expression. Empathy requires openness, compassion, connection, acceptance, and understanding. Both of these needs must be met in the context of coaching relationships in order to create a no-fault zone in which new possibilities sprout, take root, and grow.

5. *Autonomy-Community.* All of us by nature strive for autonomy and bristle when we feel our autonomy is threatened. There is a saying that goes, "You insist, I resist," reminding us of how easily a person's autonomy needs can be provoked

by the insistence of another person. Yet we all by nature are social beings who strive to belong and as a practical matter are interdependent with others around us. These two needs reflect the creative tension between "the capacity to both self-regulate and be regulated by the norms, values, and goals of the larger system" (Costa & Garmston, 2002, p. 142). Autonomy incorporates such things as choice, control, freedom, self-efficacy, power, independence, and competition. Community includes a sense of belonging, acknowledgment, to matter, to be heard, appreciation, support, and cooperation.

Universal human needs are often below the surface of awareness, but they are at the heart of life and consequently at the heart of our work as coaches. Establishing an empathic connection with teachers at this level can help them become more aware and accepting of their needs and of what they are experiencing. Such awareness also expands the range of constructive actions they can take and of behavior changes they can make. By expressing empathy for and connecting respectfully with the living energy of needs, regardless of how teachers are feeling when they show up for coaching conversations, coaches can more effectively be in relationship with teachers and move the conversations forward.

If we want [teachers] to meet the needs of all students, we need to model with them how that is possible, by meeting the needs of all teachers.

Jane Kise (2006, p. 38)

Reflecting and honoring the universal needs that are alive in teachers not only opens the door for teachers to consider alternative strategies for meeting those needs, it also releases the frustration that naturally arises when an action fails to generate desired results. By confusing strategies and needs, teachers become more attached to a single course of action, less creative and open to new ideas, as well as more controlling and demanding in how they seek to move things forward. Experiences and stories revolve around strategies, some of which work better than others at meeting needs. Strategies are, in fact, nothing but another name for the actions and struggles that form the backbone of story architecture. They influence and may even determine what happens, but they are never ends in themselves. Strategies are always means to an end, and that end is the meeting of one or more universal human needs.

Similar to permitting confusion between feelings and faux feelings, the structure of the English language can also make it difficult to distinguish between needs and strategies. It is commonplace for people to use the language of needs when we are in fact expressing strategies to meet needs. Although the following sentences use the word *need* and are grammatically correct, they do not express universal needs: "You need to stop talking so much," "You need to check homework more frequently," and "You need to rearrange your classroom." These are strategies for meeting needs; they do not represent the needs themselves.

- Needs are essential; strategies are optional.
- Needs are universal; strategies are particular.
- Needs are life giving; strategies are life pursuing.
- Needs are beautiful; strategies are functional.
- Needs are expansive; strategies are limiting.

One way for us to be alert to the confusion between needs and strategies is to notice when the object of a sentence about our needs shifts to another person (e.g., *I* need *you* to do something). Such shifts suggest that we are holding someone else responsible for how we are feeling and for getting our needs met. They refer to strategies rather than to the underlying needs themselves.

When teachers fail to understand the needs they are trying to meet, their designs and action-learning strategies often prove to be inefficient or ineffective. Evocative coaches shift that dynamic by putting the spotlight on universal needs. The third column of Table 4.2 suggests some of the needs that may underlie the judgments and feelings presented in the first two columns. When a teacher wants someone to stop talking so much, for example, she might be reflecting her needs for participation, connection, or engagement. When he wants students to turn in their homework on time, he might be feeling both his need for ease and for contributing to student learning. The desire to rearrange one's classroom might be a way to express a teacher's need for greater comfort, order, or safety. Needs always underlie strategies and designs.

When coaches understand the distinction between needs and strategies, we can hear complaints and criticisms with new ears. We can understand them as expressions of unmet needs and values (Rosenberg, 2005). Instead of responding impatiently "Oh, quit whining" (either out loud or in our heads), we can instead get curious as to the need beneath the complaint. We can assist a teacher who is complaining to become more aware of his or her needs by offering a guess as to what need may want attention. This clarity allows the complainer to consider the selection of a new strategy in service of that need. Through our conversation, it might well emerge that the teacher has competing commitments or multiple sets of needs vying for her attention (Kegan & Lahey, 2009). By guessing at the underlying needs beneath the complaints or criticisms, we can offer teachers empathy and introduce them to an empowering and open stance for looking at and meeting their needs.

The moment I saw Meredith I knew she was upset. She'd had a difficult exchange with a parent that had left her shaken. She said that this dad was known to be a bully and that the principal had told all of the teachers that they should deal only with the mom in this family and refer the dad to her. But he'd shown up when the principal was out of the building and insisted that Meredith meet with him. The conflict centered on the consequences his son had been given for engaging in bullying behavior of his own with some other children. Meredith reported that this dad had talked so fast that she couldn't get a word in edgewise. He'd essentially called her a liar, demanded to know exactly what questions she'd asked in interrogating his son, and accused her of putting words into his mouth. He insisted that his son was innocent and that Meredith was just out to get him. When Meredith tried to interrupt this tirade by describing what she'd seen, the dad changed tactics and questioned her about her level of education and where she'd received her teacher degree. I could tell she needed a great deal of empathy. I reflected her report of what the dad had said and then guessed that she may have felt angry that her integrity was being questioned as well as disappointed that her intentions to contribute to this little boy's learning were not being seen for what they were. I guessed that she was frustrated when the father spoke over her words and wouldn't stop speaking long enough to let her answer his questions because her need for respect was not being met. I also guessed that she felt frightened by the intensity of his feelings and by how fast and how loudly he was speaking, disrupting her sense of safety. Meredith nodded as I spoke. When I asked her how she felt hearing me say these things, she said that she was beginning to feel a little calmer, that I had heard her correctly, and that she was aware that she was breathing more easily. She then became more able to talk about next steps.

Tara, elementary instructional coach

Distinguish Requests

The final way for coaches to express empathy in light of the four NVC distinctions is to make requests rather than demands of teachers so as to confirm understandings and explore possibilities. After reflecting observations, feelings, and needs, coaches can immediately ask, "Would you be willing to tell me what you heard me say?" or "How do you feel when you hear me say that?" Such requests enhance both the connection between coaches and teachers as well as the connection of teachers to the life-giving elements of their own experiences. Becoming clear as to what is being said and felt enables teachers to reframe their evaluations, thoughts, and strategies and to learn more about what they want to ask of themselves and others. It is essential for coaches to make such connection requests quickly and without any sense of demand. We are not trying to correct the way teachers are telling their stories, and we are not trying to control the conversation. We are simply inviting teachers to become more aware of and give voice to what they are feeling and needing. If teachers do not want to respond to our requests, or if they respond by taking the conversation in a different direction, then it is our job as coaches to roll with that decision. The agenda and flow of the coaching session is owned by the teacher, not the coach.

Another kind of request, which we work with extensively in the next two chapters as a staple in the Inquiry–Design phase of the evocative coaching process, is an action request to explore and commit to possibilities. After receiving empathy for their feelings and needs, teachers and coaches will often find themselves in a space where new ideas can be generated and new designs can be drafted. Empathy is not an end in itself; it is a rather a condition for all that follows. Empathy creates a possibility zone such that teachers yearn to come away from coaching sessions with a definite sense of what they might pay attention to and/or do differently in the future. Inviting teachers to clearly state their intentions in the here and now as to what they are willing and able to do is itself a form of action. Instead of leaving things ill defined or coach directed, asking teachers to make clear statements of intention facilitates their learning and growth by focusing their awareness and directing their energies into action. Once again, it is essential for coaches to request, rather than to demand, such statements. If it is unacceptable for teachers to say "No" and decline such requests, then this is a situation of demand that undermines both the coaching relationship and the potential of the teacher no matter how politely the words have been spoken. If teachers experience freedom and choice in such requests, they are more likely to respond with clear statements of intention that can greatly assist them to more fully understand and meet their needs in the future.

Elevating Readiness to Change

Just as it is important for coaches to recognize and pay attention to the presenting energy of teachers at the outset of coaching conversations, it is also important for coaches to assess and recognize the stages of change that teachers may be in as they talk about and work on various areas of their performance (Prochaska et al., 1994; Moore & Tschannen-Moran, 2010). Teachers' readiness to change in any given area refers less to their outlook on life than to their sense of competence and self-efficacy in a particular domain. Teachers will be in different stages of change for different coaching projects. Requesting teachers to consider or to commit to doing new things that they may not be ready for can undermine their self-confidence and progress. For example, teachers who have negative feelings or ambivalence about the prospect of changing how they do something in the classroom are not sufficiently ready to try out new methods. Requesting, let alone pressuring or demanding, that they do so may set them up for failure and precipitate their withdrawing from the coaching process altogether. Such teachers need empathy to sort out their thoughts and feelings about the change, to understand more fully the needs and values that a change might meet, and to get to a point of confidence before making the change.

Even after teachers begin to experiment with action-learning strategies, it is not uncommon for them to lapse back into old behavior patterns over the course of a coaching relationship. That is because the stages of change do not represent a linear process. They represent a spiral dynamic in which people continuously push out and pull back over time. By being aware and mindful of the stages teachers are in, coaches are better positioned to extend empathy and to assist teachers to meet their needs through the coaching process. Such stage-specific sensitivities are important if coaches want to assist teachers to reach their goals quickly, effectively, and enjoyably.

We have already noted that resistance to change represents an access point for empathy. Such resistance typically amounts to teachers saying that they either can't or won't consider alternative ways of meeting their needs. The "I won't" people are not interested in alternatives because they are certain their strategies are right. Colleagues may feel otherwise and may be nagging them to change, but they refuse to consider the possibility. The "I can't" people would like an alternative but they have not yet found strategies they feel confident in implementing. For different reasons, both kinds of people are not even contemplating, let alone working on, making changes in their teaching (Prochaska et al., 1994). To move forward, teachers at this end of the readiness-to-change continuum need lots of empathy (Miller & Rollnick, 2002). It does not elevate their readiness to change to pressure or demand that these teachers get going or try it anyway. This is rather the time to use distinctive reflections to show that we understand and respect their feelings and needs. A coach's ability to recognize and accept that teachers do not intend to change a particular behavior unlocks the door to future possibilities. We want to clearly communicate that we respect their freedom to choose and that we want them to move forward only once they are ready, willing, and able to do so. By asking them to deepen their knowledge and understanding of both themselves and their craft, without judgment, fear, guilt, or blame, evocative coaches enable teachers to come into new relationships with themselves and to find the motivation to move forward.

When I began working with Stacy and her team, she was very resistant. She had some negative comment or some way to shoot down any idea that was offered. She'd say, "Oh, we tried that years ago and it didn't work." Or "That'll never work with the kids we've got." It was clear to me that she was very insecure as a teacher and that her negative comments were a way of protecting herself. When the team decided on a particular strategy that they wanted to see me model over a three-day period, Stacy immediately offered her class, adding, "My kids are impossible. This will never work with them!" Because the students were not very accustomed to engaging instruction, they just ate it up. They really loved it. When we got to the debrief session, Stacy started right in with her negative comments, saying how the strategy was unrealistic and didn't teach the concept, and on and on. I empathized with her feelings and needs but did not reflect back her judgments and critical comments. After hearing her out, I then said, "Stacy, you must really be doing something right in your room because your students were *so* engaged in that lesson!" For a moment, she was stunned into silence. It was though she was considering the implications. And from that moment on, she was my new best friend. Her attitude completely changed once her need for acknowledgment was met. She became open to considering new possibilities. At the end of the eight-week collaboration, her only complaint was that it wasn't long enough. She said, "I didn't get to learn all that I wanted to learn."

Julie, elementary literacy coach

By expressing empathy for feelings and needs, coaches elevate readiness and lower resistance to change. Resistance talk says more about the approach coaches are taking than about the attitudes teachers are carrying. Knight (2007) put it this way: "Teachers don't resist new ideas as much as they resist the suggestion that they are not competent and they need to be helped or improved" (pp. 69–70). Expressing empathy facilitates a life-giving connection and makes the relational field between teachers and coaches both safe and interesting. It enhances self-esteem and expands self-concept (Rosenberg, 2005). Learning to appreciate and value the underlying needs behind resistance talk without communicating a shred of judgment or demand is a challenging and yet essential part of evocative coaching. Resistance has much to teach us. Pushing back against resistance closes the door on that opportunity. Whenever we find ourselves tempted to confront resistance directly, we end up provoking more resistance and squandering the chance to dance with teachers through the fire of their frightening feelings and unmet needs. The more curious we become about the living energy of teachers' needs while suspending our judgments, interpretations, assumptions, evaluations, and agendas, the greater becomes the chance of our breaking loose a new zone of possibility and hope (Gonzales, 2006).

> *We must remember this simple truth: the human soul does not want to be fixed; it wants simply to be seen and heard.*
>
> *Parker Palmer (1998, p. 151)*

The followings shifts in attitude, orientation, and communication patterns may assist coaches to avoid provoking resistance and to elevate the readiness to change:

- *From correction to connection.* The more we seek to correct people, the more they resist change. In contrast, the more we seek to respectfully understand their experience, the more open they become.
- *From competence to confidence.* The more we claim to know, the more resistance we provoke. In contrast, the more we claim to believe in the teacher's ability to learn, the more confident they become.
- *From causes to capacities.* The more we dig for the causes of problems, the more trouble we may dig up. The more we search for capacities, however, the more excited teachers become.
- *From counterforce to counterbalance.* The more forcefully we argue against ambivalence and for change, the more we generate push-back. But the more we counterbalance teacher ambivalence by articulating our awareness of their core feelings and underlying needs, the more we generate change talk.

In the interest of being helpful, coaches may at times want to advise, educate, console, reassure, explain, problem-solve, and correct teachers (Gordon, 1970; Humphrey, 2000). Although such behaviors may occasionally be appropriate and useful in coaching conversations, especially when teachers ask for the help, they do not represent the posture of empathy and tend to interfere with expressing empathy. To stay connected with teachers and to promote their full engagement, it is often better to listen mindfully and reflectively—especially early on in the course of a coaching conversation—rather than to jump in and start using one or more of the following approaches:

- Advising or problem-solving: "Let me tell you how I think you should handle this."
- Commiserating: "Oh, you poor thing."
- Consoling or reassuring: "There now, it'll be all right."

- Correcting: "That's not how it happened."
- Educating: "This could turn into a very positive experience for you if you just . . ."
- Explaining: "I would have come by, but . . ."
- Interrogating: "How long has this been going on?"
- Prodding: "Cheer up. Get over it. It's time to move on."
- Stepping over: "Well, let's not talk about that just now."
- Storytelling: "That reminds me of the time . . ."

It is easy for coaches to fall into these common patterns of communicating. Increasing our awareness when that happens and paying attention to the resultant shifts in the relational and conversational dynamics, can assist coaches to become more evocative listeners and collaborators in the service of teacher learning and growth.

Listen!

When I ask you to listen to me
and you start giving advice,
you have not done what I asked.
When I ask you to listen to me
and you begin to tell me why I shouldn't feel that way,
you are trampling on my feelings.
When I ask you to listen to me
and you feel you have to do something to solve my problem,
you have failed me, strange as that may seem.

Listen! All I ask, is that you listen.
Not talk or do . . . just hear me.
Advice is cheap:
50 cents will get you both Dear Abby and Billy Graham
in the same newspaper.

And I can do for myself; I'm not helpless.
Maybe discouraged and faltering, but not helpless.
When you do something for me that I can and need to do
for myself, you contribute to my fear and weakness.

But when you accept as a simple fact
that I do feel what I feel,
no matter how irrational,
then I can quit trying to convince you
and get about the business of understanding what's behind

this irrational feeling.
And when that's clear, the answers are obvious,
and I don't need advice.

Anonymous

Celebrating Effort and Progress

We have spent much of our time in this chapter on how to express empathy when teachers have uncomfortable feelings and unmet needs. We have done so because that is often the way teachers show up for coaching and because these can be the most challenging of times to express empathy. That is not, however, how teachers always show up for coaching, and in many cases it is not even normally the presenting energy. That is especially true if evocative coaching is doing what it is supposed to do. The whole point of evocative coaching is to assist teachers to better understand and meet their needs so that they show up for coaching with positive emotions and success stories regarding the new steps they are experimenting with and taking in the classroom. If coaching does not lead to increased teacher self-efficacy and professional mastery, then it is undershooting its potential and missing the mark as a catalyst of learning, growth, and change.

Because effort and progress are so important to the learning enterprise, evocative coaches look for and celebrate their evidence at every opportunity. Such moments are, in fact, additional access points for empathy and more opportunities for connection. Good work should not go unrecognized or unappreciated. As coaches, we want to assist teachers to fully savor and value what their positive accomplishments and experiences have to teach them. By finding the right words to describe that positivity, both about the feelings involved and the underlying needs that are being met, teachers become more aware of what happened, why it is important to them, and how to cultivate those factors in the future. Instead of just rushing in and moving on, with a quick "thumbs up" or a "high five," evocative coaches seek to enhance the benefits of positivity by enthusiastically reflecting and appreciating the lively energy. It truly is a wonderful thing when teachers are able to say and do things that assist them to more fully meet their needs, as well as the needs of their students.

We, of course, do not want to be over the top with praise and compliments, and we certainly do not want to turn such empathy into a reward, but we do want to share the joy and satisfaction of good work and to celebrate the capacity of teachers for continued good work. If teachers do not experience coaches as authentically celebrating the best of what is, there is no way they will join up with us to create the best of what might be. If we want the coaching relationship to radiate the energy of possibility and hope, then teachers have to know not only that we believe in them but also that we see them as making progress with their goals.

The Golden Sigh

When a teacher's needs for empathy, understanding, and appreciation have been met, when coaches have listened well and communicated respect for the feelings and needs of teachers, it often evokes what we refer to as a "golden sigh." This release is sometimes accompanied by a slight nodding of the head, a signal that teachers are ready to move on into inquiry. Whether or not there is an actual sigh or nod, this is a moment when the energy shifts to looking forward and outward rather than backward or inward. It may take time for this shift to come; so do not rush it. To move on too quickly is likely to result in defensiveness, resistance, and resentment. When we are working with teachers who have experienced deep discouragement or who have felt unappreciated for a long time, it may take several sessions before their empathy needs will be met. On the other hand, the "golden sigh" may come very quickly. The key is to watch for the felt sense that something has shifted and that the readiness to change has elevated. When the need for empathy is met, teachers will be ready to take steps to improve their situations, to move from places of powerlessness and blame to places of creative action.

If the "golden sigh" does not come, then one of two things may be happening: either we are not speaking distinctly—mixing in evaluations, thoughts, strategies, and demands with observations, feelings, needs, and requests—or the teacher is just not at a moment in time when she or he can move on. Either way, it calls for coaches to change our approaches. We must first look at our intention and language. Are we truly trying to understand the teacher's experience, or are we trying to change the teacher? What are the overtones of the words we are using and the language we are choosing? Whenever an agenda to get teachers to do something that we want them to do comes out, that agenda interferes with expressing empathy. Returning to the language of NVC is one way for coaches to get back on track.

If that does not work, then a shifted-focus reflection may be helpful (Miller & Rollnick, 2002, pp. 102–103). This amounts to changing the subject and shining the spotlight on some other area of teacher experience that may be more accessible and amenable to conversation in the moment. Here, too, coaches have to be careful to stay teacher centered. We do not shift the focus to talk about what we want to talk about; we rather shift the focus to shine the spotlight on some other aspect of teacher experience in which they have more energy and readiness to change. When teachers connect with these more positive dynamics, it renews the coaching relationship, elevates the coaching conversation, and encourages teachers to tackle those tougher areas where they feel stuck or are otherwise conflicted about change. When coaches dance with teachers in this way, a shift in energy will eventually come, and often more quickly than we might expect. Like all people, at their core, teachers need to make sense of their experiences and contribute to their own learning and growth. They want to move on and be successful. Expressing empathy enables teachers to do just that.

> *The ability to reconnect, to be resilient in relationship, to move back into connection to see if mutual growth-enhancing relatedness can be reestablished is one of the most important skills [coaches] can develop.*
>
> *Judith Jordan (2004a, p. 58)*

Summary

We have reached the end of our discussion concerning Story–Empathy, the first loop or turn in the dynamic dance of evocative coaching. Although presented as different steps in the dance, it should be clear by now that Story–Empathy, the No-Fault Turn, is of one piece. As teachers tell their stories, it is important for coaches to express empathy. As coaches express empathy, teachers open up and expand their stories. The No-Fault Turn cannot be rushed; it is a key work of evocative coaching.

Expressing empathy does not mean that we feel sorry for teachers (pity), or even that we get swept up in their emotions (sympathy); it rather means that we demonstrate a respectful understanding of their experiences. When teachers feel heard in this way, trust is built and readiness to change is facilitated. Our interest as coaches is to unleash the imagination so that teachers will consider ever more creative and venturesome designs for improving their performance and quality of life. The constricted emotional space of judgmental thoughts about what is right and wrong, who is to blame, and how things should be different generates limited designs, timid approaches, and constrained solutions. The expansive awareness of core feelings and underlying universal needs generates a very different energy as a dazzling panoply of ideas and possibilities gets evoked.

To unlock that awareness and energy requires coaches to cultivate the intention and to learn the language of empathy. Being empathetic is neither accidental nor unreliable. We mindfully and consistently set our intention to accept people right where they are and just the way they are. It is not our job to instruct, fix, demand, blame, praise, judge, or otherwise do anything to change teachers.

Our intention is simply to get with them, to come alongside them, and to more fully understand them as they understand themselves.

The language of empathy presented here is the language of Nonviolent Communication. This language makes four distinctions that are helpful to coaches in reframing teacher stories and in communicating the intention of empathy:

1. Distinguishing observations from evaluations
2. Distinguishing feelings from thoughts
3. Distinguishing needs from strategies
4. Distinguishing requests from demands

By connecting with teachers at the level of observations, feelings, and needs, coaches not only maintain trust and rapport, we also create a zone of possibility as teachers encounter new ways of understanding and processing their own experience. When teachers get to the core of the matter, they release a "golden sigh" and indicate a readiness to change. At this point, it is time to move the conversation forward with Inquiry–Design.

Questions for Reflection and Discussion

1. What is the orientation of empathy? How can coaches bring that orientation into school settings?
2. What practices assist you to cultivate empathy in your personal life? In your professional life?
3. Why did Carl Rogers assert that effective communication cannot take place if the atmosphere is threatening?
4. What are your feelings and needs right now, as you think about expressing empathy with teachers? How can you express your feelings and needs distinctly?
5. Recall a person you have recently dealt with who expressed a complaint. What do you suppose may have been the underlying unmet needs and values that this person was experiencing?
6. How might you heighten your awareness of your use of communication patterns that interfere with connection? What do you notice about the energy in the conversation when these patterns are present in the conversation?
7. Recall a time when you have offered empathy in your professional or personal realms. What did that look like and where did that lead? What were the clues that the other person felt heard?

LOOP II:
THE STRENGTHS-BUILDING TURN

That is surely a major ingredient in the success of coaching. The coach has the responsibility to, first, make sure the client is paying attention to what is positive—his or her strengths, what has worked well in the past, the upside of the problem. Second, the coach steadies the spotlight on the intended change, not by issuing orders but by asking questions.

ROCK AND PAGE (2009, PP. 185–186)

As we discussed in Chapter One, it is no accident that we portray the dynamic dance of evocative coaching on a Möbius strip (refer to Figure 1.1). It is precisely the mysterious properties of Möbius strips as two-dimensional objects in three-dimensional space that drew us to the model in the first place. Möbius strips reflect the human quest for continuity and novelty to which coaching conversations also give voice. When coaches and teachers meet, it appears that two separate people, with two separate perspectives, are talking to each other and working together. In actuality, they are sharing one experience with only one surface. The dynamic dance of evocative coaching facilitates what Martin Buber ([1923]1970) described as an "I-Thou" relationship, that basic word pair that establishes an essentially interconnected and intertwined mode of existence. The coach is not in relationship without the teacher; and the teacher is not in relationship without the coach. Together, they form one relationship with one experience looking to create one possibility.

All actual life is encounter.

Martin Buber ([1923] 1970, p. 62)

That possibility, as we have seen, is the full experience and satisfaction of universal human needs. Coaches listen to stories and express empathy not as ends in themselves but in order to facilitate that need-meeting dimensionality. We want to embody the change we hope to see in schools. We want to bring something new into being, but we can only do it through relationship. So we start with the No-Fault Turn, where "I-Thou" relationships can emerge and flourish. Once that happens, once the No-Fault Turn has begun to work its magic, we can trace that line around the Möbius strip to explore new territory until we end up back where we started, at which point the dynamic dance of evocative coaching starts all over again.

> Out beyond ideas of wrongdoing and rightdoing,
> there is a field. I'll meet you there.
> When the soul lies down in that grass,
> the world is too full to talk about.
> Ideas, language, even the phrase *each other*
> doesn't make any sense.
>
> *Rumi, thirteenth century (2004, p. 36)*

The new territory that coaches and teachers have to explore, out "beyond ideas of wrongdoing and rightdoing," is the luminous realm of capacity, possibility, and fulfillment. We call this "the Strengths-Building Turn" (see Figure LII.1), because it starts where the no-fault zone leaves off and turns teachers toward the future with a new sense who they are, what they can do, and how they want to contribute in the world. This includes and yet also goes beyond their activities in classrooms and schools. It awakens in teachers and coaches alike a sense of destiny, cause, and calling (Secretan, 2004). We become the ones schools have been waiting for.

FIGURE LII.1 LOOP II: THE STRENGTHS-BUILDING TURN

To do that, evocative coaching stays focused on strengths. It may be customary and it may even appear logical to focus on teacher shortcomings and weaknesses in order to help them do better. That is generally the hope and intent of all evaluation systems. But evaluation in coaching can do more harm than good, taking us off the Möbius strip altogether. Repeated studies have demonstrated the relative ineffectiveness of focusing on and trying to fix weaknesses (Buckingham, 2007). To stay on the Möbius strip of evocative coaching and to stay connected in life-giving relationship, coaches must assist teachers to learn more about what they do well, to frame aspirations about the best they can be, and to design actions that will generate learning as to how to get there. That is the method and measure of the Strengths-Building Turn.

There is no way for coaches to fully assist teachers to make that turn while coming from the "expert" frame. Even when expertise is shared with the best of intentions, to build up rather than to tear down people, it does not have the power to move teachers all the way forward. For that, teachers must discover, come to know, and trust their own strengths, values, vitalities, and aspirations. That is the path to teacher self-efficacy and positivity. So evocative coaches use appreciative inquiries and vital observations to call out and call forth those realities. Teachers' aspirations are always there. They are always waiting and enduring, as a presence to be found. They often get scuffed, marred, and obscured by the focus on what must be done, but they never get entirely lost. Evocative coaching awakens the sleeping giant of aspiration by focusing conversations on what wants to emerge, not as a private affair for personal aggrandizement and satisfaction at the expense of others but as a common quest for excellence in education. We seek to connect with teachers around our reason for being in education at all: the quest for contribution that makes a positive difference in the world.

> *The antidote for exhaustion is not necessarily rest. The antidote for exhaustion is* wholeheartedness.
>
> *Brother David Steindl-Rast (in Whyte, 2001, p. 132)*

As we will see, working wholeheartedly in education requires new understandings, approaches, and courage (a word that comes from the old French word *cuer*, heart). It requires coaches and teachers to move from the no-fault zone into the possibility zone. It requires imaginative recitals and creative visualizations of what people want as well as clear designs regarding how to get there. It is challenging but not impossible work. At their best, the designs shift entire systems into alignment. The stories of what coaches and teachers are doing together become self-replicating. The good news spreads as entire schools are transformed, one conversation at a time.

CHAPTER 5

APPRECIATIVE INQUIRY

A world of questions is a world of possibility. [The spirit of inquiry] opens our minds, con-
nects us to each other, and shakes outmoded paradigms. [It invites] exploration, discovery,
innovation, and cooperation. . . . We have only to ask the right questions to begin.

MARILEE ADAMS (2004, PP. 7–8)

The inquiry phase of the evocative coaching process shifts the focus of the conversation from the no-fault consideration of experiences and emotions to a forward-looking consideration of strengths, vitalities, aspirations, and possibilities. When "the No-Fault Turn" of evocative coaching has done its work, by the time coaches hear the "golden sigh," teachers are primed for a positive, action-oriented conversation. "Now what?" becomes the operative question (Fortgang, 2004). Teachers want to get going on designing ways to improve their performance and quality of life. That does not mean, of course, that it is now time for coaches to take over the conversation as expert advisers. Even when coaches know design strategies that might work well in a teacher's classroom, it is better to evoke from teachers the unique approaches they can call their own. All that we have written and learned about resistance and openness to change applies as much to the latter phases of the coaching process as to the earlier phases. Whenever coaches adopt a "tell-and-sell" approach with teachers, motivation is undermined and movement is stifled. People tend to push back when they perceive that someone is trying to change them. Evocative coaches therefore take a "listen-and-learn" approach, discovering the strengths teachers can engage and eliciting the designs they may want to employ. Over time, and in the context of a coaching relationship that supports their yearnings and ambitions, most teachers will figure out for themselves how to do things better.

Curiosity is therefore a key tool in the evocative coaching toolbox. Curiosity on the part of coaches empowers teachers to find their own answers, to be more resourceful, and to discover new possibilities for moving forward. The more coaches navigate by open-minded curiosity, especially with teacher capacities, strengths, aspirations, and desires, the more teachers discover about themselves, where they want to go, and how they want to get there. At the start of a coaching relationship, coaches do not know what the outcomes will be and how things will develop. Even when teachers have a specific curriculum to follow, it is largely unknown as to how they will assimilate and implement that curriculum. Because every teacher is different, with unique internal and external resources to call upon, every teacher will follow a different path of development on the way to personal and professional mastery. Evocative coaching is a personalized learning system that generates different answers with different teachers. It is a privilege and joy to participate in and witness the discoveries teachers make and the dreams teachers realize along the way.

There are plenty of ways to ask questions and plenty of things on which to focus. We have already written about the importance of asking open-ended questions, which gives teachers the opportunity to develop their thinking more fully. "Yes-or-No" questions are simply not that evocative. It is also important to avoid asking judgmental questions, so coaching sessions do not feel like interrogations. Evocative coaches seek to calmly ask authentic learner questions that connect teachers with their passions and invite a fresh consideration of their practices (Adams, 2004). After asking a question, coaches stop and listen. Coming forward with another question too quickly communicates impatience and restricts the coaching space. The same can be said about asking too many "Why?" questions, asking leading questions with an implied right answer, and asking questions that focus on problems or things teachers are doing "wrong." Such questions stimulate defensiveness, self-doubt, suspicion, discouragement, and immobility. By demonstrating genuine curiosity about the things teachers are doing well and want to do better, evocative coaches enable teachers to become more curious about their own abilities and more willing to try new things. By exploring with confidence teacher abilities and aspirations, coaches enable teachers to become more open and inclined to put their strengths to work. That is the energy and spirit of inquiry in evocative coaching. We want teachers to discover the best of what is and to dream about the best of what might be.

Appreciative Inquiry

A process for motivating change that we have found to be particularly helpful in coaching teachers and other educators is called appreciative inquiry (AI). AI contrasts with traditional models of change that focus on weaknesses and problems to fix. Instead, with AI, teachers are encouraged to focus on their strengths and vitalities in order to rise above and outgrow their problems. To stay with the notion that all teachers are yearning and striving to meet legitimate universal needs, regardless of how ineffective or counterproductive their current strategies may be, we want to turn the spotlight of our inquiries on those things that make for openness, self-efficacy, trust, encouragement, and mobility. AI is one way to do that.

> *By celebrating what's right, we connect with our passion and find the energy to fix what's wrong.*
>
> *Dewitt Jones (2001)*

AI was initially developed as a research methodology for studying and understanding organizations by David Cooperrider and his colleagues at Case Western Reserve University (Cooperrider & Srivastava, 1987). Somewhat to their surprise, however, the process of inquiring into and studying the positive aspects of a system proved, in and of itself, to be transformational. Inquiry proved to be not only a prelude to action but a form of action. It enabled systems to become the change they hoped to see and be in the world. Over time, AI evolved into a change methodology with links to disciplines such as positive psychology, organizational development, sociology, and professional coaching (Bushe, 2007). AI is undergirded by five principles: the positive, constructionist, simultaneity, anticipatory, and poetic principles (Cooperrider & Whitney, 2005). The image of a pyramid illustrates how these principles are related to each other and work together to generate positive actions and outcomes (see Figure 5.1).

The Positive Principle

Coaches hope our work with teachers will result in positive actions and outcomes. Teachers hope their efforts with students will result in positive actions and outcomes. So how do we get that? Newton's first law of motion states that "objects at rest tend to stay at rest while objects in motion tend to stay in motion unless acted upon by an unbalanced force." Applying this law to human beings and human systems, the positive principle holds that positive actions and outcomes stem from the unbalanced force generated by positive energy and emotions. Negative energy and emotions, associated with identifying, analyzing, and fixing or correcting weaknesses, also generate an unbalanced force, but that force—which runs counter to the language of empathy—lacks the necessary orientation and magnitude to transform and propel systems in new directions. At best, root-cause analyses of weaknesses correct the problems they seek to solve. At worst, they cause a downward spiral as people become more focused on what is wrong and who is to blame.

FIGURE 5.1 FIVE PRINCIPLES OF APPRECIATIVE INQUIRY

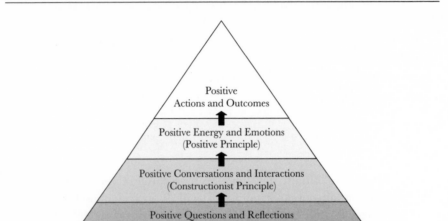

The positive principle asserts that positive actions and outcomes stem from the orientation and force generated by positive energy and emotions. Such force has the power to disrupt downward spirals and to build the inherent aspirations of people into a dynamic movement for transformational change. Inquiring into and appreciating strengths is, like empathy, a way for people to set aside their negative, internal voices and to envision and experiment with wholly new ways of understanding and doing things. Demonstrating "why it's good to feel good," these new actions and outcomes flow from positive energy and emotions because these motivational charges broaden thinking, expand awareness, increase abilities, build resiliency, bolster initiative, offset negatives, generate new possibilities, and create an upward spiral of learning and growth (Frederickson, 2002, 2003, 2009). That is the kind of energy we want to unleash in teachers and schools.

The Constructionist Principle

If positive energy and emotions hold so much potential for good, how do we get that? The constructionist principle asserts that positive energy and emotions are constructed through positive conversations and interactions with other people. The constructionist principle makes clear the importance of the social context in creating the present moment and in changing future moments. Inner work and self-talk alone are not sufficient. Different environments generate different truths and different possibilities. They even generate different dimensions of individual experience, which is what happens when coaches assist teachers to reframe their stories by asking hypothetical questions and reflecting back feelings and needs without judgment or blame.

As we noted in Chapter Three in our discussion on the power of story, people do not just make sense of their experiences through the stories they tell; they also create the reality in which they live. Stories are not just accounts of the world as people find it; they are also constructions and interpretations of the world as people understand it. "Words create worlds." If we focus our conversations on the things that are not working, then that is how the world will be for us: a tough and difficult place. If we focus our conversations on the things that *are* working, then we will start to notice and observe more of the best life has to offer. In this way, our stories can become wonderful, self-fulfilling prophecies. Zander and Zander (2000) make this point in speaking about how we make sense of life: "It's all invented anyway, so we might as well invent a story or framework of meaning that enhances our quality of life and the life of those around us" (p. 12). Coaching conversations can be viewed as an evocative way to invent life-enhancing stories and frameworks.

We live in worlds that our questions create.

David Cooperrider and Frank Barrett (2002, p. 58)

The Simultaneity Principle

If positive conversations and interactions are able to create positive worlds, how do we get that? The simultaneity principle proceeds from the following observation: conversations and interactions shift the instant we ask a new question, evoke a new story, or make a new reflection. Asking "What is the problem here?" tends to deplete the available energy and leads down a path of fault finding, blame, and defense. On the other hand, asking "What is going well here?" tends to bring positive energy, renewed hope, and creativity. The simultaneity principle views positive lines of inquiry and reflection as quick and effective ways to generate positive conversations and interactions. The energy lifts and the conversation lightens when people connect with and converse about positive things. Just as reflecting back feelings and needs without judgment or blame tends to reframe and shift judgmental thoughts and strategies in the empathy stage, so, too, do appreciative questions that focus on the positive tend to reframe and shift negative conversations and interactions in the inquiry stage.

Such questions have the ability to change things in the twinkling of an eye. They do not just begin a process that leads to a positive future; they simultaneously create a positive present by reorienting conversations and interactions around the stuff that enhances life. Our questions and reflections are fateful. "There are no 'neutral' questions," writes Kelm (2005). "Every inquiry takes us somewhere, even if it is back to what we originally believed. Inhabiting this spirit of wonder can transform our lives, and the unconditional positive question is one of the greatest tools we have to this end" (p. 54). When coaches and teachers ask such questions, we begin the process of reconstructing the worlds in which we live and work.

The Anticipatory Principle

If positive questions and reflections are of such critical importance to the tenor and substance of our conversations, where do those come from? The anticipatory principle asserts that our questions and reflections flow from the things we anticipate happening in the future. If we are filled with dread and negative thoughts about the future, then it is hard to seek out, much less to celebrate, the positive. If we are filled with hope and positive thoughts, then things tilt in that direction. Equipped with a glimpse of what things look like at their very best, we become more creative, resourceful, and resilient in looking for ways to make it so. Positive anticipation of the future beckons us forward and perfects the present.

Such anticipation becomes both the hallmark and the herald of change. It is a proleptic force that energizes the present. The word *prolepsis* means "a forward look." The anticipatory principle asserts that it takes specific, positive images of the future in order to affect the dynamics of the present. The more concrete and real the images, the more yearning and movement they create. Bennis and Nanus (1985) captured this notion when they wrote, "Vision is a target that beckons" (p. 89). Wheatley (1999) described vision as a field that is "a power, not a place, an influence, not a destination," best served by imbuing the present with "visionary messages matched by visionary behaviors" (pp. 53–54). Scharmer (2007) wrote of it as a transforming presence that happens "when our perception begins to connect to the source of our emerging future" (p. 165). That is how vision works. It infuses the present with both energy and agency.

The Poetic Principle

If positive anticipation of the future sets the stage for positive questions and reflections, how do we get that? Forming the base of the pyramid upon which all the other principles are built, the poetic principle connects hope with mindfulness and intention with attention. The more we attend to the positive, life-giving dimensions of the present moment, the more positive will be our intentions for future moments. By seeing and attending to life's poetry, we become inspired. It is not that problems disappear. Rather, other things become more important. Becoming mindful of what adds richness, texture, depth, beauty, clarity, significance, and energy to life awakens us to life's magnificent potential. It is as though life becomes a work of great poetry, filled with hopeful meter and meaning as well as movement toward positive growth and change. That is because we get more of what we focus on. What we appreciate appreciates. When we focus on problems, we get more problems. When we focus on possibilities, we get more possibilities. AI seeks to appreciate strengths. Thus, life's poetry resolves into a spiral of positive imagination.

In addition to looking for signs of the positive in the present moment, the poetic principle also incorporates the work of empathy. Empathy is another name for seeing the beauty of the need, regardless of whether or not that need is being met. Even when there is a lot of pain, or when people have a lot of anger, empathy can assist people to reconnect with the legitimacy, the universality, and the fullness of their needs. When this happens, the "golden sigh" emerges as though it were the last line of a great poem. The present radiates with new dimensions of meaning and magnificence, laying the foundation upon which the pyramid of positive actions and outcomes can be built.

When I do walkthroughs, I always leave a note for the teacher afterward. I use a short form that has a list of checkboxes for strategies and good things I may have seen, as well as a space where I write some specific commendations for the teacher. This is not the space where I would ever write, "Come see me." It's all about the positive.

Lydia, elementary assistant principal

Initiating the Learning Conversation

To help make the transition from the first turn, Story–Empathy, to the second turn, Inquiry–Design, it is helpful to sketch out the learning brief of what teachers want to focus on and how the coaching relationship will work. The parameters of the learning brief answer such questions as:

- What is the learning focus . . .
  - Of the entire coaching relationship?
  - In a particular topic or subject area?

- o Of any given coaching conversation?
- o What are the benchmarks for measuring progress?
- o What are the objectives to be realized?
- How will the coach and teacher work together?
  - o What is the role of the coach?
  - o What is expected of the teacher?
  - o How will conversations take place?
  - o Who will initiate what?
  - o How will observations be arranged?
  - o How long will the relationship last?

Delving into such questions too quickly, before Story–Empathy has established rapport and eased the fears of the teacher being coached, can damage the coaching relationship. Never asking the questions at all, or asking the questions as though they were a set of tick-boxes to be checked off, can also damage the coaching relationship. Asked at the right moment and in the right way, however, such inquiries become a reassuring and influential part of the coaching process. They help to shape, focus, clarify, and advance teacher intentions.

As coaches explore such questions, it will quickly become evident whether or not teachers are leaning forward, wanting to engage more fully, or leaning away, with a sense of wariness or disengagement. When teachers lean away, it is important for coaches to not push ahead. Instead, make an empathy guess as to what you are noticing. Teachers cannot be coached against their will, even from an appreciative, strengths-based framework. If a teacher does not want coaching, and if the coach's attempts at story listening and expressing empathy do not turn that around—if the coach never hears the "golden sigh"—then the coaching cannot go forward. That would turn the whole process into a counterproductive and unhappy arrangement. As with horse whisperers, we, too, want to "Join-Up" with teachers rather than to break them down. We want teachers to work out of willingness, not out of fear. To that end, then, the relationship as well as the conversations must be experienced as desired and voluntary, even if they did not start out that way. Teachers should always be given the choice to say "No" to coaching.

The learning brief clarifies two aspects of the coaching relationship: what the teacher wants to focus on (*topic choice*) and how she or he wants to do the work (*method choice*). On occasion, the topic is defined externally by a supervisor or curriculum resource. In this case, it is still important for teachers to feel at choice when it comes to the coaching. This can be done by asking teachers to identify the pieces they want assistance with as well as other areas of interest that may improve their teaching. The more specific the better when it comes to topic choice. "What do you want learn?" is the operative question. Clarifying objectives and benchmarks while leaving room for the unexpected to emerge gives substance to coaching conversations. The learning brief can address both long-term and near-term time frames. "What do you want to learn in your work as a teacher?" is the professional frame with the longest time horizon. "What do you want to learn through this conversation right now?" focuses on the immediacy of the moment. In between those two extremes, other near-term possibilities will emerge. Getting clarity and consent regarding the goals of coaching will assist coaches to guide and structure the inquiry and design processes. Writing up the goals, either on paper or electronically, enables coaches and teachers to review and revise them periodically over the course of the coaching relationship.

> *A design brief that is too abstract risks leaving the [teacher] wandering around in a fog. One that starts from too narrow a set of constraints, however, almost guarantees that the outcome will be incremental and, most likely, mediocre.*
>
> *Tim Brown (2009, p. 24)*

In addition to clarifying goals, the learning brief clarifies basic logistics such as how, when, where, and how long coaching conversations will take place as well as expectations regarding the approach we take as evocative coaches. The logistics should be clear and consistently adhered to because that will foster trust and engagement. The expectations revolve primarily around the understanding that evocative coaches do not come in as designated experts to tell teachers how to do things right; we come in as partners to ask questions and co-create designs. We can inform teachers that our expertise is available to them as a resource, particularly during brainstorming, as they choose. But we are not "answer people"; we are "question people." Once teachers understand and trust this, they stay engaged and active. If teachers think that coaches have the answers and are there to solve their problems, then they can sit back and relax. They do not have to work very hard, and they do not have to take full responsibility for their situations. In setting up the relationship, then, evocative coaches communicate our desire to avoid such counterproductive dynamics. We express our intention to treat teachers like adults who are already doing many things right and who have the ability to learn how to do even more things right. Most teachers welcome this frame and quickly warm up to such a coaching relationship, to the many questions we ask, and to the creative approaches we take over time.

Illuminating the Best of What Is

Discovering Strengths

Coaches who express empathy, stay positive, anticipate greatness, and evoke insight enable teachers to shine. Coaching then brings out the best in teachers, rather than the worst. Although coaching is important, serious work, evocative coaches seek to make the process enjoyable and fun. The principles and practices of appreciative inquiry enable coaches to do that. Once the parameters of the working relationship are clear, AI encourages coaches to focus on strengths rather than weaknesses. We do not want to provoke defensiveness and resistance. To avoid this eventuality, evocative coaches focus our inquiries to discover where teachers shine, what's worked in the past, in other settings, and what's working now, in this setting. What gives life? What can we celebrate? What generates positive results? What things can we build on in designing a desired action or outcome? By inquiring into the strengths, vitalities, aspirations, and possibilities that teachers bring with them to the teaching task, the spirits of both coach and teacher are energized and lifted. The issues may be weighty, but the process of AI can lighten the load in the course of moving forward. We shift into new ways of being. Instead of wrestling with problems, we soar with potential.

> *Excellence is not the opposite of failure and you will learn little about excellence from studying failure. To learn about success you have to study success. Only successful examples can tell you what excellence looks like.*
>
> *Marcus Buckingham (2007, pp. 5–6)*

Appreciative Interviews

It is important for evocative coaches to start and stay in an appreciative frame throughout the coaching process. When teachers show up with complaints, hard-to-hear messages, and painful stories, the work of Story–Empathy is to reframe the experience and relieve the negative energy. Empathy does not make things better, but it does make our relationship to things better. Empathy is part of the appreciative frame. The emphasis is not on trying to solve problems. It is rather on trying to respectfully understand the feelings and needs of people who think they have problems. Once people feel heard on this level, they open up to the consideration of what has worked in the past and what is working now. Without empathy, AI may seem dismissive of the struggles and pain people are experiencing. "How can you ask about the positive when I have so many problems? It doesn't help to put on rose-colored glasses." With empathy, AI becomes empowering and practical. "You *still* think I have strengths even though you know I have so many problems? It really helps to be seen and heard in this way." That reaction is what we hope to evoke by using AI in coaching.

AI holds that this line of inquiry is appropriate and helpful even with the most discouraged of teachers and even in the most distressed of situations. No matter how bleak and barren the situation may appear, something is always working. No matter how ineffective a teacher may seem, she or he has always had shining moments. By reconnecting teachers with these experiences through appreciative inquiries, coaching becomes evocative of learning, growth, and change. Teachers discover the emotional and professional capital to dream new dreams and design new strategies for moving forward.

AI practitioners have developed a generic, four-question Appreciative Interview Protocol that coaches can use in coaching conversations to elevate energy and emotion. The protocol assists teachers to remember, connect with, and discover the things that are important to them and that they have done well.

1. *Best experiences.* "Tell me about your best teaching experience, a time when you felt most alive and engaged. What made it so rewarding? Who was involved? How did students learn? Describe the experience in detail."

2. *Core values.* "Tell me about the things you value most deeply, things about yourself, your relationships, and your work. Who are you when you are at your best?"

3. *Supporting conditions.* "Tell me about the core, life-giving factors in your experience. What are the key ingredients, both internal and external, that enable you to be at your best and to have fun?"

4. *Three wishes.* "Tell me about your hopes and dreams for the future. If you could make any three wishes for your teaching practice come true, what would they be?"

In coaching conversations, these questions are typically adapted and tied to specific learning briefs. If teachers want to learn how to do something different in the classroom, for example, then coaches want to evoke stories, values, conditions, and wishes related to times when they have changed their methods in the past. Or, again, if teachers want to learn how to better handle a challenging discipline situation, then coaches want to evoke stories, values, conditions, and wishes related to times when teachers have successfully handled discipline situations in the past. The more closely coaches can target our lines of appreciative inquiry to what teachers want to learn, the more effective we will be in building teacher motivation and self-efficacy around the design and implementation of new approaches for teaching success.

Inquiry is the experience of mystery that changes our life.

David Cooperrider and Frank Barrett (2002, p. 59)

Inquiring into strengths lays the foundation for all that follows. It induces positive self-monitoring. That is why it is important to not rush through the inquiry process in order to get to the design step. The simultaneity principle makes clear that asking appreciative questions is transformational in its own right. By taking our time and savoring the experience of inquiry, we give our questions the space they need to work. Exploring life-giving stories, values, conditions, and wishes not only forms the basis for change; it is an appropriation of the change we seek.

It is especially important for coaches not to skip inquiring into strengths when teachers are discouraged or stuck. It may seem as though we have done enough just by expressing empathy in such situations. The point of empathy in coaching, however, is not just to help teachers feel heard, acknowledged, and understood. Empathy is not an end in itself. The point of empathy is to open up teachers to the consideration of new possibilities for moving forward. Remembering to inquire about the positive elements of teacher experiences, even when there are a lot of obvious negatives, is a way of reminding teachers that we still believe in them and that they have a lot to offer. Such implicit championing dramatically accelerates the behavior change process. When teachers are painfully aware of being "stuck in the muck" or of being conflicted about their ability to move forward, they need both empathy and inquiry into the life-giving variables of their experiences. Such discoveries are invaluable in creating the conditions for change to occur. Even when teachers bring seemingly intractable problems to the coaching conversation, it is important to help them look at things through an appreciative frame. Reframing enemy images and remembering energizing experiences assist teachers to reconnect with and leverage their assets and to marshal new resources of concentration and energy.

Kathryn is a great organizer and that's something she's always been good at. When you ask her about data, she's got it right there. When she was able to see that she could take some of these organizational skills and use them in behavior management and to structure lessons, I think it was a breakthrough. It was taking the strengths that already existed and capitalizing on them in a new way. So that's been the biggest thing—she's realized that we all have strengths and if we use them in the right way we can achieve the same results even though the way we go about it may be different than how someone else goes about it.

Danielle, elementary literacy coach

Appreciative Assessments

In addition to discovering strengths through appreciative interviews, many teachers also value a more objective look at strengths. One tool for doing so, based on the classification of strengths developed by Peterson and Seligman (2004), is the Values-in-Action (VIA) Signature Strengths Questionnaire. The questionnaire can be taken online, free of charge, by going to www.authentichappiness. sas.upenn.edu. After responding to 240 statements, respondents receive a report of their twenty-four character strengths in rank order. Although all twenty-four represent respondent strengths, the top five are identified as "signature strengths" since they are the ones that respondents tend to use most frequently, naturally, and easily. In the Peterson and Seligman taxonomy, the twenty-four character strengths are organized around six large categories called "virtues" that emerge consistently across history and culture as important for good life and work.

The VIA Taxonomy of Virtues and Strengths

I. *Wisdom and knowledge*: Cognitive strengths that entail the acquisition and use of knowledge
1. Creativity: Thinking of novel and productive ways to do things
2. Curiosity: Taking an interest in all of ongoing experience
3. Open-mindedness: Thinking things through and examining them from all sides
4. Love of learning: Mastering new skills, topics, and bodies of knowledge
5. Perspective: Being able to provide wise counsel to others

II. *Courage*: Emotional strengths that involve exercise of will to accomplish goals in the face of opposition, either external or internal
6. Honesty/authenticity: Speaking the truth and presenting oneself in a genuine way
7. Bravery: Not shrinking from threat, challenge, difficulty, or pain
8. Perseverance: Finishing what one starts
9. Zest: Approaching life with excitement and energy

III. *Humanity*: Interpersonal strengths that entail "tending and befriending" others
10. Kindness: Doing favors and good deeds for others
11. Love: Valuing close relations with others

(Continued)

---

12. Social intelligence: Being aware of the motives and feelings of self and others

IV. *Justice*: Civic strengths that underlie healthy community life

13. Fairness: Treating all people the same according to notions of fairness and justice

14. Leadership: Organizing group activities and seeing that they happen

15. Teamwork: Working well as a member of a group or team

V. *Temperance*: Strengths that protect against excess

16. Forgiveness: Forgiving those who have done wrong

17. Modesty: Letting one's accomplishments speak for themselves

18. Prudence: Being careful about one's choices; not saying or doing things that might later be regretted

19. Self-regulation: Regulating what one feels and does

VI. *Transcendence*: Strengths that build connections to the larger universe and provide meaning

20. Appreciation of beauty: Noticing and appreciating beauty, excellence, and/or skilled performance in various domains of life

21. Gratitude: Being aware of and thankful for the good things that happen

22. Hope: Expecting the best and working to achieve it

23. Humor: Liking to laugh and joke; bringing smiles to other people

24. Spirituality/religiousness: Having coherent beliefs about the higher purpose and meaning of life (Park & Peterson, 2009, p. 67)

As with the appreciative interviews, the VIA Signature Strengths Questionnaire does not ask about or focus on weaknesses. A person's twenty-fourth strength is not a weakness; it is a strength that one uses less frequently, naturally, and easily. Although we may at times lose sight of them, everyone has some experience of all the strengths. Teachers often find it quite affirming to discover and organize their strengths in this way. Posting a teacher's top five "signature strengths" in a place where both the teacher and the coach can refer to them regularly may enable teachers to tap into these strengths as they brainstorm ideas and design experiments to facilitate their learning and growth.

Observing Vitalities

In Chapter Four we wrote about the value of the Nonviolent Communication (NVC) distinction between making observations and evaluations for life-enriching communication. It is important for coaches to understand and master this distinction because the former expands awareness and evokes mobility while the latter provokes defensiveness, antagonism, and retrenchment. People shut down and want to argue with evaluations, even when they contain an element of truth. People open up and want to engage with observations, even when they contain challenging messages. Openness and engagement are two prerequisites of evocative coaching.

School settings afford coaches the opportunity to observe teachers in action. Indeed, many coaching systems work primarily with the dynamics surrounding pre-observation conferences (planning), observations (events), and post-observation conferences (reflecting) (Barkley, 2005; Costa & Garmston, 2002; Glickman, Gordon, & Ross-Gordon, 2009). Those dynamics are important because observations and the conversations surrounding them can make or break a coaching relationship. Although evocative coaching views observations as but one of many inputs in the coaching process, along with self-reports, signature strengths, emotional readiness, intrinsic aspirations, and present possibilities, we share a concern for making vital observations that contribute to the learning and growth of teachers.

To do that, coaches must observe mindfully, suspending the urge to evaluate what teachers are doing well and what they are doing poorly. Compliments and criticisms work against the evocative dynamic. When we identify things that teachers are doing as "right" and "wrong" or "better" and "worse," let alone when we reward "appropriate" and punish "inappropriate" behavior through formal and/or informal channels, we undermine the safety and potential of the coaching space. Yet evaluative and incentivizing approaches can be hard to set aside. They are so ingrained that coaches may even worry we have not added value until we point out deficiencies and make suggestions for improvement. As we have seen, however, there is a better way when it comes to facilitating adult learning and growth. Observing without evaluating is not only possible, it is crucial for observations to have their intended effect. So teachers and evocative coaches focus a nonjudgmental spotlight on what is happening in the present moment, especially on those things that demonstrate vitality, engagement, and connection. We look, for example, for smiling faces, shining eyes, eye contact, body language, room arrangement, teacher movements, student participation, energy levels, and other signs that teachers and students are enjoyably meeting their mutual needs for learning, stimulation, and growth. We look for evidence of competencies that teachers can celebrate and build on. Even struggling teachers will occasionally have such moments. By observing and appreciating those moments, they multiply in both quantity and quality to more fully meet the needs of teachers and students alike. The more fully needs are met, the more vitality results (refer to Figure 4.12). The more vitality results, the easier progress becomes.

It's not what you look at that matters, it's what you see.

Henry David Thoreau

Observing and dialoguing with teachers about their vital practices—the things they say and do that contribute noticeably to classroom vitality—expands their awareness of how their presence and techniques are landing in the room. Freed from judgments and fear of reprisals, teachers can allow themselves and the coaching conversation to fully and honestly explore both the internal and external dynamics that make for educational excellence. The International Coach Federation (ICF) and the International Association of Coaching (IAC) both identify creating awareness as a primary work of coaching. The ICF refers to creating awareness as a "core coaching competency," noting that effective coaching "helps clients to discover for themselves the new thoughts, beliefs, perceptions, emotions, moods, etc. that strengthen their ability to take action and achieve what is important to them" (2008b, p. 3). The IAC refers to it as "processing in the present," noting that masterful coaches "expand the client's awareness of how to experience thoughts and issues at the level of the mind, body, heart and/or spirit, when and as appropriate" (2009, p. 2). This holistic frame around expanding awareness is an essential part of evocative coaching. Teachers will not discover new strategies until they tackle new questions. And they won't tackle new questions until they have new information to work with. Discovering strengths and observing vitalities are two growth-fostering ways to get that new information.

Claudia was assigned to teach seventh-grade math when the math teacher left suddenly. In my first meeting with her, she was almost in a panic state. For the first few sessions I had with her, I didn't observe her teaching because she really did not feel comfortable having someone watch her teach. We just went through her plans before she taught. But I did walk by the door a couple of times, and the students appeared to be very engaged. After about four coaching sessions, she said, "I think you can come now." I said, "Are you sure?" and she said, "Yeah, I'd like you to help me figure out which students have this concept or which do not." So we did a mastery checklist with the students' names and specifically what she wanted me to look for. As she taught the lesson on polygons, I went around and watched how the kids interacted with the manipulatives. I wrote down some of the questions that they asked each other and their team, and I took pictures of their finished products. When we met after school, we looked at the pictures. I asked her, "What do you see?" And she said, "I think Jonathan has it because he's able to do this with manipulatives," and I agreed. When we finished she said, "This is so completely different than what I thought it would be." So now she e-mails me on a regular basis. "What day are you going to be here? This is a piece of content that I'm having trouble coming up with how to get kids engaged. Can you help me come up with any ideas? What do you suggest?" She's very open to brainstorming new approaches, and her students' benchmark scores really show strong improvement.

Patti, middle school math coach

Tim Gallwey (2000) refers to observing vital practices as "focusing on critical variables." By mindfully paying attention to the things that change and matter most to your desired outcome, Gallwey notes that "self-interference decreases and performance inevitably improves" (p. 58). To illustrate how this works, Gallwey tells the story of his consultations with AT&T soon after the breakup of their communication monopoly. Being in a competitive marketplace was a new experience, and the corporate culture was having a hard time adapting. "That's not how we do things here" was a spoken and unspoken rule. Fear of the future was rampant. They knew they had to do things differently, they just didn't know what or how. Gallwey was brought in to work with a customer service team, the operators who answer the phone when people call with a problem or complaint. AT&T wanted to improve the "courtesy ratings" of these operators without increasing the average time per call. It was a daunting task, to be sure. Gallwey agreed to take the assignment on two conditions. First, participation had to be voluntary. No one would be forced to take the training or use the tools. Second, "courtesy" would not be identified as the subject of the training. In fact, he eschewed the notion of a traditional training program, preferring instead to adopt a coach approach to reducing stress and improving the work experience. The assumption Gallwey made was that one would follow the other: that satisfied operators would lead to satisfied customers. But this agenda was not put on the table as either the rationale for or the intended output of the program.

Gallwey was given the freedom to go about things as he requested, freed from supervisory interference. So he began by observing the operators at work, interviewing some of them, and identifying the major obstacles. Gallwey quickly

observed that boredom was a recurrent complaint of the workplace. One operator put it this way: "After the first six weeks, there's nothing more to learn on this
job. We've heard all the problems and know how to handle them. I could do the
job in my sleep, and sometimes that's just how it feels." Gallwey also observed that
"in spite of the boredom, there was a lot of stress on the job because operator pro-
ductivity was monitored and measured closely and constantly." Finally, Gallwey
noted that the operators were frequently disgruntled by the prescribed routines
and tight controls of the system and their supervisors. Operators felt they were
being treated like children in elementary school by the system and their supervisors. These conditions produced an atmosphere of discontent, resentment, and
hostility. No wonder courtesy was in such short supply!

Gallwey's solution? To identify and explore a critical variable, something relevant that could energize the monotonous, repetitive day of a telephone operator.
Everyone agreed that the most interesting part of each call was the person on the
other end of the phone. In conversation with Gallwey and with each other, the
operators agreed to conduct an experiment: "Apart from factual information, what
can be learned by listening to the customer's voice?" To answer that question they
invented a series of "awareness exercises" that called for operators to listen more
closely to customers than they ever had before. They were to rate on a scale of 1
to 10 the various qualities they could hear in the customer's voice, like the degree of
warmth, friendliness, or irritation. The next step was to learn to express different
qualities in their own voices. They conducted a series of role-plays so that people
could observe and practice different qualities of response. Finally, they started to
track the impact of their responses on customer vitality. Choosing to express different qualities in their voices generated different responses and energies. Even
though their conversations were short and confined, the operators discovered that
they could have a small but tangible impact on a great number of people.

It is perhaps no surprise, then, that the more attention operators paid to this
critical variable, of how they were listening and talking, the more their "courtesy
ratings" improved. The measurable outcome was a byproduct of the game they
were playing. Without any specific direction to "be more courteous" or to "make
customers feel better," the operators nevertheless gravitated in that direction as
they began to have more fun on the job and more confidence in their ability to
make such a difference. Gallwey notes that he had come to anticipate such indirect results although others saw it as some kind of magic. Success, like happiness, is always a byproduct of a meaningful game. When people focus their
attention on what is happening in the immediate environment and when they are
freed to respond adaptively without pressure or fear of consequences, they will
naturally figure out ways to be more effective. In the case of the AT&T operators,
they not only improved their effectiveness; they also reported that their levels of

boredom and stress went down an average of 40 percent, while enjoyment on the job went up 30 percent. The operators were working in a new way and in a new world. AT&T ended up packaging and delivering the program to nearly 20,000 telephone operators in four regions of the country (Gallwey, 2000, pp. 34–40).

What Gallwey was able to do with the AT&T operators is what evocative coaches do with teachers and other classroom educators. First, we listen respectfully to what people have to say (story). Second, we establish trust and rapport (empathy). Then, we discover strengths and observe vitalities (inquiry) which leads naturally to increased motivation and behavior modification (design). The secret is to inquire with a beginner's mind and with no overtones of evaluation or judgment into those life-enhancing critical variables that can be experienced and observed. When we do that, when we inquire through an appreciative rather than an accusative frame, when we look for strengths and vitalities rather than weaknesses and banalities, we assist teachers to become ready, willing, and able to move forward in positive directions.

I think it's just a principle of human nature that when someone is trying to find out what's wrong with you that we have a tendency to try to contradict that. So I decided that it would be more effective that instead of trying to get at what's wrong with the teachers, we would start by looking at data on student performance that they bring. They write down the things that have really jumped out at them in terms of strengths and weaknesses in student performance. And then we share this with the team, and I take copious notes about some of the similarities and differences across teachers. Then we talk about, "So, we have all these things that students are presenting, what do you think are the biggest areas for potential growth that we could address concerning our students?" As a group we talk about that and come up with the top three to five things. We look at those things and think about what are some teaching implications. So it's never about the individual teacher or what anyone is doing wrong.

Julie, elementary literacy coach

Appreciative Classroom Observation Tools

To observe vitalities without interjecting judgmental evaluations, coaches and teachers not only want to view experience through an appreciative lens, they may also want to use observation tools that highlight the practices teachers are most interested in, excited about, and able to control. That was the secret of Gallwey's success at AT&T: he assisted operators not only to identify the life-giving dimensions of their work experience (the person on the other end of the phone) but also to quantify and track a seemingly intangible variable (the irritation level of the person on the other end of the phone at the start and end of a call) using a 10-point scale. By creating and using an observation tool, the operators found that the irritation level of the person on the other end of the phone didn't intimidate and bother them as much. Instead, that level became an opportunity to experiment with different responses and to learn different approaches. By taking the sense of threat out of the irritated voice, and by treating it as an opportunity to play a life-enriching game, the operators' performance, learning, and enjoyment all increased exponentially.

Appreciative classroom observation tools work much the same way. They can turn data gathering on what is happening in the classroom into an engaging and informative learning enterprise. By focusing on things teachers find inherently interesting and relevant to their experience and effectiveness, by noticing strengths and vitalities, the process of collecting, analyzing, and reviewing data can raise awareness, stimulate thinking, and evoke change. When teachers control both what data are collected and how the data will be used to facilitate their learning and growth, data collection becomes a source of encouragement and an invaluable ally in the coaching process.

It may be helpful to make use of an observation tool, such as one of the three mentioned following. Blank forms and additional tools that can be refined and adapted for new purposes are available online at www.EvocativeCoaching.com. In time, teachers and coaches may want to develop observation tools from scratch to inform particular coaching projects. In selecting, modifying, and using tools, three things are essential. First, teachers are at choice. They are at choice as to whether they want to use an observation tool at all and, if so, they are at choice as to what the observation tools will be, how they are to be adapted, as well as when and how the data are to be collected. Although most schools have required observation tools that are used once or twice a year as part of the teacher evaluation process, coaches do not limit ourselves to these nor allow these to be the sole source of observation data for the coaching process.

Second, evocative coaches always look for vitality. The notion that people only grow from having their mistakes observed, documented, and pointed out to them is overstated at best and counterproductive at worst. Recent research by positive psychologists suggests that identifying our weaknesses and working diligently to improve them is not the best way to promote learning, growth, and change (Buckingham, 2007). Identifying strengths and working to engage them—the "broaden and build theory" of positive emotions—has proven to be far more effective (Fredrickson, 2009). Yet a strengths-based approach to change is neither customary nor intuitive. We have had classroom observers, for example, express disappointment that they could not find anything wrong with the teaching of a particular lesson. That was their understanding of adding value. Evocative coaches understand differently. When collecting data, we go out of our way to notice and document vitalities because these are the dynamics that promote self-efficacy and teaching success.

Third, once the data are collected, evocative coaches and teachers always review the data together with appreciative eyes. No dataset is ever entirely positive. And it is easy to fall into the trap of mining the data with a fault-finding mentality. We may notice a few positive things and then pounce on the "heart of the matter": our evaluations and recommendations as to what teachers should do differently. That doesn't work in evocative coaching. The "Gotcha!" game stimulates the "fight, flight, and freeze" response of the limbic system. It causes people to strike out or withdraw and shut down. The "Shining-eyes!" game moves people in the opposite direction. When vitality is recognized and appreciated in a classroom experience, teachers open up, lean forward, and yearn for more. They find the conversation both enjoyable and engaging. That is why evocative coaches and teachers always approach classroom observation data by asking:

- What is working well here?
- What can teachers build on and celebrate?
- When were classroom participants fully engaged in the learning task?
- When did we notice shining eyes and smiling faces?

As we shall see in Chapter Six, such questions create the context for moving the coaching conversation from inquiry to design.

To be helpful, then, classroom observation tools must be freely chosen, strengths based, and enjoyably reviewed by coaches and teachers together. Unless teachers feel an absence of threat over the collection of data and how they will be used, it may be counterproductive to go down this road. Coaching presence requires an authentic respect for and appreciation of who teachers are and what they need. When coaches come from this frame, classroom observation tools may be particularly useful in the identification and strengthening of vital practices.

Student Engagement Observation Tool. The Student Engagement Observation Tool is used to assess the degree to which students are engaged in a particular activity or class period. The observer-coach scans the room in five-minute sweeps to assess the proportion of students who are on-task and off-task at any given time, as well as to capture what the teacher is up to during that time frame. A key delineates five categories of on-task behaviors and five off-task behaviors that might be observed. Identifying individual students across the period may be a challenge if the students are unfamiliar to the coach. If the students are stationary, the observer may be provided with a seating chart with the students' names for assistance in completing the chart. If students will be moving around the room during the class period, the observer may make notes of features of the students' appearance, such as gender, hair color, or prominent features of the students' clothing or accessories (e.g., glasses, purple headband, green striped shirt) rather than indicating their names. It is not always easy to discern, when students are passive, whether they are listening to the lesson or daydreaming, for example, or when they are writing, whether they are taking notes or writing a note to a friend. It is up to the observer to make his or her best guess, and to hold the data somewhat lightly when sharing the results with the teacher. In some settings, it may be appropriate to ask students what they are doing and what they are learning from the experience, but it is important to guard against distracting from the learning taking place. In advance of sharing the data with the teacher, use a highlighter to bring into focus the instances of student engagement. Tally down the columns for the total on-task sweeps for each student, and tally across the rows for the total number of students who are on task during each sweep. You might also calculate an average of the number of on-task sweeps per student (the totals of the columns), as well as a separate average of the number of students on task during each sweep (the totals of the rows).

The Student Engagement Observation Tool is very popular. For a window into how a conversation centered around this tool might look, we turn to Carly, the foreign language department chair in a suburban high school, as she offers coaching to Anna Bradley, a French teacher in her department who sought her assistance. Although Anna is a highly regarded French teacher with twelve years of teaching experience, she has sought coaching for a class where she is struggling. See Figure 5.2 for the completed Student Engagement Observation Tool that grew out of Carly's observation. Here are Carly's reflections on the session:

> When I met with Anna, she asked that I observe her French II class because she thought that her students were not doing as well as she would like and because she was concerned that she was missing some of her students. When offered several observation tools, she selected the student engagement tool. She said she was interested in knowing which of her students were on-task and which were off-task so that she could better diagnose the needs of her students. She also wanted to know what she was doing that might be triggering those different behaviors.
>
> After the observation, Anna was very interested in the results. As we examined the patterns of when students were most engaged, she noticed that during the time sweeps when she moved around the room and students performed

FIGURE 5.2 STUDENT ENGAGEMENT OBSERVATION TOOL

Teacher Observed: **Anna Bradley-French II**
Observer: **Carly – Foreign Language Department Chair**

Date: **Feb. 3**
Time of Observation: **12:25** to **1:07**

Time	Leanne	Sophia	Christopher	Jamie	Jessica	Nicole	Nick	Michael	Angelita	Lisa	Melanie	Chad	Kathryn	Ashley	Drew	Maggie	Jennifer	Caitlin	Justin	Jackie	Jordan	Total	Teacher Action
12:25	N2	N4	F3	N1	N1	N1	F4	F1	N3	N3	N1	N1	N1	F2	F1	F1	N1	F1	N1	N1	F1	N13	Lecturing
12:30	N1	N1	F1	N3	N3	N3	N3	F4	F3	N3	N3	N3	N3	N1	F1	N3	N3	F1	N1	N1	F1	N15	Lecturing/Calling on students
12:35	N1	F1	F1	N1	N1	F3	F4	N1	N3	F1	N1	N3	N1	F1	N1	N1	N1	F4	F1	N1	N2	N13	Lecturing/Calling on students
12:40	N2	N2	F1	N2	N2	N2	N2	N2	F4	N2	N2	N2	N2	N2	N2	N2	F1	N2	F1	N2	N2	N17	Circling room
12:45	N1	N5	F1	N1	N1	N1	N1	N1	N1	N5	N5	N5	N1	N1	F3	N1	F1	F4	N5	N1	N1	N17	Coaching answers
12:50	N1	F4	F1	F1	N1	F3	F4	N1	N1	N1	N3	N3	N1	F1	F2	F1	N1	N1	N1	N1	F1	N12	Checking work at board
12:55	N1	F1	F1	F4	N1	F3	F4	N1	F1	N1	N1	N1	N1	N1	F2	F3	N1	F1	N1	N1	F1	N11	Activity on overheard
1:00	N1	F1	F1	N1	N1	N4	F1	N1	N1	N1	N1	N1	N1	N1	F1	N1	N1	F1	N1	F3	F1	N14	Book activity
1:05	N1	F1	F1	F4	N1	F1	N1	N1	F1	F1	N1	N1	F1	N1	N1	N2	N1	N1	N1	F1	F1	N11	Students answering orally
..																							
Total	N9	N4	N0	N6	N9	N5	N4	N7	N5	N7	N9	N9	N8	N6	N3	N6	N7	N2	N7	N7	N3		

On Task:
N1 - on task: listening/watching
N2 - on task: writing
N3 - on task: speaking
N4 - on task: reading
N5 - on task: hands-on activity

Off Task:
F1 - off task: passive
F2 - off task: doing work for another class
F3 - off task: listening to others
F4 - off task: disturbing others
F5 - off task: playing

Observations:
Average on-task sweeps /student= 5.9
Average # students on task/sweep = 13.6
Type of On-task: N1 – 81; N2 – 20; N3 – 15; N4 – 2; N5 – 5
Top segments: Teacher circling, coaching answers; students writing, hands-on

individual practice, the highest number of students were on-task. She also noted that there were some students who were consistently on-task and some who were consistently off-task. She was surprised and concerned to see that Nick had only been on-task during four of the sweeps; she considered him to be one of her best students. She reported that she would like to follow up with him. She also wanted to rethink her activities. She hopes to vary the activities she uses more and to move around the room more frequently. Although she wants the students to assume responsibility for their behavior, she recognizes that by changing her behaviors she will create the conditions for student behavior change as well. It was rewarding to see how enthusiastic she was to receive this information and how she planned to continue to reflect on it after our meeting to find ways to continue to improve her practice.

Teacher Verbal Behaviors Observation Tool. The Teacher Verbal Behaviors Observation Tool captures instances of an array of teacher verbal behaviors during a lesson, including information giving, questioning, answering, encouraging or praising, direction giving, correcting, and redirecting. The observer-coach tallies the various verbal behaviors observed in three-minute intervals throughout the lesson. Space is also provided to capture specific comments or brief descriptions of the class activities at various points in the lesson. Figure 5.3 depicts the information gathered as Gwyn observed Jennifer Dalton, a novice teacher, during a middle school biology lesson.

As I began the meeting with Jennifer, she recounted a recent supervisory conference that she perceived to have been quite negative regarding her capability as a teacher. She conveyed hurt and confusion about the feedback she had been given. Her body language also conveyed frustration with heavy sighs, running her hands through her hair, leaning forward while describing the situation and then falling back in her chair with a defeated thud when she finished. She stated clearly that she wanted feedback that would help her improve rather than just stating that she was deficient without any guidance for improvement. I listened attentively, reflected her feelings, probed for clarification, waited for her to finish what she wanted to say, and followed up with related questions. In response to my question about what I would see in her classroom, she was very clear in describing why the lesson would progress in the flow described on the lesson plan. When I asked if there were specific areas she wanted me to focus on during the observation, she responded very generally and did not seem to know what to ask me to focus on. When I introduced the observation tools, her eyes got wide and a big smile lit her face. After reviewing several tools, she selected the Teacher Verbal Behaviors Tool.

FIGURE 5.3 TEACHER VERBAL BEHAVIORS OBSERVATION TOOL

Teacher Observed: Jennifer Dalton – Middle School Biology
Observer: Gwyn
Date: Nov. 5
Time of Observation: 10:05 to 10:48

Time	Information Giving	Questioning	Answering	Encouraging/ Praising	Direction Giving	Correcting	Redirecting	Action
10:05–10:07					///			Get into groups, KNL board
10:08–10:11		/			/		/	Talk to each group
10:12–10:14			/	/	/			"Good job"
10:15–10:17	/	/			/		/	Check with groups, prepare for visitor
10:18–10:20	/	////			/		/	Who is our visitor? Why is it important she visit? Student use NK Board
10:21–10:23		//	/					What's our problem? What do you think? What would you tell our visitor?
10:24–10:26	/	/		/				"TaDa! Definitely!" How would you summarize our project? Get back in rows
10:27–10:29		/////	//	//			/	Visitor planning handout. Are you all set? What is your question? That's a really great question.
10:30–10:32			/					

FIGURE 5.3 (CONTINUED)

Teacher Observed: Jennifer Dalton – Middle School Biology
Observer: Gwyn

Date: Nov. 5
Time of Observation: 10:05 to 10:48

Time							Comments
10:33–10:35		/	///	///	/		What could you do to figure out where germs are? Hands down, wait for Maria to think. OK, everyone, now what are your ideas?
10:37–10:39	/			/	/		Pass out markers. Two places in bldg to check germs.
10:40–10:42	/	///		/			Read paper. Where might you find saliva?
10:43–10:45	/	///		/			What else? What do you need for the experiment?
10:46–10:48	/	///	/	/	/		Write your hypothesis and check. Everyone's hypothesis looks good.
Total	4	25	10	8	11	0	5

Source: Adapted from Glickman, Gordon, and Ross-Gordon (2004).

During the post-observation conference, I provided a copy of the Teacher Verbal Behaviors Tool for her to read and keep and I described the process I used for recording the data. When I pointed out the totals, she asked, "Is that good? What should the totals be?" I assured her that the totals would vary depending on the context of the lesson. I explained that the totals serve as a lens to let her see where the majority of her behaviors were so that she could look more closely and be more aware of those behaviors and how they fit the learners she is teaching. We noted together that her high total was in the area of questioning. I had noted many of the questions she had asked during the lesson, and it was clear as we read through them that many were at the knowledge/comprehension level. We discussed the importance of developing skills in high-level questioning not only for gifted students but for all students. She then recalled another of the observation tools we had considered, the Level of Questioning tool. I asked if she might like a copy of that tool for her files. She was very excited to be given that tool and indicated that she was anxious to watch the video that we'd made of the lesson to chart her own questioning behavior using that observation tool. Before concluding, we also made note of other areas of strength, particularly the clarity of her direction giving and the appropriate use of encouragement and praise. As a novice teacher, she definitely has areas for improvement but the important thing is her growing confidence and her willingness to work toward improving her performance.

Level of Questioning Observation Tool. The Level of Questioning Observation Tool allows the observer-coach to capture the kinds of questions a teacher asks along the spectrum of the revised Bloom's Taxonomy of Educational Objectives (Anderson, Krathwohl, Airasian, Cruikshank, Mayer, Pintrich, Raths, & Wittrock, 2001, p. 28). In just her second year of teaching, Charlotte was a highly regarded third-grade teacher in an urban school that served a primarily low-income population in the southeastern United States. Charlotte invited Amy to observe while she taught a read-aloud lesson from the basal reader. When asked what in particular she wanted Amy to observe, Charlotte mentioned that she was concerned about her students' ability to comprehend the story, which took place in a snowy setting in Alaska, a context far removed from what most of her students would have experienced. She stated that she was trying to improve her questioning techniques to assist with comprehension, so she selected the Level of Questioning Observation Tool. (See Figure 5.4.)

Charlotte began by asking the class if anyone had ever heard of a famous dog race named the Iditarod. When none of her students raised their hands, she went on to explain a brief history of the race and to tell them that she was

FIGURE 5.4 LEVEL OF QUESTIONING OBSERVATION TOOL

Teacher Observed: **Charlotte Gibbs - 3rd Grade Reading**   Date: **Oct. 17**
Observer: **Amy**   Time of Observation: **10:40** to **11:10**

Cognitive Process Dimension	Factual Knowledge	Conceptual Knowledge	Procedural Knowledge	Meta-Cognitive	Total	%
Remember recognizing, recalling	~~HHH HHH~~ ~~HHH~~ /	/			17	38%
Understand explaining, clarifying, interpreting, categorizing, classifying, comparing, contrasting, inferring, predicting, extrapolating, exemplifying, illustrating	~~HHH HHH~~ ~~HHH HHH~~ //	///			25	56%
Apply applying a procedure to a familiar or an unfamiliar task						
Analyze differentiating, distinguishing, organizing, integrating, outlining, attributing	//				2	4%
Evaluate checking, monitoring, testing, critiquing	/				1	2%
Create generating, hypothesizing, planning, designing, producing						
Total of Questions Asked	41	4			45	

Source: Adapted from Anderson et al. (2001).

going to read them a story that happened during the race. As she proceeded to read aloud, she paused frequently to ask questions, sometimes in rapid fire succession, to ensure that the students were paying attention and that they understood the unfamiliar vocabulary in the story. When Charlotte arrived at the post-observation conference a couple of hours after her lesson, she had an air of hopeful expectation. She acknowledged that she was pleased with her questioning during the lesson. And sure enough, she had asked an impressive forty-five questions during the thirty-minute lesson observed. She felt pleased with the level of engagement that she had noticed from the students and felt that the dialogue that ensued from the questions had helped her students grasp a story that was set in a very unfamiliar context. When I shared the observation tool with her, her attention immediately went to the top two categories of remember and understand questions. She noticed that the bulk of her questions had been in these two categories, and that they had tended to be more factual questions than conceptual ones. I also shared some examples of questions she had asked, and she noticed that almost all of them had started with "What." We turned our attention to an exchange that had taken place when she'd asked an evaluate question about whether a decision made by a particular character had been a wise choice or not, and the insightful reflection that one of her students had offered in response. "Yes, he is a bright little boy and I sometimes worry that my attempts to support the other students are holding him back," she commented. Then a smile crept onto her face as she realized that she could easily offer him greater learning challenges just by varying the level of questions she asked. She could do more of what had just worked so well. Charlotte asked for a blank copy of the observation tool, saying she wanted to keep it in her lesson plan book because it was helpful just to have that reminder of the different levels and types of questions close at hand.

Imagining the Best of What Might Be

Evocative coaches inquire into and seek to appreciate a wide variety of inputs that teachers can build on to improve their skills and performance; these include stories of past successes, signature strengths, emotional readiness, and observations of present vitalities. But teachers and coaches are not limited to a strengths-based reconnaissance of the past and present. We can also inquire into and seek to appreciate the future. That is what Scharmer (2007) means by "learning from the future as it emerges" (p. 56) or "connecting with the Source of the highest future possibility and bringing it into the now" (p. 163). That dynamic, which Scharmer refers to as "presencing," is not just about setting a goal that is out there to work toward; it is about imagining the best of what might be in ways that infuse the present with energy, guidance, and resourcefulness. Not only can we imagine the best, we can invoke the best. Imagination serves, then, as a proleptic force that brings the future into the present moment and gets people to act as if the future is breaking in upon them. It becomes a kind of incarnation.

This effervescent dynamic is what evocative coaches hope for as we begin to explore with teachers their inherent ambitions and present possibilities. We seek to connect them with what Lance Secretan (2004) described as their "destiny, cause, and calling" (p. xxv). Why am I here? What do I stand for? How will I contribute? By inquiring into the "Why-Be-Do" of teachers' personal and professional lives, coaches inspire teachers to move beyond incremental improvements in technique to transformational shifts in attitude, orientation, and approach. When teachers are filled with passion for who they are and how they contribute with students, when they feel that passion in their bones (not giving it mere lip service), it moves teachers forward through the stages of change (Prochaska, Norcross, & DiClemente, 1994), elevates their understanding of the possible (Cooperrider, 2000), increases their positive affect (Fredrickson, 2009), and unlocks the door to self-efficacy (Bandura, 1997). The anticipatory principle of AI articulates the impact of our future outlook on present reality. Anticipating the realization of a larger vision, or what Gallwey (2000) describes as an "inherent ambition," organizes the present moment and pulls or beckons people forward (Bennis & Nanus, 1985). It enables us to outgrow, rather than to solve, our problems by getting us interested in what Carl Jung described as a "new and stronger life-tendency" (Jung, [1931]1962).

> *The greatest and most important problems of life are all in a certain sense insoluble. . . . They can never be solved, but only outgrown . . . once a higher and wider interest arises on the horizon.*
> *Carl Jung ([1931] 1962, pp. 91–92)*

Framing Aspirations

Everyone has aspirations because, as we discussed in Chapter Four, everyone has needs, and needs create aspirations. Human beings have needs that range from the most mundane to the most sublime. Subsistence-transcendence, safety-challenge, work-rest, honesty-empathy, and autonomy-community (refer to Figure 4.12) represent one way of describing the range of needs that may be alive for people, awakening the energy of aspiration. All needs are important for a sense of personal and professional fulfillment. When needs go unmet, we feel bad and strive to get them met. When needs are being met, we feel good and savor that satisfaction. Either way, human needs always comes into play when we are talking about aspiration. We know what makes us feel strong and good, and we aspire to bring that into our life and work as much as possible.

For teachers, these aspirations may be even closer to the surface. Working with students who are in the formative stages of life, developing their abilities, identities, and commitments with an evolving sense of self, teachers brush up against remarkable examples of human aspiration. Who has not been impressed, at least on occasion, by the energy, enthusiasm, learning, idealism, and altruism of children and young people? They often outdo their adult mentors and role models. Teachers have regular opportunities to both witness and cultivate that vigorous spirit; indeed, the entire teaching profession can be viewed through the lens of aspiration. Teachers who evoke and enable great aspirations are great teachers. They do more than the minimum, in all senses of the word, to inspire and infuse students with a lifelong love of learning, citizenship, and service.

If human beings are such need-meeting organisms, then why do so many needs so often go unmet? Appreciative inquiry works with one answer to that question: people become dispirited through the conversations and interactions we have with other people. Teachers may start out with idealistic notions as to what they can accomplish in education, but the more they butt heads with people who doubt their abilities, deconstruct their performance, dissect their difficulties, and demand their compliance, the more they lose sight of their inherent aspirations. Teaching is no longer a joy; it becomes just a chore.

Evocative coaching seeks to disrupt that downward spiral by taking a strengths-based approach to change. That is why we focus on discovering and observing the best of teacher abilities and experiences. By connecting teachers with the upside of their stories, those times when needs are met through the teaching life, we awaken and reawaken the aspiration to get more needs met. Instead of being discouraged and beaten down, teachers are lifted up through evocative coaching conversations to the full measure of their calling. They dare to dream the impossible dream and march to their own drummer when it comes to those Why-Be-Do questions. They stop going through the motions and start engaging their unique combinations of strengths, values, talents, priorities, sensitivities, situations, and patterns. Although human needs are universal, there is no standard-issue aspiration when it comes to teaching or any other pursuit. Each teacher understands and approaches his or her needs in a different way. They have only to capture and recapture the courage of their convictions to bring those aspirations forward.

No amount of skillful invention can replace the essential element of imagination.

Edward Hopper

Notwithstanding its individuality and complexity, framing aspirations is a key work of evocative coaching. Exploring, mapping, cultivating, and articulating aspirations are just as important as discovering strengths and observing vitalities. Aspirations represent, as it were, another dataset for coaching. What do teachers really want? What resonates with their very being and calls out their very best?

How do they imagine their future selves? How do they describe those targets that glisten and beckon in the present moment? Evocative coaches encourage teachers to dream big and to develop provocative propositions regarding the best of what might be (Watkins & Mohr, 2001). Such propositions have the most power to influence present attitudes and behavior when they are

- Grounded: Building on the best of current reality
- Daring: Boldly stretching the status quo
- Positive: Reflecting what we want to move toward, not away from
- Palpable: Sensing the future in the present, as if it was already happening, and
- Participatory: Involving all relevant stakeholders

It becomes easier for teachers to talk about their intrinsic aspirations, and to spin them out as provocative propositions, once they are connected to their strengths and vitalities. The better teachers feel about themselves and their work, the more teachers aspire to make themselves and their work even better. At their best, such aspirations go beyond yearning to the place of vision. Teachers come to see themselves and their work in new ways. The more coaches connect teachers with images that are infused with the energy and emotion of possibility, the more teachers move beyond imagining small tweaks in their performance to significant leaps forward that benefit themselves, their students, and the schools in which they serve. No wonder such coaching transforms schools, one conversation at a time. It elevates energy, improves mood, unleashes creativity, and bolsters both initiative and resilience.

Facilitating this future search requires a more creative approach to coaching than just talking about what teachers want or how teachers see the future. All talk and no play makes coaching a dull task. Evocative coaches may therefore ask teachers to close their eyes, to breathe deep and stretch, to create collages and vision boards, to draw pictures, to write poems, to coin a jingle, and to otherwise engage the right side of the brain in mindful creativity (Langer, 2005). The poetic principle of AI encourages coaches to go beyond the limitations of analysis by utilizing images, metaphors, stories, and narratives to make dreams come alive. That is when teachers truly come into the fullness of their aspirations for change. By engaging the heart and stirring the imagination, through positive mental stimulation and simulation, coaches enable teachers to generate both the willingness and the readiness to make dreams come true.

By now it should be clear that framing aspirations is a visionary practice, calling teachers to imagine both themselves and their schools at their very best. Aspirations are not isolated, egocentric visions. They are also not pipe dreams. They are rather palpable, incarnate visions that answer those larger questions in life and work regarding the contribution we make, the energy we muster, and the support we mobilize to realize the full potential of one and all. Although that may sound lofty and grandiose, it takes big dreams to stir hearts and move people to action. Unless people feel deeply connected to and passionate about a cause that is larger than themselves, they often do little more than the bare minimum, muddling along as best they can.

> *If you want to build a ship, don't drum up people to gather wood, divide the work, and give orders. Instead, teach them to yearn for the vast and endless sea.*
>
> Attributed to Antoine de Saint-Exupéry

Just because framing aspirations is a transformational and visionary practice, with plenty of opportunity for right brain engagement, the work is not complete until the left brain catches on and finds the words to describe what all those images, metaphors, stories, and narratives represent. In framing aspirations, we start with the need, give voice to the yearning, imagine its fulfillment, and frame its significance. Coaches can assist teachers to find the right words by inquiring appreciatively into values, outcomes, strengths, behaviors, motivators, and environments. All aspirations, however luminous, touch on these practical realities:

- Values: What are my principles? What do I stand for?
- Outcomes: What do I need? What do I want?
- Strengths: What am I good at? What makes me feel strong?
- Behaviors: What activities do I aspire to do consistently?
- Motivators: Why does this matter a lot to me, right now?
- Environments: What support team and structures will facilitate success?

However teachers get there, through whatever combination of creative right brain and expressive left brain activities, evocative coaching seeks to crystallize for teachers a clear understanding and statement of their personal and professional aspirations. They should be encouraged to write it down and then to summarize it in a few memorable sentences. When asked, teachers should be able to easily and passionately share their aspirations with others. An example of an aspirational statement for teaching, written in the present tense as if it were already true, might sound something like this:

My presence and way of being with my students is life affirming and inspires trust. I engage my students' intellectual curiosity and ignite their imagination about the topics we explore together. My students are confident that I value them as human beings more than I value the work we do together. My enthusiasm for our work is contagious. It motivates my students to be extraordinary learners.

Inviting Possibilities

For all their power to ignite motivation and stimulate movement, aspirational images and statements are not sufficient in and of themselves to change specific activities of individual teachers. As we will see in Chapter Six, aspirations without specific design strategies are like empty promises: they often fail to materialize. Before addressing design questions with teachers, however, one more line of inquiry can help to set the stage for determining the direction those design conversations will go: How would teachers describe their present possibilities? Were we to ask teachers that question before discovering their strengths, observing their vitalities, and framing their aspirations, we might well get a rather limited and scripted response. We might even get the party line as specified in the curriculum or a districtwide planning document. By waiting to ask that question in the wake of strengths, vitalities, and aspirations, however, we get a much broader and more personalized response. Teachers begin to think for themselves as to how they could best expand the realm of the possible.

One way to appreciate the difference between aspirations and possibilities is in terms of time frame. Aspirations are longer-term expressions of identity and mastery. They capture who teachers are and want to be in the classroom. Possibilities, on the other hand, are near-term expressions of what teachers would like to learn, explore, and do over the course of a semester or academic year. They answer the question, "What could possibly happen over the next few weeks and months that would align your life and work more closely with your aspirations?" Such immediate possibilities, like aspirations, are filled with energy, only this energy is even more intriguing and irresistible. When teachers see the possibility of learning or doing something that would help to make their future aspirations a reality, they often smile at the thought and jump at the opportunity.

Many coaching systems describe aspirations and possibilities in terms of visions and goals. Often that reduces the work of coaching to a rather linear, mechanical, and tedious process of moving deliberately from Point A to Point B. Armed with architectural and navigational metaphors, these systems envision the completed building or final destination and then commit to incremental goals for moving in that direction. Such approaches treat human motivation and movement as though they were projects to be managed, paying attention to time, materials, resources, and deliverables. "Make the plan, work the plan." Oh, if it were only that easy! Schools would have long ago closed the achievement gap and become learning organizations. Teachers would know just what to do, and students would know just what to expect. Educators would be continuously improving with many spectacular examples of performance mastery. Everything would be progressing steadily.

As everyone knows, however, that is not the case. Life is more complex and challenging than that. There are no simple solutions. But there are possibilities worth exploring, especially those that tap into existing strengths, vitalities, and aspirations. The language of possibility, as compared to the language of goals, implies less attachment to an outcome. People play with possibilities; they work at goals. And at this stage in the evocative coaching process, before we move on to design, we want teachers to stay in the place of curiosity and playfulness. We want them explore the realm of the possible, those feasible things that may be slightly out of reach but can nevertheless be grasped with a little stretch, before becoming accountable for making things happen. There is a time and place for accountability in the Design phase, as teachers commit to conducting experiments, but first they must experience freedom and trust in the identification and consideration of possibilities.

It is the extension of such autonomy to teachers that makes coaching evocative (Pink, 2009). When teachers are filled with a sense of their own strengths, vitalities, and aspirations, and when they are invited to imagine the possibilities that would make their life and work more wonderful, they get fully engaged in self-directed learning. Their energy goes up and their resistance goes down. That, in fact, is the primary sign that coaches and teachers are dancing together. If energy is low and resistance is high, then no one is happy and few possibilities are generated. The work of coaching is like pulling teeth. It is anything but evocative. If and when that happens, it is time for coaches to change our approach. Whatever we are doing is stimulating the wrong energy and triggering the wrong response. Backing off from goals that teachers "need" to work on is an important first step. Returning to Story–Empathy, until we again hear the release of the "golden sigh," is the next step. Then we can come back around to inquiry about the strengths, vitalities, and aspirations that teachers can draw upon and build on in the search for possibilities. That is the dynamic, iterative dance of evocative coaching.

Simply put, the upshot of inquiry should be an enthusiastic response to the question, "Now what?" (Fortgang, 2004). That is the question that invites possibility. If there is no enthusiasm, then something is off and coaches must adjust. If there is enthusiasm, then coaches can assist teachers to move forward by asking one or more of the following questions designed to get them thinking about new possibilities. These questions, of course, would never all be used with any one teacher on any one occasion. That would be an interrogation. The selective use of these questions, however, is an essential part of getting teachers ready for design conversations.

- What would you like to pay more attention to in your classroom?
- What variables do you think matter most?
- What possibilities do you see for yourself in the next few months?
- What changes do you think your students would really appreciate?
- What commitments have you made to yourself?
- What things can you imagine doing differently?
- What would you like to see more of in your classroom?

- How could your needs and the needs of your students be more fully met?
- How might your teaching be different a few months from now?
- What do you believe is possible?
- What things are most important to you right now? In life? In work?
- What would you like more of in your life? How is that linked to your teaching?
- What kind of environment would you like to create for your students?
- What changes would excite you and make you feel great?
- How would you describe your intentions over the next few months?
- What would your life be like if you realized those intentions? How would that feel?
- What has worked for you in other settings that you can draw on in this situation?
- What are the best things that could happen in your classroom in the near future?
- What changes would you like to experiment with in your teaching?
- What do you think are the best possible outcomes of our work together?

To answer such questions, many teachers find it helpful to relax their bodies and focus their minds (Garfield, 1984). There is no way to rush the generation of possibilities; they well up only when we come into a safe and creative space. Evocative coaches hold that space. We seek to minimize distractions and evaluations not only for ourselves, but also for the teachers we coach. We may ask teachers to close their eyes, to relax their muscles, to breathe deeply, to sense their emotions, to follow their energy, and to visualize the possibilities they imagine in vivid detail. What works for aspirations also works for possibilities: embodiment is a source of both information and inspiration. By getting teachers to focus on what they want now, to feel how it sits in their bodies, and to flesh out the particulars with whatever creative modalities they might enjoy, evocative coaches enable teachers to become more articulate, confident, and creative in the possibilities they see for change.

> *It takes courage to start a conversation. But if we don't start talking to one another, nothing will change. Conversation is the way we discover how to transform our world, together.*
>
> *Meg Wheatley (2002, p. 31)*

Coaching with Strengths, Observations, Aspirations, and Possibilities

It is common for coaches to talk with teachers about their strengths *and* their weaknesses, successes *and* their failures, triumphs *and* their tragedies, high points *and* their low points, pluses *and* their minuses. Indeed, it seems so obvious and natural to talk about both sides of the coin, that many people, including many coaches, have trouble imagining any other way to conduct a performance-oriented conversation. "We learn more from our mistakes than our successes" has become axiomatic, with cognitive neuroscience confirming just how quickly the brain works to help us avoid repeating errors. From this vantage point, it might seem necessary and valuable to make teachers face the music as to what they are doing wrong and have to change.

As we have seen, however, there is another school of thought that evocative coaching has drawn upon in the development of our strengths-based method. It may seem logical to talk with teachers about fixing their problems and correcting their weaknesses, but research indicates how this mode of inquiry can do more harm than good. Regardless of how many strengths are recognized, as soon as the weaknesses come out the limbic system reacts, and that is all people focus on and remember. It becomes a constricting downward spiral that may keep people from making the same mistake twice but that does little to facilitate higher orders of learning and growth. It generates defensive rather than expansive reactions. To achieve outstanding performance, then, a different approach is called for. Appreciative inquiry represents one such approach, firmly grounded in research and theory. AI does not pretend there are no problems; it rather assumes that people will outgrow their problems the more they focus on their strengths, vitalities, aspirations, and possibilities. AI was born in organizations as a large-group method; it works equally well, however, in one-on-one coaching. For that to happen, coaches must restrain our urge to talk with teachers about what they are doing poorly and engage our curiosity to learn about what teachers are doing well. The more we stay in that positive frame, the more we dialogue with teachers about their strengths, vitalities, aspirations, and possibilities, the more teachers will come to believe in their abilities and the more progress they will make in their classrooms.

> *The coach's task is to help teachers perceive change not as a means of discrediting their professional expertise, but of building on it.*
>
> *Michael McKenna and Sharon Walpole (2008, p. 20)*

Reviewing Data from a Strengths-Based Perspective

So how do coaches come at problems through the back door, as it were? By assisting teachers to connect the dots between the best of what is and the best of what might be. Strengths and vitalities can be viewed as datasets. They represent palpable and observable realities that teachers can draw upon as they frame their aspirations and possibilities. The more teachers know about their strengths and vitalities, the better their changes will be. It is easy for these positive realities to get lost in the continuous clamor of what must be done on a day-to-day basis, with all its difficulties and deadlines. Social cognitive neuroscientists have now pinpointed exactly how this works in the brain. Problems generate a powerful and immediate cathexis or emotional charge in the limbic system, long before the brain's frontal lobes, associated with reflective thought processes, know what is going on. Yet the cerebral cortex is not helpless, and data are among its strongest of allies. For people to set aside the "fight, flight, and freeze" reactions of their limbic systems, they require new information that reframes the situation and sets them on a different course. Positive, strengths-based data can do just that. It is the work of evocative coaching to look for those strengths and to equip teachers with an understanding of what they are doing well.

Evocative coaches take the stance that all teachers are doing some things well at least some of the time and that they are all capable of doing more things well more of the time. This stance, that all teachers have strengths and that they are using those strengths to do some things well, assists coaches to better support teachers in the building of self-efficacy. That is why evocative coaches seek to dialogue with teachers about their strengths and vitalities in the classroom. We do not use observation tools to highlight problem areas; we use observation tools to highlight possibility areas. What are teachers successfully doing now that they can build on to generate even more success in the future? Dialoguing with teachers in this way with the information gleaned from observation tools assists teachers to know themselves and to move forward in the direction of their desired future. By asking teachers open-ended questions about the best of what is going on, in light of the data provided by the observation tools, coaches not only learn more about teacher frameworks and priorities, coaches also elevate their readiness and energy for change.

Prior to coaching sessions in which data from one or more observation tools will be reviewed, take time to carefully review the data ahead of time. In reviewing, the goal is not to evaluate but to consider the data with curiosity, keeping in mind that the data captured on an observation tool never provides the teacher's entire story. Curiosity enables coaches to ask better questions during the review, use intuition to attend to what is unsaid, challenge our own assumptions about the teacher, develop a strengths-based framework through which to appreciate the teacher, and be more open to new information and energy shifts during the coaching session.

I was paired with Jessica in our peer coaching program. Jessica had taught for seven years in New York City with a very disadvantaged population, and she was having trouble making the adjustment to working with much more affluent students. She was like a fish out of water. She was used to desks in rows, while our school is arranged around tables to facilitate discussion. She would dominate the discussion, which let the students get away with opting out of participation. I could see that she had been a really great teacher in the inner city—she was good at drawing kids out of their shells, but that was not really necessary in our context. Jessica and I arranged that we would visit each other's classrooms on alternating weeks and that we would meet every week to discuss whichever class we'd observed. At our first meeting, we set up a sheet for our observations, with a column for strengths and a column for questions about what we'd seen. After I'd observed in her classroom the second time, I questioned her about student participation, and about when the conversation seemed most lively. I asked how she could encourage more of that dynamic. We talked about the importance of silence and how it gave students the time to think. We also processed her feelings about silence. After we talked about this for a while, she said, "The next time you observe me, map who talks for how long and time the silences." So I mapped the conversation, drawing lines between who spoke and for how long. Then she did the same for me in my classroom for comparison sake. When we reviewed the map of my class, she noticed that I was calling on the boys more than the girls. The boys were definitely more engaged as a result of my questions. So we both had something to work on. We didn't do the mapping again for a couple of months, but when we did, we both had improved.

Matt, high school department chair

Noticing and Elevating Teacher Energies

The process of noticing and elevating teacher energies never ascends on a straight line. Teachers circle around with a waft of emotions and needs even in the face of the most appreciative of inquiries. Evocative coaches anticipate this circling round and learn to dance with teachers in ways that honor their experience and bolster their confidence. This is particularly important in the wake of classroom observations. When teachers are feeling down and discouraged about the way a lesson went, returning to Story–Empathy enables them to renew and restore their energies. When teachers are feeling excited and hopeful, inquiry into strengths, vitalities, aspirations, and possibilities enables them to enlarge and expand their energies. That is the give and take of the evocative coaching dance. By noticing and responding to teacher energies as they are in the moment, evocative coaches assist teachers to set aside their judgmental voices and to reconnect with their best qualities, experiences, and intentions. To do this dance successfully, evocative coaches pay continuous attention to changes in teacher affect. When teachers pull back, it may be time for more empathy. When teachers lean forward, it may be time for more inquiry. There is no hard and fast rule, but there is the sense of keeping just the right amount of tension on the line. Too little tension and coaching becomes little more than a chat. Too much tension and coaching becomes a chore. The right amount of tension enables teachers to develop their passion and to move forward, often dramatically, in their paths of development.

To elevate teacher energies, evocative coaches may want to ask any of the following or similar questions, based upon the Appreciative Interview Protocol discussed earlier in this chapter. Following up an appreciative question with "What else?" communicates confidence that more good stuff is there and invites the kind of elaboration that can build energy and enthusiasm for change.

- What was the best part of this experience? What else?
- What stands out for you as a shining success? What else?
- What can you celebrate about what happened here? What else?
- Who do you remember as being particularly engaged? What was happening at the time?
- What values are reflected in how you handled this lesson? What else?
- How did this lesson connect with your sense of purpose? How else?
- What needs did this lesson meet for you? What else?
- What needs did this lesson meet for your students? What else?
- What enabled this lesson to be as successful as it was? What else?
- When did you feel most comfortable and confident? When else?
- What things did you have in place that helped you to be successful? What else?
- What could assist you to be even more successful the next time? What else?

Positive Reframing

As we have seen, appreciative inquiry does not gloss over negative experiences with rose-tinted glasses. It does not pretend that everything is wonderful when it is obviously not. AI does, however, avoid inquiring into the root causes of what is wrong. It also resists the temptation to characterize any human experience, including any teaching experience, as a total failure. That is never a helpful or wholly accurate description. The natural human tendency to notice problems and react to pain can lead people down the rabbit hole of discouragement, distress, and despair. We can easily extrapolate problems into catastrophes, especially if we lose perspective on what is going right. This tendency crops up in coaching when teachers want to start coaching conversations with problems that are identified as the "issue of the day." They assume that coaches want to dig into difficulties and tear into troubles. Indeed, the mere fact of coaching is often seen through a negative frame, as if coaching were nothing but a remediation plan for subpar players.

In evocative coaching, we do not show up as either Fix-It-Up Chappies or Know-It-Alls. We rather show up as partners in the search for whatsoever things are true, noble, reputable, authentic, compelling, gracious, beautiful, and praiseworthy. We trust that those things are always there, no matter how tough the situation, and we collaborate with teachers in the inquiry to find them. We are steadfast in our search for strengths, vitalities, aspirations, and possibilities. By assisting teachers to stay focused on this quest, we enable them to reframe negative experiences in positive terms. Story listening makes clear how many ways there are to tell a story. By imagining different vantage points, pivot points, and lesson points, it is always possible to find things to appreciate and build up rather than to depreciate and tear down. Evocative coaches proceed with the unshakable conviction that good things can always be found. Such perspective and confidence are infectious. Teachers quickly calm down, believe more in themselves, and generate new possibilities for moving forward. If even one student was engaged for even one moment, that is the moment evocative coaches want to notice and nurture. "What happened there?" and "How can we get more of that?" is the drift of a conversation that has taken a positive turn. That is the drift evocative coaches work for in each and every conversation.

To facilitate positive reframing, coaches may want to ask one or more of the following strengths-based questions. They affirm the importance of not just making lemonade out of lemons, but also of appreciating what goes into making the lemonade and how it tastes. Evocative coaches assist teachers to value the best of every experience, no matter how difficult or trying, in order to generate the life-giving energy that facilitates change.

- Tell me how you got through this and what's possible now.
- What did you try that worked, even if only a little bit?
- How did this experience make a positive contribution to your development?
- What's the silver lining here?
- When, if ever, did things start to go better and look up?
- How else can you describe this situation?
- What is the best thing your students might say they learned today?
- What was the best thing you did for yourself in this situation, no matter how small?
- What values did you hold true to even though it was a tough class?
- How did you manage to keep things from getting any worse?

If teachers can think of nothing positive to say in response to such inquiries, encourage them to go back further in time. Perhaps there was another tough class, lesson, or subject that turned out better in the end. If that invitation fails to land, remembering instances of successful perseverant effort in other areas, inside or outside of school, may get the conversation back on track. When multiple positive reframing efforts come up empty handed, teachers may not be ready for "the Strengths-Based Turn" of Inquiry–Design in the evocative coaching conversation. Going back to "the No-Fault Turn" of Story–Empathy is, then, the way to gradually move forward to a new "golden sigh." Such is the coaching dance when it comes to working with strengths, vitalities, aspirations, and possibilities.

Moving Through Ambivalence

Ambivalence, the felt sense of conflicting feelings about alternative possibilities, is another form of negative energy that teachers may experience and move through as they contemplate their options for performance improvement. Ambivalence is, essentially, an internal dynamic as teachers come to terms with competing commitments, attachments, assumptions, and emotions. It is not that one possibility is good and the other is bad; it is that all possibilities have value and meet different needs. Until and unless teachers are able to sort out and appreciate those dynamics, they will not take effective action.

The first step in moving through ambivalence is accepting it as a common and perfectly normal state of mind (Miller & Rollnick, 2002). There is nothing *wrong* with them when teachers feel ambivalent. Fighting against ambivalence is counterproductive. The more teachers try to force themselves to go one way or another, the more stress, frustration, and strain they will experience. They may find themselves saying one thing and doing another. For these reasons, it is important for coaches not to be impatient with ambivalence. As much as we might like to tell teachers what to do and to push them to get going, such strong-arm tactics usually do more harm than good. There is a "tough love" school of coaching that takes pride in its ability to force an outcome, but those outcomes are seldom effective or enduring. Effective and enduring changes require a more evocative approach.

The second step in moving through ambivalence is understanding what it has to teach us (Gonzales, 2006). Through our facility with Story–Empathy–Inquiry, evocative coaches are well equipped to guide teachers through the process of exploring and resolving ambivalence, on at least a tentative or provisional basis. We seek to appreciate the beauty of all the needs teachers are trying to meet until one rises to the surface as being the most compelling for now. The following questions can assist teachers to work through their dilemmas:

- How do you see the possibilities before you? How else do you see them?
- What choices are you facing? How else would describe those choices?

- Where do you feel the possibilities in your body? What can you learn from that?
- Who could you talk with about your quandary? Who else could you talk with?
- What do you know for sure about your options? What don't you know?
- How do you know what you know about the possibilities before you? How could you test what you know?
- What needs are you trying to meet? What else? What else?
- What values would you honor by going one direction? By going another? And another?
- What benefits do you see to one course of action? To another? And another?
- What concerns do you have regarding one possibility? Regarding another? And another?
- What strengths would be called upon if you went one way? If you went the other?
- How do you feel when you contemplate going one way? Going another way?
- On a scale of 0 to 10, how valid are the reasons for doing one thing? For doing another?
- On a scale of 0 to 10, how good do you feel when you think about the reasons for doing one thing? For doing another?

The point of such questions is to get teachers to talk through their ambivalence without any sense of judgment, pressure, or bias. Coaches cannot afford to be attached to an outcome. We want teachers to find their own answers and to chart their own course so that motivation is high and progress is more likely once teachers start moving forward on a path of self-directed learning.

The final step in moving through ambivalence is field testing one or more of the possibilities, as discussed further in the next chapter. Teachers are not required to figure everything out ahead of time in their minds, once and for all and forever. Teachers are encouraged to play with possibilities, to prototype, trying one or more on for size to see how they work, what they learn, and what they enjoy most. If they move in one direction and their energy goes up, they won't be ambivalent for long. They'll be more than ready for design. If their energy goes down, Story–Empathy–Inquiry will eventually assist them to find a new path. By exploring stories, reflecting feelings, understanding needs, appreciating strengths, noticing vitalities, and cultivating aspirations, all teachers will sooner or later move through ambivalence to engage in the powerful work of design conversations.

From SWOT to SOAP

A well-known strategic planning method known as the SWOT (Strengths, Weaknesses, Opportunities, and Threats) analysis is generally credited to the late Albert S. Humphrey (1926–2005) through his work at the Stanford Research Institute.

The analysis makes use of a four-quadrant matrix that looks at internal/external dynamics on one axis and helpful/harmful dynamics on the other. Putting them together, the analysis walks individuals or organizations through a detailed consideration of their strengths, weaknesses, opportunities, and threats. Once identified, the analysis seeks to help people capitalize on strengths, overcome weaknesses, exploit opportunities, and mitigate threats. For all their apparent logic and widespread utilization, SWOT analyses often fail to generate successful change and may actually harm performance. That is because they pitch people into battles against often intractable weaknesses and threats. SWOT is just another form of problem solving, and not a very effective one at that. As one study of twenty companies conducting SWOT analyses concluded, "It's time for a product recall" (Hill & Westbrook, 1997).

In working with teachers, evocative coaches make use of a different metaphor to generate better results. Instead of SWOT analyses, we opt for SOAP (Strengths, Observations, Aspirations, and Possibilities) inquiries. We use strengths, observations, aspirations, and possibilities to discover the best of what is and to imagine the best of what might be. In this way, SOAP lathers up new realities, imbuing the entire process with wonder, awe, fun, surprise, joy, satisfaction, and deep relationship. Such qualities are among the biggest differences between SWOT and SOAP. SWOT is filled with a sense of urgency and threat as gaps are identified and targeted for mitigation or elimination. The militaristic imagery is no accident; SWOT is common practice in warfare (Sutherland & Stavros, 2003). But teachers are not at war, and SOAP inquiries represent a better way to change. The acronym makes that clear with its implied cleansing power. SOAP has a way of washing away the grime of discouragement and making dreary perspectives sparkle anew. Strengths, observed vitalities, aspirations, and possibilities invigorate teachers with can-do energy and ready teachers for the design thinking and design conversations that are yet to come.

Summary

Although inquiry is presented here as a distinct step in the coaching dance, it is an integral part of every other step as well. Story listening is all about inquiry, as coaches attend to and explore teacher stories from different vantage points, pivot points, and lesson points. Expressing empathy, in which coaches attempt to compassionately understand and reflect the feelings and needs of teachers, is also a form of inquiry, albeit without the question mark. Design conversations, filled, as we shall see, with brainstorming ideas, exploring inertia, and designing experiments, are similarly driven by inquiry. There is no way to coach without asking questions. Yet, all questions are not created equal. Some questions invite only short, one-word answers. Other questions come with an implied right answer. And many questions focus on some problematic aspect of human experience in order to analyze, diagnose, evaluate, educate, correct, compare, and problem-solve. Although people usually ask such questions to figure out what people are doing poorly in order to help them do it well, they are neither encouraged nor frequently used in the evocative coaching process.

Evocative coaches use appreciative inquiries to learn more about the life-giving energies and experiences of teachers. We want to learn what they care about and what they are doing well in order to facilitate the requisite openness to change. We seek to bring their assets into the foreground so they can better invest them in high-yield strategies. The more teachers know about their strengths and vitalities, with the help of appreciative interviews, assessments, observations, and dialogues, the more prone teachers will be to frame aspirations and invite possibilities. The former flows naturally into the latter. Appreciating the best of what is through life-giving inquiries generates the best of what might be through life-enhancing designs. Positive energy generates productive energy. Such inquiries not only get teachers ready for change, they are, in important senses, change itself. The more teachers focus their attention on the things they are doing well, the better their teaching becomes. Awareness is action because what we appreciate, appreciates. Inquiry intervenes. "Awe," to quote Joseph Campbell, "is what moves us forward." That is the power of strengths-based inquiries to shift not only individual teachers but entire schools and school systems, one conversation at a time. The essence of coaching is asking good questions. Such inquiries reintroduce us to wonder, connection, and possibility—the necessary components and prerequisites of change.

Questions for Reflection and Discussion

1. What has been your best experience of building on strengths at work? How did you feel when those strengths were called upon and came out? What did that experience lead to?
2. Why is it important for evocative coaches not to rush teachers into Inquiry–Design until we have first set the stage through Story–Empathy?
3. How might you incorporate the four questions that constitute the generic Appreciative Interview Protocol into an ongoing coaching relationship?
4. Take the VIA Signature Strengths Questionnaire at www.authentichappiness .sas.upenn.edu. What are your top five strengths? How can you use these when coaching?

5. When observing teachers in the classroom, why is it important to avoid praising and criticizing their attitudes and actions? What can we do instead?

6. How can we turn performance improvement into an enjoyable game? What things might we pay attention to and notice?

7. What is the value of appreciative classroom observation tools? How might their use contribute to the quality of the coaching conversation? What do evocative coaches look for when observing teachers?

8. When teachers have difficult experiences in the classroom, how can coaches assist them to reframe those experiences in positive terms?

9. Write out a one- to three-sentence aspirational statement for yourself as a coach, teacher, and/or educator. Share the statement with at least three other people in the week ahead.

CHAPTER 6

DESIGN THINKING

The positive lens refers to . . . our capacity to construct better organizations and technologies through positive discourse. Joining a positive lens onto organizing with the transformative power of design thinking opens new horizons and uncovers previously overlooked possibilities for creating organizational and social well-being.

MICHEL AVITAL AND RICHARD BOLAND (2007, P. 3)

As coaches do the Story–Empathy–Inquiry dance with teachers, motivation and movement pick up steam. Teachers feel better about themselves, their experiences, and their abilities. They understand more fully what they are doing and what needs they are trying to meet. As a result, the mounting energy and motivation for change are palpable. Teachers frame aspirations and identify possibilities that they not only yearn to see realized, but that they now believe can be realized. In short, teachers become inspired.

Such inspiration is the first space of what is now being called "the design thinking process" (Brown, 2008, 2009, 2010; Kelley, 2001, 2005; Martin, 2009). In the face of ever-more complex and challenging problems and opportunities, design thinking is proving to be a way for people and organizations to stimulate innovation, increase self-efficacy, and advance creativity in order to better meet human needs. The process requires empathy, integrative thinking, optimism, experimentalism, and collaboration as designers pass through three spaces: inspiration, ideation, and implementation (Brown, 2008). It combines intuition with analysis to create value (Martin, 2009). In other words, the design thinking process engages the same attributes and makes many of the same moves as the evocative coaching process, with the same intended results: assisting people to better meet both their own needs and the needs of others within the constraints of human systems.

Design thinking . . . starts off with really trying to serve people's needs. It connects constraints with creativity, enabling us to look at old problems with new eyes and generate new possibilities.

Tim Brown (2010)

Evocative coaching seeks first to inspire teachers to imagine and trust the realm of possibility; it then invites teachers to dance in that realm. Inspiration without the dance of ideation and implementation, intuition without analysis, has little impact and quickly fades. Put them together, however, and the realm of possibility can become reality. That is why design thinkers work with the formula: Innovation = Inspiration + Ideation + Implementation. Evocative coaches therefore take special note of when teachers appear ready to implement new ideas so that we can effectively encourage and collaborate with them to brainstorm those ideas, select the ones they want to try out, design and conduct a variety of prototypes and learning experiments, and integrate the learning into their daily practices. When Design successfully follows Story–Empathy–Inquiry in this way, one round in the dynamic dance of evocative coaching is finished. Coaches and teachers generate new value in a fulfilling way such that they look forward to getting out on the dance floor and doing it all over again.

All this happens when teachers learn to trust themselves and their highest of aspirations through Story–Empathy–Inquiry–Design. By viewing and treating teachers as resourceful and creative partners in the process of performance improvement, both during coaching conversations and in classroom applications of design innovations, coaches assist teachers to develop not only a "can-do" attitude but also the "can-do-much-more" attitude that represents the hallmark of self-efficacy: the belief that one has the capability to organize and execute a course of action to achieve a desired outcome (Bandura, 1997). The design step in "the Strengths-Building Turn" nurtures that belief by assisting teachers to see a way forward, aligning their aptitudes, interests, abilities, and actions with the procedures, systems, technologies, roles, resources, relationships, structures, and stakeholders that make up their professional lives.

As we have seen, aspirations and possibilities describe who teachers want to be and what they seek to accomplish. Big-picture aspirations describe attractive ideals that may take many years to achieve. Present possibilities describe intriguing initiatives that may be taken and realized within a month, semester, or academic year. Together, aspirations and possibilities constitute a purpose statement that is necessary but not sufficient for motivation and movement. They identify what teachers want—they inspire teachers—but unless and until teachers do the work of designing, committing to, and experimenting with action-learning strategies, aspirations and possibilities are unlikely to be realized. Without this work, aspirations and possibilities represent a form of New Year's resolutions, which tend to be heavy on outcomes and light on action strategies. "To lose weight," for example, one of the most common of all New Year's resolutions, does not specify how that will happen. It states an aspiration and an intriguing possibility without stating the requisite behavior changes. As a result, for all their desirability, more than half of all New Year's resolutions go unfulfilled. Or, as an anonymous saying goes, "A New Year's resolution is something that goes in one year and out the other."

A key factor in assisting teachers to change their behaviors, then, is building the behavioral and environmental infrastructures that will support and help them realize their desired possibilities. Inviting teachers to design specific action-learning experiments as to what they will be doing differently when, and encouraging them to secure the necessary organizational resources, are essential parts of the coaching process. Although no design is ever perfect, since designs must be continuously adapted to ever-changing, real-world conditions, few human endeavors succeed without design thinking and planning. Possibilities without planning are little more than pipe dreams. Investing the time and effort to develop creative and yet feasible designs is what gets people moving forward. Without design conversations, coaching becomes something of a cruel joke. It pumps up teachers without giving them the tools to do the job. It gets teachers excited about their capacity and vision for change without mapping out how to get started, what route to follow, and how to adapt in the face of adversity. It makes clear the destination without providing a path of development. Through the design conversation, however, all this begins to shift. Teachers come up with new, actionable ideas and commit to the ones they view as particularly doable, exciting, and impactful. They also devise ways to reengineer their classrooms, teams, and other environments to better support those commitments.

As in every other aspect of the evocative coaching model, the coach does not prescribe or tell teachers what their designs should be. That posture is fraught with multiple dangers. It may generate resistance rather than openness, create a power-over rather than a power-with dynamic, and set up teachers for struggle and failure—even when they take the advice—because they are in the difficult and oftentimes awkward position of having to implement someone else's ideas. Coaching leads teachers through the process of discovering that they are capable of great things and then creates the space for compelling visions, desired outcomes, and transformational action-learning strategies to emerge. There is never anything final about the designs that teachers and coaches cook up together for realizing aspirations and possibilities. Progress in living systems such as schools is never linear. Setbacks and surprises are inevitable. Experimental designs therefore require continuous learning, dialogue, and updating in order to be fulfilled and fulfilling.

Dan was a frustrated first-year teacher. He came to our school primarily as a football coach and was assigned to teach in my department. I was his assistant coach, so on the field he was "the boss" and in the classroom I was "the boss." That made for a very collegial relationship. He had good instincts as a coach, so when I'd see him using a successful strategy with his players I'd talk about how he could use the same approach in the classroom. He has really grabbed hold of the idea of using coaching strategies in his teaching. He's grasped a larger conception of teaching that goes beyond just dispensing information. As a result, he's much more enthusiastic about teaching. He's come back for his second year really eager to plan our units together and to continue to try out new teaching strategies.

Luke, high school department chair

Therein lies the true promise of evocative coaching: that teachers might develop strong, intrinsic motivation to improve their performance and quality of life with a high sense of self-efficacy. Evocative coaching does this by encouraging continuous, self-directed learning with its Möbius strip model of Story–Empathy–Inquiry–Design. As teachers go around and around the Möbius strip, dancing with coaches through multiple turns and iterations, the dreams get bigger and the designs get better for teaching success.

Calling Forth Motivation and Movement

Educators, psychologists, and, most recently, neuroscientists have all delved deeply into questions concerning human motivation and agency. What piques people's interest in doing something new? What moves us into action? What keeps us going in the face of challenges and setbacks? What enables us to successfully achieve new levels of competence and mastery? Such questions lie at the core of the coaching task, and evocative coaching answers those questions with a research-based model that emphasizes the importance of valuing intrinsic motivation and supporting self-efficacy to improve performance in tasks such as teaching (Pink, 2009). Intrinsic motivation, self-efficacy, and trust are the precursors of change.

Numerous authors have helped to popularize these concepts with the general public. Alan Deutschman (2007), for example, documented the ineffectiveness of those things we traditionally rely on to motivate and foster lasting change: "facts, fear, and force." Facts are not effective because human beings are not as rational as we think we are. Fear does not serve long-term change because people cannot stay afraid forever. At best it is a short-term motivator. And force is ineffective because people can be very clever in the strategies they come up with to resist and retaliate. Deutschman claims the "three Rs" are a more effective path: *relating* to people who inspire and sustain hope, *reframing* our thinking with positive, inspiring, and emotionally relevant perspectives, and *repeating* new routines that teach and train new behavior. Daniel Pink (2009) described the ineffectiveness of extrinsic motivation (rewards and punishments, incentives and threats) on dynamic, non-routine, empathic tasks. Such motivators crush creative problem solving. To foster intrinsic motivation, Pink documents the value of autonomy, mastery, and purpose. When people have control over their task, technique, time, and team, and when they have a clear sense of direction, they will more quickly and assuredly develop the mastery of skills necessary to be successful. More recently, academic researchers are spreading the good news of positivity (e.g., Ben-Shahar, 2009; Fredrickson, 2009; Kashdan, 2009). They want people to know how to arrange life in ways that will facilitate happiness, success, and fulfillment.

Motivation comes with being alive. Gallwey (2000) described people as having "inherent ambitions"; and Rosenberg (2005) wrote of our natural inclination to meet "universal needs." The desire to meet needs does not have to be planted in people like seeds in order to grow. Those seeds are preexisting. They can fail to take root and thrive, however, if we do not weed and feed the soil. That is the work of evocative coaching. By reducing interference and adding resources, we cultivate motivation and move teachers to action.

Intrinsic motivation and self-efficacy are important in coaching because they are inextricably related to the effort, persistence, and resilience that teachers bring to their teaching practice (Tschannen-Moran, Woolfolk Hoy, & Hoy, 1998; Tschannen-Moran & McMaster, 2009). They literally change the brain (Begley, 2007; Rock & Page, 2009). The more teachers desire to improve their teaching, the more confidence they have in their ability to do so, and the more encouragement they receive to devise their own way forward, the more inspired, curious, and creative they become in setting new goals, exploring new territory, and tackling new challenges (Kashdan, 2009). Bandura (1986, 1997) holds that human behavior is determined by three factors that interact with each other in dynamic and reciprocal ways: cognitive factors (such as what we believe and how we feel about what we can do), environmental factors (such as our support networks and role models), and behavioral factors (such as what we ourselves experience and accomplish). Bandura's work recognizes the importance of both social and cognitive processes in arousing ambition, constructing reality, and regulating behavior. A growing body of evidence from positive psychologists and neuroscientists confirms Bandura's hypothesis: human motivation and self-efficacy beliefs are affected by all three factors (cognitive, environmental, and behavioral).

Working with and aligning those factors are therefore critical components of design thinking and conversations.

There is a well-known circular dynamic within belief and action: the more confidence we have in our ability to do what we want to do, the more likely we are to invest the energy and effort to do it; similarly, the more success we have in doing what we want to do, the more likely we are to do it again and to try things that may be even more ambitious. The opposite is also true: the less confidence we have, the less likely we are to take action; similarly, the less success we have, the less likely we are to do it again or to try things that may be even more ambitious. As Henry Ford once said, "Whether you think you can or think you can't, you're right." The job of coaching is to assist teachers to think they can. Until and unless teachers believe they are able to discover ways to improve their performance, they will not envision or pursue performance improvement strategies. That is the power of motivation, self-efficacy, and trust: they move people to action. Nothing is more thrilling than making progress toward a self-directed goal. The more teachers experience success in their chosen areas of interest, the more confidence they gain and the more progress they make. It is an upward spiral.

> *You need to be optimistic in order to be creative. And confident. In fact, if you don't have confidence that you can create solutions, you won't create solutions.*
>
> Tim Brown (2010)

The first three stages of the evocative coaching process, Story–Empathy–Inquiry, are all designed to inspire and awaken such confidence by extending freedom and trust, reframing experiences, understanding emotions, and elevating energies in positive terms. From the moment of first contact, and by virtue of our very presence, it is important for coaches to convey our certainty that teachers have what it takes to learn what they want to learn and to achieve what they want to achieve. Our certainty is greater than their doubt. When teachers have difficult stories to tell, coaches look for vantage points that open up new perspectives through which successes can be seen. When teachers have difficult emotions to process, we look for language that will quiet judgmental, nay-saying internal voices through authentic mourning. When teachers have difficult problems to solve, we look for strengths and vitalities that can assist teachers to outgrow their problems through natural learning. Once teachers believe they have what it takes to get beyond their difficulties and to be successful, the primary work of coaching is done.

Many disciplines have sought to understand how best to call forth motivation and movement from people. Bandura's (1997) social cognitive theory identified four things that support self-efficacy and move people to action: verbal persuasion, physiological and affective states, vicarious experiences, and enactive mastery experiences.

Positive psychology has studied those dimensions by looking at positive relationships, positive energy and emotions, positive images, and positive actions (Cooperrider, 2000; Fredrickson, 2009). Neuroscientists are now documenting how these factors influence and change the brain (Thatchenkery & Metzker, 2006; Siegel, 2007; Rock & Page, 2009). Taken together, these disciplines make a case statement for evocative coaching. They explain how Story–Empathy–Inquiry–Design both inspires people and moves them to successful, perseverant action. If we hope to get teachers interested in and able to improve their teaching, then we have to support their best thinking, unleash their best energy, tap into their best examples, and design their best action-learning strategies. We have to take full advantage, in other words, of the design thinking process.

Positive Relationships

One of the most important of all factors, if not *the* most important factor when navigating our way through a change process, is our relational environments. When people we love and respect champion our abilities and encourage our exploration of new frontiers, we are much more likely to open up, to get into gear, and to bounce back from hardship or disappointment. That is the fundamental insight upon which evocative coaching is based. It doesn't work to tell teachers what to do and to demand their cooperation. Such approaches backfire because they get interpreted as negative evaluations of teacher competence and as formulaic prescriptions for performance improvement. Such dynamics inhibit and often doom our efforts at change. What works are positive relationships that broker encouragement, extend respect, cultivate trust, reframe failure, endorse competence, model excellence, and challenge teachers to be the best they can possibly be. What works are evocative relationships that liberate teachers to do more than they might otherwise have thought possible.

Because positive relationships are so important in the change process, evocative coaches seek not only to cultivate positivity in our own relationships with teachers but also to impact the quality of the relational networks that teachers affiliate with both inside and outside their school environments. This book aims to make coaching relationships evocative of change. But coaching relationships are not sufficient, in and of themselves, to meet all the motivational and learning needs of teachers. Appreciative inquiry, with its social constructionist principle, makes clear the importance of taking a whole-system approach. Inviting teachers to connect with others they trust, who share a passion for the possible and who endorse new learning strategies, is therefore an essential part of the design process in evocative coaching. We talk actively with teachers about how to find and create pockets of support within their school environments and other social networks, including virtual networks on the Internet. Through encouraging the use of appreciative frameworks, coaches assist teachers to have positive effects on organizational culture. In this way, teachers develop not only their own abilities; they also serve as catalysts for transforming schools one conversation at a time.

> *The tie between flourishing and enjoying good social relations is so strong and reliable that scientists have called it a necessary condition for flourishing.*
>
> *Barbara Fredrickson (2009, p. 191)*

When Bandura (1997) described "verbal persuasion" as a source of self-efficacy, he was referring to the verbal inputs people receive regarding their performance and prospects for success. All the voices in a school community, including those of colleagues, supervisors, students, and parents, influence the self-efficacy of teachers. Evocative coaches pay attention to how those voices sound, starting with our own. Since coaches work explicitly with teachers to improve performance, our communications regarding their ability to be successful carry special weight. As Bandura noted, "It is easier to sustain a sense of efficacy, especially when struggling with difficulties, if significant others express faith in one's capabilities than if they convey doubts" (p. 101). The more teachers struggle, the more reminding they need as to their capabilities. By communicating appreciation that is sincere, based on teacher-specific strengths and vitalities, evocative coaches do much to bolster self-efficacy. By assisting teachers to find and build supportive relational networks, we strengthen teacher self-efficacy and contribute to the collective efficacy of successful schools.

The posture of evocative coaches with teachers is that "you have what it takes to succeed." Unless we believe in the ambitions and innate abilities of teachers, we cannot assist them to achieve their educational vision. If we find ourselves questioning teachers' desires and capabilities, and if we do not believe they have what it takes to succeed, then we have to either turn around our attitude or hand off the coaching relationship to someone who does believe in them. We cannot persuade someone of something of which we are not ourselves persuaded. The first three steps of the evocative coaching process benefit both coaches and teachers alike with the conviction that teachers can be successful. If it doesn't happen right away, persistently inquiring into teacher strengths and observing classroom vitalities will eventually make a difference. Mindfulness and patience, remembering that it takes time and effort to overcome inertia, can assist coaches to stay hopeful when the going is slow.

In the work of verbal persuasion, it is better to recognize teachers for their unique strengths and observable vitalities than to compliment them in general or vague ways. Generalized compliments fail to offer specific feedback as to the causes of success and often come across as judgmental evaluations (albeit in a positive frame). Such compliments may even provoke skepticism and resistance if they are perceived as insincere or if we come across as working too hard to persuade teachers they can do something. Targeted recognitions, on the other hand, leave teachers with a clear sense of the strengths and vitalities they can build on to be successful. Such recognitions can always be identified and offered, even when teachers struggle or express doubts and insecurities. Verbal persuasion does not mean that we try to talk teachers out of their bad feelings. It does not mean that we deny frustration or disappointment. Instead, through empathy, we connect with teachers, understand their needs, and communicate trust in their ability to figure things out and get on track. By keeping our eyes and ears open for those glimmers of evidence that all is not lost and that some things are still working well (or at least well enough), we radiate a calm energy of confidence, assisting teachers to believe anew in themselves and in their abilities.

Tiffany had a very positive attitude and was always willing to try something new. I noticed that from listening to her working with her teammates. She never shut anything out. She was always willing to try. And so I made sure I encouraged her by noting things that were going well. After a math lesson was over, I'd give her a thumbs up or I'd stop by later or I'd put a little note in her mailbox and say, "I saw a lot of busy workers when I went past your room today." Just to let her know that I was noticing and appreciating what was happening. She would say, "We haven't had any behavior problems and everybody's been getting their work done!" or "Look how well they did on this quiz!" She was noticing that she was well planned and that she felt comfortable and confident when she was working.

Robin, elementary math coach

The positive relationships coaches have with teachers often compete with other relationships and other voices in the school and school district. The teachers' lounge is a notorious locus for stories and complaints about the obstacles to working in the system or teaching certain students. When a respected veteran teacher, for example, consoles a novice teacher about a lesson gone awry with messages about the overwhelming impediments to learning posed by the environment, the verbal persuasion may drive down the novice teacher's sense of self-efficacy and work at cross purposes to the coaching agenda. Bandura (1994) noted that it is far easier to discourage someone with our words than to encourage them. The wrong words spoken at the wrong time can undermine confidence and produce disappointing results. That is why design conversations often include discussion of how teachers can defuse and redirect such discouraging inputs. The same approaches that evocative coaches use to reframe stories, process emotions, and elevate energies can be used by teachers in casual conversations to shift organizational realities. Asking people to describe their best experiences, what works in their classrooms, and what got them into teaching in the first place are ways to turn the tables on the downward spiral. For coaching to transform schools, evocative conversations must spread to all organizational levels.

Positive relationships have the most influence on self-efficacy when they are viewed as having credibility, trustworthiness, and expertise (Bandura, 1997). How coaches carry and conduct ourselves is therefore an important part of building teacher self-efficacy. When coaches are known to be effective educators, this may increase the impact of our commendations. So, too, when coaches come across as mature and respectful in our demeanor. Verbal persuasion alone is limited in its power to create enduring increases in perceived efficacy, but it can increase initiative and bolster self-change when it comes on good authority and is within realistic bounds. As Bandura (1997) noted:

> To the extent that persuasive boosts in perceived efficacy lead people to try hard enough to succeed, self-affirming beliefs promote development of skills and a sense of personal efficacy. . . . To raise unrealistic beliefs of personal capabilities, however, only invites failure that will discredit the persuaders and further undermine the recipients' beliefs in their capabilities. (p. 101)

Positive relationships that increase self-efficacy strike a balance between challenging people too much and not challenging them enough. Evocative coaches know how to do that with the teachers we work with. There is no one-size-fits-all formula. Depending upon where teachers stand in the change process, from still thinking about it to taking action, evocative coaches work with teachers to pursue their inherent ambitions, to set appropriate goals, to work through setbacks, and to identify the relevant skills to be learned over time. When this happens, the coaching relationship becomes a wellspring of inspiration, ideation, and innovation. It becomes the kind of relationship that evokes willingness, readiness, and ability to change.

Positive Energy and Emotions

One reason that positive relationships are so effective with motivation and movement is that they build positive energy and emotion. We saw this in our discussion of the five principles of appreciative inquiry in Chapter Five. Positive energy and emotions are not just matters of attitude and self-talk. They are also cooked up through positive conversations and interactions with other people. Once that happens, once teachers are feeling good, research indicates that all kinds of good things follow (Fredrickson, 2009). Teachers become:

- More receptive and creative
- More interested in learning new ways of doing things
- More trusting and connected to others
- More aspirational and future oriented
- More curious and innovative
- More resilient and persistent
- More positive and friendly
- More patient and helpful
- More relaxed and fun loving

That is why we spend so much time assisting teachers to feel good about their experiences and capabilities. Even when things don't work out the way they would like, we want teachers to appreciate the richness of their experiences and the reach of their capabilities. We want them to have a felt sense of excitement regarding the contribution they can make with their students. When the feeling is right, action follows. When the feeling is off, resistance or retreat follows. If teachers are filled with stress or anxiety, for example, about trying a particular approach or teaching a particular lesson, then their willingness and success are sure to suffer. If teachers are filled with anticipation and vitality, however, then their confidence and self-efficacy are sure to soar. That is what we hope for through evocative coaching sessions: we want teachers to recognize, understand, and leverage their emotions in the pursuit of doable strategies that work.

This was Bandura's (1997) point about the impact of physiological and affective states on self-efficacy. Feelings matter. Butterflies in our stomach and quivering hands lower self-efficacy. Energy in our body and a smiling face support self-efficacy. Understanding this, evocative coaches assist teachers to become physically and emotionally comfortable with, rather than intimidated by, the prospect of changing their approach. All the data in the world will be for naught if a teacher's physical sensations and emotional reactions are negative. There is a reason why the word *motion* is embedded in the word *emotion*. The two are integrally related. When we elevate our emotions, we get into motion. Similarly, when we get into motion, we elevate our emotions. Mental and physical pathways are integrally interconnected (Pearsall, 1998). The brain changes as the body works (Rock & Page, 2009). Humorist and stress coach Loretta LaRoche (1998) points out that if we get our bodies to smile or laugh out loud, sooner or later our minds will decide that we must be happy. It is not always clear which comes first, the emotion or the motion, but it is clear that coaches have to work with both if we hope to increase teacher self-efficacy.

If stress is defined as stimulation, then distress represents either too much or too little stimulation. The former provokes anxiety while the latter produces boredom. In the extreme, both are distressing to the point of impaired performance and disability. *Eustress*, literally defined as "good stress," is when we are engaged in an activity but not overwhelmed, in control of our experience but not bored. Psychologist Mihaly Csikszentmihalyi (1997) has referred to this threshold level of stress as "flow." This is the sweet spot that evocative coaches seek to hit with teachers, both during the coaching conversation itself—challenging teachers to stretch their thinking and feeling, while being affirmative and empathetic to avoid distress—and after the coaching conversation is completed, as teachers actively pursue new possibilities and experiment with new designs. Giving respectful attention and understanding to physiological and affective states, both during and between coaching sessions, can assist coaches and teachers in finding that sweet spot.

When teachers have trouble finding the right balance, perhaps due to a preponderance of negative energy and emotion, it is important to not minimize or dispute their feelings. Such confrontations invalidate and discredit teacher experiences and make matters worse. Instead, evocative coaches will want to return to the Story–Empathy dance, exploring new vantage points and communicating an understanding of a teacher's core feelings and underlying needs. Some teachers will appreciate the invitation to check in on their physiological and affective states, getting a sense of how and where their emotions are manifesting in their bodies and gently listening to what those "felt senses" are trying to say. This process, known as "focusing" (Gendlin, 1981), can help teachers develop a positive relationship with their negative feelings.

Assisting teachers to notice, understand, accept, and appreciate what is happening on an emotional level while they are experimenting with behavior change helps them to discover and claim the things that fill them with energy and hope. Self-efficacy increases as teachers feel connected to themselves in positive ways. Instead of forcing themselves to do things that generate distress, which usually means doing things poorly, evocative coaches encourage teachers to design action-learning experiments that are within the liminal threshold of their abilities. When teachers are empowered to design action-learning experiments that work for them—when the locus of control shifts from the external to the internal frame—energy and emotions become more positive and the prospects for change increase proportionally.

Positive Images

There is abundant evidence that visual and mental images impact both motivation and movement. The observation of successful role models and the visualization of successful personal achievement are tried and true methods when it comes to performance improvement. Athletes have long recognized and worked with the dynamics of "developing positive pictures" to relax the mind and to influence how their bodies respond to a set of circumstances (Lynch & Scott, 1999). There is a mind-body connection that can be cultivated and leveraged for peak performance in any area of interest, including the classroom. Evocative coaches ply this dynamic to facilitate teacher learning and growth. We want teachers to know what success looks like and to imagine their own successful handling of situations.

Research indicates that positive images and positive self-monitoring are particularly effective ways to facilitate change. In one experiment, Kirschenbaum (1984) compared a set of bowlers who received lessons on effective bowling and whose performances were then videotaped as a learning tool. The bowlers were divided into two groups to watch clips of their performances. One group was shown only their positive moments, times when they hit the mark. This group was told to notice what they were doing right and to build on that. The other group was shown only their negative moments, times when they missed the mark. This group was told to notice what they were doing wrong and to correct that. Both groups improved their performances after watching the video clips, but the group shown only positive images evidenced significantly more improvement than the group shown only negative images. And the most unskilled bowlers who watched only their positive moments evidenced the most improvement (more than 100 percent) of all the subgroups. Since then, similar results have been obtained in other settings, and neuroscientists have documented how positive visual and mental images change the brain (Begley, 2007; Rock & Page, 2009; Thatchenkery & Metzker, 2006). It is not just that positive images have a lot of technical value; it is also, and more important, that positive images bolster self-efficacy such that we become more centered, confident, and perseverant in our ability to figure out ways to be successful.

> *By rehearsing and focusing with visualization correctly, you not only prepare for your best performance, you also are able to plan for and offset potential speed bumps along the way.*
>
> *Jerry Lynch and Warren Scott (1999, p. 34)*

The impact of positive images underlies Bandura's (1997) discussion of how vicarious experiences support self-efficacy. The more exposure we have to people successfully doing a target activity, such as teaching a particular subject or a particular group of students, the more we come to believe that it is possible for us to do that as well. Positivity is infectious. What we see gets internalized and actualized. Vicarious experiences become mental images that stimulate and change the brain as though we ourselves were doing the activity. When we observe examples of successful performance by multiple people we trust and identify with, we come away with new ideas and an affirmative sense of possibility. We find ourselves thinking:

- "This must not be so hard."
- "People are making this work here."
- "If they can do it, I can do it."

From there, it doesn't take long before we start trying things out for ourselves and designing our own strategies for doing things better. Repeating our prototypes and experiments on multiple occasions can then make new behaviors an integral part of our way of being and doing (Deutschman, 2007).

Two preconditions must be met for role models to become positive images with positive effects: similarity and collegiality. The more similar an observer perceives a role model to be, the greater the impact on self-efficacy. When a role model with whom an observer identifies closely performs well, self-efficacy is enhanced. When such a role model struggles or has great difficulty with a task, self-efficacy is damaged. Evocative coaches therefore pay attention to both the perceived similarity and the competence of role models. We want them to be approachable and to do well.

We also want role models to have a collegial, high-trust relationship with the observer. In the absence of a positive relationship, even successful role models can generate negative associations and images. When teachers feel threatened by or don't want to observe role models, evocative coaches respond with empathy rather than force. Teachers may be afraid of being embarrassed, for example, or they may not have developed sufficient trust in the coach to make themselves vulnerable in this way. Evocative coaches take pains to avoid such counterproductive dynamics. We never take a know-it-all or I-can-do-it-better attitude. We also avoid the implication that there is only one right way to teach a lesson. We make clear that observing positive role models is but one way among many to gain ideas and confidence for the planning and conduct of lessons. It increases awareness and provides grist for the mill in future coaching sessions. Role models are not instructing or demonstrating the correct way to do something. The point of classroom demonstrations is for coaches and teachers to have a good time together as they plan, handle, and reflect on the activities. They are opportunities for inspiration, exploration, and collaboration. If those dynamics do not characterize the experience, coaches can end up doing more harm than good.

Suzanne finally agreed to let me model a component of the curriculum we were implementing with her ninth-grade English students (after lying to a supervisor in my presence that I had never offered to do so). "But why just a component of the lesson?" asked Suzanne, "You might as well teach the whole ninety-minute block." When I showed Suzanne my lesson plans for the day, she replied flatly, "Oh, they'll never be able to do all that." But it went really well. Maybe a little *too* well. The students were busy and engaged from bell to bell. At the end of the lesson, they *applauded*. I told them, "No, don't applaud, really, please don't applaud." In the wake of the lesson, my relationship with Suzanne has become even more strained. Although I was painfully aware of what Suzanne's low expectations were costing the students, my attempt to show Suzanne a better way may have been received as an attempt to show her up.

Melissa, high school literacy coach

In addition to observing positive role models, there are many other ways to evoke positive images in teachers' minds. The Appreciative Interview Protocol, for example, as we saw in Chapter Five, works because it calls to mind successful past experiences. The more vivid the story, the more vivid the image and the more power it has to bolster self-efficacy. Once again there is a brain-based link to why this works. When coaches and teachers exchange best experience stories as to strategies they have successfully worked with or used in the past, teachers have a sense of temporality, as though those experiences are being viewed in the present moment (Brown, 1990). The positive images stimulate the brain as if those experiences were happening again. The images become a form of vicarious experience that can positively affect performance. Positive images have the same effect when they flow from looking forward to a positive future. Four matched groups of world-class Soviet athletes, in preparation for the 1980 Winter Olympic Games, followed different training regimens. Each group had a different mix of physical and mental training (100/0, 75/25, 50/50, and 25/75). There was a direct correlation between the amount of time spent in mental training, including relaxation and visualization, and the degree of performance improvement in their sport. The group that spent 75 percent of their time visualizing their performance behaviors and outcomes and only 25 percent of their time in strenuous physical training improved the most of all (Garfield, 1984, p. 16).

Positive mental imagery, whether cultivated through recollection or anticipation, enhances motivation and movement. That is why evocative coaching conversations may include creative, psychosomatic exercises that assist teachers to cook up and connect with such imagery. It may be human nature to notice, analyze, and solve problems, but that does not make it the best or most effective strategy to use. Indeed, tackling problems head on often provokes discouragement and resistance because the brain becomes painfully aware of what is wrong. Such awareness is demotivating and debilitating, immobilizes people, and reduces brain plasticity—the ability of the brain to change and rewire its synapses over time (Rock & Page, 2009). Instead, evocative coaches take a different approach. We inquire into strengths, reframe problems as opportunities (Deutschman, 2007), and cultivate positive energy through relaxation and visualization exercises. Coaching sessions can include, for example, times when teachers close their eyes, breathe deeply, relax their bodies, imagine new behaviors, visualize different approaches, and anticipate positive outcomes. Such exercises are especially important as teachers engage in design thinking and design conversations. The clearer the picture of what those designs look like at their very best, the more successful teachers will be when it comes time to experiment with putting those designs into practice.

Positive Actions

"Nothing breeds success like success," the old saying goes. Although positive actions can be viewed as the desired effect of positive relationships, positive energy and emotions, and positive images, they can also be viewed as a causal agent. The single most powerful source of efficacy-relevant information is mastery experiences (Bandura, 1997). Accomplishing a desired task does more than anything else to cultivate positivity and successful, perseverant effort. With teachers, self-efficacy beliefs are raised, for example, when they witness improvements in student performances as a result of their teaching. This contributes to optimism that future performances will likely be proficient, resulting in greater effort and persistence (Guskey, 1988; Ross, 1992; Tschannen-Moran et al., 1998). The more often teachers experience success as a result of their actions, the better they will feel about themselves and about the coaching relationship. As a result, they become more willing to attempt even more challenging and creative initiatives over time.

Since positive actions are both cause and effect vis-à-vis self-efficacy, evocative coaches collaborate with teachers on designing actions that have a high probability of success. We want teachers to experience quick wins because these help teachers stay on the winning path over time. Although it is valuable for experimental designs to be research based, it is essential for them to be warmly embraced. Even the most proven of educational methods will not work if teachers do not accept and feel confident about using them. Conversely, even the most unconventional of methods can be made to work when teachers have pride of ownership and a high degree of confidence in their ability to make them work. The dance between standardization and personalization is an integral part of evocative coaching, with the primary criteria being the intended outcomes and the self-efficacy of teachers. When the outcomes align with the standards designed to encourage the achievement of every student, and when the enthusiasm and confidence of teachers are high regarding the strategies they want to attempt, then the design work of evocative coaching is well underway.

To do this dance, evocative coaches use a combination of objective and intuitive data to provide transformational feedback to teachers through the process of designing and implementing action-learning strategies. Teachers easily lose sight of their progress when they have setbacks or don't reach their goals as quickly as they would like. On such occasions, it is important for evocative coaches to go back to discovering strengths and observing vitalities. Things may not have gone as a teacher might like, but what can we celebrate that did go right? An unfailingly positive orientation on the part of the coach is an essential part of evocative coaching. We assist teachers to remember past success, and we commend teachers for even the most nascent and modest of accomplishments in each and every coaching conversation. That is especially important when teachers have experienced a situation that they would frame as a setback or failure; on such occasions, evocative coaches assist teachers to reframe such stories through story listening and to turn such experiences into opportunities for authentic celebration and mourning.

Strengths-based questions such as these avoid catastrophizing setbacks and condemning teachers:

- What parts of the experience can we celebrate?
- What skills were you using well?
- What approaches were working in some ways or for some students?
- What hopes did you have for this lesson?
- What helped you to get through it?
- What might have happened if you had chosen to do something differently?
- What would you say is the moral of the story?
- How can you build on this experience for even better results next time?

By mining difficult experiences for their positive core, evocative coaches can reconnect teachers with their sense of self-efficacy.

When teachers come up with new ideas they would like to experiment with in the classroom, it is important for coaches to interview them regarding their confidence level with that approach. If teachers set overly complex experiments or overly ambitious goals, they may experience more setbacks than successes, which can put them on a downward spiral. Lowering self-efficacy in this way can have long-lasting, negative effects and is to be avoided whenever possible.

Coaches should be careful to not unduly influence teachers in the setting of behavioral strategies with our ideas, energy, and enthusiasm. This can result in teachers not being honest about their confidence level or taking on strategies that are more important to the coach than to the teacher. Avoid making suggestions that teachers can interpret as being what the coach wants them to do or thinks they *should* do. When teachers ask for a suggestion, it is better to brainstorm ideas together than to make either a pronouncement or a prescription. By developing and asking teachers to choose from a universe of possibilities, the decision making remains in their hands, where it belongs.

When I first started working with Rosa she confided in me that reading and writing were her least favorite areas of teaching. English is a second language for her and she'd struggled so much in learning English that she didn't feel confident in passing those skills along to her students. She said that she didn't know how to structure the time during the literacy block, so her lessons felt choppy and she didn't think she was doing any part of it well. We came up with a lot of ideas together and once she picked a strategy she would try it out right away. We worked on putting a structure into place for the literacy block. Then I modeled some of the strategies we had talked about with the grade-level team. She got really excited because right away she saw improvement in her lessons and the student's response in terms of their excitement about reading and the types of language they were using to discuss the reading.

Julie, elementary literacy coach

Repeating new behaviors helps teachers to be successful and to become more confident because skills and performance improvement is neither a linear nor terminal process; it is an ongoing and iterative process with unanticipated loops, twists, and turns (Deutschman, 2007). New skills and habits of mind need to be learned, practiced, and mastered, and that won't happen from one or two attempts. Repetition is the key. We certainly do not use repetition to drill things into teachers that they don't want to learn. We focus, instead, on the intrinsic motivation and self-efficacy of teachers in order to discern and co-construct those scenarios where repetition becomes an ally of change. When the relationship is right and the desire is there, "Practice, practice, practice" ends up being adopted as a positive way for moving forward. What methods represent good practice? What approaches fit best with an individual teacher's interests and abilities? Just because a new approach doesn't work the first time does not mean it won't work the next time. Knowing when to try again and when to move on to a different approach is another aspect of the evocative coaching dance. Coaching is about innovation—assisting teachers to change and to try new things in the service of student achievement as well as personal and professional development. When the relationship, energy, emotions, and images are right, positive strategies and actions can emerge. Evocative coaching assists teachers to stay on a positive path of development.

Coaching Tools for Design Thinking

As we have seen, it is the work of evocative coaching to help teachers achieve desired outcomes and enhance their quality of life. To do this, coaches must not only inspire teachers, we must also assist teachers to come up with new ideas and to implement those ideas in the classroom. We must, in other words, engage teachers in design thinking. Until and unless teachers move from possibility to prototype to practice, until and unless teachers come to experiment with and appropriate new behaviors, evocative coaching will not have realized its full potential. Evocative coaches therefore strive to make sure that teachers come away from each coaching session with a clear understanding of what they will focus on and/or do differently in the days and weeks ahead. That represents the "homework" that comes out of coaching. To develop such behavioral strategies, evocative coaches engage teachers in brainstorming design ideas, exploring inertia, and designing S-M-A-R-T action-learning experiments. Each of these is considered in turn.

Brainstorming Design Ideas

Brainstorming design ideas is the first coaching task when assisting teachers to approach their present possibilities. If coaching fails to generate new ideas for moving forward, then coaching fails to be evocative. Yet it is not always easy to engage teachers in brainstorming. When coaches are perceived to have a lot of instructional expertise and pedagogical prowess, teachers ask coaches to give them the answers and tell them what to do. What could be simpler than listening to the expert, getting advice, hearing how to solve problems, and adopting the suggestions? As we have seen, for all its simplicity and familiarity, such didactic approaches are fraught with hazards when facilitating adult learning and lasting behavior change. That is why evocative coaches redirect such requests, and even our own desire to add value to a design conversation, by proposing a brainstorming session in which we can work together with teachers to come up with ideas. By co-creating multiple possibilities in this way, teachers remain active and empowered in the search for more effective instructional approaches. Coaches are confirmed as one voice among many on the way to a teacher's professional mastery.

There is a difference between brainstorming ideas and sharing information, and evocative coaches keep that distinction in mind. When teachers pose a procedural question, for instance, such as how to file a grade report, how to get reimbursed for out-of-pocket expenses, or how to access policy manuals, it is best to just provide that information if the coach knows the answer. Nothing is more frustrating than the appearance of a cat-and-mouse game, where the coach is apparently withholding information to see if teachers will come up with it on their own. It can even be frustrating for coaches to express empathy at these points, unless there are chronic and widespread contributing factors (which could be an excellent focus for brainstorming). As one teacher noted, "It is infuriating to receive empathy when I need information." Notwithstanding all that has been said about the limits of didactic approaches and expert advice, there are times to just tell teachers what they want to know. There is no hard and fast rule for identifying those times, but the concept of brief and facilitative answers comes into play. If teachers ask a question and we proceed to take over the conversation for extended periods of time, if the energy shifts from one of co-creation to one of coach-creation, then that was probably an instance when brainstorming ideas as to how teachers could figure that out for themselves would have worked better and been more in keeping with the evocative coaching model. For the substantive work of design thinking, we prefer brainstorming because it generates new and better ways of doing things.

Brainstorming, the playful and rapid generation of possibilities, is an essential part of how evocative coaching conversations move teachers forward. The more often we engage in brainstorming with teachers and the more ideas the process generates, the more we will facilitate teacher learning, movement, growth, and change. Brainstorming helps teachers to get out of their own way, to think outside the box, to come up with innovative ideas, and to entertain notions they might not otherwise consider. It is a great way to break through bottlenecks and infuse strategies with energy.

If at first an idea is not absurd then there is no hope for it.

Albert Einstein

Tom Kelley (2001), the general manager of IDEO, a leading design consultancy based in Palo Alto, California, and affiliated with the new Stanford d.school (d. for design), identified "seven secrets for better brainstorming" in his book *The Art of Innovation*:

1. *Sharpen the focus.* Edgy is better than fuzzy. Clarify and focus the topic on what you are trying to accomplish with the end user. Getting teachers to focus on the needs of specific students and

classes will generate more and better ideas than generic conversations about improving instructional strategies.

2. *Set playful rules.* Don't start to critique, evaluate, or debate ideas until the brainstorming session is done. Bold, wild, and exaggerated ideas are all encouraged when brainstorming.

3. *Number your ideas.* Identify a minimum number of ideas you want to generate and then number them as you go along. Don't be afraid to shoot for big numbers. At IDEO, they report that a team can usually come up with at least a hundred ideas in an hour.

4. *Build and jump.* Not every idea has to be unique. Build on each other's ideas. Introduce small variations. Combine and expand on ideas. Or take a jump, either back to something that came before or forward to something new that begins to pop.

5. *Leverage the space.* Write down the flow of ideas in a visible medium and make your notes part of the space. This can be extremely low-tech, using Post-it notes and folders or pads of paper with cluster diagrams. When people reenter that space and see the notes, they recapture the mindset that emerged in the first place. The space remembers.

6. *Stretch your mental muscles.* Warm up with fast-paced word games or brainstorm something completely off topic, like ten different brands of soda, to get the mind in brainstorming mode.

7. *Get physical.* Good brainstorms are also "bodystorms." Don't just sit there and talk, move around, act out, role play, dramatize, sketch, diagram, point, or do whatever else will stimulate the generation of new ideas. (Adapted from Kelley, 2001, pp. 56–62)

Coaches and teachers can easily apply these seven secrets for better brainstorming in coaching sessions. In design discussions, evocative coaches watch for brainstorming opportunities. Seizing the moment, coaches can propose a time of brainstorming in which coaches and teachers work together to generate ideas until they have come up with six or more. Teachers are often relieved to learn that they do not have to come up with all the ideas themselves. Such an approach also gives teachers time to think when the coach is putting an idea on the table. From the coach's vantage point, brainstorming is a way to put forward ideas that teachers might never come up with on their own or might otherwise resist, without coming across as either authoritative or prescriptive. Warming up, writing things down, keeping ideas visible in the coaching space from session to session, and engaging our bodies are all good suggestions for coaches and teachers to employ. Cluster diagrams can facilitate brainstorming because of how they show and stimulate relationships between ideas. Once teachers get used to brainstorming during coaching sessions, they may even start proposing it themselves. That is because brainstorming is both fun and productive, albeit challenging and hard work. To come up with so many creative possibilities in a relatively short period of time stretches the mind and the conversation beyond its normal limits. Such stretching capitalizes on and enhances teachers' willingness to change.

> *When conversation between a coach and a teacher comes alive, ideas can bounce around like balls in a pinball machine, and people can start to communicate so well that it becomes difficult to see where one person's thoughts end and another's begin.*
>
> *Jim Knight (2007, p. 46)*

Designing experiments without brainstorming can cut short opportunities for both teacher motivation and success. The operational task is to generate and test out multiple ideas for skill and performance improvements instead of getting wedded too quickly to a single course of action. Timing is an important consideration when it comes to brainstorming in coaching sessions. Brainstorming too early can overwhelm teachers and provoke resistance. Failing to brainstorm at all can squander the potential of the moment, either because no new possibilities are generated or because one possibility takes over the energy of the conversation before others are considered. Running with the first idea that comes up limits professional development and may even send teachers in the wrong direction. As French philosopher Émile Chartier once quipped, "Nothing is as dangerous as an idea when it is the only one you have" (in O'Hanlon & Beadle, 1997, p. 31).

We had a lot of conversations, even just standing in the hall in the morning when kids were coming in the building for five or ten minutes. Just brainstorming things or sending an e-mail saying, "Oh, I thought of this" or "When you start that unit next week, think of this." I'd send an e-mail and pretty soon somebody would run down to my office and say, "Oh, show me what it is. I want to see!" So I would show them and pretty soon I'd have somebody else down there or somebody else would send me an e-mail and say, "Hey, I want to see it too!" They got that excited about it because I would never say, "You did it wrong." I was just encouraging. I listened to them and I'd clarify so I was sure I understood what they were talking about.

Robin, elementary math coach

Exploring Inertia

In many respects, design thinking and evocative coaching can both be framed as processes for shifting inertia. We do not want to push or force teachers to change, we want to invite and inspire them to make that move for themselves. And that starts, as we have seen, with an empathetic understanding of current conditions and practices. Things are the way they are, and people are doing what they are doing, for a reason. If teachers or administrators could make everything better on their own, by snapping their fingers, they would have done so long ago and there would be no need for the intervention or assistance of coaches. For better or for worse, that is not the case, so mentoring and coaching have both been adopted as increasingly popular and common approaches for facilitating improvement with underperforming teachers. When seasoned and competent teachers take novice or underperforming teachers under their wings, as mentors or peer-development partners, great opportunity exists to apply the principles and practices of evocative coaching. Unfortunately, that is not always the case and such interventions—based primarily on problem solving and advice giving—may not generate the desired improvements in teacher performance (Lipton & Wellman, 2003, p. 26). When teachers fail to improve, failed mentoring or coaching may become a basis for teacher dismissal rather than a basis for changing our stance and approach.

The evocative coaching model promises to help more teachers make greater improvements because of how Story–Empathy–Inquiry–Design facilitates motivation and movement as a design thinking process. The adroit use of the evocative coaching model helps to dislodge what Kegan and Lahey (2009) describe as our natural "immunity to change." Teachers who get attached to underperformance do so as a result of a constellation of underlying relational, emotional, motivational, cultural, and political factors. No real progress can be made until teachers move beyond those factors. Based on our experience, evocative coaching can assist teachers to do just that. Experiences get reframed, emotions get understood, and energies get elevated. When that happens, when teachers get infused with positivity, they leap at the suggestion to do creative brainstorming of new ideas and they look forward to designing and conducting the requisite action-learning experiments. The whole experience is fun and productive. Coaches may even find it challenging to shut down a brainstorming process. There is that much energy and enthusiasm.

Sometimes, however, brainstorming falls flat and teachers fail to thrive. They may not participate wholeheartedly, or even at all; they can't or won't come up with any or hardly any new ideas. There is just too much inertia and attachment to the status quo. When that happens, the attempt at brainstorming can become a painful experience. Teachers may view the process and the coach with suspicion. No one is having any fun, and the chances of success are slim to none. At such critical junctures it is time for coaches to return to Story–Empathy–Inquiry. Evocative coaches do not view and disparage uncooperative behavior as a sign that there's something wrong with the teacher; we view it as a sign that there is something wrong with the approach we are taking. If teachers are not choosing to dance with us, evocative coaches assume that teachers have good reasons for sitting tight and doing just what they are doing. Until those reasons are understood, accepted, and appreciated, until teachers come into a compassionate understanding of the stories, judgments, feelings, and needs that surround their inertia, no transformation is possible and no improvement is likely. Fortunately, all teachers have that capacity.

In addition to story listening and expressing empathy using the tools introduced earlier in this book, another tool that coaches can use for exploring inertia is the "immunity to change map" process developed by Kegan and Lahey (2009). If teachers are willing to talk honestly about what is going on with them using the four questions on the map (see Figure 6.1 for an example), and if they are willing to test their big assumptions, Kegan and Lahey demonstrate how they can move from being unconsciously "immune" to change to being consciously "released" from the hidden, self-protective attachments that have been holding them back. That is what distinguishes this process from problem solving. It is not designed to solve problems; it is rather designed to facilitate a deeper understanding of our attachment to the status quo (a form of Story–Empathy) so that different decisions can be made if we so choose to do so (a form of Inquiry–Design). Kegan and Lahey assert that our current mindsets are managing our anxieties and concerns brilliantly—keeping things right where they are and just the way they are for good reasons—and that in order to move forward and be successful with change we must become conscious of how these "immune systems" are operating.

The simplicity of the map, a four-column worksheet based on four questions, belies its sophistication and power as to the things it gets people to think about. The first column asks the question, "What are you committed to doing that would make you more successful?" To get on the map, these "visible commitments" or "improvement goals" should meet four criteria: (1) they should be viewed as true by the person or persons filling out the worksheet; (2) they should be viewed as chosen by them, rather than as assigned or imposed by someone else; (3) they should be viewed as areas where there is room for improvement; and (4) they should be viewed as important by them. Even teachers with great inertia have some consciousness of the things they try to do for teaching success. These are the things that go in column 1.

FIGURE 6.1. IMMUNITY MAP WORKSHEET

Name: Anna Bradley   Date: March 16

Commitment (Improvement Goals)	Doing/Not Doing Instead (Behaviors that work against the goals)	Hidden Competing Commitments	Big Assumptions
I am committed to providing engaging and meaningful instruction to my students to spark their interest in and facility with French. I am committed to showing up well prepared for every lesson. I am committed to showing up fully present and engaged for every lesson.	I rely on tried-and-true activities and set patterns of instruction for most class periods. I stand at the front of the room for much of the class period. I spend more time talking than encouraging the students to talk or work independently.	Worry Box: I'm worried that if students are more active then it will create a chaotic environment, and that problematic students will interfere with the learning of others. I'm concerned I won't cover all of the material. I want to maintain order and stay in control of my classroom. I want to demonstrate my facility with teaching French. I want to limit the time I spend planning so that I don't overwork and burn out.	If I fall behind on my pacing guide, I'll never catch up. If I don't cover all of the material, the students won't be well prepared to go on in French. If the students do the talking, they won't get the information they need. If I give the students more responsibility, they may practice the wrong things and reinforce erroneous information. If these things happen I will lose the respect of my colleagues and administrators.

Source: Adapted from Kegan and Lahey (2009).

The second column asks the question, "What are you actually doing or not doing that works against those first column commitments?" Teachers may state, for example, that lesson planning is important (a column 1 commitment) but that they only get around to it half the time (a column 2 behavior). The more specific and observational the better when it comes to the items in the second column. One should be able to capture these behaviors (or the lack thereof) on a video camera. The point is to notice and become aware of these behaviors, not to figure out what to do about them or why they are happening.

The third column asks the question, "What are the hidden or competing commitments that keep the column 2 behaviors in place?" Once again, we are not trying to change anything. We are trying to increase awareness of and explore the attachments that tether us to whatever we are doing now. On the one hand, we say we want to do the things in column 1. On the other hand, we are actually doing and not doing the things in column 2. Why is that? What commitments fuel those column 2 behaviors? To get at the hidden or competing commitments, Kegan and Lahey (2009) suggest that we may want to identify a list of worries in column 3 that arise when we imagine trying to do just the opposite of the things in column 2. These worries, in the "Worry Box," can then be framed as commitments to keep those things that one is worried about from occurring. Column 3 makes sense of the column 2 behaviors, often as an outgrowth of our need for protection and security.

The fourth column asks the question, "What are the big assumptions that underlie those column three commitments?" In other words, "What mindsets keep this system in place?" These big assumptions or mindsets make sense of the column 3 commitments and make further sense of the column 2 behaviors, often involving a mix of relational, emotional, motivational, and political factors. To identify the big assumptions, one can take each item in column 3 and complete the following sentence: "I assume that if I did not stay committed to _____, then something bad will happen—and not just something a little bad, but something BTB (Big-Time Bad)." Write down that BTB as a big assumption. Such assumptions display a certain view of the world, a certain mindset, and explain how column 3 commitments help to avoid the BTB conclusion.

At this point, with a much greater understanding of our "immunity to change," Kegan and Lahey suggest that people are better able to explore the reality of their big assumptions by designing and conducting field tests. How do our fears hold up in the real world? What nuances can we discover? What happens if we push the envelope with a gentle nudge? To answer such questions through field testing, Kegan and Lahey recommend several criteria: the tests must be safe, modest, actionable, researcher-like (interested in getting data, not results), and focused on only one big assumption at a time. After doing a test and collecting data, it is important to generate multiple interpretations of the data in order to decide what of the big assumption is worth keeping and what is worth letting go. Through repeated testing of our big assumptions in this way, we can release our attachment to the status quo, shift inertia, and facilitate readiness to change.

Figure 6.1 represents a completed Immunity Map Worksheet for Anna Bradley, whom we met in Chapter Five, a teacher whose visible commitments included varying the types of activities she uses and moving around the room more frequently. After several weeks, however, Anna wasn't making much progress toward these goals. She and her coach would design action-learning experiments during their coaching sessions, but when she got to her classroom she didn't get around to doing them. Old habits die hard. She expressed her frustration to her coach. She was discouraged about her apparent inability to follow through on her commitments. Through the Immunity Map, Anna discovered that she had commitments to maintaining order in her classroom, staying on her pacing guide, and limiting the time she spent in planning that were competing with her commitment to vary her instruction and move around the room. Once she examined the Big Assumptions behind the seeming incompatibility of these two sets of commitments, she saw ways to redesign her experiments so as to field test her Big Assumptions one at a time. This helped Anna to take action and move forward.

Framing Innovations as Experiments

However we get there, whether immediately upon the heels of a creative brainstorming process (for teachers ready to change) or after looping back to express empathy, increase awareness, and shift inertia (for teachers not ready to change), the final stages in the design thinking process are to design, map out, and then to conduct action-learning experiments that will assist teachers to learn more about themselves and about how they can be successful in life and work. Such initiatives are verbal commitments with a twist: they represent hypotheses that teachers want to test out rather than plans that teachers have to make work. The difference is subtle but significant. Teachers are all too familiar with the rolling out of plans that they did not create. They are also familiar with the frustrations that come from not being able to implement such plans successfully. Failed school improvement plans quickly undermine self-efficacy and make inertia even weightier. The framing of new initiatives as experiments conveys a very different energy. There is no way to fail at an experiment of one's own choosing. Whether or not things work as expected, the data gathered are intrinsically interesting, useful, and valuable. When scientists conduct experiments, they engage in "win-learn" rather than "win-lose" activities; that is how we want teachers to view their activities in the living laboratory of the classroom. Data are collected, understandings are revised, and approaches are modified until things work and fit together through a process of "trial and correction." That is the approach we take when assisting teachers to master new skills through action-learning experiments. If something works, great! Try it again to see if it works again. If something doesn't work, great! Try it again or try it differently, based upon a new hypothesis, until something does work. Evocative coaches carry and communicate the conviction that teachers can always find things that work.

The process of "trial and correction" does not have to be taught. It is how human beings learn to walk. What has to be taught is framing professional learning processes as trial and correction rather than as "trial and error." Those first few tentative baby steps occur after months of watching other people walk upright. These role models provide a vicarious experience that awakens in toddlers the desire and ambition to walk. At the appropriate developmental moment, the role models begin to encourage the young ones. They stand the toddlers upright, hold their hands, and move them forward. With outstretched arms, they cheer and cajole until the brave youngsters take their first, unsupported steps. Those first few steps typically lead to two eventualities: falling down and rousing applause. Everyone present, including the child, smiles and laughs at those obviously awkward and relatively unsuccessful first attempts. There is no criticism or blame. There are no errors and no talk of failure. On the contrary, toddlers are cheered on, encouraged to try again and again until they master the art. Ironically, we seldom have more fun and get more cheers for walking than when we barely know how and often fall over. The joy is in the process of trial and correction, and so we remain steadfast in our attempts until success is achieved.

Scientists understand this joy as well. They call it "the scientific method." Identify a puzzle. Develop a theory. Test the theory. Fall down. Change the variables. Change the method. Change the theory, if necessary. But stick with the process until a discovery is made. One can almost feel the excitement. Many scientists report that they learn more from unexpected rather than expected developments. By coaching teachers to frame innovations as experiments and to positively reframe unexpected outcomes as valuable learning experiences, we enable them not only to bounce back from setbacks but also to avoid getting attached to the notion of "failure." Failure is not an option in learning, because failure never happens. Experiments may not work out as expected, but they always provide valuable data upon which we can design and build future experiments.

> We've got a saying around IDEO: "Fail often to succeed sooner." Failure is the flip side of risk taking, and if you don't risk, odds are you won't succeed.
>
> Tom Kelley (2001, p. 230)

It is important for teachers to be at choice in the design and planning of the experiments they want to conduct. Coaches risk generating resistance and jeopardizing teacher success when we do that work for teachers. Instead, we invite teachers to pick ideas they view as intrinsically interesting, important, valuable, enjoyable, and possible to conduct. If a large number of possibilities have been generated through brainstorming, encourage teachers to identify the top two or three that hold the most appeal. Each can be considered, briefly, before settling upon the one or two to develop further. Coaches may want to ask questions like:

- What ideas stand out as the best ideas? What attracts you to them?
- Which ones would push you the most?
- Which ones would be the most fun?
- What would it take to succeed with them?
- What do you hope to learn from them?
- What makes them worth pursuing?
- How do they compare to other approaches?
- How easy would they be to implement?
- What strengths might you leverage?
- What kind of an impact might they have?
- What ideas would never fly at this school? Which ideas stand a chance?
- When have you tried something like this before?
- Which ones do you want to try first?

Eventually, it will become clear as to what experiments teachers want to conduct. At that point, asking teachers, "On a scale of 0 to 10, how important would you say it is to conduct this experiment at this time?" can validate that teachers are contemplating something they really want to do. Once teachers pick a number, coaches can follow up with two questions:

1. What led you to pick X and not a lower number?
2. What would make it a higher number?

Such questions may lead teachers to either modify their ideas or to go off in entirely new directions. There is no point in designing unimportant action-learning experiments. They must be related to that larger, positive vision of who teachers are and where they want to go in the future. Experiments must also be grounded in the reality of what teachers know and have accomplished in the past. That is why evocative coaches spend so much time with Story–Empathy–Inquiry. Those phases of the evocative coaching process pour the foundation for aspiring, presencing, brainstorming, and experimenting. They assist teachers to enhance not only their effectiveness in the classroom but also their sense of meaning, learning, and joy in life.

They enable teachers to design innovations that will assist them to become more effective.

> *Teaching is such a rich and artful activity than no manual comes close to capturing all that is involved in the healthy, joyous, effective interactions between teachers and students.*
>
> *Jim Knight (2007, p. 29)*

Making Experiments S-M-A-R-T

Good action-learning experiments are S-M-A-R-T experiments, that is, they are Specific, Measurable, Attainable, Relevant, and Time bound. Teachers know what they are going to do differently in the wake of a coaching session when their designs meet the S-M-A-R-T test. Teachers are *specific* about *how* and *when* they will do *what* and with *whom* to test their theory and increase their level of success. Requirements for materials and resources are also specified. Setting a specific *time frame* for the experiments increases the likelihood that the experiments will happen. It is the difference between putting something on your schedule now versus "getting around to it" when there is time. The more detailed the specifics, the easier it is to *measure* and understand the results of experiments. Did they work out as expected or not? Inquiring minds want to know. To answer that question, teachers must be very clear as to what their experiments are designed to do and accomplish in the first place. S-M-A-R-T experiments, whether designed to test changes in awareness or behaviors, represent the "homework" that comes out of each and every coaching session. Such "homework" assists teachers to be more accountable in their path of development and helps coaches to be more supportive and responsive to teacher actions over time.

As we have learned from our discussion on motivation and movement, it is very important for teacher experiments to be *attainable* and *relevant*. Unless teachers feel confident in their ability to conduct an experiment, the experiment may not be attainable and may do more harm than good. Experiments typically represent incremental steps in the direction of a desired outcome, not quantum leaps that accomplish everything at once. "Time," it has been said, "was invented so everything doesn't happen at once." S-M-A-R-T experiments reflect that understanding of time. If teachers want to conduct particularly ambitious experiments, it is not the coach's place to say "No" or to get in the way. It is the coach's place, however, to check in on the reality of those experiments by asking, "On a scale of 0 to 10, how confident are you that you will be able to conduct this experiment as planned?" If we hear an answer of 7 or above, we can be reasonably confident that the teacher will follow through on the design. If we hear a lower number, or if the teacher's affect is not congruent with the number he or she picks, then we can ask the same two follow-up questions as when asking about importance:

1. What led you to pick X and not a lower number?
2. What would make it a higher number?

Both questions communicate the coach's certainty that teachers are already doing some things well and that they have the ability to design and successfully conduct experiments that will assist them to do more things better in the future. Encourage teachers to modify their experimental designs, changing their goals or aligning their environments, until their confidence and corresponding energy level is 7 or higher. Sometimes a small change will make a big difference. Other times teachers will want to scrap the experiment altogether and start over. The basic principle, when it comes to making experiments S-M-A-R-T is to not over-promise and underdeliver. When that happens, confidence is eroded and growth is stunted.

It is also important for experiments to be seen as relevant by teachers to their stated aspirations and possibilities. Teachers will not have enthusiasm for and should not be pushed to conduct "make work" experiments. The change process will be hindered if teachers go through the motions of learning without seeing how those motions may contribute to their personal growth and professional development in the classroom. Asking about the importance of an experiment using the 0 to 10 scale is one way to get at that. So, too, is talking about expected outcomes and designing a series of experiments that build on each other over time. "If this works, then we might try that" is a great conversation to have to in-crease the sense of an experiment's relevance. Be sure teachers understand that they may turn away at any point from an experiment. Teachers are always at choice. If they seem intrigued by a particular idea, but intimidated by the chal-lenge, keep working with them to make the experiment S-M-A-R-T. We want teachers to feel stretched but not so far outside their comfort zone as to be anx-ious and fearful. We want teachers to be "in the zone" and to have "flow" expe-riences (Csikszentmihalyi, 1990, 1997, 2000). Evocative coaches empower teachers to take on greater challenges than they might otherwise think are pos-sible, while encouraging a scaling back of experiments that are too far out of reach.

Great teachers are not great because they know what to do. Great teachers are great because they can always think of something else to do.

Stephen Barkley (2005, p. 155)

In the process of designing and conducting experiments, teachers should be encouraged to identify backup strategies and to modify procedures as necessary and appropriate. The reason we have put the word "homework" in quotes is because no experimental design ever takes precedence over teacher discretion. Conducting design experiments is more about innovation than implementation. They represent our best guess as to how things might work better, but the unexpected happens and improvements can always be made. When teachers understand that experiments are just that, experiments, then they will approach performance improvement with a sense of freedom and curiosity rather than of pressure and compulsion. They will not wait for the next coaching session to reflect on possible changes and to design new experiments. They will eagerly adopt that attitude for themselves in the way they handle their classrooms and the things they talk about with their colleagues.

Mapping Out S-M-A-R-T Experiments

Scientists design and conduct action-learning experiments for a living. In so doing, they have developed templates that help their experiments to be successful. Such templates typically involve:

- *Hypothesis:* An assertion that you want test or explore
- *Materials:* Things you need to conduct the experiment
- *Procedures:* How the experiment will be conducted
- *Observations:* What happens when the experiment is conducted
- *Recording:* How the observations are recorded in real time
- *Conclusions:* How the data are viewed as relating to the hypothesis

In working with the data and in drawing their conclusions, scientists test their results for statistical significance to guard against the possibility that the results emerged by chance. Although the S-M-A-R-T action-learning experiments designed through evocative coaching do not have to meet those same rigorous requirements, a design template can assist teachers to move into action by adding procedural clarity and reducing performance anxiety. We want teachers to conduct their experiments as prototypes and field tests. The design thinking mantra, "Fail often to succeed sooner" (Kelley, 2001, 2005) speaks to the task at hand. It is all about trial and correction. The Experimental Design Template captures the following elements of S-M-A-R-T action-learning experiments:

- *Ownership.* The teacher's name and the date the experiment was designed.
- *Focus.* Is this more of a professional or personal experiment? Evocative coaching works with both because the two realms impact and interact with each other.

- *Summarize experiment and state hypothesis.* In broad strokes, what will she (or he) do and what does she think will result from bringing a new awareness and/or trying a new approach in the classroom? Include theories regarding how the experiment might improve student learning and/or make her own life better.
- *Relevance to personal aspirations/professional standards.* How is the experiment related to a teacher's long-term, big-picture aspirations? How is it related, if at all, to professional standards?
- *Strategies or activities (specific as to what, where, and how).* Describe the details of the experiment itself. What will the teacher do and where/how will the teacher do it? Be as specific as possible.
- *Supporting systems and resources.* What and who does the teacher want to have on hand in order to conduct the experiment? Again, be as specific possible as to what the teacher requires and how the teacher wants to set up the supporting conditions.
- *Timeline.* When and how often will the experiment take place? If the timeline includes benchmarks or milestones before the next coaching session, make them explicit.
- *Confidence level.* How confident is the teacher, on a scale of 0 to 10, that she will be able to conduct the experiment? Revise the experiment, resources, and/or timeline until the teacher's confidence is 7 or higher.
- *Data collection and reporting.* How will the teacher observe, capture, and report on the results of the experiment? Will the coach be involved? Will the teacher collect her own data? If so, how? Will logs, video/audio recording, and/or reflective writing be used? If so, include any requisite equipment in the space for supporting systems and resources. Will other people provide feedback? If so, how will that information be registered and reviewed?

The Experimental Design Template in Figure 6.2 depicts an experiment designed by Jennifer Dalton, whom we met in Chapter Five as she sought to enrich the level of questioning in her classes. Jennifer wanted to build upon the insights she gleaned from her coaching conversation with Gwyn and to conduct an experiment to try out using a wider array of questions. She realized that she already had a video recording of a lesson on hand, and that gave her the idea that she could set up the equipment on her own and not have to wait for the next time that Gwyn was available to observe. Jennifer decided to conduct her own experiment, tallying the number and types of questions she asked. She also planned to watch for the level of student engagement as a result of her new questioning strategy.

The Experimental Design Template should not be understood as a set of talking points, although the items will certainly be talked about. The template's primary function is to serve as a writing tool to capture the details of action-learning

FIGURE 6.2. EXPERIMENTAL DESIGN TEMPLATE

Name: Jennifer Dalton   **Date:** Nov. 5   **Focus:** (Professional) Personal

Summarize Experiment and State Hypothesis:

I want to ask questions across the whole range of Bloom's Taxonomy because I think it will increase student engagement and learning. I also think I will enjoy the intellectual challenge of framing these questions.

Relevance to Personal Aspirations/Professional Standards:

Asking more high-level questions is directly aligned with my vision of being an outstanding teacher, fostering outstanding learning in my students. I am excited by the prospect of making this happen more consistently.

Strategies or Activities (Specific as to What, Where, and How):	Supporting Systems and Resources:	Timeline:
• Teach a lesson and record it using a video camera.	The Levels of Questioning Observation Tool	Video record a lesson and review the recording before Friday.
• Watch the video recording of my lesson and chart my use of the levels of questioning.	A video camera and tripod to record my lesson	
• Write my lesson plans for the next week, including specific questions at the varying levels for each section of the plan.	A good list of higher-level questions, gleaned from the Internet	Search for sample questions and develop lesson plans over the weekend.
• Teach a new lesson and video record it again, paying attention to how the students respond to questions, whether higher-level thinking is evoked, and whether students are more engaged or less engaged as a result.		Teach from new plans next week, recording the lesson

Confidence Level (On a Scale of 0 to 10): 7 . *Revise the strategy, systems, resources, and/or timeline until confidence is 7 or higher.*

Data Collection and& Reporting:

In the new lesson, I will check off the questions I have prepared as I use them. I will review those I have asked and those I did not ask to see if there is any pattern evident. I will notice evidence of student vitality in the discussion.

experiments so they can be reviewed from one coaching conversation to the next. If teachers want to work on multiple goals at the same time, then one template should used for each activity. The more carefully teachers think about, visualize, and write down their experimental design, the more likely it is that they will take creative, innovative actions in the classroom that will move them forward in their personal and professional mastery.

> *I don't play the puck where it is; I play it where it's going to be.*
>
> *Wayne Gretzky*

Experiments are not always of sufficient size and scope to map out using the Experimental Design Template. When teachers decide to take an action that they can easily and quickly handle, they can usually move forward on the basis of a simpler plan. Some actions are within reach during coaching conversations themselves. That's when the "Do it now!" principle comes into play. If teachers can do something now, like putting something on their calendars or rearranging some part of their classroom, encourage them do it immediately. When progress is made in this way during coaching sessions, it elevates self-efficacy, positivity, and mobility. Other actions, more singular and incremental in nature, can be mapped out using an abbreviated form of the Experimental Design Template. Whatever form it takes, the key is to walk away from coaching conversations with a clear picture as to what teachers will do when and with whom, captured in such a way as to facilitate commitment and accountability.

Awareness Experiments

In Chapter Four we described the readiness-to-change spectrum as representing a continuum from "I won't," "I can't," or "I may" on one end, to "I will" in the middle, to "I am" and "I still am" on the opposite end (Moore & Tschannen-Moran, 2010, pp. 34–39). Teachers in the early stages of change are usually not ready to test out new behaviors. They need more time to think, feel, and learn about what changes they may want to make. In addition, we have also introduced the concept of "natural learning," where people rely less on "how-to-do-it" instructions and evaluations and more on "I-can-do-it" ingenuity and observations (Gallwey, 2000; 2008; 2009). For natural learning to be facilitated, teachers may want to design and conduct awareness experiments that can assist them to pay attention to critical variables, those things that change and are crucial to our desired outcomes. In Chapter Five we described how Gallwey (2000) designed an awareness experiment for AT&T operators that indirectly resulted in significant performance and quality of life improvements.

Evocative coaches make frequent use of awareness experiments both with teachers who are in the early stages of change and with teachers who want to conduct their own natural-learning experiments. Instead of deciding to field test a behavior-change strategy, awareness experiments are conducted when teachers decide to shift their focus onto those critical variables that influence the quality and outcomes of their teaching experience. The Appreciative Classroom Observation Tools presented in Chapter Five are well suited for awareness experiments. Although teachers may use them to field test a behavior-change strategy, such as moving around the room more, they can also use them with no agenda other than to increase their awareness as to what they are already doing and how it is impacting instruction.

Both awareness and behavior-change experiments can be designed and mapped out as S-M-A-R-T experiments using the Experimental Design Template (Figure 6.2). It is not that behavior-change experiments are S-M-A-R-T while awareness experiments are fuzzy. What teachers decide to field test rather has to do with their preferred learning style and readiness to change. Teachers in the later stages of change, who are eager to imagine and try new things, may leap at the thought of prototyping and testing a behavior change. Other teachers, however, and perhaps most teachers, will not be sure as to the exact changes they want to make and their capacities for doing certain things in new ways. Or they may just be more autonomous and self-directed adult-learners. Whenever coaches experience resistance to brainstorming and/or designing behavior-change experiments, expressing empathy and increasing awareness of the vital practices they are already doing in the classroom can open up teachers to the consideration of new possibilities. "What can we learn?" is the orientation behind every experiment, and the more awareness gets heightened the more learning gets generated.

Confirming Commitment

Once an action-learning experiment has been designed to be S-M-A-R-T, and once it has been mapped out using the Experimental Design Template, coaches can increase motivation and movement by confirming both the teacher's understanding of the design and the teacher's commitment to conduct the experiment and see it through. Once the design template has been completed, coaches may want to invite teachers to read it through from beginning to end, noticing any outstanding issues or inconsistencies. This need not take a long time, but it helps to concretize the design when the entire scope is reviewed in one fell swoop. Teachers should be encouraged to make changes at any point, until it accurately reflects their intentions.

After confirming that teachers understand and are happy with what they will be attempting to focus on and do, coaches can check in on the commitment level of teachers to move forward with either closed-ended or open-ended questions. Closed-ended question, such as "Are you ready to move forward?" or "Are you happy with this design?" reduce commitment to a single "Yes" or "No" answer. Although closed-ended questions are generally discouraged, they can be helpful when confirming and increasing readiness to change. Open-ended questions, such as "How ready are you to move forward?" or "On a scale of 0 to 10, how happy are you with this design?," give teachers a little more freedom to express their feelings and needs in relation to the design. This can be especially helpful when coaches sense that teachers may yet have traces of reluctance or ambivalence. The point of confirming commitment is to make sure that teachers are ready, willing, and able to move forward so they have the greatest possible chance for success.

Around and Around the Möbius Strip: Back to Story

Once teachers have designed and committed themselves to one or more S-M-A-R-T experiments, completing a separate Experimental Design Template for each one, the coaching session is effectively complete. The teacher's job is to go forth and conduct the experiment as a prototype, following the design and innovating improvements in real time. Unless coaches have been asked to participate in the experiment, either as observers or as participant-observers, coaches will receive all their information about how the experiments went from teacher reports and data sources such as contemporaneous notes, student work samples, or audio and/or video recordings. These reports and data may come to coaches in the form of interim updates, through e-mails or spot encounters, or as formal parts of subsequent coaching sessions. However they come, evocative coaches recognize that all reporting and data on teacher activities are themselves stories and the beginning of a new round of coaching conversations.

- What went well? And why?
- What did you learn?
- How did the students respond?
- What surprised you?
- What did you like?
- How did you feel before, during, and after the experiment?
- What would you like to build on in the future?

All that we have learned about Story–Empathy–Inquiry–Design comes back into play. When teachers have one story to tell, coaches listen attentively and explore it from different angles. Whether teachers feel elated or disappointed, we reflect our understanding of their feelings and needs. Watch for the "golden sigh." Inquire about their best experiences, observed vitalities, and present possibilities. Once coaches have assisted teachers to process the experiment from a strengths-based perspective, it is time to brainstorm new ideas and design new experiments for continued learning, growth, and change. From there, the dance whirls around again to another twist of capacity building and strengths creation.

> *[Coaches and teachers] are partners in an ancient human dance, and one of teaching's great*
> *rewards is the daily chance it gives us to get back on the dance floor.*
>
> *Parker Palmer (1998, p. 25)*

Because teachers design and conduct their own experiments in evocative coaching, they also own the evaluation of those experiments. As with every aspect of the evocative coaching process, the more we support teacher autonomy and purpose the more we generate teacher motivation and mastery (Pink, 2009). It is not the role of the coach to decide whether or not the teacher did a good job. It is also important for coaches to not get attached to the design as sketched out on the design template. If a teacher does something differently or doesn't do anything at all, that may reflect the creative brilliance of an improvisation or that may be related to the "immunity to change." Either way, it represents another opportunity for Story–Empathy–Inquiry–Design to work its magic. No matter what happens, evocative coaches have ample opportunities to facilitate a successful coaching process. Our presence communicates that we trust teachers and their abilities to find the answers they need. One way or another, through the repeated application of Story–Empathy–Inquiry–Design, teachers will experience breakthroughs and find ways to make things work.

Summary

Although we titled this chapter "Design Thinking," and although Design is presented as the final step in the dynamic dance of evocative coaching, in reality the whole of evocative coaching represents a design thinking process. Story–Empathy–Inquiry–Design ebbs and flows through the same, three, iterative, nonlinear, overlapping spaces that design thinkers have carved out for their own process: inspiration, ideation, and implementation (Brown, 2008, 2009). Our Möbius strip model loops back through these spaces, over and over again, as ideas get refined and new directions get explored. Story listening, expressing empathy, and appreciative inquiry inspire teachers with an awareness of what is happening in the present moment and an ambition to transform what might be happening in future moments. Design thinkers in engineering and other fields point out how these same practices assist them to get a good, accurate, and sympathetic understanding of what people are dealing with in the here and now so as to generate good, relevant, and energetic designs for making things better in the future. It is all about mustering inspiration and gaining insight into the mystery of what's going on and how to make things better (Martin, 2009).

To make this work with teachers in the classroom, evocative coaches need to take time with these steps and not move prematurely into the work of designing action-learning experiments. Without inspiration, the work of ideation and implementation becomes just another chore. With inspiration, they take off and soar. Then, and only then, are teachers ready for that final step of the coaching process. With strong intrinsic motivation, high self-efficacy, positive energy, emotion, and images, as well as a deep-seated eagerness to change, teachers are ready to turn their aspirations into actions and their possibilities into realities. Nothing succeeds like success, so evocative coaches collaborate with teachers to design action-learning strategies that generate quick wins in a fulfilling manner.

Three tools are helpful to the design process. Creative brainstorming is a fun way to put lots of new ideas on the table without the coach coming across as the expert who prescribes what teachers should do. Exploring inertia assists teachers to come into a new relationship with themselves and their "immunity to change." If they are not responding to the coaching process with enthusiasm, and are not doing well in the classroom, then respectfully exploring the attachments and assumptions that are tethering teachers to the status quo can shake loose the process. Designing S-M-A-R-T experiments is the tool in the design process that forwards the action. Such experiments can be used to test the "immunity to change," to raise awareness, and/or to design new actions that teachers may want to repeat on the way to significant performance improvements. No coaching conversation should end without some sense of what teachers will do differently in the days and weeks ahead. Instead of framing this "homework" as an assignment to be completed, it is better for coaches and teachers to frame it as an experiment to be conducted. This frame reduces the fear of failure, increases the fun factor, and makes learning the primary goal of all new behaviors. It gives juice to the work of enhancing teacher performance.

Questions for Reflection and Discussion

1. What role do success stories play in evocative coaching? How can those stories best become a part of evocative coaching conversations?
2. In what ways are quick wins important to teacher success? How can coaches use the confidence scale to arrange for quick wins?

3. How do positive images, words, and emotions affect the human brain? How does this relate to human behavior?

4. What role does visualization play in performance improvement? How can evocative coaches bring visualization exercises into our work with teachers?

5. How can coaches assist teachers to turn "thinking about something" into a S-M-A-R-T, action-learning experiment?

6. How do our Big Assumptions interfere with our ability to change? How can coaches bring this into the coaching process when teachers are stuck?

7. Imagine a change you'd like to make in your own life. What actions are you avoiding that keep you locked in your current position? What actions do you take that help maintain the status quo? What BTB (Big-Time Bad) things are you worried would come to pass if you started (or stopped) taking those actions? How might you safely test your assumptions?

8. Think of a time when you successfully made a change, maybe in breaking a bad habit or positioning yourself for a new opportunity. What role did the three Fs (facts, fear, and force) play? How about the three Rs (relationships, repetition, and reframing)? What experiments did you conduct along the way?

PART THREE

EVOCATIVE COACHING IN PRACTICE

CHAPTER 7

ALIGNING ENVIRONMENTS

A prerequisite [for innovation] is an environment—social but also spatial—in which people know they can experiment, take risks, and explore the full range of their faculties. It does little good [to conduct experiments] in an environment that dooms their efforts from the start. The physical and psychological spaces of an organization work in tandem to define the effectiveness of the people within it.

TIM BROWN (2009, P. 32)

Our design conversations with teachers regarding S-M-A-R-T (Specific, Measurable, Attainable, Relevant, and Time bound) experiments, discussed in Chapter Six, are not complete until we pay specific and detailed attention to the laboratories in which those experiments are to be conducted. Physical scientists understand the integral connections among environments, researchers, and experiments. Many experiments simply cannot be conducted unless the right equipment, materials, financing, energy, human resources, and other factors are in place. "No one is an island," to paraphrase poet John Donne, and that is never more true than in the conduct of S-M-A-R-T experiments designed to facilitate learning, growth, and change. In the design phase of evocative coaching, we not only assist teachers to figure out what they will do on their own, we also assist them to think through how they might better shape, structure, modify, and align their environments so as to support their experiments and make their teaching as effective and fulfilling as possible.

Throughout this book we have written about and alluded to the importance of working with teachers not as isolated individuals but as contextualized ones. The constructionist principle of appreciative inquiry holds that we are not only situated in many different environments but also that those environments work to create the realities and potentialities of our experiences. Teachers know this. They know that many different things affect their ability to enjoy their work, to improve their performance, and to enhance their quality of life. At the start of coaching, teachers may view those things as givens, outside their control, just the way things are, and reasons why things are not going to get any better. We've sat with that discouragement on many occasions. But through story listening, expressing empathy, discovering strengths, observing vitalities, framing aspirations, inviting possibilities, and designing experiments, coaches awaken hope. Maybe new things are yet possible if one is willing to give them a try.

Trying new approaches is, of course, the whole point of coaching. But in the absence of supportive environments, teachers can end up feeling more frustrated and disheartened than before they tried. When their needs for support, resources, and encouragement go unmet, they can become discouraged and cynical. Sometimes, when teachers are asked to assess their confidence about a proposed experiment on a scale of 0 to 10, they may choose a low number because of environmental factors. Once that happens, it can become harder for teachers to try again. As we have seen, unless teachers have quick wins and at least some degree of success with their experiments, their self-efficacy is diminished, and they may become even more resistant to change. That is why evocative coaches pay so much attention to aligning environments as we work with teachers to build their energy, stoke their possibilities, and design their experiments. It is not enough to just bolster the resolve, develop the skills, and change the behaviors of teachers; performance improvement is not a bootstrap, self-help project. It does not happen in isolation from other people or systems. It happens in the context of many environments that must be designed and arranged to support the intentions, capacities, and actions of teachers. Design thinking is therefore systems thinking. There are certainly limits as to how much coaches and teachers can affect school environments, but to ignore them or to pretend they don't exist is to limit the effectiveness of evocative coaching.

Understanding Environments

"We shape our environments and they, in turn, shape us."

Winston Churchill

The concept of an environment often conjures up images of nature, since that is the context in which environments often get the most attention. In global ecosystems, there is a recognition that individual quality of life is affected, for better or for worse, by the quality of such external factors as air, water, light, noise, minerals, organisms, and other influences. In the contest between individual initiative and environmental impact, environments always win. The best of efforts on the part of individuals cannot overcome the worst of environments, unless things begin to shift. Environments are that influential and that important.

By way of analogy to the natural world, many environments in the educational world can be identified that affect the ability of teachers to achieve desired outcomes and enhance their quality of life. To mention only a few of the most obvious:

- *Classroom environments.* These include the furniture, equipment, materials, and resources available to teachers in their classrooms as well as how things are arranged, laid out, and designed to support teaching effectiveness. Teachers cannot be effective unless they pay attention to these dynamics.
- *Relational environments.* Teachers are in multiple relationships, both professional and personal, that affect the quality of their teaching and the ability to improve their teaching. Who else can they call upon and work with in the classroom? What are the dynamics in the school? How do their relationships affect how they show up at work? Relationships both help and hinder teacher efforts; evocative coaches pay attention to reducing interference and increasing support.
- *Cultural environments.* Beyond specific webs of relationships, teachers also find themselves in organizations with distinct cultures, messages, and ways of doing things. "We've never done it that way before!" has killed more than one good idea. When teachers get excited about trying new things, when coaches and teachers brainstorm new ideas and design S-M-A-R-T experiments, cultural environments may undermine or support their execution. Arranging for support and sharing success stories can influence cultural environments, making teacher experiments both more productive and more satisfying.
- *Technology environments.* Technology is an essential part of education in the modern world. What technology is available and how well it works is as important to teacher success as teachers' ability to understand and interact with the various interfaces. Evocative coaches work with teachers to optimize their technology environments as well as their ability to make use of those environments.
- *Financial environments.* How many times does a lack of money become the reason why something cannot be done? How many times do teachers buy supplies with their own money or do parents have to pitch in for classroom activities that are outside the budgets of schools? Teachers may not control the financial resources available to them in their classrooms and schools, but those resources affect their performance as much as any other environment. Coaching teachers to find creative solutions to the financial constraints posed by their environments can help alleviate the stress teachers experience by resource shortages.
- *Recovery environments.* If there is a single message that virtually every coach confronts in the course of our work with teachers, it is the message of overload and overwhelm. Teachers experience more demands today than ever before, and it shows in manifold ways, including increased health problems and reduced enthusiasm for teaching (Gallwey, 2009). Such messages and stories provide

fertile material for empathy but they also provide opportunities for coaches and teachers to design environments for recovery and renewal. Full engagement requires a rhythm of work and rest, seriousness and play, that teachers and many coaches too often neglect (Loehr & Schwartz, 2003). Paying attention to the rhythm of teachers' lives is not beyond the scope of evocative coaching; indeed, it lies at the heart of sustainable change.

Reviewing the environments listed here, which are a sampling rather than a complete inventory of the things that affect teacher performance, makes clear the complexity of the evocative coaching task. Teachers know this complexity on deep, emotional levels. When coaches talk with teachers about change, their many environments are lurking in the background. Ambivalence, reluctance, and resistance to change do not flow just from internal dynamics; they also flow from the impact of environmental realities and potentialities. When coaches express empathy for teachers' feelings and needs generated by stressful environments that do not fully support their goals, the more teachers feel understood when it comes to the complaints, assumptions, and values that lie beneath the surface of their experiences. When teachers perceive that coaches have a respectful and sympathetic grasp of what they are up against and dealing with, the more open teachers become to the possibility of designing change.

Once that openness is there, once we hear the "golden sigh," it is time for coaches to use appreciative inquiry and design thinking not only to assist teachers to improve their own skills and techniques but also to align their many environments in ways that support their efforts. We work with teachers to reengineer and shift their environments as part of the coaching process (see Appendix D.9). The section for "Supporting Systems and Resources" on the Experimental Design Template (refer to Figure 6.2) is not just a place to list materials and equipment. It is a place where teachers can take note of any and all necessary environmental supports, including systems, structures, resources, supplies, physical arrangements, placements, tools, and relationships.

> *Simple, easy adjustments to your environment can be done through several different ways. The three major ways I have found to shift your environment and shift your goals is through reminders, surroundings, and people.*
>
> Scott Young (2006)

Such considerations are an essential part of evocative coaching conversations; they assist teachers to be more successful with their experiments. If a system or resource cannot be arranged to be supportive, then securing such support may itself become a design experiment. Given the very real power limitations that many teachers and coaches have within school systems, there may be a lack of self-efficacy or courage when it comes to designing and conducting environmental experiments. Yet evocative coaching does not shy away from such bold conversations. We can at least ask such questions and participate in the brainstorming process about how to make it so. In the end, if teachers decide "to accept what they cannot change," evocative coaches can facilitate serenity as well as alternative action. If, however, teachers decide to address an environmental condition, and if they are successful at shifting environments into alignment, they may well have an impact that goes far beyond improving their own skills and performance in the classroom. Other members of the school community may be brought into the process. New sources of materials and resources may be found. New purchases may be made. The arrangement of furniture and equipment may be changed. Old assumptions and patterns of how things get done may give way to new understandings. If and when this happens, teachers and coaches may become catalysts for transforming schools, one conversation at a time. The entire scope of the educational process may be affected as the improvements made by one teacher percolate into school culture, such that those cultures more fully embody the vision of "schools that learn" (Senge, 2006; Senge et al., 2000).

> I think one of the biggest challenges of coaching, whether you are coaching teachers or athletes on the athletic field, is to get the individuals to see their relationship to the larger whole.
>
> *Luke, high school department chair*

Flow

One way to understand the design thinking that goes into aligning environments is through understanding the dynamics of a process called "flow." *Flow* is a term that was coined by the famed psychologist Mihaly Csikszentmihalyi (1990, 1997; Nakamura & Csikszentmihalyi, 2002) as he researched the conditions that made for optimal human experience. Csikszentmihalyi set out to examine what made for peak human performance across a variety of human endeavors. What he learned was that whether the performance was in the realm of music, chess, golf, or mountain climbing, the state that performers described when they were at their best was remarkably similar. This state, called flow, is the experience of being both fully immersed in and unusually successful with an activity. "Flow is the state in which people are so involved in an activity that nothing else seems to matter; the experience itself is so enjoyable that people will do it even at great cost, for the sheer sake of doing it" (Csikszentmihalyi, 1990, p. 4). A person in flow experiences a feeling of complete and energized focus in an activity, with a high level of enjoyment and fulfillment. The components of a flow-producing activity are that the activity has clear goals and the participant receives direct feedback on progress toward meeting that goal. The participant feels confident and in control of the activity as well as the ability to concentrate on the activity. As a result of being in flow, any worries and concerns the participant has disappear, and the subjective experience of time is altered. Not all of these components need to be present together for flow to be experienced, but some combination of them is required.

Flow happens when teachers are fully immersed in the process of growth and change. To reach that state of full engagement, the activity needs to be intrinsically interesting and just within reach of their abilities. If the activity is too challenging, then it is overwhelming and stressful. If the activity is not challenging enough, then it is boring and tedious. The sweet spot—the flow spot—is where the level of challenge perfectly matches the skills, training, strengths, and resources of the performer (Csikszentmihalyi, 2000). Athletes sometimes speak of this experience as being "in the zone." Coaches want to assist teachers to enter that state as often as possible while working on their instructional strategies. By conducting experiments that are neither too hard nor too easy, but rather perfectly suited for their interests, abilities, and environments, teachers will enhance their self-efficacy to take on even more daring and creative experiments in the future. Such flow moments are inherently pleasurable and even timeless. They successfully walk the tightrope between anxiety and boredom, arousal and fatigue, chaos and control, effort and ease, challenge and support. They build on each other to make teachers more competent and coaching more evocative.

Teachers will not fully benefit from their S-M-A-R-T experiments unless those experiments are designed to help teachers walk that tightrope and get into flow. And their ability to do that depends upon the interface between teachers and their environments. When their environments are chaotic, overwhelming, under-resourced, conflicted, or otherwise antagonistic, the odds of getting into flow go down. When their environments are controlled, manageable, well resourced, consenting, and otherwise supportive, the odds of getting into flow go up. Coaches and teachers pay close attention to these dynamics in designing S-M-A-R-T experiments. What are the givens? What can be changed? Understanding and working successfully with teacher environments is central to elevating both the energy and self-efficacy of teachers, in order to assist them to realize their sense of calling and purpose. Flow studies can help us figure out how to make that happen.

Navigating the River of Change

Keeping with the metaphor of "flow," we can draw upon the analogy of a river to explore the dynamics of change in schools. The river of change is sometimes calm, often turbulent, always moving, and ever dynamic. Even when we become frustrated at the seemingly slow pace of change, we can be assured that nothing is ever really staying the same. A Buddhist teaching holds that we never step into the same river twice. Neither do we show up at the same school with the same teachers twice. Each day, each conversation presents a new opportunity to foster productive change.

The Rapids

Coaches are often called upon to coach teachers, particularly novice teachers or those struggling with a challenging new teaching assignment, in the rapids. A kayaker entering a narrow passage or shallow water recognizes in that environment the potential for danger. The swiftly moving water and the many sharp rocks, both visible and submerged, pose potentially life-threatening hazards. Well-trained and experienced kayakers may encounter the rapids with a sense of exuberance and enthusiasm, confident in their skills to successfully meet the challenge. Those with less experience, however, may find themselves in the grip of fear. This fear, if it is too intense, may contribute to a debilitating decrease in performance that adds to the danger. It works much the same way with teachers facing a challenging instructional situation. Teachers who have skills and resources that are up to the challenge may feel energized and enthusiastic in anticipation of having to draw upon their best teaching skills. Teachers whose skills and resources are not up to the challenge may anticipate and conduct the same experiment with a sense of anxiety that can interfere with performance and contribute to poorer outcomes all around. Fear has a way of constraining and riveting attention to the source of the fear. That constriction limits the range of options that are considered, creating a potential for a downward spiral of ineffective interventions.

The theory of flow suggests two possible courses of action when we find ourselves coaching a teacher who is overwhelmed, anxious, and afraid. The first is to reduce the level of challenge, perhaps by designing environments with more support and resources as well as less interference and obstacles. Interference can be reduced by modifying externalities and managing focus. Teachers generally know what externalities they would like to change, and those should be discussed and modified as much as possible. Teachers do not always realize how their cognitive, physiological, and affective states come into play. These, too, can be seen as environments. What are teachers focusing on? What voices are they listening to? They may be distracted by noncritical variables. They may suffer from low self-efficacy by remembering past failures rather than successes. They may try to control outcomes rather than the processes, mechanics, and conversations involved with getting to outcomes. The more interference teachers experience from non-supportive environments, the louder the noise from both external and internal sources, the more teachers are up against in their ability to succeed (Gallwey, 2000, 2008, 2009). Coaches can assist teachers to regroup and refocus through a variety of conversational and personal practices. Who can they talk with? Where can they go for empathy? How can they lower the volume on their own negative self-talk? How can they relax their minds, reduce their anxiety, and manage their stress? Assisting teachers to talk through these dynamics can expand their awareness of options in the present moment (Domar & Dreher, 2001, p. 184). Encouraging them to conduct awareness experiments can help them focus more on observable, critical variables and less on evaluative, internal voices. By mustering support in these ways, evocative coaches assist teachers to be more successful.

The second course of action suggested by the theory of flow is to work on adding tools to the instructional toolkits of teachers, equipping them with more skills for the task at hand. Optimal performance involves not just minimizing interference but also maximizing resources. The more the resources, the more teachers enhance their ability to succeed. Coaches can assist teachers to develop their skills by inviting them to design experiments that would make them feel more confident. What strengths could they leverage and borrow from in developing new skills? How could they arrange their environments so as to make their weaknesses irrelevant? What training opportunities would they enjoy experiencing? Who could they collaborate with? What other resources are already available in the system that they could call upon? What resources could they find outside the system? How could they practice new behaviors in small, pilot, low-risk environments? Our job, as evocative coaches, is to assist teachers to minimize interference and maximize resources, aligning environments as much as possible, so that teachers experience moments of flow that become the stuff of wonder and joy.

The Doldrums

Coaches may also find ourselves called upon to coach teachers in the doldrums, navigating through slow, deep waters. These are teachers for whom teaching is no longer a challenge. These may be veteran teachers who have been teaching the same subject matter for a long time, or they may be teachers who have cultivated effective strategies for buffering themselves from the demands of seemingly never-ending reform initiatives. Such teachers may have adopted a defensive posture toward new initiatives, projecting an attitude that "this too shall pass." Teachers in the doldrums may have too many skills for the challenges at hand, which result in boredom and a lack of initiative, or they may be discouraged from years of pressure and a lack of acknowledgment for their efforts. Coaching teachers through the doldrums requires effective use of Story–Empathy–Inquiry–Design. Through story listening, expressing empathy, appreciative inquiries, and design thinking, we connect and/or reconnect such teachers with their aspirations and we quicken their awareness of new possibilities. These new possibilities may mean letting go of old strategies, cultivated over the course of a career, for resisting administrative directives and attempts to force them to change. This letting go does not come easy. It requires us to cultivate an evocative quality of conversation that loosens the moorings and engages teachers in the quest for educational excellence.

Our ability to engage teachers in such evocative conversations, as we have seen repeatedly, depends upon both our presence and our approach. Haim Ginott (1975), describing a note he penned as a young teacher, could well have been characterizing the consciousness of an evocative coach:

> I have come to the frightening conclusion that I am the decisive element. It is my personal approach that creates the climate. It is my daily mood that makes the weather. I possess tremendous power to make life miserable or joyous. I can be a tool of torture or an instrument of inspiration; I can humiliate or humor, hurt or heal. In all situations, it is my response that decides whether a crisis is escalated or de-escalated, and a person humanized or de-humanized. If we treat people as they are, we make them worse. If we treat people as they ought to be, we help them become what they are capable of becoming. (pp. 15–16)[*]

The most important thing to remember as we coach teachers in the doldrums is to respect and empathize with their needs and desires. As we noted in Chapter Four, teachers are not lazy, crazy, stupid, or wrong for feeling the way they feel. They have their reasons. They need empathy not judgment. When coaches cultivate strong bonds of connection and understanding with teachers, they are more able to reframe their negative energy and reawaken their positive desire. Story listening and empathy reflections are paramount. By understanding rather than critiquing their lethargy we increase our chances of hearing the "golden sigh," that release of pent-up emotion and nod of recognition. Once we deescalate the crisis and rehumanize the teacher, we can work more confidently and directly with appreciative inquiries and design thinking. Energy mounts for design conversations,

---

[*] This quote, as it appears here, is often misattributed to Goethe.

including talk about aligning environments, that bolster self-efficacy, increase positivity, and make possible new efforts for teachers to get themselves into flow.

By following the teacher's lead, evocative coaches ease our way into such collaborative and co-creative conversations. By remembering that we are in partnership rather than in charge, attending more to the teacher's feelings than to our own thoughts and opinions, we become genuinely inspired and inspiring. It is a two-way street. At their best, coaching conversations may feel intense, exciting, deep, powerful, and moving, but not hard. These moments are the peak experiences of coaching sessions that happen in conversation with teachers about their strengths, vitalities, aspirations, and possibilities. In these pivotal moments, teacher feelings, needs, and desires translate into the willingness and ability to change. That is because these moments inspire teachers to generate new ideas, to discover new insights, and to uncover new capacities, all of which lead to bold actions that can positively alter their future (Bushe, 2007). Since teacher potential is often more than they recognize, evocative coaches are not afraid to consider design experiments and environmental modifications that may stretch teachers beyond their initially perceived limits. When the relationship is right, and the necessary supports and scaffolding are aligned, teachers appreciate being called to go beyond what they're imagining to increase the odds of success.

When I became social studies department chair, I knew I was going to have to do something about Charles. Charles had been teaching history the same way for twenty-three years, mostly lecturing. He was burned out. The kids found him boring. He asserted that he was a teacher not an entertainer. He said that the kids had changed and he'd made up his mind that he was not going to change. When I met with him after I'd visited his classroom a few times, I started by asking about how he felt about the situation. He opened up right away. He said that he was frustrated and tired. He said that he'd been successful in the past but that the kids just didn't care about history anymore. It seemed like a relief to him to be able to share all that. When that outpouring subsided, I told him that my goal was to help him feel good about what he was doing again. I told him that I was not going to give him a list of things to do or fix but that together we would come up with strategies to try. I asked him what used to make him feel inspired. It turns out he'd been a Peace Corps volunteer in Africa and that's what had inspired him to become a teacher. We found a way to incorporate that experience, the era of the '60s, and the history of Africa into his teaching. Once he got reconnected to his passion, his teaching in all of his courses improved.

Matt, high school department chair

Managing Clouds, Wind, and Thunder

As we have noted, teachers do not work in a vacuum, and coaching does not work in isolation from other environments. The role of the coach in designing experiments with teachers is to make sure they do not overlook or ignore important aspects of the system. Thus, the need arises to coach the teacher *and* the environment. Talking with teachers about how they can align their environments to be supportive of their designs is essential for coaching success. People do not change by themselves, solely from the inside out. Rather, change also happens from the outside in, as we engage in conversations with others. Because of how interdependent human behavior is, it is very important for coaches to include environments, systems, communities, organizations, networks, movements, relationships, processes, policies, practices, structures, and resources in coaching conversations. If we coach without paying attention to these larger dynamics, we are coaching less than half the situation.

I first met Ron at a summer professional development conference. He went out of his way to say how excited he was that I would be working as a math coach in his building and that he couldn't wait to get started. But when I started working in his school in the fall, every time we would arrange a time to meet during his planning period, he would be gone when I showed up, or else he'd have an excuse about how he needed to go do something else. I think I know why he was so resistant. The teachers in that school have been scrutinized so much in the past six or seven years because they are an underperforming school. They have just been inundated with interventionists of every kind.

Patti, middle school math coach

Clouds of Climate

When we consider our environment in the largest sense, as our habitation on planet Earth, our concerns may turn to issues of climate and the extent to which the conditions are conducive for human thriving. The analogy of climate as conditions conducive to human thriving has been applied to organizations, and more specifically to schools, through research spanning nearly five decades (Tschannen-Moran, Parish, & DiPaola, 2006). School climate involves the quality of the interpersonal relationships in a school and how well these relationships support the school's core mission. Research in school climate draws our attention to attitudes and norms that govern interpersonal relationships in schools, such as academic press, or the degree to which academics are taken seriously and academic success is honored within the school community and community engagement, or the degree to which the school productively engages parents and members of the surrounding community in support of its mission. Teacher professionalism, which assesses the degree to which teachers perceive their colleagues to uphold professional norms of conduct, influences whether teachers go beyond minimum contractual obligations. And collegial leadership is the degree to which the principal is friendly, accessible, and open to suggestions from teachers.

To draw this analogy further, we can imagine the clouds of collective emotion that sometimes seem to settle over a school and remain for a sustained period of time. In some schools, the climate can be compared to a bright blue sky with only a few high, fluffy clouds. These sunny schools are energetic and happy places where the enthusiasm and sense of purpose are contagious. In other schools, dark clouds, heavy with rain and threatening to storm, seem to fill the sky. In these gloomy schools, energy is low and a collective depression seems to characterize most of the interactions as inhabitants dwell on the school's many failings. Resentment tends to run high in these schools, which can lead to resistance and outright sabotage of change initiatives. We want to pay attention to these atmospheric conditions as we coach, since they are likely to influence the energy and openness teachers feel for change. We also want to assist teachers to think through how to adapt to those environmental conditions as part of the design process.

> *Educational institutions are full of divisive structures, of course, but blaming them for our brokenness perpetuates the myth that the outer world is more powerful than the inner.*
>
> *Parker Palmer (1998, p. 36)*

Winds of Collective Efficacy

It is not just individuals who have beliefs about their efficacy that can affect motivation and performance; groups too can take on collective beliefs about their capacity to accomplish their collective work. School faculties take on beliefs about whether they have what it takes to bring about student learning for the population served by the school (Goddard, Hoy, & Woolfolk Hoy, 2000; Tschannen-Moran & Barr, 2004). If we think about the collective emotions in a school as the clouds in the atmosphere, we might think of the collective efficacy beliefs as the wind. When the wind is at our back, it can speed our progress and reduce the effort needed to move ahead in the directions we want to go. Such is the case when the collective efficacy beliefs among a faculty of teachers are high. They bring with them a high level of energy and motivation for adaptation and striving for ever-higher goals. In schools where the collective efficacy is low, an abiding sense of futility and discouragement presents a strong headwind, making progress difficult. Again, paying attention to the level of collective efficacy in the team, department, and school in which the teacher we are coaching functions may provide insight about the teacher's motivation and readiness for change. It may also provide grist for the mill in cultivating strategies suited to particular contexts.

Thunder of Conflict

There are moments in all schools when the clouds of emotion gather and the winds of efficacy blow, when a high pressure system meets a low pressure system, and the thunder of conflict resounds. Conflict is an inevitable part of life in schools, as it is in all social systems. It would be unrealistic to imagine that we could eliminate conflict in schools; schools are places with limited resources that must be shared between competing interest groups. When it is handled well, conflict can be a constructive force for positive change. When it is handled poorly, however, it can siphon away energy from the core mission of the school, leaving participants feeling wounded, hunkering down into protective warring encampments (Uline, Tschannen-Moran, & Perez, 2003).

As we coach teachers, we need to be aware of the level of conflict in their working relationships and the extent to which that conflict is handled constructively. Whether there is "hot" conflict, with open animosity between individuals and teams, or whether the conflict is "cold," with individuals stewing in sullen, resentful silences, the conflict will affect a teacher's readiness and willingness to engage in the change process. Offering empathy for the negative emotions that have been aroused in the midst of the conflict as well as the needs that are not being met is always the first step; from there, it may be possible to work with teachers to design experiments for resolving conflicts constructively so that they do not continue to drain teachers of zest, energy, and focus for the teaching task.

Nonviolent Communication, discussed extensively in Chapter Four as a tool for expressing empathy, is also an effective tool for resolving conflicts. The process starts by honoring conflict as an opportunity to learn what is alive in people and to find common ground at the point of our common humanity. All people have and are trying to meet the same universal needs, regardless of whether or not their current strategies are working. The process also helps to ensure that conversation about a conflict stays away from personal attacks and insults. People can vigorously debate differing points of view or different approaches to a problematic situation without impugning the integrity, motives, or character of others. The process then seeks to make sure that constructive conversations take place. Suppressing conflict and deferring to authority do not work over the long run. Speaking cleanly, eschewing

judgment and blame, and constraining our communication to observations, feelings, needs, and requests, can work to alleviate and resolve conflict when it clears
up misunderstandings, and helps people to see the beauty of each other's needs
(Gonzales, 2006). Much conflict and much unhappiness is generated by playing
the game of "Who's right?" When we choose to stop playing that game, then
the amount of unproductive conflict is reduced. When we put our energies into the
respectful understanding of another's experience, we are more likely to find
mutually satisfying solutions.

Ripples in a Pond

With so many different layers and levels of complexity, the notion that coaches
can work with teachers to modify and align environments in support of their
S-M-A-R-T experiments may sound hard to believe. How can teachers and
coaches influence an entire hallway, department, school, or school system? Isn't
that the work of principals, superintendents, and school boards? Is it really possible for one teacher to make that kind of difference? Can lightning really flash
from one classroom to an entire web of environments? According to Bill Byham
(1992), that is often the only way it ever starts. One person has to catch the energy
and run with the ball.

Evocative coaching is about assisting teachers to do just that. We evoke energy, aspiration, and designs for successful learning. We talk not only about what
teachers can do for themselves, but also about what they can do with others. We
consciously ask environmental design questions in the process of developing and
confirming S-M-A-R-T experiments because we know not only that environments
are important but also that they are malleable.

One process for working with environments, described as the "ABC Inquiry
Model" by Jane Magruder Watkins and David Cooperrider (Watkins & Mohr,
2001, pp. 154–168), is a process we like to call "Ripples in a Pond." After teachers design S-M-A-R-T experiments, and as part of the conversation regarding
the Experimental Design Template, coaches can invite teachers to work with three
concentric circles in order to better understand and map out their strategies for
influencing the environmental factors related to their experiments (see Figure 7.1).
The analogy is to throwing a stone into a pond, producing ripples in all directions. That is what happens when teachers conduct experiments. Their efforts
generate ripples that touch their students, classrooms, colleagues, and schools.
Until and unless they factor those ripples into their design, their experiments will
not be S-M-A-R-T. Coaches and teachers can think through these factors together
as part of the coaching process. Coaches can invite teachers, for example, to

FIGURE 7.1. RIPPLES IN A POND PROCESS

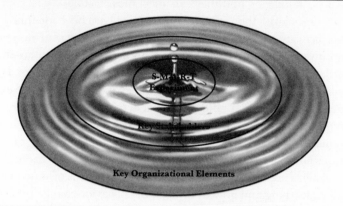

Key Stakeholders	Key Organizational Elements
• Students	• Materials
• Other teachers	• Supplies
• Team members	• Curriculum
• Guidance department	• Standards
• Administrators	• Structures
• Parents	• Policies and procedures
• Volunteers and donors	• Technology resources
• Board members	• Funding sources
• Etc.	• Etc.

imagine conducting the experiment, throwing it into the pond of their classroom and school environment, anticipating reactions and other factors that may come into play. The more vivid and concrete these mental simulations become, the more they assist teachers to successfully conduct their experiments when they come to the real thing.

When it comes to school environments, the ripples in the pond represent at least two types of rings as they spread out from teacher experiments. The first ripple involves the people the experiment touches; the second includes the organizational elements that may come into play. Who will be affected by this experiment most directly? Who will be affected indirectly? What students will be involved? Who might be called upon to help out? Who might resist the effort? How will it land with parents? How will it land with family members and friends? Teachers can think through all the key stakeholders and put them on the diagram in the first ring. They can then do the same with the organizational elements. What policies, procedures, systems, resources, materials, equipment, technologies, budgets, norms, standards, and other aspects of the school may be affected by the S-M-A-R-T experiment? The more specific teachers can be in imagining these various environmental factors, both human and systemic, the more successful they will be in imaging how they can affect those factors.

Once all of the environmental factors have been identified and appreciated, teachers are asked to consider how they might nudge or move those factors in a positive direction. We want to incorporate and build on supportive resources in order to outgrow and move beyond the inevitable challenges. Two considerations will make it easier for teachers to conduct and have a positive experience with influencing their environments: "What actions can the teacher take?" and "What requests can the teacher make?" Note that these questions focus on teacher actions and requests, not on outcomes. We don't know the outcomes of teacher experiments. That is why we frame them as experiments in the first place. Experiments are not about success or failure, in terms of outcomes; they are rather about learning and growth through the behavior-change process. Framing questions in terms of what teachers can focus on and do to align their many environments to carry out and enjoy their experiments supports the intention of evocative coaching and assists teachers to better meet their developmental needs. Once environments begin to shift, they support the design of new experiments not only for one teacher but for others as well.

Stories as Catalysts for Transformation

To align environments in organizations is never an easy task; in schools and school systems it is an especially difficult task, because of the many different stakeholders who can influence those environments. There is no single person with final authority to say, "This is how we will do things." Instead, school cultures are born out of complex and shifting interactions among a wide variety of individuals and constituencies. That is both good news and bad news about aligning environments. On the one hand, it means there is no single person responsible for setting the tone and culture of the organization. On the other hand, it means that every single person is responsible for setting the tone and culture of the organization. Teachers and coaches can make over a school, one conversation and one story at a time. Tim Brown (2009) describes this opportunity by way of analogy to bees and ants:

> Anthills and beehives are good examples of complex nonhierarchical systems in which the behavior of the system is the result not of centralized command and control but of a set of individual behaviors that, when repeated thousands of time, achieve predictable results. But when it comes to colonies of humans, we have to reckon with the additional factors of individual intelligence and free

will (often to the despair of designers, police officers, and high school teachers). The implication is that we must think differently. Instead of an inflexible, hierarchical process that is designed once and executed many times, we must imagine how we might create highly flexible, constantly evolving systems in which each exchange between participants is an opportunity for empathy, insight, innovation, and implementation. Every interaction is a small opportunity to make that exchange more valuable to and meaningful for all participants. (pp. 187–188)

That is how we view the interactions between coaches and teachers: they represent small opportunities to evolve entire systems. What starts in the one-on-one exchanges between coaches and teachers and leads to design experiments can spread out in every direction like those ripples in a pond. When coaches and teachers communicate what they are working on with others, the systems and structures in schools shift into alignment. When coaches and teachers share the stories of their design experiments, including details as to how things went, what worked well, and what things were helpful to them, the news begins to spread. Such stories can have a huge influence on school environments. They convey not only information but inspiration. They become what Chip and Dan Heath (2007) refer to as "ideas that stick" and what Richard Dawkins (2006) famously called "memes"— those self-propagating, self-replicating ideas that change behavior, perceptions, and attitudes. When coaches and teachers spread the word as to their work together, through evocative stories and appreciative inquiries, they not only align environments, they become catalysts of school transformation.

That is our hope and belief when it comes to evocative coaching: the good work we do in one-on-one coaching conversations will diffuse and disseminate on its own. We don't have to discipline or force ourselves to make that happen. Good news is contagious. When teachers have good experiences through coaching, they naturally want to tell others. We just have to let it happen. Design thinking and innovation can thereby make their way into school cultures such that teachers can have even more success in the future. That infusion can do more to align environments over time than any policy statement or top-down pronouncements. When it percolates up, through simple, unexpected stories of success that concretely and credibly stir people's emotions it sticks (Heath & Heath, 2007), schools become cultures of learning that are more likely to rise to the full measure of their calling.

We have no illusion that a single success story, a single meme, can transform schools overnight. But we do believe that coaching stories have that power over time, and we encourage coaches to become advocates and storytellers in schools regarding the design experiments that teachers are working on. Without violating trust or confidentiality, respecting what teachers are willing and not willing to share, coaches can become subtle and yet powerful voices in the school transformation process. Brief conversations with administrators, other teachers, and staff can become forums for spreading the news. Meetings and professional development sessions can become opportunities to feature the news. The more such stories spread around, the more enthusiasm replaces discouragement and the more hope replaces despair. When that happens, the self-efficacy of teachers translates into the collective efficacy of schools. People come to believe that they have what it takes to facilitate student learning and to generate school success.

Summary

Evocative coaching is not just an inside-out activity; it is also an outside-in activity. We do not just call for motivation and movement from within; we also call for systems to support motivation and movement from without. This is an essential part of designing S-M-A-R-T experiments. Experiments are not relevant (the R in S-M-A-R-T) unless they account for and ameliorate the very real and complex webs of environments in which teachers live and work. Aligning those factors to better support teachers may be all they need to move forward with greater confidence and success.

That is what happens when coaches and teachers work together to align environments: teachers get into flow. Environmental alignment can affect both the challenge and the skills sides of the flow equation. The right environments can bring the challenge down, if necessary, while others can bring the skills up, enabling and supporting teachers to conduct their S-M-A-R-T experiments with full engagement, improvising in the moment to facilitate not only their own learning and growth but also the successful and vibrant education of their students.

Questions for Reflection and Discussion

1. What do you make of the claim that "in the contest between individual initiative and environmental impact, environments always win"? Can you think of examples from your own experience that bear this out?
2. Tell a story about a time when you experienced flow. What was going on? Who was involved? How does your experience align and differ with the description of flow developed by Mihaly Csikszentmihalyi?
3. How could you experience flow more often in your own life and work? What environmental modifications would help you to do so?

4. What is the climate like where you work? How does it affect you and the teachers you are working with?
5. How can coaches assist teachers to work through conflicts productively? Brainstorm six useful ideas.
6. How can teacher actions and requests affect school environments? What can we realistically hope to achieve in this regard?
7. What are your learning goals in relationship to coaching? What are three strategies you might try in pursuit of your learning goals? What environmental modifications would each strategy require?
8. How could you become more of a story ambassador, spreading the message as to the good things that are happening through your coaching and in your school? What story would you tell, and who could you tell it to within the next few days?

CHAPTER 8

COACHING CONVERSATIONS

The coach dances with [teachers] to facilitate the unleashing of potentials and the experience of change. The dialogue dance creates motivation and energy. . . . It creates readiness for change, the power to change, and the leverage for change. In this dance, new frames of mind are co-created for facilitating that change. The dialogue is a dance around support, celebration, accountability, fun, and actualizing potential. It's a dance for enabling dreams to come true. Do you want to dance?

L. MICHAEL HALL AND MICHELLE DUVAL (2005, P. 6)

By now it should be clear how much value we place on the work of coaches in schools. We truly believe that schools can be transformed one conversation at a time. For this to happen, coaches and other school leaders tasked with improving the quality of instruction and solving the problems of practice must come to embody both the presence and artistry of the evocative coaching process. We must carry ourselves as instruments of inspiration and humanization (coaching presence), and we must learn the steps of the coaching dance (story listening, expressing empathy, appreciative inquiry, and design thinking) all the way through to aligning environments. At first, as with all dances, these steps may feel unfamiliar, awkward, and confusing. We may be clumsy and stilted in their application. Toes can get stepped on, we trip, we do not always get the timing just right.

That dynamic may occasion discouragement and prompt some coaches to give up on the dance before it has time to work. If we hang in there, however, with lightheartedness and a sense of humor, practicing the dance steps until the choreography begins to take shape in our minds and in our interactions with the teachers we coach, all this begins to change. As time goes on, we become more graceful and light on our feet as we go through the motions. Things begin to shift in our conversations and in our presence with others. When we know the steps well, and know the choreography of how they go together, we become undercover agents of transformational change. Teachers may not realize exactly what we are doing or how it is happening. They may just begin to notice more lightness in their step and more hope in their hearts as they experience more success with their students and in other areas of their lives. They may even have the sense of doing it all themselves, because new attitudes and actions will have been evoked from within.

Such is the promise of evocative coaching. When coaches trust and practice the process, we increase our ability to make significant contributions to the professional development of teachers and to the learning climate of schools. To that end, then, we seek in this chapter to describe the choreography of coaching conversations. How do the steps come together to facilitate change? How do we navigate our way through the ebbs and flows of the coaching process? What does the evocative form look like, whether we are interacting in the context of a scheduled coaching appointment or a brief hallway encounter? When do we circle back and when do we move forward? Evocative coaching does not depend for its effectiveness upon how much time and structure we have available for a coaching conversation. It depends upon our ability to connect and dance with teachers in the moment as partners on the never-ending journey of learning how to teach better. Story–Empathy–Inquiry–Design (S-E-I-D) represents the four dance steps; within those steps we recognize eight movements that choreograph the method so that more teachers make more significant improvements over time.

The Great 8: Choreographing the Coaching Dance

To successfully and enjoyably dance with a partner, one must know not only the steps of the dance; one must also have a sense of their progression, flow, and destination, and then one must practice the steps until they become second nature. Where are we starting? How are we moving? What is the rhythm? Where are we ending? As the dance advances, it is critical to monitor multiple contingencies in real time. The unexpected happens, and when it does, adjustments must be made to keep the dance in sync and moving forward. It is a case of continuously processing in the present (see Appendix D.4). What is going on? What am I doing? What is my partner doing? How can we stay or get back in step? Such questions and sensitivities are essential to making dances work. Dances that turn out well are not necessarily the ones that go according to plan. They are the ones that come together in a graceful fashion, with a sense of mutuality and destiny. When the chemistry and composition are right, dances are beautiful to behold.

That same beauty is possible in evocative coaching conversations. We may not be physically dancing with teachers, but we are seeking to move together through the coaching process in ways that co-create a new reality. We are not always taking the lead, and we are not always following. We are rather moving back and forth among these different steps, exploring stories, empathizing with feelings and needs, inquiring into strengths, or developing and prototyping designs, intuitively initiating and responding in ways that bring out the best in teachers. We want teachers to feel engaged, intrigued, open, willing, stimulated, supported, and challenged by the conversation. We do not want to be wandering around aimlessly or getting out of sync through the coaching process. We want to know where we are and where we are going. We want to know when it is time to circle back and when it is time to move forward. We want to pick up on and recognize the signals and cues so that things come together and teachers realize their full potential. The more we do that, the more we pay attention, "Join-Up" with teachers, and navigate with curiosity, the more evocative coaching becomes.

The steps of Story–Empathy–Inquiry–Design are represented on a Möbius strip because they are not linear or progressive. The underlying relational, emotional, motivational, cultural, and political dynamics of teachers in schools are as complicated as any human endeavor. Coaches learn to notice and respond to those dynamics in adaptive ways. We learn to evoke a spiral dynamic in our conversations, iteratively moving around and around the dance floor with Story–Empathy–Inquiry–Design so as to generate ever-higher levels of professional mastery and maturity. We learn when to push and when to pull. We learn not only to expect the unexpected but to leverage the unexpected for creativity, growth, and change (Von Oech & Willett, 2002). We learn to bring out the best in teachers, regardless of where they start in competence, experience, willingness, and vision. By engaging teachers in the dance of self-directed learning and performance improvement through evocative coaching, we enable teachers to more fully rise to the challenge of not only meeting student achievement standards but also creating schools where learning is Job One.

To conceptualize how Story–Empathy–Inquiry–Design look and feel in practice, as coaching conversations move from the beginning through the middle to the end, we have found it helpful to use the device of the "Great 8": initiate, elaborate, validate, appreciate, extrapolate, innovate, deliberate, and activate. These eight lyrical movements give us one more way to approach and conceptualize the dance. Each movement represents a subset in the Story–Empathy–Inquiry–Design coaching model. By presenting them here, at the end of our discussion, we aim to create a clear and vivid picture, a mental simulation, of how evocative coaches work and what we do with teachers. The more hands-on the descriptions, and the more clearly we can picture the process, the more elegant we will be when it comes time to execute the dance. Appendix A summarizes the principles and sample question lists organized around the Great 8 and may be an especially helpful tool for getting a sense of what the evocative coaching dance looks, sounds, and feels like. Beginning coaches may want to use Appendix A as a ready reference guide for mastering the evocative coaching process in schools.

The Great 8 Movements of Evocative Coaching

Story Listening
1. Initiate
2. Elaborate

Expressing Empathy
3. Validate

Appreciative Inquiry
4. Appreciate
5. Extrapolate

Design Thinking
6. Innovate
7. Deliberate
8. Activate

Story Listening

The stories teachers bring to coaching conversations are at the heart of the enterprise. For a coach who has been trained to listen well, those stories provide crucial information about the teacher's values, feelings, needs, experiences, and thinking. Stories reveal who teachers are as human beings and what they think is going on in their worlds. Stories represent the currency of evocative coaching. They not only represent a down payment on the changes teachers want to make, they also represent the sum principal and the interest that accrues over the course of the coaching relationship. Through the alchemy of evocative coaching, stories become pure gold. Inviting teachers to tell their stories (initiate) and to explore different facets of their stories (elaborate) are the two opening movements of any coaching conversation.

1. Initiate

We know a man who has become enamored with learning to dance the tango. Just before the music begins, he always slips on his reading glasses. Curious, we asked why he did that; he explained that doing this dance well requires a close read of his partner's facial expressions and movements. So it is with coaching. It requires a close read of our partner so that we can make adjustments to the tone and style of what we are bringing to the coaching conversation. When coaching conversations begin, we do not initiate them by focusing attention on the learning brief or by reviewing the "homework" from the last session. There will be time enough for that later; first, we seek to read, understand, and connect with the presenting energy of the teachers we are coaching. That is how we establish, and reestablish, trust and rapport. That is also how we hone our instincts about how that particular coaching dance might go. Evocative coaches take pains to renew trust and rapport at the outset of each and every conversation. To avoid coming across as being in a hurry to get down to business, we begin each and every encounter with at least a brief check-in as to how teachers are feeling in that moment. We initiate coaching with a clear expression of interest in and concern for their humanity. We want to know how they are doing as human beings, not just how their work is going or how things went with their S-M-A-R-T (Specific, Measurable, Attainable, Relevant, and Time bound) experiments. With the use of one or more opening questions, we communicate authentic compassion for and engagement with the teacher as a person. In so doing, we elevate positivity and readiness to engage.

Our hope, of course, is that teachers show up with lots of positive energy that can be easily built on and developed over the course of the coaching conversation. Many times, however, teachers show up with an awareness of one or more painful problems that may be afflicting them either personally or professionally. They may evidence great frustration, discouragement, anxiety, or even despair. When that happens, it is up to the coach to reflect those negative emotions and to guess at unmet needs in ways that communicate acceptance, understanding, and hope. As long as coaches communicate a respectful understanding of a teacher's experience as well as a calm sense of confidence that success can yet be arranged, the energy will generally drain out of their distress, enabling teachers to regroup and contemplate other dimensions of their experience in the service of learning, growth, and change.

Throughout the check-in process, evocative coaches look for openings to ask those first, fateful "How did you grow?" questions. We want to elicit learning stories in a developmental frame. "What has challenged and excited you since the last time we met?" is the basic orientation. Once teachers start telling those stories, remembering something that went well or sharing something that they learned, they often gain perspective and connect with their explicit as well as latent abilities to make things work. There may not yet be any notion of how that will happen, let alone any specific designs, but an opening presents itself to consider anew the possibilities for change. When that happens, the foundation for moving forward has been laid.

As much as we want teachers to get to that place of integration and readiness, pressing to make it happen is generally counterproductive. Jumping to conclusions, making assumptions, or putting words in teachers' mouths can damage trust and rapport and set back our ability to engage with teachers in designing experiments and aligning environments. To initiate coaching, then, we respect how teachers show up, what they are ready to share, and when they are ready to go deeper. If we get that right, if we ask those first "How did you grow?" questions at the right moment and in the right way, teachers will open up and share what is on their hearts. If we give them a chance to express themselves fully, teachers will often run with their stories in surprising and productive ways. Such "Follow-the-Teacher" conversations represent a shift from traditional training and development activities; they enable teachers to move forward positively by taking charge of their own personal and professional evolution.

> *Relationship building is a subtle, unconscious dance between two partners, hinging on each person's ability to send and accept bids for emotional connection.*
>
> *Jim Knight (2007, p. 24)*

Before the Session. To initiate coaching conversations in this way, coaches have to get into the right frame of mind before coaching conversations ever begin. To some extent, this mindset reflects how coaches care for and carry ourselves in every minute of every day. We cultivate daily mindfulness, self-care, and reflective learning practices such as those we discuss in Chapter Nine. In addition, however, we take time—ideally before each and every coaching session—to pause, gather our thoughts, and frame our approach with individual teachers. What Tim Gallwey (2000, pp. 141–164, 2009, kl. 1771–1888) calls the "S.T.O.P. Tool" (Step back, Think, Organize our thoughts, before Proceeding) is important for coaches to make use of before the start of coaching sessions. That S.T.O.P. may be, in fact, the most important part of the session. It enables evocative coaches to clear our minds, set our intentions, frame our questions, and get into the coaching mindset. Taking a few deep breaths, at that point, can assist coaches to be completely present and teacher focused.

Some coaches find it helpful to review the following key points before coaching sessions:

- *Confidence is contagious.* The more we communicate our certainty that teachers can be successful, the more likely it is that teachers will be successful. The operative question: "What do I believe is possible, now?"
- *What we appreciate, appreciates.* The more we focus on what teachers want rather than on what they don't want the more energy and ideas teachers will have for moving forward. The operative question: "What do I want to appreciate, now?"
- *Listen until we don't exist.* Slow down and listen with full attention. The more we set aside our own agenda, in favor of listening for the teacher's agenda, the more teachers will discover about themselves and discern their own answers. The operative question: "What do I want to listen for, now?"

• *Respect the truth.* The more we reveal teachers to themselves, through empathy and inquiry, the more progress they will make toward their visions. Do not be afraid to share what it is there. The operative question: "How do I want to connect, now?"

• *Trust our intuition.* The more deeply we listen to our own instincts and inklings during coaching conversations, the more deeply teachers will connect with their instincts and inklings. That is what leads to the intuitive dance of coaching. The operative question: "What is my gut saying, now?" (Adapted from Moore & Tschannen-Moran, 2010, p. 135)

To initiate coaching conversations in this way, we must affirm, respect, and honor the confidentiality of the coaching conversation and the coaching space. Coaching in a location where others can overhear the conversation is usually not ideal for evocative coaching. We want teachers to feel comfortable enough to open up and freely share whatever is on their minds. It is our job as coaches to make sure the space supports that intention. No matter how friendly, warm, respectful, considerate, and purposeful we may be as coaches, the dynamics of confidentiality in the coaching environment can undermine our best efforts. Working to make that space conducive to coaching speaks volumes to teachers. It lets them know that they can count on us to watch their backs and to care appropriately for the information and stories they share with us. The goal is to create a relational space in which trust and rapport can grow. Until that happens, coaching conversations will be superficial, and the potential of coaching to generate transformational change will not be realized.

> One thing that the teacher I was working with realized was that what we discussed and implemented for her students never left the classroom. It didn't matter how negative she perceived her circumstances to be, the administrators in the building were not informed about the specifics of our collaboration. She really realized that I was being truthful with her that I was not there to evaluate her teaching. I tried never to make her feel inadequate.
>
> *Patti, middle school math coach*

The First Coaching Session. Although everything we have just written applies to initiating every evocative coaching session, the first session with any given teacher deserves special comment because it represents the first, fateful impression of our presence and energy, of who we are and how we work, and of what our agenda is with that teacher. Through the way we initiate and handle ourselves in the first coaching session, teachers will decide whether or not we can become trustworthy partners in their professional development. That is especially challenging when we have been assigned to coach a struggling teacher. Such teachers already know, or think they know, why we are there: to make them do things they do not want to do in ways they do not want to do them. They may also think we are there to spy on them for the principal or other authority figures. When that happens, evocative coaches have a lot of unlearning and trust building to do with teachers. That is difficult, but not impossible, when we apply the principles of evocative coaching.

The initial conversation is key in establishing the quality of the relationship as non-threatening and productive.

Matt, high school department chair

We start, then, by introducing ourselves without taking too much time or calling too much attention to our credentials. We say enough to gain respect without overtalking. We express our passion for excellence in education, our desire to get to know them, and our interest in working with them not as their boss or supervisor but as their partner and collaborator. "We bring good things to life" was not just a good motto for General Electric; it is also a good motto for how evocative coaches seek to work with teachers. After introducing ourselves in this way, check in with teachers to see whether or not they have any questions about our background, our role, or anything else that may be on their minds. Handle any questions respectfully, honestly, and succinctly in order to reassure teachers that we will listen to them and take them seriously. Do not ramble on at any point.

It is important to communicate our understanding of and ability to protect their confidentiality. Assure teachers that we respect their right to privacy and that we are fundamentally prudent in the protection of those rights within the limits of institutional regulations and the law. Many coaches state explicitly how they will handle inquiries from the principal that are evaluative in nature, saying, for example, that we will invite the principal to make a joint observation and that afterward we will be willing to listen to the principal's concerns. As a general rule, however, coaches commit to not sharing concerns with the principal unless we perceive that something illegal or immoral is going on, in which case we commit to sharing those concerns with the teacher before making them known to the principal. Such clarifications represent the ethical foundation of coaching.

Once we have a beginning sense of trust and rapport, it is time to introduce teachers to how evocative coaching works. This is best done by getting as quickly as possible into the flow of story listening, expressing empathy, and appreciative inquiry. In other words, the best way to explain coaching is to coach. The main distinctions to get across are that we are not showing up to observe and evaluate their teaching, to identify and fix their problems, or to tell them what to do. We are the facilitator of a discovery process that will enable them to better reach their goals and develop themselves professionally. On occasion we may make suggestions or share advice, but that is not our primary role. Our primary role is to help teachers find their own answers and achieve exceptional results even in the face of challenges. Communicate confidence that this approach often assists teachers to do better and reach higher than they would otherwise. Ask teachers to confirm that this is acceptable, and address any additional questions or concerns they may have. If they seem especially wary or troubled, reflect those feelings and needs with a stated desire to understand them fully, to accept them right where they are, and to work with them only in ways that they will enjoy and appreciate. Stay here, if necessary, until we hear a "golden sigh" regarding the coaching relationship itself. There is no point in pushing forward until a vital connection is made.

When that connection is made, or at least beginning to emerge, and once basic understandings are shared, immediately shift to a "How did you grow?" story invitation that will get teachers talking about their experiences in positive ways. That sets the tone for all that follows, including the discovery of strengths, the observation of vitalities, the framing of aspirations, the inviting of possibility, and the engagement of design thinking. Once teachers are talking in this way, we have successfully initiated the evocative coaching relationship and conversation.

When I start a coaching relationship, I start off by just observing to get a sense of the dynamics in the classroom and the needs of the kids. I got off to a rough start with one of the teachers I coached, though. I thought I was well known and respected in the building where I was coaching, so when I was assigned to coach Natalie I just decided to drop by unannounced to observe her reading block. Well, her reading block was just before lunch, and I arrived in her classroom just as another teacher was delivering her lunch from a fast food restaurant. It was apparently her habit to eat her lunch while she was teaching reading. Catching her "in the act," so to speak, did not get our relationship off to a good start. I've learned to make arrangements in advance for my first observation with a teacher and to clarify what I will be doing.

Danielle, elementary literacy coach

2. Elaborate

As we saw in our discussion on story listening in Chapter Three, teachers may need encouragement to elaborate the details and dimensions of their stories. That is true throughout coaching conversations. Sometimes when we make a story invitation or, later in the session, when we ask an appreciative question, teachers will respond with a truncated version of some event, a factoid rather than a story. When that happens, it is our job to ask them to elaborate. They may assume that we do not want to know about the details, as if they are unimportant or irrelevant. Evocative coaches learn how to ask for details in ways that make sense. "Tell me more" is one of our favorite responses to elicit elaboration. Look for details as to what was done and what kind of effect it had on people. We want to get a sense of the emotion. Ask about what led up to and grew out of an experience.

Once we have the gist of the story, including the situation, search, and shift (Drake, 2008), we may want to invite teachers to retell their stories from different vantage points ("Who else?"), pivot points ("How else?"), and/or lesson points ("What else?"). Such invitations expand the range of possibility. The objective is not to interrogate teachers and not to beat stories to death. It is rather to explore stories, to kick them up a notch, to play with them, and to see what other truth and light might come from them. Retelling stories from different point of views, hypothesizing as to what might have happened if different decisions had been made, and constructing more than one "moral of the story" are all ways to do that. Such inquiries expand the range and energy of teachers as to the genesis and arc of their stories. What may have seemed obvious at one point may no longer seem so self-evident. Experiences are the raw materials that coaches and teachers have to work with in coaching; whether through storytelling or shared observation, evocative coaches assist teachers to squeeze as much learning as possible from the experiences they deem significant.

Remember that story invitations at the start of coaching sessions are open-ended, positive-leaning, growth-oriented questions that are not limited to whatever design experiments teachers may have specifically agreed to work on in prior coaching sessions. A more general question (e.g., "Tell me a story about something that's gone well for you this week") enables coaches to connect teachers with some positive energy even if their design efforts did not turn out as they had hoped. This raises the bar of the possible for the rest of the session. Teachers should not, of course, be prevented from jumping right in to talk about their "homework"—how their action-learning experiments went—from the last session. But that is not how we phrase those first story invitations, and we do not rush to get there. We want teachers to elaborate on their stories of possibility and hope, wherever they may be found. The stories they come up with in response to more general questions may even have taken place outside of the school environment; evocative coaches do not discourage such reflections and disclosures. Whatever comes out, we seek to communicate genuine interest in teacher stories and a certain ease in hearing them through.

On the other hand, just as there are teachers who are reluctant to share the details of stories, there are also teachers who can't stop talking about them. These teachers are verbal processors and can easily take up an entire coaching session with their stories, never getting to the work of design thinking that is so crucial to calling forth motivation and movement. Elaboration is therefore a judgment call, like many things in coaching, as to when there is too much and when there is too little. Either way, coaches can move the conversation forward through speaking up with distinctive empathy reflections that show we understand and respect the teacher's core feelings and universal needs. Most people who talk too much or talk too little do not feel understood. For them, navigating with empathy is the way to move things forward without coming across as either disrespectful or pushy. The longer we work with teachers, the more trust and rapport we have, the easier it becomes to step in, to tie off rambling conversations, and to bring things back to center.

Expressing Empathy

As evocative coaches, empathy is one of the greatest gifts that we give teachers. Feeling fully heard, in many cases, is enough in and of itself to free teachers to be able to move forward. Generative conditions grow out of the vital connection that coaches make with teachers during coaching conversations. In evocative coaching, we are careful to empathize with teachers by reflecting our guesses as to their core feelings and underlying needs, sidestepping the thoughts and judgments embedded in their stories. It is our job as coaches to suspend the urge to critique, appreciating the value of and the urgency behind their efforts to make and maintain behavioral changes. Change is challenging enough without piling on assessments as to whether or not someone is doing things right. By establishing a "no-fault zone" in which teachers can blamelessly and shamelessly open up and share, and by communicating confidence in teacher capacities to find a way forward, evocative coaches make it possible for teachers to learn from their experiences and to move on. The "no-fault zone" becomes a "possibility zone" in which coaches and teachers can dance and make progress together.

3. Validate

In many respects, expressing empathy means validating teacher experiences. This is quite different from evaluating teacher performance. When expressing empathy, we do not critique teachers' decisions, strategies, and outcomes as being good or bad, right or wrong, correct or incorrect, better or worse. We do not agree or disagree as to whether we would handle things the same way. Such evaluation tasks have their place in schools, but not as part of evocative coaching conversations. Our goal in coaching is to validate the efforts teachers make, the needs they are trying to meet, the feelings that surface through their experiences, and the progress they are making. While observing vitalities, these are the kind of the things coaches look for. Where do we notice effort? How do we discern needs? Where do we see feelings? How can we witness learning? Where do we observe at least glimmers of proficiency? The more coaches attend to and validate these aspects of teacher experiences, the more motivation teachers muster for personal growth and professional development.

> *People are not machines. When their needs, emotions, and needs are not considered, their productivity decreases, as does their overall level of commitment.*
>
> *Jane Kise (2006, p. 162)*

Such validation is a crucial part of evocative coaching conversations, both when teachers are excited and when teachers are intimidated by their stories and the prospect of change. The key is for teachers to connect the dots between their feelings and needs. Sometimes coaches may just want to ask, "How are you feeling about that?" "What's the most important thing here?" "What would you like to accomplish?" With the right tone, such questions can communicate respect and interest. They can encourage teachers to go deeper without putting them off or intimidating them. The emotional charge of the teacher's reply will indicate whether the question landed correctly or not. Did the teacher appreciate or resent the question? If the teacher pulls back in response to such questions, coaches may express empathy for the feelings and needs that teachers are experiencing in the coaching space itself. Feeling validated at any level facilitates learning, growth, and change at every level.

As simple as it is to ask direct and open-ended questions about how teachers are feeling, that is not always the best way to explore, understand, and validate teacher experiences. For one thing, teachers may not be able to identify their feelings and needs. To ask directly about them may put teachers on the spot. For another thing, teachers may be suspicious as to the intentions of the coach. "What will the coach do with that information?" If there are any trust issues between the coach and teacher, asking direct, open-ended questions about feelings and needs can do more harm than good. It is often better, then, for coaches to validate teacher experiences by reflecting what we imagine they may be going through with authentic, judgment-free feeling and need words. Such empathy guesses or empathy reflections communicate our sincere desire to understand and respect teacher experiences, no matter how difficult or troubling. Expressing empathy in this distinctive way invigorates teachers when the right words are finally found.

It is important for evocative coaches to avoid and limit communication patterns that are incompatible or interfere with expressing empathy. It is not helpful to judge, label, demonize, shame, compare, demand, reward, or punish teachers in the course of evocative coaching conversations. Advising, commiserating, consoling, correcting, educating, explaining, interrogating, and telling our own stories must also be limited and used with discretion. Grace and rhythm fail to characterize the dance in the absence of openness, understanding, and mutuality.

Empathy helps to facilitate these qualities when teachers feel heard at the level of their feelings, needs, and values. When teachers share about times when their lessons went particularly well, an evocative coach might express empathy by offering the following reflection and connection request: "It sounds like you're feeling excited and ready to take action because your needs for clarity and contribution are being met. Does that seem right?" We want to savor their excitement, deepen their enthusiasm, and celebrate their progress. When teachers make judgmental or cynical comments about their abilities or situations, a coach might offer the following reflection and request: "I'm guessing that you're feeling hesitant and nervous because your needs for competence and control are not being met. Does that hit the mark?" We want to calm their nervousness, understand their concern, and appreciate their intention.

The awareness generated by attending to life-affirming and life-alienating emotions in this way, combined with the request that teachers confirm and clarify the reflection, provides an opening for teachers to connect with their needs and values and to think about how they want to meet them. It also makes clear our intent to understand rather than to judge their experience. Allow time for silence and processing before moving forward in the coaching process. Invite teachers to corroborate and expand on empathy guesses; then express gratitude for whatever they come up with. Be sure teachers feel heard and respected before moving on. Celebrate progress at every opportunity. Watch for the "golden sigh." By acknowledging the life force that is stirring in teachers, evocative coaches increase the likelihood of coaching success.

Appreciative Inquiry

After coaches have established trust and rapport with teachers, and after teachers have shared, explored, and received empathy for their stories, it is time for two more movements in the evocative coaching process: appreciate and extrapolate. Interviewing teachers regarding their best experiences, core values, generative conditions, and heartfelt wishes elevates self-efficacy, enhances motivation, and energizes action. It gets teachers in the mood for change. That is especially true, and all the more amazing, when struggling teachers come to see themselves in new, more positive lights. It becomes possible, then, to develop a clear learning brief— what teachers will work on and how coaches will assist them—and to pursue a robust inquiry into teachers' strengths, vitalities, and possibilities. Extrapolating from the best of what is to the best of what might be takes inquiry to a whole new level. It engages the imagination and assists teachers to frame compelling aspirations of their best personal and professional selves.

The learning brief represents the swing from Story–Empathy to Inquiry– Design. Addressed too early, before Story–Empathy has worked its magic, the learning brief may undermine trust and rapport as well as limit the realm of the possible. If it is never addressed at all, however, coaching conversations will lack focus and direction as teachers move forward through Inquiry–Design. The brief should be clear without being overly detailed. We seek to be neither too general nor too specific as to our intentions. The learning brief is not rocket science; it is simply agreeing on the focus of our conversation and nature of our relationship.

Even when coaching is mandated around a clear issue of concern, the learning focus has to be clarified and agreed to by both the teacher and the coach. On occasion, a focus will jump out immediately. Often, however, coaches and teachers will float different topics for consideration until one topic clearly rises to the surface as an area of interest. When that happens, it can be useful to summarize the understanding and then to ask teachers how much energy they have around that topic on a scale of 0 to 10. If energy is low, there may be another topic worth pursuing. Or, it may be possible to invigorate the energy by discussing their energy rating. When teachers have ambivalence as to the learning focus, the conversation should continue until they clearly identify something on which they would like to concentrate. Evocative coaching is not just an engaging conversation; it is an engaging conversation with a clear focus that coaches and teachers agree to work on together.

Although an initial coaching session may clarify parameters for the entire coaching relationship, it is also important on a session-by-session basis to clarify the focus of that particular coaching conversation. If the learning brief, negotiated during the first coaching session, represents the macro level of the coaching project, then the brief for each subsequent coaching conversation represents the micro level of the coaching project. It clarifies where teachers want to go today, in this moment, with this conversation. After an effective session opening, with the wise use of Story–Empathy, it is time to frame the learning brief in order to move on with Inquiry–Design.

4. Appreciate

As we learned in Chapter Five, evocative coaches take a strengths-based approach to inquiry. We seek to discover the best of what is happening now in order to build those dynamics into the best of what might be possible in the future. What we appreciate, appreciates. Evocative coaches do not spend much time inquiring into, analyzing, and fixing problems. Rather, we target our inquiries to focus on strengths, vitalities, aspirations, and possibilities. In so doing, we assist teachers to reconnect with their joy and to realize their full potential. It is especially important for coaches to approach struggling teachers, who may be very resistant to change, in this way, since they have deep unmet needs both for validation and appreciation. That is usually possible with just about anyone. Everyone has shining moments, even teachers who struggle. No situation is so bleak and barren as to be totally without beauty, promise, and merit. The secret is to find a vantage point from which these glimmering facets can be seen. Empathy starts that process, because it validates the positive core behind even the most negative of messages. Appreciative inquiry continues the process by shining a spotlight on what teachers can celebrate about the past, savor about the present, and aspire to in the future.

The benefits of appreciating the positive dimensions of life are plentiful. They include generating optimism and positive energy, reminding teachers of their capabilities, cultivating resilience, inducing wider visual search patterns, expanding novel and creative thoughts, creating more inclusive and flexible mindsets, as well as stimulating more of the behaviors that created previous success (Cohn, Fredrickson, Brown, Conway, & Mikels, 2009). The primary objective of appreciating strengths and observing vitalities is to connect teachers with their "destiny, cause, and calling"—that place of deep longing and contribution that brought them to teaching in the first place (Secretan, 2004). The better teachers feel about themselves, the stronger teachers feel about their capabilities, and the more passion they feel about their work, the more successful they will be in designing experiments that move them forward.

The more we know about our strengths, the better our changes will be.

Evocative coaches make use of a wide variety of tools to explore a wide variety of strengths in teachers. Story listening is itself a tool, as teachers self-report on their experiences. Through story listening we expand awareness and increase readiness to change. To explore the learning focus, evocative coaches return to story listening while using an adapted version of the generic Appreciative Interview Protocol (see Appendix A). We adapt it to ask teachers specific questions about their stated learning interest. "When have you been the most successful with that in the past?" "When did you feel most comfortable and confident?" "What values did you express?" "What were the life-giving factors?" Inquiries such as these both reveal and magnify teacher capacities, proficiencies, competencies, creativities, energies, and opportunities. They launch coaches and teachers into a spiral dynamic of meaning making, strengths building, vitality boosting, and vision casting. This is the dynamic we hope to generate by appreciating the best things teachers can build on for their own learning and growth.

Our tone of voice, pacing, and our comfort with silence as teachers respond to our appreciative inquiries are as important to creating this spiral dynamic as the questions themselves. The best inquiries in the world will fail to land correctly if they are asked in the wrong way or with an implied right answer. Speaking too quickly after an inquiry is voiced, either to try and help teachers respond or to get teachers to see our point, also diminishes or even negates its effectiveness. We want teachers to sit with our strengths-based questions and to receive our vitality-oriented observations so that our questions and observations sink in and call forth both motivation and movement. If the teacher appears to be straining, the coach's changing approaches, adding variety, using humor, engaging the body, being creative, or going the extra mile in our communications and actions can keep the coaching conversation moving forward. That is the dynamic dance of evocative coaching. As we move through conversations with teachers, our presence, inquiries, and reflections bring out the best in teachers and encourage their learning in interesting and informative ways.

When teachers tell stories with strong, negative emotional charges, evocative coaches respond first with empathy reflections and then with appreciative inquiry. Instead of dissecting the experience to figure out what went wrong, we look for ways to see the strengths that may be shining through. This appreciative approach is not meant to deny the existence of problems; it is rather meant to shift the spotlight away from the train wrecks and onto the positive aspects of experience. Those aspects are always there. If teachers really want to talk about the problem, evocative coaches can bring them back to a positive frame with appreciative reflections and questions that look for the diamond in the rough. "How did this experience contribute to your development?" "What's the silver lining here?" "How else might you describe this situation?" "What did you learn about yourself and your values today?" "What did you learn about your students?" Inquiries such as these represent the work of appreciative reframing championed by Deutschman (2007) and others as one of the keys to successful and lasting behavior change. When coaches stay in that frame, teachers will eventually follow. By appreciating strengths and vitalities, it is possible to quicken the interest of teachers in the life-affirming and life-giving dimensions of their own experience.

In addition to using appreciative questions to explore what teachers remember and how teachers view their experiences, evocative coaches can use many other tools for discovering and building on strengths. The VIA Signature Strengths Questionnaire, for example, available at www.authentichappiness.sas.upenn.edu, can help teachers identify their virtues and character strengths that can be leveraged for motivation and movement in the classroom. Of even greater importance may be the observation tools that assist coaches to make appreciative observations when we visit the classroom or participate in design experiments. Observation is fraught with dangers, since it is so easy for evaluations to sneak into our vocabulary and tone. Although performance evaluations are often mandated in schools, they can interfere with the work of evocative coaching. Evocative coaches prefer to stay focused on the vital things that can be seen and heard when making observations. We look for shining eyes and smiling faces as teachers engage students in learning activities. Observation tools such as the Student Engagement, the Teacher Verbal Behaviors, and the Level of Teacher Questions Tools (see Chapter Five) can assist coaches to stay focused in this appreciative direction. Learning how to make life-giving observations without communicating life-draining evaluations is an essential part of the coaching dance. When teachers know that their coaches see positive value in what they are doing and how they are interacting with students, however fledgling their efforts, all manner of things become possible.

Coaching conversations go from engaging to productive when they move from empathy to inquiry. Appreciating strengths and vitalities enables coaches and teachers to drill down to the heart of the matter without getting stuck on the problem. That is when coaching becomes a dance of self-discovery for teachers, enabling them to think differently about the learning focus and even to see themselves in new lights. "Aha!" experiences are not uncommon. Frequently teachers will say things like, "I've never thought about that before," or "I never realized that until now." By appreciating teachers' strengths and vitalities, coaches build and harvest positive energy and emotion. Such reconnection provides the fuel for all that follows in aspiring, presencing, brainstorming, and designing.

5. Extrapolate

Once teachers have connected with the best of what is, once teachers have fully appreciated their strengths and vitalities, they naturally start aspiring and feeling the possibilities for the best of what might be. Such extrapolation is the second phase of the appreciative inquiry process. It often goes beyond incremental improvements to a bold statement of who teachers are and how teachers teach when they are at their very best. Such boldness can be encouraged by coaches through the questions we ask, as long as we do not ask them too soon. To invite teachers to frame great aspirations will often sound empty, inauthentic, impossible, and even insulting to a struggling teacher who is caught in the grip of negative emotions and performance reviews. "Yeah, right" and "Who are you trying to kid?" are more likely to be the reactions of such teachers than free and willing engagement in the process of conceptualizing how their identity and behavior might change to support personal and professional mastery.

You can tell people that they have to do something. You can be directive. And they may do what they have to do, but it won't be effective because it doesn't really change people's deeply held beliefs about teaching. It doesn't ultimately help students.

Luke, high school department chair

That is why it is so important to validate teacher experiences and to appreciate teacher strengths before asking teachers to extrapolate to the even more positive and constructive frame of aspiration and possibility. Discouraged and aggravated teachers are not prone to aspire to new heights. They are not even prone to cook up small improvements in their life and work. Until teachers receive empathy for their negative emotions, and until they connect with positive emotions through appreciative inquiries into their strengths and vitalities, not much will take off in the way of vision casting. After their mood elevates, however, evocative coaches will find teachers much more inclined to contemplate and work on future possibilities.

When teachers hang back, tap dancing away from challenge and commitment, we may want to talk with them about their ambivalence. Do not tell teachers what to do or push them to get on with the program since that usually exacerbates their resistance to change. Stay focused on expressing empathy until there is a deep and shared understanding of what is going on (Rosenberg, 2005). Invite teachers to weigh the pros and cons of the status quo and of the alternatives they see (Prochaska, Norcross, & DiClemente, 1994). Guide teachers through a focusing process to gain a felt sense of what this energy is trying to teach them (Gendlin, 1981). Explore the underlying and competing commitments that may be anchoring their "immunity to change" (Kegan & Lahey, 2009). The point is to not grow impatient or insistent with teachers. The point is to receive and explore ambivalence as a gift. There is something valuable to learn from it.

Extrapolation seeks to move teachers from an appreciative inquiry of the present and past to an appreciative inquiry of the future. The aspirations of teachers, both long and near term, are part of how the future breaks into the present. It is another way of coming at the reality that problems represent. Instead of coming at them directly, focusing on what we want to eliminate and get rid of, aspirations come at them indirectly, through the lens of what we want to cultivate and get more of. As teachers increase their awareness of how the future is inbreaking, as teachers increase their felt sense of how the future wants to be (Scharmer, 2007), the more they will move away from a place of ambivalence and resistance to a place of clarity and enthusiasm regarding their visions and goals. Instead of reacting to the worst of what is, teachers will start "preacting" to the best of what might be.

Presence is not what is evanescent and passes but what confronts us, waiting and enduring.
Martin Buber ([1923] 1970, p. 64)

That, at least, is what we hope for out of the appreciative inquiry phase: a strong felt sense and a clear, compelling statement of what the future is calling teachers to be and do. Using the best of what we know about the brain, including its creative-imaginative and analytic-declaratory capacities (Medina, 2008), we want teachers to connect with and give voice to a vision of who they are and how they teach at their very best. To that end, evocative coaches invite teachers to frame not only their long-term aspirations but also their more immediate possibilities in terms that beckon them forward. What would make life more meaningful and productive? What possibilities do they see as being within their reach and what aspirations do they hear calling out their name? Capturing such aspirations and inviting such possibilities in words and images, framed in the present tense as if they were already true, is an essential part of the evocative coaching dance. Before moving on to design thinking, we first elevate the readiness to change and bolster teachers' self-efficacy for making dreams come true.

Design Thinking

We described in Chapter Six how the whole of evocative coaching can be viewed as a design thinking process. Story–Empathy–Inquiry generates inspiration. The word *inspiration* means both "stimulation of the mind or emotions to a high level of feeling or activity" and "something, such as a sudden creative act or idea that is inspired" (American Heritage Dictionary). In other words, inspiration is both a process and an outcome. By definition, inspiration is evocative. It invests ideas with emotional energy and moves people to action. That is exactly what happens when we engage teachers with story listening, empathy reflections, and appreciative inquiries. We inspire both eagerness and the ability to change. That is why evocative coaching works: teachers find the inspiration to more fully and freely generate and implement ideas for change. Without Story–Empathy–Inquiry there is little hope for Design when coaching in schools. By dancing with teachers using Story–Empathy–Inquiry, however, coaches move teachers to innovate, deliberate, and activate their designs into being. These final three movements of the Great 8 have the power to turn aspirations into actions and possibilities into realities. They give teachers the chance, through brainstorming, choosing, and experimenting, not only to discover ways to improve their own skills and performance but also to design ways to transform school environments, one conversation at a time.

6. Innovate

If coaching is about anything at all, it is about encouraging teachers to generate and try out new ideas to help them be more successful. As we have seen, however, that does not mean that coaches show up with all the answers. Regardless of how much data may stand behind us and regardless of how great those ideas may sound to both coaches and teachers alike, prescriptions as to how teachers can improve their performance will generally not translate into effective actions. That is either because teachers may harbor an undercurrent of resentment at an outside expert telling them what to do or because they do not have enough ownership in the idea to stay with it long enough, through thick and thin, for it to become part of their behavioral repertoire. The key, then, is to generate innovative ideas through brainstorming.

Brainstorming is the process of rapidly generating a large number of ideas in the service of aspirations and possibilities. Once long-term aspirations have been framed and once short-term possibilities have been invited, identified, and claimed, the next logical question is, "How do we get there?" Assisting teachers to brainstorm answers to that question is an important part of evocative coaching. On occasion, teachers will be able to come up with a large number of ideas all on their own. Coaches can ask, "What else? What else? What else?," and the ideas just seem to pour out of them. More often, however, teachers have a hard time coming up with so many ideas. They may even have a hard time coming up with one idea. Evocative coaches can then offer to participate in the process as an active and collaborative partner. Coaches and teachers can take turns throwing out ideas, without pausing to evaluate their relative merit or feasibility, putting forward possible approaches that build and bounce from one to another. This co-creative process assists coaches to step out from wearing the expert hat and assists teachers to step up to generating and playing with out-of-the-box possibilities. Brainstorming encourages and tends to produce such wild and crazy ideas, since everyone knows they may never fly. This is all part of what makes brainstorming so evocative and fun.

Through the brainstorming process, coaches will be able to notice what is happening with the energy of teachers. Are they getting into it or are they pulling back? Are they having fun, or is this just another chore? If the energy is waning, then coaches may want to generate less ambitious and more realistic ideas. If the energy is waxing, then coaches may want to generate more ambitious and less conservative ideas. The point is to come up alongside teachers, to match their energy, and to move the process forward. Picking a number of ideas to generate ahead of time (6 to 10 is a good range) makes sure that the process does not stop prematurely. Often, through brainstorming, the best ideas come out at the end, when coaches and teachers alike warm up to the process.

Make sure the ideas are numbered and captured on paper as they get generated. Someone has to write them down before they can be reviewed, prioritized, and acted upon. One easy approach is for coaches and teachers to each have a pad of Post-it notes on which to write down their ideas. Afterward, the Post-it notes can be placed on poster board or on the inside of a file folder for both immediate viewing and future reference.

> *It is difficult to live another's answer, regardless of the amount of goodwill with which it is offered.*
>
> *Peter Block (2002, p. 6)*

7. Deliberate

Once coaches and teachers have come up with a large number of possibilities through brainstorming, it is time for teachers to prioritize those ideas, choosing the ones they want to do something about and designing S-M-A-R-T experiments that can assist them to learn and grow. Such deliberations, which are an essential part of the evocative coaching process, flow naturally upon the heels of inspiration and ideation.

To prioritize the ideas, ask teachers to identify the three they find most interesting and promising. Both qualities need to be present. We do not want teachers to pick ideas that represent the party line in the school system, just because they are the party line. We also do not want them to pick ideas that they think the coach wants them to pick. Coaches do not tell teachers what to do for many reasons, not the least of which is that we never really know what will work. We invite teachers to choose the ideas they want to pursue in order to see what comes of them. We want teachers to pick ideas they see as intrinsically interesting and valuable. To do that, we navigate with curiosity:

- Which ideas would be easy for you to work with successfully?
- Which ideas would be the most fun?
- Which ideas stand out as the best ideas?
- Which ideas would push you the most?
- Which ideas might have the greatest impact?
- Which ideas build on what you are already doing well?
- Which ideas would require you to learn new skills?
- What makes these ideas worth pursuing?

Questions such as these enable coaches and teachers to explore and prioritize ideas together. Once teachers have narrowed it down to three ideas, we carefully consider each to get them to pick the one or two they want to work with in the days and weeks ahead. Explain the concept of conducting S-M-A-R-T experiments as a way of field testing ideas rather than implementing plans, if teachers are not already familiar with the concept. We frame innovations as experiments because we want to learn what works. We make no assumptions and have no failures. Whether a design works or not, we physically and/or mentally raise our arms and say, "How fascinating!"—"rerouting our attention to the higher purpose at hand" (Zander & Zander, 2000, p. 103). There is no way to fail with an experiment; that is what makes experiments such fun and profitable ways to learn. We make experiments S-M-A-R-T because that framework helps to make sure they happen. Experiments that are designed and never conducted do not teach us much at all.

Teachers are more likely to act on what they say, not on what they hear.

In designing S-M-A-R-T experiments, it is important to invite teachers to think through whether they would rather design an awareness experiment or a behavior-change experiment. The two often overlap and both have real value in the evocative coaching process. Awareness experiments do not commit the teacher to a particular course of action or behavior change. They simply invite the teacher to pay attention to one or more of the critical variables that may be impacting their performance and quality of life. Behavior-change experiments start with an if-then hypothesis—"If I do this, then I may get that"—regarding something a teacher would like to do differently in their way of working. The goal of both kinds of experiments is to increase motivation and facilitate movement through self-directed, no-fault learning projects.

It is also important in designing S-M-A-R-T experiments to invite teachers to think through what would help to make their experiments successful. It is seldom sufficient just to bolster their resolve, shift their focus, or change their technique. Effective teaching requires the use and alignment of multiple resources, within classrooms, school buildings, and school systems. By assisting teachers to think through these environmental dynamics, their experiments will be more successful and their self-efficacy will be raised. What help do they want from other people? What materials do they want to have on hand? How do they want to design the physical space? What technology is required? How do they want to manage their time? Questions such as these are the stuff of good lesson planning, but in the conversation between coaches and teachers they take on new dimensions.

That is especially true when teachers view their environments as being dysfunctional and as having their own "immunity to change" (Kegan & Lahey, 2009, pp. 87–124). When the culture of a school or school system does not support the learning framework of S-M-A-R-T experiments, ambivalence and resistance may again become part of the coaching dance. Teachers may end up tap dancing around matters of choice and commitment. In such instances, it may be helpful to invite teachers to design a S-M-A-R-T experiment around environmental alignment. What could teachers do to affect the system? Assisting teachers to play with that question may be exactly what they need to kindle or rekindle their passion and commitment. Such conversations and experiments move teachers beyond the realms of their own skills and classrooms to the larger context of how other key stakeholders and organizational elements can better support their progress.

As important as supportive environments are to teaching success, evocative coaches do not allow the lack of environmental support to become a reason or an excuse for teachers to not have any professional improvement aspirations or designs at all. As we noted in Chapter Seven, the smallest of design experiments can trigger large and growing ripples in a pond. Evocative coaching views teachers as being fully responsible for their own feelings, frameworks, actions, and commitments. They are always able to respond by creating some measure of new possibilities, initiatives, understandings, and competencies. Challenging and assisting teachers to do that is the work of evocative coaching. How can teachers do more of what works now and do it even better in the future? By continuing to ask appreciative inquiries, reminding teachers of their strengths, vitalities, aspirations, and possibilities, most teachers will find the energy and vision to change.

Tiffany was a new third-grade teacher, having just completed her master's degree. She was young and fresh, with lots of ideas, but she couldn't put it all together. She was creative about coming up with ideas, thinking on her feet to come up with an example of a problem or a strategy or a skill. She could get up and teach an awesome lesson, but in the follow-up things would get jumbled. The kids weren't getting enough practice and enough repetition because there wasn't as much planning there. When she had the kids divide into groups or go to centers, everything was kind of haphazard. When I would plan with her, we would talk about how she was going to teach this unit. She came up with all these neat ideas and I wrote them down on index cards. I said, "Okay, see these four ideas that you came up with? We're going to make them into four different centers because they're all feeding off these great ideas." We got buckets and gathered all of the materials that would be needed for each center right then and there. When the kids got engaged in the centers, they were focused on skills that were related to the lesson that she had just taught. Because everything was there, and well planned out, she could do small group instruction and never have to be interrupted by students at the centers not knowing what to do. The design experiment worked great and she decided to keep using the process.

Robin, elementary math coach

---

8. Activate

Forward movement is made possible when teachers believe they have what it takes to activate the plans they have made. If teachers do not believe they have what it takes to move forward, or if they believe that their circumstances make progress impossible, they will not take action, learn, or grow. Understanding this dynamic, evocative coaches support self-efficacy and positivity throughout the coaching session. By acknowledging what teachers have brought to the table, the good work they have done in brainstorming, and their capacity to conduct experiments that will assist them to see their dreams through to fruition, coaches enable teachers to move forward and leverage success.

Once a S-M-A-R-T experiment has been designed, invite the teacher to restate and summarize what she will focus on or do in her own words. Whenever possible, commit the plan to writing by using the Experimental Design Template (refer to Figure 6.2). Be sure teachers sound committed and ready to participate fully in the experiment. Reflect the energy and emotion of teachers until the prospect of conducting an experiment is clearly a life-giving proposition. To move teachers into action, it can be helpful to ask one or more of the following scale questions:

- On a scale of 0 to 10, how important would you say it is to conduct this experiment at this time? (Clarifies willingness)
- On a scale of 0 to 10, how ready are you to conduct this experiment at this time? (Clarifies readiness)
- On a scale of 0 to 10, how confident are you that you will conduct this experiment at this time? (Clarifies ability)

Explore the numbers teachers come up with by asking two follow-up questions:

1. What led you to pick that number and not a lower number?
2. What would make it higher number?

Continue to talk about the numbers they select, redesigning the experiment as necessary, until teachers end up with numbers of 7 or higher. That usually indicates that teachers are ready, willing, and able to conduct and learn from an experiment. Lower numbers may indicate that teachers find the experiment to be either too challenging or too boring. When teachers think about an experiment, when they rehearse and simulate it in their minds, we want them to get into the sweet spot of "flow" (Csikszentmihalyi, 1990, 2000) where the challenges are stimulating but not overwhelming, where their skills are stretched but not broken. Those are the experiments worth conducting with a high probability of success.

Experimental designs are not complete until teachers decide how they want to collect, report, and reflect on their data. As much as possible, their observations and data collection should take place in real time rather than after the fact. This can be done through concurrent note taking, recording with audio or visual equipment, inviting the coach or someone else to observe the experiment in action, and/or getting student feedback. The value of different approaches and observational tools can be discussed with teachers, who may decide to use more than one method simultaneously. When coaches are asked to observe S-M-A-R-T experiments, it is important to look for strengths and vitalities rather than to focus on weaknesses and deficiencies. Identifying observable things that go well can assist and empower teachers to design new experiments that build on those positive dimensions. If an experiment doesn't go according to plan, notice the ways in which teachers are modifying or improvising on their experiments in order to be more successful. Evocative coaches not only affirm this level of autonomy and spontaneous engagement, we recognize that it is the only way effective teaching happens.

After an observation, teachers will not be the only ones with new stories to tell. Now both coaches and teachers will have new information to talk about. The more we can look together with appreciative eyes at, observational data collected in real time the better, because that is the data that can best serve teacher learning and growth. The observational tools described in Chapter Five and available at www.EvocativeCoaching.com can assist coaches in that task. They often prove to be effective conversation pieces as teachers seek to make sense of their experiences, to process their feelings, and to frame new aspirations for the future.

Championing teachers is a good way to wrap up evocative coaching sessions. It is just as helpful to end coaching sessions as it is to begin them with trust, rapport, and positivity. Celebrate the best to bring out the best. Invigorate learning with recognition. Endorse the work, the aspirations, and the experiments. Honor the feelings and needs. Champion the courage, creativity, and possibility that teachers are bringing into the world. Let teachers know that we believe not only in their ability to be successful but also in the surprising discoveries they will make along the way.

W. H. Murray (1951) of the Scottish Himalayan Expedition famously addressed this dynamic when he wrote:

> Concerning all acts of initiative and creation, there is one elementary truth, the ignorance of which kills countless ideas and splendid plans: that the moment one definitely commits oneself, then Providence moves too. All sorts of things occur to help one that would never otherwise have occurred. A whole stream of events issues from the decision, raising in one's favor all manner of unforeseen incidents and meetings and material assistance, which no one could have dreamed would come his or her way. I have learned a deep respect for one of Goethe's couplets:
> "Whatever you can do, or dream you can, begin it.
> Boldness has genius, power, and magic in it." (pp. 6–7)

Summary

Evocative coaching is different from instruction, supervision, or evaluation. We do not tell teachers what to do and then induce them to do it. We call forth that desire and empower that ability. Since evocative coaching conversations are different in their orientation and approach than typical didactic methods, it helps to have a sense of the movements to make. At a high level, Story–Empathy–Inquiry–Design reflects the dance steps. On a more granular level, the Great 8 choreographs those steps so that coaches can better handle the transitions, iterations, and directional flow of coaching conversations. When coaches initiate, elaborate, validate, appreciate, extrapolate, innovate, deliberate, and activate the learning and growth of teachers, we have made a lasting contribution to the transformation and betterment of schools.

Questions for Reflection and Discussion

1. Which of the Great 8 movements resonate most with your experience? Which present a challenge for you?
2. What helps you to get into a coaching frame of mind before a coaching session?
3. How do you start a coaching session in order to facilitate the development of trust, rapport, and positivity? What questions do you like to ask at the start of a coaching session?
4. How do you deal with teachers who talk too much? Who talk too little? What does how much teachers talk reveal about their needs?
5. Why might it be better to offer an "empathy guess" rather than to ask directly about teacher feelings and needs?
6. When teachers are having a hard time coming up with new ideas, what is a good way for coaches to help them out?
7. Why does it help teachers for coaches to do some of the brainstorming? How can coaches do that without taking over or dominating the process?
8. What are some good ways to capture the data from S-M-A-R-T experiments? Why is this important?

CHAPTER 9

THE REFLECTIVE COACH

Reflection-in-action is essential to the process by which individuals function as agents of significant organizational learning.

DONALD SCHÖN (1983, P. 338)

In this book, we have introduced the notion of evocative coaching as an effective and enjoyable way to promote learning, growth, and change with teachers and other educators. Our teacher-centered, no-fault, strengths-based approach may have challenged your own assumptions and approaches as to how to go about this important work. It is time now to reflect on what we have presented, in light of your own experience, in order to fashion your own approach to coaching, a definition-in-action that will clarify, facilitate, and empower your way of being with the people you coach.

Coaching the Self

Just as coaches invite teachers to reflect on their experiences in order to generate new stories and design new actions, coaches take the time to do that for ourselves and for each other. We read books like this one and reflect upon our coaching experiences in order to facilitate our own continuous growth and progress. Donald Schön (1983) coined the phrase "reflective practitioner" as he made the case that this quality of both "reflection-*in*-action" and "reflection-*on*-action" is part and parcel of how professionals do our work. Reflective practice involves thoughtfully considering critical incidents in one's own experiences and applying professional knowledge to practice. It is through such reflection that

artistry enters the work of a profession, taking practice beyond the mere application of technical knowledge. Schön described the far-reaching consequences for
schools that truly embraced reflective practice:

> In a school supportive of reflective teaching, teachers would challenge the
> prevailing knowledge structure. Their on-the-spot experiments would affect not
> only the routines of teaching practice but the central values and principles of
> the institution. Conflicts and dilemmas would surface and move to center stage.
> In the organizational learning system with which we are most familiar, conflicts
> and dilemmas tend to be suppressed or to result in polarization and political
> warfare. An institution congenial to reflective practice would require a learning
> system within which individuals could surface conflicts and dilemmas and
> subject them to productive public scrutiny, a learning system conducive to the
> continual criticism and restructuring of organizational principles and values.
> (pp. 335–336)

Coaches assist teachers to become reflective practitioners when we enable
them to examine their teaching methods and determine what works best for their
students without fear or presuppositions. As coaches, we become reflective practitioners when we pay attention to our own story, actively engage in self-empathy,
inquire into our own strengths, vitalities, aspirations, and possibilities, and design our own S-M-A-R-T (Specific, Measurable, Attainable, Relevant, and Time
bound) experiments for personal and professional growth.

Hearing Our Own Stories

Deep story listening is something we can do for ourselves as well as for others. How
often do we stop and listen to the stories we are telling in our own life? In *The Artist's
Way*, Julia Cameron (1992) recommends the discipline of writing three pages every
morning. Write less, she cautions, and we won't go deep enough. Write more, and
we will probably burn out before it becomes a daily habit. Deep listening as a daily
habit is the point of her discipline.

We can also listen to our own stories by practicing mindfulness—the nonjudgmental awareness of what is happening in the present moment—throughout
the day and, as we have noted, in those significant moments right before the start
of coaching sessions. The ability to practice mindfulness during coaching sessions,
reflection-*in*-action, is a core coaching skill. When coaches model that ability and
presence, teachers open up and gain that ability for themselves. It is only in the
practice of mindfulness that we come to understand the meaning of mindfulness

and its effect on our professional practice. By practicing mindfulness in our every-day lives, and showing up mindfully for our coaching sessions with teachers, we enable teachers to learn, grow, and develop beyond what they might otherwise have imagined possible. To that end, coaches can ask ourselves the following questions before, during, and after coaching:

- Where am I?
- What is going on around me?
- What do I notice that's unexpected or surprising?
- What am I thinking about?
- What am I feeling?
- How can I enhance my experience of coaching?

Coaches would also do well to incorporate silence as a habit in our daily routines. Becoming comfortable with silence can be supported by an ongoing practice of contemplation or cultivating other silent moments throughout the day. It is hard to effectively listen well and utilize silence in coaching if we have not learned to do so in our daily lives. Before the start of coaching sessions, coaches may find many of the follow practices to be helpful:

- Take five deep, slow breaths.
- Close our eyes for five seconds.
- Stand straight with our weight evenly distributed.
    - Lift the right arm and left leg at the same time.
    - Return to starting position and repeat with left arm and right leg.
    - Return to starting position and dangle and shake arms loosely at our sides.
- Become aware of our breathing.
- Place our hands on our chest and become aware of our heart beating.
- Say out loud any of the following statements. Let them sink in.
    - I am grateful for this opportunity to connect and make a difference.
    - I evoke trust, rapport, and positive energy.
    - I have an opportunity to make a pivotal contribution.
    - I am open to and curious about what will unfold.
- Do whatever other activities (art, music, movement, etc.) bring us into the present moment and prepare us for coaching. (Adapted from Moore & Tschannen-Moran, 2010, pp. 21–22)

It is not possible to coach masterfully in a state of feeling overwhelmed, fatigued, stressed, burned out, or in despair. Therefore, self-care on the part of the coach translates into coaching effectiveness. Mindfulness contributes to the cultivation of our strengths through taking the opportunity to quiet our mental chatter (Silberman,

2007). Paying attention to the rhythm of work and rest, of energy out and energy in, is an essential part of self-management for conveying coaching presence. The more things we do that fill us with energy, the more likely it is that we can serve as inspiring role models for the teachers we coach. Without doing the things that make life worth living, including adequate time for rest and recovery, it is quite difficult to share renewing energy with others. We pay attention to energy dynamics when we work with teachers in designing S-M-A-R-T experiments; we attend to those same dynamics in our own personal and professional practices.

Self-Empathy

Authentic empathy and complete acceptance represent the compassionate core of the work of evocative coaching. Every time someone tells us a story about his or her life, every time we step back to reflect and organize our thoughts, we have the opportunity to connect with both the facts and the feelings. An awareness of one's own feelings and needs is crucial if coaches want to be an empathic presence with teachers. When coaches notice and share what is happening with us in the present moment ("My stomach is churning right now"), the teachers we are working with often respond with greater awareness and openness of their own.

When coaches find it difficult to give teachers empathy, it may mean we are not receiving enough empathy in our own lives. Since coaches should not expect or demand to receive empathy from teachers, we must be sure to get it from other sources. Regular self-empathy, as well as mutual empathy with significant others, are essential practices for authentic coaching presence. By connecting deeply with and understanding our own feelings and needs, coaches grow our empathy muscles and open the way for relational authenticity with others (Jordan, Walker, & Hartling, 2004). To become aware of both our feelings and the needs behind our feelings, we might practice focusing (Gendlin, 1981) or we might write in a journal about our feelings and needs, referring to the lists of feeling and need words presented in Chapter Four. We can also become aware of and write down our thoughts about those feelings and needs. Preface any intrusive thoughts with the words, "The story I'm telling myself is . . ." Remember that the story of our thoughts and recollections are but one version of reality.

Self-empathy is a critical ingredient for coaches in managing our emotions during coaching sessions. The more we know about what is going on with us, the less we will allow our own events, feelings, opinions, and worries to get in the way of our being present in the moment. Although coaches widely recognize the importance of creating a generative relational space with teachers, it is sometimes difficult to maintain a calm, safe, judgment-free posture in the face of poor teaching. It becomes even more difficult when those behaviors persist in spite of a coach's best efforts to support self-responsibility and behavior change. Being mindful of our own energy and emotional reactions in relation to the teachers we are working with is an essential part of evocative coaching. Examining our own reactions and feelings can be done in the moment (reflection-*in*-action) or outside of coaching sessions (reflection-*on*-action), alone or with a mentor coach, in order to facilitate our competence and development as coaches.

When conversations with teachers trigger emotional responses, when we start viewing teachers as irritating or uncooperative, it helps to notice the things we are saying to ourselves and then to explore the underlying feelings and needs. What are we really feeling when we "feel" that teachers are being uncooperative? Coaches may be more invested in an outcome than the teachers. We may want to push hard to make change happen more quickly. When such thoughts come up, it is important to remember that such thinking interferes with empathy and provokes resistance to change. Such change-promoting efforts are usually counterproductive because they encourage resistance talk rather than change talk, which hinders the advancement of the teacher's agenda and the work of coaching in general. Although we may be momentarily frustrated with a teacher, that often says more about us than about the teacher. Becoming curious about the needs that are motivating teacher behaviors can begin to shift things in a positive direction. Recognizing that both poor teaching behaviors and poor engagement with the coaching process are expressions, however unfortunate, of a teacher's unmet needs can facilitate empathy and relieve frustration. Change is not likely until and unless the needs of teachers are fully and respectfully recognized and expressed.

Coaching will not succeed unless the intention and presence of the coach is purely to understand the teacher's experience. The more coaches try to manipulate behavior or force an outcome, the more likely our actions will increase rather than decrease resistance. When that happens, our actions work against rather than support the motivation to change. Self-determination and adult-learning theories make it clear that the human propensity for personal growth toward integration and cohesion only happens when change is freely chosen, in the moment, through the interplay of competence, autonomy, and relatedness (Markland, Ryan, Tobin, & Rollnick, 2005).

Inquiring into Our Own Professional Practice

Our effectiveness as coaches will not only be enhanced by modeling the practice of self-empathy but also by modeling appreciative inquiries and continuous curiosity into our own professional practice. We can always observe ourselves in the moment with a metacognitive, or "thinking about our thinking," awareness. This "sensemaking" is likely to be more explicit when things are going either worse or better than expected (Weick, 1995). Significant gaps between expectation and observation invite us to make a bigger investment in our own learning by taking more time to S.T.O.P. (Step back, Think, Organize our thoughts, before Proceeding), to use one of the tools described following, and to design our own S-M-A-R-T experiments around the questions we bring to our practice.

Self-Observation

Self-reflection can be facilitated by using appreciative observation tools such as those we offered to teachers in the inquiry phase of the evocative coaching process (see Chapter Five). To make such observations, coaches may want to solicit the permission of the teacher we are coaching to audio and/or video record one or more coaching sessions. It is important to assure the teacher that this is for our own learning and growth as a coach and that we will delete the recording after we have finished reviewing it. We review the recordings in the search for vitalities that enhance the coaching dynamic. These vitalities are the things we want to broaden and build on in our professional practice as coaches. Several self-observation tools are available for download at www.EvocativeCoaching.com, or coaches may want to construct their own around their particular learning focus.

> *Doing and thinking are complementary.*
>
> *Donald Schön (1983, p. 280)*

Preparing Notes and Written Debriefs. Many coaches like to take notes during coaching sessions, although this can interfere with teacher learning if the coaching session is face to face and too many notes are being taken. We do, however, want to capture the salient points. In addition to the notes taken during the coaching session, it may be helpful to take five to ten minutes immediately after the coaching session for a written debrief, documenting:

- What did we notice?
- When were energies high?
- How did we feel during the session?
- What questions got a reaction?
- What promises were made?
- What would we like to build upon and develop in the next session?
- What would we like to explore further?

These are just a start to the questions we can ask ourselves and write about as reflective practitioners. And there is no better time to do that than immediately following a coaching session. Creating such written debriefs assists with continuity from one session the next when coaches take the time to review those notes in those moments before future coaching sessions.

Charting Talk Time. In evocative coaching sessions, teachers do more of the talking. Coaches are encouraged to adopt a W.A.I.T. and S.E.E. attitude: Why Am I Talking? and Stop Explaining Everything. A teacher talking always represents a measure of vitality. One simple way to find out what proportion of the coaching conversation coaches and teachers talk is to review an audio recording of the coaching session and tally minute-by-minute totals of who was speaking, in terms of "idea chunks" or in ten-second intervals, like the time sweeps in the Student Engagement Observation Tool in Chapter Five. After charting a coaching session with Kelly, Rob reflected on his intention of allowing of Kelly to talk more using the Talk Time Chart (see Figure 9.1).

FIGURE 9.1. CHARTING TALK TIME

Teacher: Kelly   Date: Nov. 3
Coach: Rob   Time: 2:45–3:10

Minute	Teacher	Total	Coach	Total
0:00	⧸⧸⧸⧸ //	7	⧸⧸⧸⧸ /	6
1:00	⧸⧸⧸⧸ /	6	⧸⧸⧸⧸ /	6
2:00	⧸⧸⧸⧸ /	6	⧸⧸⧸⧸ //	7
3:00	⧸⧸⧸⧸	5	///	3
4:00	⧸⧸⧸⧸ //	7	//	2
5:00	⧸⧸⧸⧸	5	////	4
6:00	⧸⧸⧸⧸ ////	9	////	4
7:00	/	1	⧸⧸⧸⧸ ///	8
8:00	/	1	⧸⧸⧸⧸ ⧸⧸⧸⧸ /	11
9:00	/	1	⧸⧸⧸⧸ ⧸⧸⧸⧸ /	11
10:00	/	1	⧸⧸⧸⧸ ⧸⧸⧸⧸	10
11:00	⧸⧸⧸⧸	5	⧸⧸⧸⧸ //	7
12:00	⧸⧸⧸⧸ //	7	⧸⧸⧸⧸ /	6
13:00	/	1	⧸⧸⧸⧸ ////	9
14:00	⧸⧸⧸⧸	5	⧸⧸⧸⧸ ////	9
15:00	⧸⧸⧸⧸ ////	9	////	4

(Continued)

FIGURE 9.1. (*CONTINUED*)

Teacher: Kelly   Date: Nov. 3
Coach: Rob   Time: 2:45–3:10

Minute	Teacher	Total	Coach	Total
16:00	////	4	##/	5
17:00	##/	5	##/ //	7
18:00	//	2	##/ ##/	10
19:00	//	2	##/ ////	9
20:00	//	2	##/ ///	8
21:00	////	4	//// //	7
22:00	//	2	///	3
23:00	##/ /	6	////	4
24:00	##/ //	7	//	2
25:00	##/	5	////	4
26:00				
27:00				
28:00				
29:00				
30:00				
31:00				
32:00				
33:00				
34:00				
35:00				
Total		115		166

When I charted my coaching session with Kelly, I noticed that although things started out in a fairly balanced way near the beginning of the conversation, I shifted into more of a teaching stance and started to talk more than Kelly. I got engaged in reminding her about the various levels of questioning. After that, the balance of the conversation shifted back more toward Kelly as Kelly began to imagine how she might prepare for her lessons by writing down questions at higher levels of reasoning. I noticed that as I sought to endorse this idea and to encourage Kelly in this effort, that I had once again done more of the talking.

Although it was not a scientific count (and was not meant to be), Rob noted that he had scored himself as contributing 169 "data chunks" to Kelly's 113. Although evocative coaching sessions will not always have the teacher talking more than the coach, or even have a 50/50 balance, that happens more often than not in evocative coaching conversations. Through charting talk time, Rob became persuaded that the teachers he coached would have greater opportunities for meaning making and would ultimately take more responsibility for their learning if he encouraged them to do more of the talking. As he reflected on the conversation with Kelly, he saw opportunities when he might have asked more questions to draw out more of Kelly's own thinking. He took it as a personal challenge to try to tip the balance more in Kelly's direction in the next coaching session, because that is where he noticed the most vitality.

Charting Coach Behaviors. Throughout this book we have identified numerous behaviors that coaches may use in our work with teachers. Some of the more important include attentive listening, asking questions, offering reflections, clarifying focus, brainstorming ideas, designing actions, aligning environments, and celebrating progress. There are many others. The International Coach Federation (2008b), for example, has identified eleven core coaching competencies; the International Association of Coaching (2009) has identified nine coaching masteries (reprinted with permission in Appendix D). We have also identified behaviors that are not compatible with or conducive to the evocative coaching dynamic.

To become more aware of our behaviors during coaching sessions, coaches can identify the behaviors we want to notice, record the coaching conference, and then chart our behaviors in one- or two-minute time intervals. Emma reflected on an audio recording of her coaching conversation with Rachel (see Figure 9.2).

One thing that I noticed was that I spent a great deal of time listening throughout the coaching session, which I felt really good about. I felt like I was attentive to Rachel and did not dominate the conversation. I also noticed that I asked a lot of questions, especially near the beginning and in the middle of the coaching session as I was trying to invite her to tell her story and to inquire into her successes as she recounted what had happened with her last experiment. I only asked her to elaborate once, but it didn't seem that necessary because she was very open in her sharing. I only made empathy guesses in a few places, nearer the beginning of the session. I don't know if it would have been helpful to do more of that or not. That skill does not come as easily for me, and it seems like it might have interrupted the flow of the conversation if I had tried to interject more when I was feeling a little awkward about it. I'm glad that I kept my presenting to a minimum.

FIGURE 9.2. CHARTING COACH BEHAVIORS

Coach: Emma
Teacher: Rachel

Date of Conference: 2/10
Time of Conference: 1:40–2:10

Time Interval	1. Listening	2. Questioning	3. Presenting	4. Reflecting	5. Clarifying	6. Brainstorming	7. Designing	8. Aligning	9. Celebrating	10. Humor
2	///	////		/						
4	////	//								
6	///			//						
8	///									
10	///	//			/					/
12	////	//							//	
14	/	/	/							
16	////	/				/	//		/	
18	///	//		/		/	//			
20	//	/					/			
22	/	/					/			
24	//	/	//							
26			/				/	/		
28	/						/			
30										
32										
34										
36										
38										
40										
42										
44										
46										
Total	35	17	4	4	1	2	8	1	3	1

We did brainstorming during two segments (four minutes total). This seemed like enough because she already had some ideas of what she wanted to work on and what she wanted me to observe. I didn't want to dissuade her when she was taking a lot of initiative about her own learning. Negotiating the learning parameters took a little longer because we had to figure out the logistics of when I would come into her room and I also needed a seating chart to be able complete the observation tool she wanted me to use. We did some celebrating of her successes during three segments because she was feeling really pleased with the progress she is seeing in her students since we have begun trying our experiments!

The ten categories at the top of the chart (listening, questioning, presenting, reflecting, clarifying, brainstorming, designing, aligning, celebrating, and humor) reflect the behaviors that Emma wanted to learn more about in terms of how she was using them in coaching Rachel. She had been striving to ask more questions and to do less presenting, which she clearly accomplished and was very happy about. She also wanted to use more humor, which she only used once. By charting her behaviors in two-minute increments, Emma also noticed how her role shifted during different portions of the coaching conversation. Many other behaviors can also be charted, and there is no "one right balance" of behaviors that coaches are trying to achieve in every coaching conversation. Our goal is to be aware of and responsive to the needs of the teachers we are coaching, in the context of their many environments, making "just-in-time" moves that meet teacher needs and evoke teacher engagement. Through self-observation and charting our behaviors, we gain an opportunity to reflect on our contribution and role in coaching conversations.

Noticing Evocative Coaching Style Points. To illuminate the evocative coaching process, we have already identified two loops or turns (No-Fault and Strengths-Building), four steps (Story–Empathy–Inquiry–Design), and eight movements (initiate, elaborate, validate, appreciate, extrapolate, innovate, deliberate, and activate). Dare we add sixteen style points as observable dimensions of the evocative coaching dance? Recognizing the limitations of numbered diagrams, which imply a far more linear and hierarchical form than evocative coaching conversations ever actually take, we nevertheless see value as reflective practitioners to sketching out the style points as in Table 9.1.

After audio recording a coaching conversation, Holly used the sixteen style points to observe and reflect on a coaching conversation she had with Adam regarding the use of technology in the classroom. (See Figure 9.3.) This conversation was particularly positive and productive for both teacher and coach. Holly

TABLE 9.1.   THE EVOCATIVE COACHING DANCE

LOOP I: The No-Fault Turn	LOOP II: The Strengths-Building Turn
Step 1: Story Listening	**Step 3: Appreciative Inquiry**
1. *Initiate*	4. *Appreciate*
i. Establishing rapport	viii. Discovering strengths
ii. Appreciative questions	ix. Observing vitalities
iii. Attentive listening	5. *Extrapolate*
2. *Elaborate*	x. Framing aspirations
iv. Exploring stories	xi. Inviting possibilities
Step 2: Expressing Empathy	**Step 4: Design Thinking**
3. *Validate*	6. *Innovate*
v. Offering reflections	xii. Brainstorming ideas
vi. Celebrating progress	7. *Deliberate*
vii. Clarifying focus in the Learning brief	xiii. Designing experiments
	xiv. Aligning environments
	8. *Activate*
	xv. Confirming Commitment
	xvi. Session feedback

was pleased with how the session began and with her conscious decision to not plow directly into the problems with the school's data system that Adam had been experiencing. That emerged later, as the focus of the learning brief, once some positive energy had been generated through story and empathy. Holly noted that she did not do brainstorming during the session; she reasoned that Adam was primarily looking for information about how to do his data entry more efficiently and that she knew some procedures that could help. An idea that Adam had mentioned in passing about getting parts of the data entry done at different times of the day did find its way into the experimental design. Overall, Holly thought it had been a productive session.

Noticing Body Language. To learn more about how well we are responding to teachers in the moment and facilitating a sense of flow, coaches can request a teacher's permission to video record a coaching conversation. This can feel threatening to some teachers, so be sure to explain that it is for our own learning and growth and will be deleted afterward. When we have time to reflect on the experience (and close enough in time that it is still fresh in mind), watch the video with

FIGURE 9.3. NOTICING EVOCATIVE COACHING STYLE POINTS

Teacher: Adam   Date: September 7, 2009
Coach: Holly   Time: 11:00 AM

Elements	Observed	Notes
Establishing rapport	Yes __X__ No _____	Adam showed up lots of positive energy today. I listened to several stories about his weekend.
Appreciative questions	Yes __X__ No _____	I avoided asking directly about the problems he was having with the computers. Stayed focused on what he liked and what he wanted.
Attentive listening	Yes __X__ No _____	Got distracted at one point; mindfully brought myself back with a deep breath.
Exploring stories	Yes __X__ No _____	Adam told a story about how much time it took to do data entry for the students. We explored doing it at different times of day.
Empathy reflections	Yes __X__ No _____	Adam had lots of energy around adventure and creativity. I tried to reflect that back.
Celebrating progress	Yes __X__ No _____	I celebrated his weekend adventures noting "we can make good use of that energy" together.
Clarifying focus	Yes __X__ No _____	Adam stated he wants to focus on how the computer systems were affecting his teaching. A clear learning brief.
Discovering strengths	Yes _____ No __X__	He talked primarily about his frustrations with the slow and unreliable computers in his classroom. I just let him talk.
Observing vitalities	Yes __X__ No _____	I asked him to enter some data while I watched. I noticed and commented on things he was doing well; also saw things he could improve.
Framing aspirations	Yes __X__ No _____	Adam stated that he would like the computers to feel like a joy, rather than an interruption.
Inviting possibilities	Yes __X__ No _____	He talked about learning the systems better, and he wanted to know if there were ways to batch some of the data entry.
Brainstorming ideas	Yes _____ No __X__	Did not do any brainstorming. I asked if he would like me to show him some new procedures, and he was all ears.
Designing experiments	Yes __X__ No _____	After I was done demonstrating procedures, we designed an experiment that included using the new procedures at different times of the school day. He agreed to keep track of his feelings.
Aligning environments	Yes __X__ No _____	Adam asked if I could be present while he conducted his first experiment, and I agreed.
Confirming commitment	Yes __X__ No _____	We put the dates on the calendar and Adam indicated he had a confidence level of 10, that he would do it, especially if I showed up!
Session feedback	Yes __X__ No _____	I asked Adam what he liked best about our session. He said he appreciated my teaching as well as my non-judgmental attitude.

the sound turned off. Pay attention to both your own body language and that of the teacher to see what they might reveal about how each person was feeling during various segments of the coaching conversation. Observe actions, reactions, adaptations, repetitions, facial expressions, inclinations, shifts, accommodations, and other salient factors. Look for evidence of vitality. When did eyes light up and faces smile? What were we pleased with and what would we like to do more of in future coaching sessions? As Tim reflected on a coaching conversation with Jeff, a second-year teacher who had struggled during his first year, he became aware of dynamics that had escaped him during the coaching session itself.

> I noticed that as we began, Jeff looked pretty apprehensive. He was sitting up very straight in his chair and his face looked tight. I looked more relaxed and confident, which I was glad to see because I was a little nervous myself about how I would do with this new approach to coaching. As we engaged in rapport building, I was leaning forward slightly and I kept my eyes on him. Occasionally I nodded or smiled slightly. He seemed to visibly relax. When we moved to the story phase, he became more animated. He began to gesture with his hands more. At one point, he shared something that was amusing and we both smiled more broadly and nodded. When I tried to respond to his story with a distinctive reflection, I was the one who was more visibly tense. I looked a little confused as I tried to think about what need he was trying to meet. He kept his eyes on me through this sort of awkward moment, and we seemed to have had enough momentum up to that point that we were able to move through it.
>
> During the inquiry phase, I noticed that I seemed somewhat impatient. I kept twisting my pen and I shifted in my seat. I wasn't aware of it at the time but seeing myself do this made me conscious of the need to be more patient and thoughtful in my discussions with teachers. It is apparent that I need to be more aware of the nonverbal messages I send. During this phase, Jeff became much more confident and excited about the process than he had been at the beginning. He was visibly pleased when reviewing the observation tools and selecting the one he wanted me to use when I visited his classroom. As we wrapped up, we were both smiling and there seemed to be a positive spirit between us. I was glad that even though there were some parts of my own behavior that I want to work on in the future, that the outcome of the coaching conversation still seemed to be so positive.

Asking for Feedback

Because coaching promotes teacher development within a learning partnership, it is important for coaches to occasionally solicit feedback from teachers.

This feedback is important both for our own learning as well as to enable us to adapt the coaching process to better support the learning and growth of the teachers we are working with. Asking teachers to share input and to make suggestions on how the coaching process can become more productive and enjoyable increases their sense of engagement as well as their autonomy and responsibility. Unless teachers are asked directly for such feedback, they often will not tell us if, when, and how they would like the coaching to be different. Soliciting honest input at periodic intervals during the coaching program builds the coaching relationship by making it clear to teachers that we are devoted to their success and that we will do whatever it takes to facilitate that success. Appreciative inquiries such as the following can therefore move the relationship forward in positive directions:

- What is the best experience you've had so far through the coaching process?
- What do you value most about our coaching relationship?
- What about our process has helped you to reach your goals and move forward?
- If you had three wishes for our coaching relationship, wishes that would make the relationship serve you better, what would they be?

Soliciting feedback using these and other appreciative inquiries is quite different from soliciting constructive criticism. By focusing on positive experiences, values, conditions, and wishes regarding what teachers like and want rather than what they do not like and do not want, coaches and teachers are empowered to be honest in our mutual pursuit of making the coaching relationship as productive and as enjoyable as possible.

Remind teachers that they can send us feedback at any time and that we will always take their suggestions seriously. Encourage the use of e-mail or written notes to communicate post-session thoughts. Evocative coaches become better coaches when teachers articulate the kind of approaches and dynamics that are most motivating and effective. By asking teachers to talk about the things that are working well and that they would like more of in the course of a coaching relationship, and by taking their ideas seriously, we model our commitment to lifelong learning and we reduce the likelihood that teachers will act out their resistance to change by undermining the coaching process itself.

Coaching is not a service profession; it is a modeling profession.

Jay Perry (2005, p. 7)

As teachers are sharing their thoughts in response to a request for feedback, listen for what is unspoken but conveyed by a teacher's tone and hesitations. Ask for clarification if we sense that there may be uncomfortable or hard feelings. Use empathy reflections to better understand the feelings and needs.

When we receive suggestions or criticism, we should be prepared to use them well. Thank teachers for the input and use it to grow stronger as a coach. Take notes and follow up on the points raised as soon as possible. Avoid the urge to explain our actions or intentions. Review audio and video recordings of coaching sessions to get a sense of the dynamics teachers have raised. Without violating confidentiality or becoming defensive, it may also help to talk with a mentor coach or other coaching colleagues about points of concern. As with all of evocative coaching, the goal is to build on the things that are working well and to outgrow the things that are working less well. Letting teachers know how we are handling and seeking to grow through their concerns to improve our coaching supports trust and models the very frame of learning, growth, and change that we want teachers to bring to their teaching. Modeling an attitude of openness and lack of defensiveness may be as powerful as anything we do as coaches.

Design Action-Learning Experiments

Some people are natural-born coaches, with amazing aptitude for story listening, expressing empathy, appreciative inquiry, and design thinking. Others have developed their coaching skills through life experience. Even the best talents, however, can benefit from formal training and mentoring—followed by years of practice, more training, and more mentoring to improve mastery. Learning and growth for evocative coaches never stops. Just as for teachers, it is a lifelong journey. Once we have inquired into our own coaching practice, we can use the same design thinking process for our own professional development that we use to evoke and support the professional development of teachers.

1. Frame an evocative aspiration of who we are and how we work as a coach.
2. Identify near-term possibilities that support that aspiration.
3. Brainstorm ideas for realizing those outcomes. Be creative! Go for quantity, not quality.
4. Select the top three ideas that would strengthen our coaching presence and practice.
5. Design a S-M-A-R-T awareness and/or behavior-change experiment around one of those ideas.
6. Use the Experimental Design Template (refer to Figure 6.2) to clarify and document the details of the experiment.

7. Explore and modify both personal and professional environments so they support the experiment.
8. Conduct the experiment.
9. Collect data through notes, written debriefs, recordings, and/or feedback.
10. Reflect and report on the experiment, with reference to the data, through deliberation, writing in a journal, and/or talking with a mentor coach or coaching colleague.
11. Notice the feelings and needs stimulated by the experiment.
12. Inquire into strengths and vitalities that can be built on in the future.
13. Design new experiments based upon past experiments.
14. Select a new possibility to work with when we are ready to go around again.

Coaches can continue to build our skills by reading books on coaching. Many of the references in this book represent excellent resources for coaching; at the end we make recommendations for further reading around specific concepts introduced in this book. Attending workshops and conferences on coaching, including events sponsored by professional education and coaching associations, is another good way to continue our learning and growth. Some of those events may give special attention to coaching in schools as it relates to specific subject areas (e.g., reading or math), levels of schooling (elementary, middle, or high), or particular coaching philosophies and programs. Coach training programs are also available, including one specifically designed for evocative coaching (for more information, see www.EvocativeCoaching.com).

Professional Coach Code of Ethics

Because the work that coaches do with people may place teachers and other coachees in a vulnerable position, the coaching profession is guided by a set of professional ethics (Williams & Anderson, 2006). The field of coaching is self-governing and a number of coaching organizations have articulated standards and ethical codes of conduct. Two of the best known are the International Coach Federation (www.coachfederation.org) and the International Association of Coaching (www.certifiedcoach.org). In its code of ethics, the International Coach Federation (2008a) defines coaching as "partnering with clients in a thought-provoking and creative process that inspires them to maximize their personal and professional potential." The model of coaching presented in this book certainly reflects that definition. Elsewhere, the International Association of Coaching (2003) notes that coaches are expected to "maintain high standards of competence" in our work and to "uphold standards of ethical conduct that reflect well on the individual coach as well as the profession at large." To that end, evocative coaches are expected to uphold the following minimum standards of conduct and practice, adapted from IAC and ICF ethical codes:

1. Coaches will carefully explain and strive to ensure that, prior to or at the initial meeting, teachers understand the nature of coaching, the nature and limits of confidentiality, and any other terms of the coaching agreement or contract.

2. Coaches will always act with integrity and represent ourselves in an honest and fair manner, being cognizant of our particular competencies and limitations.

3. Trust and responsibility are at the heart of the coaching profession. It is expected that coaches will treat teachers with dignity and respect, being aware of cultural differences and the teacher's right to autonomy, privacy, and confidentiality.

4. Coaches do not knowingly engage in behavior that is harassing or demeaning to persons with whom we interact in our work.

5. Because coaches' professional judgments and actions may affect the lives of others, we are alert to and guard against personal, financial, social, organizational, or political factors that might lead to misuse of our influence.

6. It is recommended that coaches appropriately document our work in order to facilitate provision of services later by us or by other professionals, to ensure accountability, and to meet other legal requirements or agreements.

7. Coaches maintain confidentiality when creating, storing, accessing, transferring, and disposing of records under our authority in accordance with professional standards and any applicable laws and agreements.

8. Coaches take precautions to ensure and maintain the confidentiality of information communicated through the use of telephone, voice mail, computers, e-mail, instant messaging, facsimile machines, and other information technology sources.

9. Coaches do not share confidential information with others without obtaining the prior consent of the teacher or unless the disclosure cannot be avoided. Furthermore, coaches share information only to the extent necessary to achieve the purposes of the consultation. Coaches inform teachers about such disclosures and review their possible ramifications.

10. Coaches must notify the appropriate authorities if teachers disclose that they intend to harm or endanger, or that they are harming or endangering, themselves or others.

11. Coaches will respect the teacher's right to terminate the coaching relationship at any point during the process, subject to the provisions of the agreement

or contract. Coaches will be alert to indications that the teacher is no longer benefiting from our coaching relationship and will discuss with the teacher terminating the relationship on that basis, including appropriate referrals to other coaches or professional services.

Conclusion

The teacher-centered, no-fault, strengths-based approach to coaching presented in this book is not universally practiced by the coaching profession. Some take the "tough love" approach of telling teachers what they're doing wrong and how they need to shape up. Others prefer to train and incentivize teachers to adopt new ways of doing things with evidence-based curricula and methods. Evocative coaching, however, seeks to facilitate self-directed learning based upon the inherent interests and abilities of individual teachers. We yearn for teachers to discover and freely choose to use the methods and approaches that work best for their students, in response to the Story–Empathy–Inquiry–Design process we have described in this book. Then, and only then, will those methods come alive and take root for individual teachers. Then, and only then, will we have called forth motivation and movement in teachers, through our conversations and way of being with them, so they achieve desired outcomes and enhance their quality of life.

Judy was a seasoned special education teacher. She'd been teaching for more than forty years and was getting ready to retire. She'd been teaching as long as I've been alive! She was scared to death of technology but she came to me because if it was something that could help her students, she wanted to learn it. I started by assuring her that I would be there beside her every step of the way and that we would start exactly where she was at. I spent a lot of time one-on-one with her, and when she was in group trainings I would make sure to position myself close to her to offer support. I let her know that I don't know everything. I'd let her watch me make mistakes and recover. I started by asking her to tell me about a student she was not getting through to. And then I'd help her design something to meet that student's needs. Once she saw the success with her students, she was sold. She started coming up with projects on her own and bringing them to me, saying, "Look what I did!"

Nancy, technology integration coach

The stories we've heard from coaches who have implemented this philosophy persuade us that we are on the right track. Story–Empathy–Inquiry–Design is not only an easy flow to remember, it is a powerful model for facilitating learning, growth, and change. The best curricula and methods in the world mean nothing if teachers are not interested in using and mastering them. That desire, as well as the confidence that it is doable, must be awakened from within. It cannot be imposed. It cannot be mandated. And it cannot be reduced to a one-size-fits-all rollout. It must be appropriated, practiced, tweaked, and developed one teacher and one conversation at a time.

We have seen how evocative coaching conversations can make teachers come alive in just this way. We have witnessed how Story–Empathy–Inquiry–Design can become a tool for making all the other tools work. Yet this easy-to-remember formula takes a lifetime to master. We are so much more accustomed to giving advice and promoting ideas, and we think of that as being so much more efficient, that even the thought of doing otherwise can be unsettling. Yet the evocative coaching model promises to be both more effective and more efficient in the long run. It enables teachers to engage fully in their developmental paths and to take quantum leaps forward in their professional masteries. By exploring motivation and facilitating movement, by building trust, understanding feelings, identifying strengths, observing vitalities, crafting visions, brainstorming ideas, and designing experiments, evocative coaches assist teachers to become the professionals they always hoped to be.

In order to do that, evocative coaches leverage the secret sauce of connection, generosity, and joy. Without these qualities, coaching is just hard work that everyone dreads. With these, coaching becomes a welcome respite in the pressure cooker of daily requirements. When teachers look forward to coaching conversations, when they see them as stimulating opportunities to reflect on their experiences, to share their feelings, to meet their needs, and to generate new ideas for moving forward, then coaching has found its rightful place in the learning community.

That is our hope for both evocative coaching and the educational landscape. We want to improve instruction and to transform schools, one conversation at a time. When trust becomes the hallmark of individual coaching relationships, it has the potential to spill over and to make life more wonderful for entire teams, departments, schools, and districts. When people experience the power of Story–Empathy–Inquiry–Design to promote their own personal and professional growth, they gain the energy as well as the wisdom to apply those practices in their classrooms and in their workplace relationships. The dynamics begin to radiate out and spiral around as people aspire to new heights and celebrate small victories along the way. This is the opportunity we have as evocative coaches: reconnecting ourselves and other educators in the noble work of making a positive difference in the lives of our students, families, and communities.

Questions for Reflection and Discussion

1. Recall and tell a story about a wonderful experience you had in coaching some-one, a time when you felt really pleased by the quality of the connection and what grew out of your work together.

2. What practices assist you to maintain a "nonjudgmental awareness of what is happening in the present moment"? How often do you do them?

3. What helps you to offer yourself empathy? How does that relate to coaching? How are you feeling right now? Have you noticed an improvement in your capacity to articulate your feelings as you have practiced self-empathy?

4. What needs have been met as you have read this book and engaged with the ideas it presents? What feelings have been stimulated?

5. What are your preferred strategies for reflection? Do you like to keep a journal, converse with a mentor coach, take time for silence, or do something else? Describe how you might strengthen your current practices.

6. What self-observations would you consider using in your own professional development as a coach? What would you like to learn? Which coaching behaviors come most naturally to you? Which ones are most challenging? How can you play more to your strengths in coaching?

7. Consider each of these questions:
   - On a scale of 0 to 10, how willing are you to implement the evocative coach-ing model? What led you to pick that number?
   - On a scale of 0 to 10, how important would you say it is for you to implement the evocative coaching model? Why didn't you pick a lower number?
   - On a scale of 0 to 10, how confident are you that you can implement the evocative coaching model? What would it take to make that number higher?

8. What is one action-learning experiment that you would like to conduct to strengthen your presence and practice as an evocative coach in the next month?

EVOCATIVE COACHING PRINCIPLES, QUESTIONS, AND REFLECTIONS

Evocative Coaching Principles

Adult Learning Principles Relevant to Evocative Coaching

- Adults are autonomous and self-directed.
- Adult learning builds on a wide variety of previous experiences, knowledge, mental models, self-direction, interests, resources, and competencies.
- Adults are relevancy oriented. They must see a reason for learning something, often connected to the developmental tasks of their social roles.
- Adults are solution focused. Instead of being interested in knowledge for its own sake, adult learning seeks immediate application and problem solving.
- Adult learning needs to be facilitated rather than directed. Adults want to be treated as equals and shown respect both for what they know and how they prefer to learn.
- Adults need specific, behavioral feedback that is free of evaluative or judgmental opinions.
- Adults need follow-up support to continue and to advance their learning over time.

Humanistic Psychology Principles Relevant to Evocative Coaching

- People are inherently creative and capable.
- The human brain is hardwired to enjoy novelty and growth, which leads to an inherent joy of learning.
- Learning takes place when people actively take responsibility for constructing meaning from their experience (either confirming or changing what they already know).
- The meanings people construct determine the actions they take.
- Every person is unique, and yet all people have the same universal needs.
- Empathy, mutuality, and connection make people more cooperative and open people up to change.
- "People don't resist change; they resist being changed" (Borwick, 1969, p. 20).
- The more people know about their values, strengths, resources, and abilities, the stronger their motivation and the more effective their changes will be.

Principles of Evocative Coaching Presence

- Give teachers our full, undivided attention.
- Accept and meet teachers where they are right now, without making them wrong.
- Ask and trust teachers to take charge of their own learning and growth.
- Ensure that teachers are talking more than we are.
- Enable teachers to appreciate the positive value of their own experiences.
- Harness the strengths teachers have to meet challenges and overcome obstacles.
- Reframe difficulties and challenges as opportunities to learn and grow.
- Invite teachers to discover possibilities and find answers for themselves.
- Dialogue with teachers regarding their higher purposes for teaching.
- Uncover teachers' natural impulse to engage with colleagues and students.
- Assist teachers to draw up a personal blueprint for professional mastery.
- Support teachers in brainstorming and trying new ways of doing things.
- Maintain an upbeat, energetic, and positive attitude at all times.
- Collaborate with teachers to design and conduct appropriate learning experiments.
- Enable teachers to build supportive environments and teams.
- Use humor to lighten the load.
- Inspire and challenge teachers to go beyond what they would do alone.

The Two Turns, Four Steps, Eight Movements, and Sixteen Style Points of Evocative Coaching

TABLE AA.1   THE EVOCATIVE COACHING DANCE

Loop I: The No-Fault Turn	Loop II: The Strengths-Building Turn
Step 1: Story Listening	**Step 3: Appreciative Inquiry**
1. Initiate	*4. Appreciate*
i. Establishing rapport	viii. Discovering strengths
ii. Appreciative questions	ix. Observing vitalities
iii. Attentive listening	*5. Extrapolate*
2. Elaborate	x. Framing Aspirations
iv. Exploring stories	xi. Inviting Possibilities
Step 2: Expressing Empathy	**Step 4: Design Thinking**
3. Validate	*6. Innovate*
v. Offering reflections	xii. Brainstorming ideas
vi. Celebrating progress	*7. Deliberate*
vii. Clarifying focus in the learning brief	xiii. Designing experiments
	xiv. Aligning environments
	8. Activate
	xv. Confirming commitment
	xvi. Session feedback

Story Listening Principles, Questions, and Reflections

- The map is not the territory; the story is not the experience.
- Stories help people make sense of experience and move people to action.
- The questions we ask determine the stories we hear.
- Mindful listening means listening with calm energy, an open mind, and focused attention.
- Silence encourages teachers to think deeply and understand themselves more fully.
- Reflections help teachers to see themselves in a new light.

1. Initiate

Opening, Energy Questions

- How would you describe your energy right now, on a scale of 0 to 10?
- What three adjectives might describe how you're feeling right now?
- What's especially present for you in this moment?
- How would you describe your mood right now?
- What color might capture how you feel right now?
- What's on your mind right now?
- How are you showing up for this coaching session?
- What is stirring inside you?
- What song could be the theme song for your day?
- What object can you see that reflects how you are right now?
- What physical sensations are you most aware of right now?
- What's alive for you right now?

2. Elaborate

"How did you grow?" Story Invitations

- Tell me the story of how you came to be a teacher.
- Tell me the story of how you came to take on this particular teaching assignment.
- Tell me a story that illustrates what has been working well for you.
- Tell me a story about a time when you handled a tough situation well.
- Tell me a story about a time when you made a real contribution.
- Tell me a story that illustrates what you love most about your work.
- Tell me a story about a time when you had a lot of fun in the classroom.
- Tell me a story about a time when you felt strongly connected to one of your students.
- Tell me a story that illustrates how your values come through in your teaching.
- Tell me a story about an experience in the classroom that taught you a valuable lesson.
- Tell me a story about a time when you felt respected and honored as a teacher.
- Tell me a story about a time when you tried something new.
- Tell me a story of a time when your lesson plan went surprisingly well.
- Tell me a story that illustrates what helps you to do your very best.
- Tell me a story from your first year of teaching and an insight that emerged from that.

Listening for Attributions

- What is the overarching theme? Does it lie more with danger or opportunity?
- Where is the locus of control? Does it lie more with the teacher or with others?
- How is the problem defined? Does it use more enemy or ally images?
- What is the language of capacity? Does it lie more with skills or resources?
- How is the objective defined? Does it lie more with metrics or morale?
- What is happening with energy? Is it emptying out or filling up?
- What is happening with values? Are they being honored or compromised?
- What is happening with needs? Are they being met, denied, or sacrificed?

Listening for Story Variants

- Imagine vantage points: "Who else?" How might others tell this story?
- Imagine pivot points: "How else?" How might things have gone if you had done something different?
- Imagine lesson points: "What else?" What other lessons can this story teach us?

Expressing Empathy Principles, Questions, and Reflections

- Enable teachers to compassionately reflect on their own experiences.
- Read, respect, and work with teachers' emotions as guideposts to their truth.
- Offer "empathy reflections" or "empathy guesses" to see if we understand teacher feelings and needs.
- Seek to connect rather than to correct.
- Get comfortable with "messy" feelings; don't rush teachers when they feel ambivalent or stuck.
- Communicate confidence in teacher capacities and respect for teacher intentions.

3. Validate

Expressing Empathy with Nonviolent Communication

- Distinguish observations from evaluations.
- Distinguish feelings from judgmental thoughts.
- Distinguish underlying, universal needs from particular strategies.
- Distinguish requests from demands to facilitate connection and action.

Avoid Communication Patterns That Are Incompatible with Expressing Empathy

- Moralistic judgments: "What a terrible thing to do!"
- Diagnostic labels: "You must have ADHD."
- Enemy images: "You'd better watch yourself, he's out to get you."
- Guilt trips: "You should have known better—look at the mess you've made!"
- Making demands: "You don't have a choice. Do it or else!"
- Denying choice or responsibility: "There was nothing you could have done."
- Rewards and punishments: "If you do this, you'll be in big trouble."
- Making comparisons: "If you were just more like _____."
- One-upping: "That's nothing; wait till you hear what happened to me."

Limit Communication Patterns That Interfere with Expressing Empathy

- Advising or problem solving: "Let me tell you how I think you should handle this."
- Commiserating: "Oh, you poor thing."
- Consoling or reassuring: "There now, it'll be all right."
- Correcting: "That's not how it happened."
- Educating: "This could turn into a very positive experience for you if you just . . ."
- Explaining: "I would have come by, but . . ."
- Interrogating: "How long has this been going on?"
- Prodding: "Cheer up. Get over it. It's time to move on."
- Stepping over: "Well, let's not talk about that just now."
- Storytelling: "That reminds me of the time . . ."

Appreciative Inquiry Principles, Questions, and Reflections

Parameters of the Learning Brief

- What is the learning focus . . .
  - Of the entire coaching relationship?
  - In a particular topic or subject area?
  - Of any given coaching conversation?
  - What are the benchmarks for measuring progress?
  - What are the objectives to be realized

- How will the coach and teacher work together?
  - What is the role of the coach?
  - What is expected of the teacher?
  - How will conversations take place?
  - Who will initiate what?
  - How will observations be arranged?
  - How long will the relationship last?

4. Appreciate

- Discover and celebrate the best of what is.

Generic Appreciative Interview Protocol

1. *Best experiences.* "Tell me about your best teaching experience, a time when you felt most alive and engaged. What made it so rewarding? Who was involved? How did students learn? Describe the experience in detail."
2. *Core values.* "Tell me about the things you value most deeply, things about yourself, your relationships, and your work. Who are you when you are at your best?"
3. *Generative conditions.* "Tell me about the core, life-giving factors in your experience. What are the key ingredients, both internal and external, that enable you to be at your best and to have fun?"
4. *Three wishes.* "Tell me about your hopes and dreams for the future. If you could make any three wishes for your teaching career come true, what would they be?"

Appreciative Questions to Build Energy and Enthusiasm for Change

- What was the best part of this experience? What else?
- What stands out for you as a shining success? What else?
- What can you celebrate about what happened here? What else?
- Who do you remember as being particularly engaged? What was happening at the time?
- What values are reflected in how you handled this lesson? What else?
- How did this lesson connect with your sense of purpose? How else?
- What needs did this lesson meet for you? What else?
- What needs did this lesson meet for your students? What else?
- What enabled this lesson to be as successful as it was? What else?
- When did you feel most comfortable and confident? When else?
- What things did you have in place that helped you to be successful? What else?
- What could assist you to be even more successful the next time? What else?

Appreciative Questions to Reframe Difficult or Trying Experiences

- Tell me how you got through this and what's possible now.
- What did you try that worked, even if only a little bit?
- How did this experience contribute to your development?
- What's the silver lining here?
- When, if ever, did things start to go better and look up?
- How else might you describe this situation?
- What did you learn about yourself and your values today?
- What did you learn about your students?
- What was the best thing you did in this situation, no matter how small?
- What values did you hold true to even though it was a tough class?
- How did you manage to keep things from getting any worse?

5. Extrapolate

- Imagine and invoke the best of what might be.

Appreciative Questions That Frame Aspirations

- Values: "What are your principles? What do you stand for?"
- Outcomes: "What do you need? What do you want?"
- Strengths: "What are you good at? What makes you feel strong?"
- Behaviors: "What activities do you aspire to do consistently?"
- Motivators: "Why does this matter a lot to you, right now?"
- Environments: "What support team and structures will facilitate success?"

Framing Aspirations as Provocative Possibilities

- Grounded: Building on the best of current reality
- Daring: Boldly stretching the status quo
- Positive: Reflecting what we want to move toward, not away from
- Palpable: Sensing the future in the present, as if it was already happening
- Participatory: Involving all relevant stakeholders

Appreciative Questions That Invite Possibilities

- What would you like to pay more attention to in your classroom?
- What variables do you think matter most?
- What possibilities do you see for yourself in the next few months?

- What changes do you think your students would really appreciate?
- What commitments have you made to yourself?
- What things can you imagine doing differently?
- What would you like to see more of in your classroom?
- How could your needs and the needs of your students be more fully met?
- How might your teaching be different a few months from now?
- What do you believe is possible?
- What things are most important to you right now? In life? In work?
- What would you like more of in your life? How is that linked to your teaching?
- What kind of environment would you like to create for your students?
- What changes would excite you and make you feel great?
- How would you describe your intentions over the next few months?
- What would your life be like if you realized those intentions? How would that feel?
- What has worked for you in other settings that you can draw on in this situation?
- What are the best things that could happen in your classroom in the near future?
- What changes would you like to experiment with in your teaching?
- What do you think are the best possible outcomes of our work together?

Appreciative Questions to Move Through Ambivalence

- How do you see the possibilities before you? How else do you see them?
- What choices are you facing? How else would describe those choices?
- Where do you feel the possibilities in your body? What can you learn from that?
- Who could you talk with about your quandary? Who else could you talk with?
- What do you know for sure about your options? What don't you know?
- How do you know what you know about the possibilities before you? How could you test what you know?
- What needs are you trying to meet? What else? What else?
- What values would you honor by going one direction? By going another? And another?
- What benefits do you see to one course of action? To another? And another?
- What concerns do you have regarding one possibility? Regarding another? And another?
- What strengths would be called upon if you went one way? If you went the other?
- How do you feel when you contemplate going one way? Going another way?
- On a scale of 0 to 10, how valid are the reasons for doing one thing? For doing another?
- On a scale of 0 to 10, how good do you feel when you think about the reasons for doing one thing? For doing another?

Design Thinking Principles, Questions, and Reflections

- Innovation = Inspiration + Ideation + Implementation
- Invite teachers to co-create new possibilities through brainstorming.
- Make clear that our ideas are not prescriptions to be followed but options to be considered (among many others).
- Assist teachers to choose possibilities they find intrinsically interesting and valuable.
- Approach teachers as the decision makers at all times.
- Harness teacher strengths to meet challenges and overcome obstacles.
- Design awareness and/or behavior-change experiments as appropriate.
- Be sure learning experiments have a high probability of success.
- Play with "homework" in a no-fault zone.
- Enable teachers to build supportive environments and teams.

6. Innovate

Basic Protocols for Brainstorming

- Set a minimum number of possibilities to generate.
- Set a time limit to keep things moving rapidly.
- Withhold judgment or evaluation of possibilities.
- Encourage wild and exaggerated possibilities.
- Let no possibility go unsaid.
- Build on the possibilities put forth by others.
- Combine and expand possibilities.
- Go for quantity rather than quality.

Seven Secrets for Better Brainstorming (adapted from Kelley, 2001, pp. 56–62)

1. *Sharpen the focus*. Edgy is better than fuzzy. Clarify and focus the topic on what you are trying to accomplish with the end user—in this case, the students themselves. Focusing on the needs of students will generate more and better ideas than focusing on what teachers need to learn.

2. *Set playful rules*. Don't start to critique, evaluate, or debate ideas until the brainstorming session is done. Bold, wild, and exaggerated ideas are all encouraged in brainstorming.

3. *Number your ideas.* Identify a minimum number of ideas you want to generate and then number them as you go along. Don't be afraid to shoot for big numbers. At IDEO, they report that they can usually come up with at least a hundred ideas in an hour.

4. *Build and jump.* Not every idea has to be unique. Build on each other's ideas. Introduce small variations. Combine and expand on ideas. Or take a jump, either back to something that came before or forward to something new that begins to pop.

5. *Leverage the space.* Write down the flow of ideas in a visible medium and make your notes part of the space. This can be extremely low-tech, using Post-it notes and folders or more high-tech, using laptops and projectors. When people reenter that space and see the notes, they recapture the mindset that emerged in the first place. The space remembers.

6. *Stretch your mental muscles.* Warm up with fast-paced word games or brainstorm something completely off topic, like ten different brands of soda, to get the mind in brainstorming mode.

7. *Get physical.* Good brainstorms are also "bodystorms." Don't just sit there and talk, move around, act out, role play, dramatize, sketch, diagram, point, or do whatever else will stimulate the generation of new ideas.

7. Deliberate

Questions to Prioritize and Choose Ideas

- What ideas stand out as the best ideas?
- What attracts you to them?
- Which ones would push you the most?
- Which ones would be the most fun?
- What would it take to succeed with them?
- What do you hope to learn from them?
- What makes them worth pursuing?
- How do they compare to other approaches?
- How easy would they be to implement?
- What strengths might you leverage?
- What kind of an impact might they have?
- What ideas would never fly at this school?
- What ideas stand a chance?
- When have you tried something like this before?
- Which ones do you want to try first?

Experimental Design Components

- *Ownership*. The teacher's name and the date the experiment was designed.
- *Focus*. Is this more of a professional or personal experiment? Evocative coaching works with both because the two realms impact and interact with each other.
- *Summary of experiment and statement of hypothesis*. In broad strokes, what will she (or he) do and what does she think will result from bringing a new awareness and/or trying a new approach in the classroom? Include theories regarding how the experiment might improve student learning and/or make her own life better.
- *Relevance to personal aspirations/professional standards*. How is the experiment related to a teacher's long-term, big-picture aspirations? How is it related, if at all, to professional standards?
- *Strategies or activities (specific as to what, where, and how)*. Describe the details of the experiment itself. What will the teacher do and where/how will the teacher do it? Be as specific as possible.
- *Supporting systems and resources*. What and who does the teacher want to have on hand in order to conduct the experiment? Again, be as specific possible as to what the teacher requires and how the teacher wants to set up the supporting conditions.
- *Timeline*. When and how often will the experiment take place? If the timeline includes benchmarks or milestones before the next coaching session, make them explicit.
- *Confidence level*. How confident is the teacher, on a scale of 0 to 10, that she will be able to conduct the experiment? Revise the experiment, resources, and/or timeline until the teacher's confidence is 7 or higher.
- *Data collection and reporting*. How will the teacher observe, capture, and report on the results of the experiment? Will the coach be involved? Will the teacher collect her own data? If so, how? Will logs, video/audio recording, and/or reflective writing be used? If so, include any requisite equipment in the space for supporting systems and resources. Will other people provide feedback? If so, how will that information be registered and reviewed?

Environments to Consider When Discussing Alignment

- Classroom environments
- Relational environments
- Cultural environments
- Technology environments
- Financial environments
- Recovery environments

8. Activate

Questions to Confirm Importance, Readiness, and Confidence

- On a scale of 0 to 10, how important would you say it is to conduct this experiment at this time?
- On a scale of 0 to 10, how ready are you to conduct this experiment at this time?
- On a scale of 0 to 10, how confident are you that you will conduct this experiment at this time?

Follow-Up Questions

1. What led you to pick X and not a lower number?
2. What would make it a higher number?

Appreciative Questions for Reviewing Experimental Data

- What went well?
- What did you learn?
- How did the students respond?
- What surprised you?
- What did you like?
- How did you feel before, during, and after the experiment?
- What would you like to build on in the future?

APPENDIX B

PRACTICE EXERCISES

Appendix B includes practice exercises that invite students to practice and reflect on the skills introduced in this book. Instructors who are using this book for a class may want to use these exercises as classroom experiences and homework assignments to enhance student learning. The exercises are designed to bring alive the principles of evocative coaching. Blank copies of the tools and templates in this book are available for download at www.EvocativeCoaching.com.

Chapter 1: What Is Evocative Coaching?

After you read Chapter One, write a coaching platform that puts into words your hopes for yourself as a coach. A coaching platform states clearly and concisely what you consider the purpose of coaching in education to be as well as how you frame your aspirations and view your possibilities for fulfilling that purpose. What are the basic values, beliefs, and ethical standards that will inform your coaching practice? How do you hope to enhance the professional development of the teachers with whom you work?

Chapter 2: Coaching Presence

Arrange to hold a one-on-one conversation with a classmate or professional colleague whom you do not know well about a lesson learned during his (or her) first year of teaching. Request permission to audio record the conversation, explaining that it will be used only for your reflection to support the development of your listening skills and that it will be deleted afterward. Spend a few minutes to develop trust and rapport and then ask your conversation partner to share his experiences, reflections, and lessons learned through her first year in education.

Afterward, listen to the recording to get a sense your coaching presence—of how well you were processing in the moment, staying connected, and facilitating the flow of the conversation. Pay attention to both the words that were being said and to the way they were being said. Notice factors such as pacing, tone, hesitations, silence, energy, level of comfort, and emotional reactions. Listen for evidence of vitality and signs of tension. The following qualities might show up when coaching presence is being fully demonstrated: engagement, lightness, fun, happiness, joy, openness, compassion, trust, co-creation, building on ideas, cross-fertilization, evolution, "Aha's," surprise, curiosity, and/or wonder. The following qualities might show up when coaching presence is not being fully demonstrated: resistance, discomfort, anxiety, pull backs, constrictions, redirects, antagonism, judgments, and/or boredom.

Write a reflective essay about what you noticed and how the things you said and did aligned with the intentions you articulated in your coaching platform. Describe the adjustments you made, if any, during the conversation to mirror your partner's affect, to process signs of discomfort, to draw your partner out, and to keep your partner engaged. What were you pleased with and what would you like to do differently in future conversations?

> Resources: A willing conversation partner, audio-recording equipment, and your coaching platform

Chapter 3: Story Listening

Find a person with whom you can practice storytelling and story listening. Recall and be prepared to share a significant event in your professional practice or personal life that involved at least one other person. When it is your turn to listen, be sure to listen attentively, mindfully, quietly, and reflectively. Create a nonjudgmental coaching space where stories can be told in different ways. Draw your partner out with open-ended questions by asking her (or him) to tell the story three different times, in three different ways:

1. Invite your partner to tell the story as it happened and as she experienced it. Be sure she describes the relevant characters, intent, actions, struggles, and details.

Who was doing what to whom? What was going on? What did your partner learn from the experience?

2. Invite your partner to tell the story again, only this time from the vantage point of one of the other characters. Pause to contemplate what that character experienced and felt. Then invite your partner to role-play the other character and retell the story accordingly. What lessons did that character take away from the experience?

3. Invite your partner to tell the story one more time, only now from a hypothetical perspective. What would have happened had your partner made a different decision at a critical juncture? How might things have turned out differently? Pause to contemplate the critical juncture and the different decision. Retell the story as if it had happened that way.

Change roles and repeat the storytelling/story listening process. After the exercise is complete, engage in a reflective conversation as to what those storytelling and story listening experiences were like. What was the hardest story to tell? What was the easiest? How comfortable did you feel? What new things came to light? What new lessons emerged from the experience that were not identified after the first telling of the story? Complete the exercise by writing a reflective essay on how you might use this technique while coaching teachers in schools. Include reflections on how this technique interfaces with and might serve your coaching platform.

Resources: A willing conversation partner and your coaching platform

Chapter 4: Expressing Empathy

Find a person with whom you can practice expressing empathy. Invite your partner to remember a time when he (or she) received a hard-to-hear message that he would be willing to share. If he can't think of such a time, invite him to recall one of his pet peeves or a time when he felt annoyed with someone. Pause until your partner has a specific example in mind, remembering how he felt at the time and how he still feels about it now. When he is ready, invite your partner to share the story fully.

As your partner shares his story, look for opportunities to distinguish observations from evaluations, feelings from thoughts, needs from strategies, and requests from demands.

1. When you hear an evaluative or demeaning description, be careful not to repeat those assessments. Instead repeat only what was seen or heard. If those

details are missing, you might ask your partner to clarify what a person would have seen or heard if the event was captured on a video.

2. When you hear a causal judgment or "faux feeling" word, you might venture a guess as to the core feelings that were alive for your partner at the time and are alive now.

3. When you hear a strategy for how things should have been done differently, whether back then, now, or in the future, you might venture a guess as to the underlying needs that your partner is trying to meet and value.

4. After you venture your guesses as to your partner's feelings and needs, you might request that your partner describe what he heard you say or share how he feels in response to your guesses. Strive to help your partner feel understood.

Reverse roles so that you can share with your partner in the same way. When both partners have shared fully and feel "complete," debrief the experience with your partner to capture what you learned about yourself and about expressing empathy. Reflect on how this way of sharing and reflecting might be useful in coaching conversations with teachers. When would it be appropriate and helpful? When might it not be? How can empathy become a more regular part of our conversations and a more life-giving part of our lives?

Chapter 5: Appreciative Inquiry

Arrange to visit a teacher's classroom to observe her (or his) teaching and to have a subsequent coaching conversation with that teacher. Inform the teacher that the focus of the observation will be on discovering strengths and noticing vitality: the things she is doing well in the classroom that are facilitating student learning and enjoyment. During the observation, look for signs of full engagement, both on the part of the teacher and the students. Be sure to take note of shining eyes and smiling faces. Capture your observations of vitality with brief but specific notes so that you can share them later with the teacher in the coaching conversation. Do not attempt to script everything that is said and done.

Prior to the start of the coaching conversation, review your notes and prepare yourself to take an appreciative, strengths-based approach. Remember that you are not going to make suggestions as to what the teacher should be doing differently. For this exercise, you are only going to focus on the things that are going well. Notice and set aside any negative judgments that cross your mind. Remember the mantra: "What we appreciate, appreciates."

Get permission from the teacher to record the coaching conversation, explaining that it is only for your own reflection and growth as a coach and will be deleted afterward. Start the conversation with the intention to connect with respect. Learn how the teacher is feeling in the moment with a brief check-in. Build trust and rapport. Before sharing your observations with the teacher, ask her the following, appreciative interview questions:

1. What was your best experience during that lesson, a time when you felt alive, engaged, and happy with what was going on? Describe that moment in detail.
2. What do you value most about teaching and yourself as a teacher? How does that come through in your teaching?
3. When things go well in your classroom, what helps you to be successful? What enables you to be at your very best?

Offer your own strengths-based, classroom observations in ways that confirm and bolster the teacher's answers to the appreciative interview questions. Be sure to note how your observations connect with her core values, inherent ambitions, and generative conditions. Affirm the teacher's competence and thank the teacher for the opportunity to share together.

After the session, as you listen to the recording, reflect on the extent to which you were able to maintain a strengths-based focus and orientation. Were there times when the conversation reverted to focusing on deficits and fixing problems? How did you bring it back around to a discussion of strengths, vitalities, aspirations, and possibilities? Write a reflective essay about the inquiry behaviors you exhibited during the coaching conference, citing specific examples. Compare these behaviors to your stated beliefs in your coaching platform.

Resources: A teacher willing to be observed and to have a coaching conversation afterward, an audio-recording device, and your coaching platform

Chapter 6: Design Thinking

Find some colleagues who are willing to engage with you in a brainstorming session focused on generating new ideas around the following question: "How can teachers respond to an encounter with an irate parent without making the situation worse?" Although you can do this exercise in a dyad with only one colleague, it may be more fun and instructive if you can arrange to work in small groups of six to ten people.

Review the rules of better brainstorming presented in Chapter Six. Remember to avoid critiquing and debating ideas as they emerge. Go for quantity rather than quality. Don't be afraid to put wild and crazy ideas on the table. Build on each other's ideas. If one idea triggers a new or related idea for you, capture it quickly and share it with your brainstorming partner(s). You may want to post some of these rules where you can see them while brainstorming.

Warm up by brainstorming universal need words. Such words appear on the Wheel of Needs in Chapter Four (Figure 4.2) but don't look at the diagram while brainstorming. Just call out as many needs as you can remember or imagine. See how many words you can generate in two minutes' time.

Now turn to the question at hand: "How can teachers respond to an encounter with an irate parent without making the situation worse?" Go back and read the story of Meredith's encounter with an irate dad in Chapter Four (at the end of the section on distinguishing needs). Take a few moments to imagine that you were in Meredith's place. Keep time and give yourself twelve minutes to brainstorm at least twenty-seven ideas that might help Meredith with her situation. See if you can come up with more ideas than that. Groups may want to designate a recorder to write down and number the ideas on a flip chart or they may want to have participants write down their own ideas on Post-it notes or small slips of paper and post them on the walls.

After all the ideas are out on the table, invite each participant to survey the ideas and select the three ideas they like best. If ideas have been posted on the walls, participants can apply three colored sticky-dots or make three distinct marks to register their preferences. Notice patterns of energy and interest. Debrief from the experience together and then write a reflective essay on what you learned from the experience and on how you might use brainstorming in your work with teachers. What kinds of situations lend themselves to brainstorming? How might this process be adapted to one-on-one conversations with teachers following a classroom observation? How else could brainstorming become a part of schools that learn?

Resources: Colleagues willing to brainstorm with you, newsprint, easel pads, markers, and/or Post-it notes, colored sticky-dots, and your coaching platform

Chapter 7: Aligning Environments

Answer the following question in writing with regard to your own professional practice and context. Remember to think about all the elements identified on the Ripples in a Pond diagram in Chapter Seven (Figure 7.1).

What environmental factors, if they were to be better aligned with my professional aspirations, would enhance my ongoing professional development and assist me to experience more energy, enjoyment, and fulfillment at work?

Select one factor that you would like to work on. Work alone or with a partner to brainstorm at least seventeen ideas as to how you might be able to influence or shift that factor in a positive direction. Pick one idea and design an awareness and/or a behavior-change experiment to serve as a field test of your thinking. Map out your experiment using a blank copy of the Experimental Design Template described in Chapter Six (example provided as Figure 6.2). Complete the Template in its entirety, including your confidence level on a scale of 0 to 10. If your confidence level is less than 7, find ways to increase it to 7 or higher either by exploring your feelings and needs or by revising your Design so that it seems more doable. Change roles and repeat the process so that both partners have mapped out an environmental alignment experiment they want to conduct.

Write a reflective essay on what you learned. What worries surfaced for you in the design phase of the process? How did you manage those fears? What surprised you most about how the experience went? What lasting effects, if any, do you think your experiment will have? How can you use this process in your work with teachers to serve your coaching platform?

Resources: A willing conversation partner, brainstorming resources such as newsprint, paper, markers, and/or Post-it notes, your coaching platform and blank copies of the Experimental Design Template

Chapter 8: Coaching Conversations

Arrange to conduct a full coaching cycle with a teacher, including a classroom observation.

1. During your initial meeting, establish trust and rapport through story listening and expressing empathy. Keep listening and reflecting until the teacher communicates he or she feels heard, understood, and ready to move forward. Then, work with the teacher to set a clear learning brief for the observation. In light of that brief, ask the teacher to select a nonevaluative observation tool that aligns with her learning goals (examples provided as Figures 5.2, 5.3, and 5.4). For this exercise, it is required that you select an observation tool *other than* the one used in your school or district for evaluations. Work out the logistics of the observation. Arrange to audio record this session.

2. Conduct the observation, using the observation tool selected by the teacher during the first meeting.

3. Conduct a follow-up coaching conversation to explore teacher strengths and to review the data from the observation. Arrange to video record this session. Be sure to focus on vitalities that celebrate and bring out the teacher's best. Brainstorm and co-create ideas with the teacher as to what she would like to focus on or do differently in the future. Assist the teacher to pick one idea and to design a S-M-A-R-T (Specific, Measurable, Attainable, Relevant, and Time bound) action-learning experiment around that idea. Complete the Experimental Design Template (example provided as Figure 6.2) for the experiment. Schedule a follow-up coaching conversation with the teacher, either face to face or on the telephone, to share stories and move the experience forward.

4. Following the experiment, conduct a third coaching conversation to reflect on lessons learned and changes yet to be made. Design new experiments as appropriate. Audio record this session, using a telephone recording device if the session is done on the telephone.

During the final coaching conference, ask for feedback on the process from the teacher. Useful feedback questions might include:

- What was most valuable part of this coaching process?
- Is there anything you'd like to change about how we did things?
- What suggestions do you have for me as I continue my development as a coach?

You may want to communicate by e-mail after the final coaching session to check in, express gratitude, and encourage continued experimentation. From the recordings, chart your coaching behaviors using the Charting Coach Behaviors Tool (example presented as Figure 9.2). Write a reflective essay based on these data and your experience. Describe your behaviors, the teacher's reaction, and the ways that you were able to adapt your behaviors based on those reactions. Cite specific examples. Compare these behaviors to your stated beliefs in your coaching platform and what you have learned about coaching. In what areas did you feel pleased with your behaviors and in what areas do you see room for further growth? Along with your reflective essay, turn in your completed Charting Coach Behaviors Tool, the observation tool you used in the classroom, and a copy of the completed Experimental Design Template you developed with the teacher.

Resources: A teacher willing to engage in a coaching cycle, audio-recording and video-recording equipment, copies of blank classroom observation tools (examples provided as Figures 5.2, 5.3, and 5.4), blank charting coach behaviors tool (examples provided as Figure 9.2), and your coaching platform

Chapter 9: The Reflective Coach

Through the exercises in this book, you have inquired into, appreciated, and learned more about your coaching presence, strengths, vitalities, and aspirations. Now it is time to imagine the possibilities for becoming an even more evocative coach.

Brainstorm and write out at least seven things you could focus on and do to support your continued growth and development as a coach. Identify one idea that seems particularly interesting and attractive. Make sure it is clearly connected to your coaching platform and long-term learning goals as a coach. Be sure it feels challenging without being overwhelming.

Design an action-learning experiment to field test and explore your idea within the next three months. Map out the experiment using the Experimental Design Template to make sure your design is S-M-A-R-T (Specific, Measurable, Attainable, Relevant, and Time bound). Be sure to describe your rationale for conducting the experiment, the activities or steps you will do, the necessary resources, as well as a timeline with dates and milestones. If you decide to conduct two or more experiments, complete a separate Experimental Design Template for each one.

Write a reflective essay to describe what you learned. How has the experiment contributed to your professional growth? How has your coaching evolved? What new aspirations and possibilities has it awakened and unlocked for you as an evocative coach?

Resources: Blank copies of the Experimental Design Template and your coaching platform

CONTENT REVIEW QUESTIONS

Chapter 1: What Is Evocative Coaching?

1. What are the limitations of the "tell-and-sell" approach as well as "constructive criticism"? What are the benefits of the "listen-and-learn" approach as well as "creative curiosity"?
2. In your own words, how would you define evocative coaching?
3. In what ways does evocative coaching differ from expert advising when it comes to facilitating learning and growth? What concerns, if any, does this shift raise for you?
4. Describe the four steps of the Story–Empathy–Inquiry–Design (S-E-I-D) model of evocative coaching. In what sense do they come together as a dynamic dance?
5. What is the relationship between awareness and action? How can the two work together to promote "natural learning"?
6. What are the five concerns of coaching? How does the S-E-I-D model pay attention to those five concerns differently from traditional models of supervision?

Chapter 2: Coaching Presence

1. How do you understand the following statement? "Evocative coaching cannot be reduced to a tool or technique." What does coaching presence have to do with the coaching process?

2. What are the five facets of trust and how do they relate to coaching?
3. How do coaches establish trust and rapport? Why is this important?
4. How can coaches observe and motivate teachers without interfering or demanding compliance?
5. What dynamics are important for coaches to foster in the coaching space? How can those dynamics be extended in other settings as well?
6. What is meant by the phrase, "My certainty is greater than your doubt"?
7. Why is a judgment-free environment important to coaching? How does it promote learning and growth?
8. Which is more important when it comes to teacher learning and growth: a coach's subject matter expertise or change management expertise? Explain your perspective.

Chapter 3: Story Listening

1. Why do evocative coaches pay so much attention to the stories teachers tell?
2. What are the limitations of "How did it go?" questions? What are the benefits of "How did you grow?" questions?
3. What is the difference between a story and an explanation? What value do you see in each? Why does evocative coaching give story such priority?
4. What's the difference between open-ended and closed-ended questions? How can we ask open-ended questions that generate stories more than explanations?
5. What are three different ways to explore teacher stories? What is the value in doing so?

Chapter 4: Expressing Empathy

1. What are the differences among pity, sympathy, and empathy? How do the first two work against change? How does empathy facilitate change?
2. Name the four access points for empathy identified in this chapter. Why are stories about villains, victims, victors, or vindicators particularly fertile ground for empathy?
3. What are the four distinctions made by Nonviolent Communication for facilitating the communication process?
4. What's the difference between observations and evaluations? How are the former helpful in assisting teachers to reframe their stories and experiences?
5. What's the difference between causal judgments or "faux feelings" and core feelings? How are the latter helpful in assisting teachers to reframe their stories and experiences?

6. What's the difference between universal needs and particular strategies? How are the former helpful in assisting teachers to reframe their stories and experiences?
7. Why do emotions figure so prominently in the behavior change process?

Chapter 5: Appreciative Inquiry

1. What are the five principles of appreciative inquiry and how do they support positive actions and outcomes?
2. What's the difference between inquiry and interrogation? How do evocative coaches avoid coming across as interrogatory?
3. What represents a better strategy for fostering change—building on strengths or fixing weaknesses? Why?
4. Name five appreciative inputs that coaches can work with in developing teacher strengths. Which ones have you most often used in your own work with teachers?
5. What elements go into a learning brief between coaches and teachers? When is the right time to negotiate and clarify such a brief in the context of a coaching relationship?
6. "Ambivalence is a normal part of life." How does this statement relate to evocative coaching?
7. Name five considerations that go into framing aspirations as provocative propositions. How can coaches assist teachers to frame aspirations like that for themselves?

Chapter 6: Design Thinking

1. How would you define teacher self-efficacy? Why is it so important to teacher success?
2. What are the four sources of self-efficacy according to Albert Bandura? How has positive psychology discussed and framed these four sources? Discuss how they are related and how they may be different.
3. What's the difference between generalized compliments and targeted recognitions? How do the latter help to support teacher self-efficacy?
4. What's the difference between eustress and distress? How can coaches assist teachers to get into the "flow" zone?
5. What's the difference between conducting an experiment and implementing a plan? Why is the former so helpful to teacher learning, growth, and change?

6. What sense do you make of the following statement: "People don't learn through 'trial and error' but through 'trial and correction.'"? How can we use that understanding in coaching?

7. What does the S-M-A-R-T acronym stand for, and how is it helpful in designing experiments that work?

8. What are the differences between big picture aspirations and present possibilities? Between present possibilities and S-M-A-R-T experiments? Discuss the role of each in design thinking.

9. How would you describe the difference between awareness and behavior-change experiments? Give an example of each.

10. When teachers ask for advice, what are the limitations, if any, associated with just giving it to them?

Chapter 7: Aligning Environments

1. When rebuilding England at the end of World War II, Winston Churchill said, "We shape our environments and they, in turn, shape us." What did he mean by that? How does that play out when improving teacher performance?

2. How do we keep environments from becoming an excuse as to why teachers cannot make changes or be successful?

3. How would you define school climate? Why is it an important element to pay attention to in coaching?

4. How does collective efficacy facilitate or impede teacher growth?

5. How might coaches and teachers spread the word concerning their work together with other people in their school communities? What difference might this make?

Chapter 8: Coaching Conversations

1. What is the difference between evaluation and coaching? How do they support each other? How do they interfere with each other?

2. Can all teachers benefit from the appreciative approach of evocative coaching? Don't some teachers just need to face the music as to what they are doing wrong? Explain.

3. What do we validate when we express empathy? What is the difference between validation and evaluation?

4. What sense do you make of the following statement: "Things are the way they are for a reason. When teachers don't respond to coaching, that doesn't mean

there's something wrong with the teacher. It means there's something wrong with our coaching."

5. How does expert energy come out in coaching? When is it helpful? When is it hurtful?

6. How can coaches assist teachers to make lifelong learning a satisfying framework and fulfilling experience?

7. Consider the following statement: "Evocative coaching does not depend for its effectiveness upon how much time and structure we have available for a coaching conversation." What do you make of that? Do you really think that's true?

Chapter 9: The Reflective Coach

1. What are the two turns, four steps, eight movements, and sixteen style points of evocative coaching? How do the turns work together to facilitate learning and growth in teachers?

2. What does it mean that evocative coaches take a "teacher-centered, no-fault, strengths-based approach" to facilitating professional development in teachers?

3. Why is it important for coaches to be "reflective practitioners"? What does that mean?

4. How can coaches become more mindful in our daily lives? In our work with teachers?

5. What kinds of feedback are we looking for from teachers regarding our work with them as coaches? How can we best discover things that we can build on and improve?

6. What does confidentiality mean in coaching? How can evocative coaches best involve principals and other supervisors in the coaching process?

7. How could the evocative coaching model become an integral part of everyday conversations in educational communities?

APPENDIX D

THE IAC COACHING
MASTERIES® OVERVIEW

www.CertifiedCoach.org

The purpose of the International Association of Coaching (IAC) Coaching Masteries® is to provide the basis and standards for a truly independent certifying body, without allegiance to any coach training schools or organizations. Through the masteries, the IAC aims to create a vehicle for evaluating effective coaching in the moment. The IAC certification focuses on masterful coaching skills that are observable and can be measured by IAC certifiers during recorded, half-hour sessions with two different clients.

The IAC Coaching Masteries® were developed by an international team of coaches with the aim to produce clear standards and measures for what constitutes the highest level of coaching and that can be understood in any culture around the world. Following is a description of the masteries including the titles, definitions, effects, and key elements. They are reprinted here with permission. A more complete description of the masteries is available to IAC members, including a list of distinctions, effective behaviors, ineffective behaviors, and measures for each mastery.

1. Establishing and Maintaining a Relationship of Trust

Definition: Ensure a safe space and supportive relationship for personal growth, discovery and transformation.

Effect:
1. The client is open to sharing and receiving.
2. The client perceives the coach as a personal advocate.
3. The client sees transformation and growth as manageable.
4. The client has realistic expectations of results and responsibilities of coaching.

Key Elements:
1. Mutual respect and acceptance.
2. Confidence and reassurance.
3. The client feels safe to share fears without judgment from the coach.

2. Perceiving, Affirming and Expanding the Client's Potential

Definition: Recognizes and help the client acknowledge and appreciate his or her strengths and potential.

Effect:
1. The client has greater appreciation of personal capabilities and potential.
2. The client is more willing to take actions beyond current paradigms or strategies.

Key Elements:
1. Being in empathy with the client.
2. Recognizing a wider range of possibilities.
3. Encouraging and empowering the client.
4. Challenging limiting beliefs.
5. Recognizing strengths of client and awareness of where strengths support personal and organizational goals (where appropriate).

3. Engaged Listening

Definition: Give full attention to the words, nuances, and the unspoken meaning of the client's communication; the coach is more deeply aware of the client, his/her concerns and the source of the issue, by listening beyond what the client is able to articulate.

Effect:
1. The client feels understood and validated—not judged.
2. The client communicates more effortlessly and resourcefully.

Key Elements:
1. The coach focuses on what the client expresses, both verbally and nonverbally.
2. The coach listens beyond what the client articulates.
3. The coach is alert to discrepancies between what the client is saying (words) and the client's behavior and/or emotions.

4. Processing in the Present

Definition: Focus full attention on the client, processing information at the level of the mind, body, heart and/or spirit, as appropriate. The coach expands the client's awareness of how to experience thoughts and issues on these various levels, when and as appropriate. The coach utilizes what is happening in the session itself (client's behavior, patterns, emotions, and the relationship between coach and client, etc.) to assist the client toward greater self-awareness and positive, appropriate action.

Effect:
1. The client is free to express and engage with present reality.
2. The client is unencumbered by past or future preoccupations or concerns.
3. The client benefits from coaching insight and support on all levels.
4. The coach is highly attuned to subtle communications from the client.

Key Elements:
1. The coach is aware of the dynamics occurring within the session, within the client, and between coach and client, and understands how the dynamics are affecting the client and the coaching.
2. The coach has a simultaneous and holistic awareness of the client's communications at all levels.
3. The coach is able to discern whether the client is communicating from the past, present, or future.
4. The coach allows the client the opportunity to process and clarify the coach's questions and comments.
5. The coach allows the client the opportunity to process his or her own thoughts and responses.

5. Expressing

Definition: Attention and awareness to how the coach communicates commitment, direction, intent, and ideas—and the effectiveness of this communication.

Effect:
1. The coaching interaction is enhanced with the client being at ease and trusting.
2. The client is open to understand and/or question any communication from the coach.

Key Elements:
1. Respect.
2. Attentiveness.
3. Client-focused.
4. Clarity.
5. Appropriateness.

---

6. Clarifying

Definition: Reduce/eliminate confusion or uncertainty; increase understanding and the confidence of the client.

Effect:
1. The client and the coach move forward in a more directed way.
2. Increased possibilities.
3. Decreased uncertainty.
4. Uncovering the unknown.

Key Elements:
1. Identify the most important issues while respecting client's preferences and limitations.
2. No judgment by the coach, no leading toward a particular destination.
3. Identify key values and needs.
4. Facilitate alignment of purpose, vision, and mission.
5. Identify blocks to progress.

7. Helping the Client Set and Keep Clear Intentions

Definition: Helps the client become or remain focused and working towards intended goals.

Effect:
1. The client feels capable.
2. The client is clear about what he or she wants to accomplish or transform.
3. The client is inspired by the possibilities.
4. The client moves forward purposefully.

Key Elements:
1. Inquiring into the client's intentions and goals.
2. Staying mindful to what is most important.
3. Clarifying direction of progress.
4. Periodically reviewing, revising, and/or celebrating the process and intentions.

8. Inviting Possibility

Definition: Creating an environment that allows ideas, options, and opportunities to emerge.

Effect:
1. The coach enables expansion of thoughts and actions.
2. The client's awareness is expanded.
3. The coach helps client transcend barriers.
4. The client is willing to leave his/her comfort zone.
5. The client has more options.

Key Elements:
1. Trust, openness, curiosity, courage, and recognition of potential.
2. The coach and the client communicate through exploration and discovery.
3. Identify "internal" possibilities (e.g., personal greatness, higher purpose) and "external" possibilities (e.g., resources, memes).
4. Possibilities are generated by the coach, the client, or a collaboration of the two.

9. Helping the Client Create and Use Supportive Systems and Structures

Definition: Helping the client identify and build the relationships, tools, systems, and structures he or she needs to advance and sustain progress.

Effect:
  The client is confident and secure in moving forward, knowing that resources are available or can be created.

Key Elements:
1. The coach suggests possible support systems and structures appropriate to the client's needs.
2. The coach prompts the client to identify support systems and structures the client has but is not utilizing effectively.
3. The coach assists the client to identify areas in which the client feels a need for support and structure.
4. The client understands the value of appropriate support systems.
5. The client's progress toward their goals or intentions is more sustainable.

REFERENCES

Adams, M. (2004). *Change your questions change your life: Seven powerful tools for life and work.* San Francisco: Berrett-Koehler.

Alderfer, C. P. (1972). *Existence, relatedness, and growth: Human needs in organizational settings.* New York: Free Press.

Anderson, L. W., Krathwohl, D. R., Airasian, P. W., Cruikshank, K. A., Mayer, R. E., Pintrich, P. R., Raths, J., & Wittrock, M. C. (Eds.). (2001). *A taxonomy for learning, teaching, and assessing: A revision of Bloom's Taxonomy of Educational Objectives.* Boston: Allyn & Bacon.

Avital, M., & Boland, R. J. (2007). Managing as designing with a positive lens. In M. Avital, R. J. Boland, & D. L. Cooperrider (Eds.), *Advances in appreciative inquiry: Designing information and organizations with a positive lens* (Vol. 2, pp. 3–14). Oxford, UK: Elsevier Science.

Bacon, T. R. (2006). *What people want: A manager's guide to building relationships that work.* Mountain View, CA: Davies-Black.

Baier, A. C. (1994). *Moral prejudices.* Cambridge, MA: Harvard University Press.

Balick, M. J., & Lee, R. (2003). The role of laughter in traditional medicine and its relevance to the clinical setting: Healing with ha! *Alternative Therapies, 9,* 4.

Bandura, A. (1986). *Social foundations of thought and action: A social cognitive theory.* Englewood Cliffs, NJ: Prentice Hall.

Bandura, A. (1994). Self-efficacy. In V. S. Ramachaudran (Ed.), *Encyclopedia of human behavior* (Vol. 4, pp. 71–81). New York: Academic Press. (Reprinted in H. Friedman [Ed.], *Encyclopedia of mental health.* San Diego: Academic Press, 1998).

Bandura, A. (1997). *Self-efficacy: The exercise of control.* New York: W. H. Freeman.

Barkley, S. A. (2005). *Quality teaching in a culture of coaching.* Lanham, MD: Scarecrow Education.

Begley, S. (2007). *Train your mind, change your brain: How a new science reveals our extraordinary potential to transform ourselves.* New York: Ballantine.

Ben-Shahar, T. (2009). *The pursuit of perfect: How to stop chasing perfection and start living a richer, happier life*. New York: McGraw-Hill.

Bennis, W., & Nanus, B. (1985). *Leaders: The strategies for taking charge*. New York: Harper & Row.

Block, P. (2002). *The answer to how is yes: Acting on what matters*. San Francisco: Berrett-Koehler.

Bohm, D. (1996). *On dialogue*. London, UK: Routledge.

Borwick, I. (1969, January). Team improvement laboratory. *Personnel Journal*, 18–24.

Brown, M. H. (1990). Defining stories in organizations: Characteristic and functions. In J. Anderson (Ed.), *Communication yearbook* (Vol. 13, pp. 162–190). Newbury Park, CA: Sage.

Brown, T. (2008). Design thinking. *Harvard Business Review*, June 2008, 1–9.

Brown, T. (2009). *Change by design: How design thinking transforms organizations and inspires innovation*. New York: HarperCollins.

Brown, T. (2010). Why we all need more design thinking. www.forbes.com/2010/01/14/tim-brown-ideo-leadership-managing-design_print.html (Retrieved 1/29/2010)

Bryk, A. S., & Schneider, B. (2002). *Trust in Schools: A core resource for school improvement*. New York: Russell Sage Foundation.

Buber, M. ([1923]1970). *I and Thou: A new translation, with a prologue and notes by Walter Kaufmann*. New York: Charles Scribner's Sons.

Buck, D. (2006). Become a coach. www.coachville.com/home/html/tjl_connection (Retrieved 12/18/2008)

Buckingham, M. (2007). *Go put your strengths to work: Six powerful steps to achieve outstanding performance*. New York: Free Press.

Bushe, G. (2007). Appreciative Inquiry is not (just) about the positive. *Organization Development Practitioner, 39* (4), 30–35.

Butler, J. K. (1991). Towards understanding and measuring conditions of trust: Evolution of a conditions of trust inventory. *Journal of Management, 17,* 643–663.

Butler, J. K., & Cantrell, R. S. (1984). A behavioral decision theory approach to modeling dyadic trust in superiors and subordinates. *Psychological Reports, 55,* 81–105.

Byham, W. C. (1992). *Zapp! in education: How empowerment can improve the quality of instruction and student and teacher satisfaction*. New York: Fawcett Columbine.

Cameron, J. (1992). *The artist's way: A spiritual path to higher creativity*. New York: Tarcher.

Campbell, P. A., & McMahon, E. M. (1997). *Bio-spirituality: Focusing as a way to grow*. Chicago: Loyola Press.

Cohn, M. A., Fredrickson, B. L., Brown, S. L., Conway, A. M., & Mikels, J. A. (2009). Happiness unpacked: Positive emotions increase life satisfaction by building resilience. *Emotion, 9*(3), 361–368.

Cooperrider, D. L. (2000). Positive image, positive action: The affirmative basis of organizing. In D. L. Cooperrider, P. F. Sorensen Jr., D. Whitney, & T. F. Yaeger (Eds.) *Appreciative inquiry: Rethinking human organization toward a positive theory of change* (pp. 29–53). Champaign, IL: Stipes.

Cooperrider, D. L., & Barrett, F. (2002). An exploration of the spiritual heart of human science inquiry. *Reflections: The SoL Journal, 3* (3), 56–62.

Cooperrider, D. L., & Sekerka, L. E. (2003). Toward a theory of positive organizational change. In K. S. Cameron, J. E. Dutton, & R. E. Quinn (Eds.), *Positive organizational scholarship: Foundations of a new discipline* (pp. 225–240). San Francisco: Berrett-Koehler.

Cooperrider, D. L., & Srivastava, S. (1987). Appreciative inquiry in organizational life. *Research in Organizational Change and Development, 1,* 129–169.

Cooperrider, D. L., & Whitney, D. (2005). *Appreciative inquiry: A positive revolution in change*. San Francisco: Berrett-Koehler.

Costa, A. L., & Garmston, R. J. (2002). *Cognitive coaching: A foundation for renaissance schools.* Norwood, MA: Christopher-Gordon.

Cox, E. (2006). An adult learning approach to coaching. In D. R. Stober & A. M. Grant (Eds.), *Evidence based coaching handbook: Putting best practices to work for your coaches* (pp. 193–217). Hoboken, NJ: Wiley.

Crane, T., & Patrick, L. (2007). *The heart of coaching: Using transformational coaching to create a high-performance culture* (3rd ed.). San Diego: FTA Press.

Csikszentmihalyi, M. (1990). *Flow: The psychology of optimal experience.* New York: Harper & Row.

Csikszentmihalyi, M. (1997). *Finding flow: The psychology of engagement with everyday life.* Cambridge, MA: Basic Books.

Csikszentmihalyi, M. (2000). *Beyond boredom and anxiety.* San Francisco: Jossey-Bass.

d'Ansembourg, T. (2007). *Being genuine: Stop being nice, start being real.* Encintas, CA: PuddleDancer Press.

Dawkins, R. (2006). *The selfish gene* (30th anniv. ed.). New York: Oxford University Press.

De Waal, F. (2006). *Primates and philosophers: How morality evolved.* Princeton, NJ: Princeton University Press.

De Waal, F. (2009). *The age of empathy: Nature's lessons for a kinder society.* New York: Harmony Books.

Deutschman, A. (2007). *Change or die: The three keys to change at work and in life.* New York: HarperCollins.

Domar, A. D., & Dreher, H. (2001). *Self-nurture: Learning to care for yourself as effectively as you care for everyone else.* New York: Penguin.

Drake, D. B. (2008). Thrice upon a time: Narrative structure and psychology as a platform for coaching. In D. B. Drake, D. Brennan, & K. Gørtz, *The philosophy and practice of coaching: Insights and issues for a new era* (51–71). San Francisco: Jossey-Bass.

Elmore, R. F., Peterson, P. L., & McCarthey, S. J. (1996). *Restructuring the classroom: Teaching, learning, and school organization.* San Francisco: Jossey-Bass.

Fortgang, L. B. (2004). *Now what?: Ninety days to a new life direction.* New York: Tarcher/Penguin.

Frankl, V. E. ([1959] 2006). *Man's search for meaning.* Boston: Beacon Press.

Fredrickson, B. L. (2002). Positive emotions. In S. J. Lopez & C. R. Snyder (Eds.), *Handbook of positive psychology* (pp. 120–134). New York: Oxford University Press.

Fredrickson, B. L. (2003). The value of positive emotions: The emerging science of positive psychology is coming to understand why it's good to feel good. *American Scientist, 91,* 330.

Fredrickson, B. L. (2009). *Positivity: Groundbreaking research reveals how to embrace the hidden strength of positive emotions, overcome negativity, and thrive.* New York: Crown.

Freire, P. (2000). *Pedagogy of the oppressed* (30th anniv. ed.). New York: Continuum International.

Fullan, M. (2003). *The moral imperative of school leadership.* Thousand Oaks, CA: Corwin.

Gallwey, W. T. (2000). *The inner game of work.* New York: Random House.

Gallwey, W. T. (2008). *The inner game of tennis: The classic guide to the mental side of peak performance.* New York: Random House.

Gallwey, W. T. (2009). *The inner game of stress: Outsmart life's challenges and fulfill your potential.* New York: Random House.

Garfield, C. A. (1984). *Peak performance: Mental training techniques of the world's greatest athletes.* New York: Warner.

Gendlin, E. T. (1981). *Focusing.* New York: Bantam.

Ginott, H. (1975). *Teacher and child: A book for parents and teachers.* New York: Avon.

Glickman, C. (2002). Foreword. In A. L. Costa & R. J. Garmston, *Cognitive coaching: A foundation for renaissance schools* (pp. xi–xiii). Norwood, MA: Christopher-Gordon.

Glickman, C. D., Gordon, S. P., & Ross-Gordon, J. M. (2009). *SuperVision and instructional leadership: A developmental approach* (8th ed.). Englewood Cliffs, NJ: Prentice Hall.

Goddard, R. D., Hoy, W. K., & Woolfolk Hoy, A. (2000). Collective teacher efficacy: Its meaning, measure, and impact on student achievement. *American Research Journal, 37,* 479–508.

Gonzales, R. (2006). *The embodied spirituality of NVC.* 3 DVD set. Prescott, AZ: Prescott Center for Nonviolent Communication. www.prescottnvc.org/DVD

Gordimer, N. (1976, October 21). Nadine Gordimer: The solitude of a white writer (an interview with Melvyn Bragg). In *The Listener,* 514. Reprinted in N. T. Bazin & M. D. Seymour (1990), *Conversations with Nadine Gordimer* (pp. 73–77). Jackson: University Press of Mississippi.

Gordon, T. (1970). *Parent effectiveness training.* New York: Wyden.

Guskey, T. (1988). Teacher efficacy, self-concept, and attitudes toward the implementation of instructional innovation. *Teaching and Teacher Education, 4*(1), 63–69.

Hall, L. M., & Duval, M. (2004). *Meta-coaching volume I: Coaching change for higher levels of success and transformation.* Clifton, CO: Neuro-Semantics.

Hall, L. M., & Duval, M. (2005). *Meta-coaching volume II: Coaching change for transformational change.* Clifton, CO: Neuro-Semantics.

Hartman, A. (1991). "Words create worlds." *Social Work, 36,* 275–276.

Haven, K. F. (2007). *Story proof: The science behind the startling power of story.* Westport, CT: Libraries Unlimited.

Heath, C., & Heath, D. (2007). *Ideas that stick: Why some ideas survive and others die.* New York: Random House.

Hill, T., & Westbrook, R. (1997). SWOT analysis: It's time for a product recall. *Long Range Planning, 30*(1), 46–52.

Horse whisperer. (2009). http://en.wikipedia.org/wiki/Horse_whispering (Retrieved 2/27/2009)

Howe, R. L. (1993). *The miracle of dialogue.* San Francisco: HarperCollins.

Humphrey, H. H. (2000). *Empathic listening.* http://empathymagic.com/articles/Empathic%20Listening%20'0061.pdf (Retrieved 7/6/2009)

International Association of Coaching. (2003). *IAC ethical principles.* www.certifiedcoach.org/ethics/IACethics.pdf (Retrieved 7/6/2009)

International Association of Coaching. (2009). *IAC coaching masteries® overview.* www.certifiedcoach.org/learningguide/PDFs/IAC_Masteries_Public.pdf (Retrieved 7/6/2009)

International Coach Federation. (2008a). *ICF code of ethics.* www.coachfederation.org/includes/media/docs/Ethics-2009.pdf (Retrieved 7/6/2009)

International Coach Federation. (2008b). *ICF professional coaching core competencies.* www.coachfederation.org/includes/media/docs/CoreCompEnglish.pdf (Retrieved 7/6/2009)

Jaworski, J. (1998). *Synchronicity: The inner path of leadership.* San Francisco: Berrett-Koehler.

Johnson, C. (1999). Metaphor vs. conflation in the acquisition of polysemy: The case of *see.* In M. K. Hiraga, C. Sinha, &. S. Wilcox (Eds.), *Current issues in linguistics theory: Cultural, psychological, and topological issues in cognitive linguistics* (Vol. 153, pp. 155–169). Amsterdam and Philadelphia: John Benjamins.

Jones, D. (2001). *Celebrate what's right with the world.* DVD. St. Paul, MN: Star Thrower Distribution.

Jordan, J. V. (2004a). Relational awareness: transforming disconnection. In J. V. Jordan, M. Walker, & L. M. Hartling (Eds.), *The complexity of connection: Writings from the Stone Center's Jean Baker Miller Training Institute* (pp. 47–63). New York: Guilford.

Jordan, J. V. (2004b). Therapists' authenticity. In J. V. Jordan, M. Walker, & L. M. Hartling (Eds.), *The complexity of connection: Writings from the Stone Center's Jean Baker Miller Training Institute* (pp. 64–89). New York: Guilford.

Jordan, J. V., Walker, M., & Hartling, L. M. (Eds.). (2004). *The complexity of connection: Writings from the Stone Center's Jean Baker Miller Training Institute*. New York: Guilford.

Joseph, S. (2010). The person-centred approach to coaching. In E. Cox, T. Bachkirova, & D. Clutterbuck (Eds.), *The complete handbook of coaching* (pp. 68–79). London, UK: Sage.

Jung, C. G. ([1931]1962). Modern psychology offers a possibility of understanding. In R. Wilhelm, *The secret of the golden flower: A Chinese book of life*. San Diego: Harcourt Harvest.

Kashdan, T. (2009). *Curious? Discover the missing ingredient to a fulfilling life*. New York: HarperCollins.

Kegan, R., & Lahey, L. L. (2009). *Immunity to change: How to overcome it and unlock the potential in yourself and your organization*. Boston: Harvard Business School Press.

Kelley, T. (2001). *The art of innovation: Lessons in creativity from IDEO, America's leading design firm*. New York: Doubleday.

Kelley, T. (2005). *The ten faces of innovation: IDEO's strategies for defeating the devil's advocate and driving creativity through your organization*. New York: Doubleday.

Kelm, J. B. (2005). *Appreciative living: The principles of appreciative inquiry in personal life*. Wake Forest, NC: Venet.

Kirschenbaum, D. (1984). Self regulation and sport psychology: Nurturing an emerging symbiosis. *Journal of Sport Psychology, 8*, 26–34.

Kise, J. A. G. (2006). *Differentiated coaching: A framework for helping teachers change*. Thousand Oaks, CA: Corwin.

Knight, J. (2007). *Instructional coaching: A partnership approach to improving instruction*. Thousand Oaks, CA: Corwin.

Knowles, M. S. (1950). *Informal adult education*. New York: Association Press.

Knowles, M. S. (1990). *The adult learner: A neglected species* (4th ed.). Houston: Gulf.

Knowles, M. S., Holton, E. F., & Swanson, R. A. (2005). *The adult learner: The definitive classic in adult education and human resource development*. Houston: Gulf.

Kohn, A. (1999). *Punished by rewards: The trouble with gold stars, incentive plans, A's, praise, and other bribes*. New York: Houghton Mifflin.

Kramer, R. M., Brewer, M. B., & Hanna, B. A. (1996). Collective trust and collective action: The decision to trust as a social decision. In R. Kramer & T. Tyler (Eds.), *Trust in organizations* (pp. 357–389). Thousand Oaks, CA: Sage.

Langer, E. (2005). *On becoming an artist: Reinventing yourself through mindful creativity*. New York: Ballantine.

LaRoche, L. (1998). *Relax—you may only have a few minutes left: Using the power of humor to overcome stress in your life and work*. New York: Villard.

Lieberman, A. (2005). *The roots of educational change: International Handbook of Educational Change*. Dordrecht, The Netherlands: Springer.

Lindeman, E. (1926). *The meaning of adult education*. New York: New Republic.

Lipton, L., & Wellman, B. (2003). *Mentoring matters: A practical guide to learning-focused relationships*. Sherman, CT: MiraVia.

Loehr, J. (2007). *The power of story: Rewrite your destiny in business and in life*. New York: Free Press.

Loehr, J., & Schwartz, T. (2003). *The power of full engagement: Managing energy, not time, is the key to high performance and personal renewal.* New York: Free Press.

Lynch, J., & Scott, W. (1999). *Running within: A guide to mastering the body-mind-spirit connection for ultimate training and racing.* Champaign, IL: Human Kinetics.

Lyubomirsky, S. (2007). *The how of happiness: A new approach to getting the life you want.* New York: Penguin.

Manske, J., & Manske, J. (2005). *Radical compassion: Integrating Nonviolent Communication.* http://radicalcompassion.squarespace.com/files/handouts (Retrieved 1/28/2010)

Markland, D., Ryan, R. M., Tobin, V. J., & Rollnick, S. (2005). Motivational interviewing and self-determination theory. *Journal of Social and Clinical Psychology, 24,* 6.

Martin, J., Feldman, M., Hatch, M. J., & Sitkin, S. (1983). The uniqueness paradox in organizational stories. *Administrative Science Quarterly, 28,* 438–453.

Martin, R. (2009). *The design of business: Why design thinking is the next competitive advantage.* Boston: Harvard Business School Press.

Maslow, A. H. (1943). A theory of human motivation. *Psychological Review, 50*(4), 370–396.

Maslow, A. H. (1954). *Motivation and personality.* New York: Harper.

Maslow, A. H. (1968). *Toward a psychology of being.* Princeton, NJ: Van Nostrand.

Max-Neef, M. (1992). Development and human needs. In P. Ekins & M. Max-Neef (Eds.), *Real life economics: Understanding wealth creation* (pp. 197–214). New York: Routledge.

McClelland, D. C. (1987). *Human motivation.* New York: Cambridge University Press.

McKee, R. (1997). *Story: Substance, structure, style, and the principles of screenwriting.* New York: HarperCollins.

McKenna, M. C., & Walpole, S. (2008). *The literacy coaching challenge: Models and methods for grades K–8.* New York: Guilford.

Medina, J. (2008). *Brain rules: Twelve principles for surviving and thriving at work, home, and school.* Seattle: Pear Press.

Miller, W. R., & Rollnick, S. (2002). *Motivational interviewing: Preparing people for change* (2nd ed.). New York: Guilford.

Mishra, A. K. (1996). Organizational responses to crisis: The centrality of trust. In R. Kramer & T. Tyler (Eds.), *Trust in organizations* (pp. 261–287). Thousand Oaks, CA: Sage.

Moore, M., & Tschannen-Moran, B. (2010). *Coaching psychology manual.* Philadelphia: Lippincott Williams & Wilkins.

Murray, W. H. (1951). *The Scottish Himalayan expedition.* London, UK: J. M. Dent.

Nakamura, J., & Csikszentmihalyi, M. (2002). The concept of flow. In S. J. Lopez & C. R. Snyder (Eds.), *Handbook of positive psychology* (pp. 89–105). New York: Oxford University Press.

O'Connor, J., & Lages, A. (2007). *How coaching works: The essential guide to the history and practice of effective coaching.* London: A & C Black.

O'Hanlon, B., & Beadle, S. (1997). *A guide to possibility land: Fifty-one methods for doing brief, respectful therapy.* New York: Norton.

Palmer, P. (1998). *The courage to teach: Exploring the inner landscape of a teacher's life.* San Francisco: Jossey-Bass.

Park, N., & Peterson, C. (2009). Strengths of character in schools. In R. Gilman, E. Scott Huebner, & M. J. Furlong (Eds.), *Handbook of positive psychology in schools* (pp. 65–76). New York: Routledge.

Pearsall, P. (1998). *The heart's code: Tapping the wisdom and power of our heart energy.* New York: Broadway Books.

Peirce, P. (1997). *The intuitive way: A guide to living from inner wisdom.* Hillsboro, OR: Beyond Words.

Pervin, L. A. (2003). *The science of personality.* New York: Oxford University Press.

Perry, J. (2005). *Master Coach series vol. 4: The fan club game.* Laguna Hills, CA: CreativeU.

Peterson, C., & Seligman, M.E.P. (2004). *Character strengths and virtues: A handbook and classification.* New York: Oxford University Press.

Pink, D. (2005). *A whole new mind: Moving from the information age to the conceptual age.* New York: Penguin.

Pink, D. (2009). *Drive: The surprising truth about what motivates us.* New York: Penguin.

Preskill, H., & Catsambas, T. T. (2006). *Reframing evaluation through appreciative inquiry.* Thousand Oaks, CA: Sage.

Prochaska, J. O., Norcross, J. C., & DiClemente, C. C. (1994). *Changing for good.* New York: HarperCollins.

Roberts, M. (2002). *Horse sense for people: The man who listens to horses talks to people.* New York: Penguin.

Roberts, M. (2009). *The man who listens to horses: The story of a real-life horse whisperer.* New York: Ballantine.

Rock, D., & Page, L. J. (2009). *Coaching with the brain in mind: Foundations for practice.* Hoboken, NJ: Wiley.

Rogers, C. (1968). *Freedom to learn.* Columbus, OH: Charles E. Merrill.

Rogers, C. (1980). *A way of being.* New York: Houghton Mifflin.

Rogers, C. (1989). *On becoming a person: A therapist's view of psychotherapy.* New York: Mariner Books.

Rogers, C., & Farson, R. E. (1957). *Active listening.* Chicago: University of Chicago Industrial Relations Center. www.gordontraining.com/artman2/uploads/1/ActiveListening_RogersFarson.pdf (Retrieved 6/5/2009)

Rosenberg, M. B. (2005). *Nonviolent communication: A language of life.* Encinitas, CA: PuddleDancer Press. www.cnvc.org

Rosenthal, R., & Jacobson, L. (2003). *Pygmalion in the classroom: Teacher expectation and pupils' intellectual development.* Norwalk, CT: Crown House.

Ross, J. A. (1992). Teacher efficacy and the effects of coaching on student achievement. *Canadian Journal of Education, 17,* 51–65.

Ruby, P., & Decety, J. (2004). How would you feel versus how do you think she would feel? A neuroimaging study of perspective taking with social emotions. *Neuroscience, 16,* 988–999.

Rumi. (2004). *Rumi: Selected poems.* Trans. by Coleman Barks. New York: Penguin.

Scharmer, C. O. (2007). *Theory U: Leading from the future as it emerges.* Cambridge, MA: Society for Organizational Learning.

Schön, D. A. (1983). *The reflective practitioner: How professionals think in action.* Cambridge, MA: Basic Books.

Scott, S. (2004). *Fierce conversations: Achieving success at work and in life, one conversation at a time.* New York: Berkley Books.

Seashore Louis, K., Kruse, S., & Marks, H. M. (1996). School-wide professional community: Teachers' work, intellectual quality, and commitment. In F. W. Newman & Associates (Eds.), *Authentic achievement: Restructuring schools for intellectual quality* (pp. 179–203). San Francisco: Jossey-Bass.

Secretan, L. (2004). *Inspire! What great leaders do.* Hoboken, NJ: Wiley.

Seligman, M.E.P. (2006). *Learned optimism: How to change your mind and your life*. New York: Pocket.

Senge, P. M. (2006). *The fifth discipline: The art and practice of the learning organization*. New York: Doubleday.

Senge, P. M., Cambron-McCabe, N., Lucas, T., Smith, B., Dutton, J., & Kleiner, K. (2000). *Schools that learn: A fifth discipline fieldbook for educators, parents, and everyone who cares about education*. New York: Doubleday.

Senge, P. M., Scharmer, C. O., Jaworski, J., & Flowers, B. S. (2004). *Presence: An exploration of profound change in people, organizations, and society*. New York: Doubleday.

Shafir, R. Z. (2000). *The Zen of listening: Mindful communication in the age of distraction*. Wheaton, IL: Quest.

Siegel, D. J. (2007). *The mindful brain: Reflection and attunement in the cultivation of well-being*. New York: Norton.

Silberman, J. (2007). *Mindfulness and VIA signature strengths*. http://pos-psych.com/news/jordan-silberman/20070327179 (Retrieved 7/6/2009)

Silsbee, D. (2008). *Presence-based coaching: Cultivating self-generative leaders through mind, body, and heart*. San Francisco: Jossey-Bass.

Stevens, N. (2005). *Learn to coach: The skills you need to coach for personal and professional development*. Oxford, UK: How to Books.

Stober, D. R. (2006). Coaching from the humanistic perspective. In D. R. Stober & A. M. Grant (Eds.), *Evidence based coaching handbook* (pp. 17–50). Hoboken, NJ: Wiley.

Stoll, L., & Seashore Louis, K. S. (Eds.). (2007). *Professional learning communities: Divergence, depth and dilemmas*. Berkshire, UK: Open University Press.

Stone, D., Patton, B., & Heen, S. (1999). *Difficult conversations: How to discuss what matters most*. New York: Penguin.

Sutherland, J., & Stavros, J. (2003, November). The heart of appreciative strategy. *AI Practitioner*. www.aipractitioner.com/Pagefiles/articles_0311.htm (Retrieved 7/6/2009)

Thatchenkery, T., & Metzker, C. (2006). *Appreciative intelligence: Seeing the mighty oak in the acorn*. San Francisco: Berrett-Koehler.

Tschannen-Moran, B. (2010). Skills and performance coaching. In E. Cox, T. Bachkirova, & D. Clutterbuck (Eds.), *The complete handbook of coaching* (pp. 203–216). London, UK: Sage.

Tschannen-Moran, M. (2004). *Trust matters: leadership for successful schools*. San Francisco: Jossey-Bass.

Tschannen-Moran, M. (2009). Fostering teacher professionalism: The role of professional orientation and trust. *Educational Administration Quarterly*, *45*, 217–247.

Tschannen-Moran, M., & Barr, M. (2004). Fostering student achievement: The relationship between collective teacher efficacy and student achievement. *Leadership and Policy in Schools*, *3*, 187–207.

Tschannen-Moran, M., & McMaster, P. (2009). Sources of self-efficacy: four professional development formats and their relationship to self-efficacy and implementation of a new teaching strategy. *Elementary School Journal*, *110*(2), 228–245.

Tschannen-Moran, M., Parish, J., & DiPaola, M. F. (2006). School climate and state standards: How interpersonal relationships influence student achievement. *Journal of School Leadership*, *16*, 386–415.

Tschannen-Moran, M., Woolfolk Hoy, A., & Hoy, W. K. (1998). Teacher efficacy: Its meaning and measure. *Review of Educational Research*, *68*(2), 202–248.

Uline, C., Tschannen-Moran, M., & Perez, L. (2003). Constructive conflict: How controversy can contribute to school improvement. *Teachers College Record*, *105*, 782–815.

Von Oech, R., & Willett, G. (2002). *Expect the unexpected (or you won't find it): A creativity tool based on the ancient wisdom of Heraclitus.* San Francisco: Berrett-Koehler.

Watkins, J. M., & Mohr, B. J. (2001). *Appreciative inquiry: Change at the speed of imagination.* San Francisco: Jossey-Bass/Pfeiffer.

Weick, K. E. (1995). *Sensemaking in organizations.* Thousand Oaks, CA: Sage.

Wheatley, M. J. (1999). *Leadership and the new science.* San Francisco: Berrett-Koehler.

Wheatley, M. J. (2002). *Turning to one another: Simple conversations to restore hope to the future.* San Francisco: Berrett-Koehler.

Whyte, D. (2001). *Crossing the unknown sea: Work as a pilgrimage of identity.* New York: Riverhead.

Williams, P., & Anderson, S. (2006). *Law and ethics in coaching.* Hoboken, NJ: Wiley.

Wooten, P. (1996). Humor an antidote for stress. *Holistic Nursing Practice, 10*(2), 49–55.

Young, S. H. (2006, August 1). Make a goal-friendly environment. *Blog Post.* www.scotthyoung.com/blog/2006/08/01/make-a-goal-friendly-environment (Retrieved 10/7/2009)

Zand, D. E. (1997). *The leadership triad: Knowledge, trust, and power.* New York: Oxford University Press.

Zandee, D. P. (2008). The poetics of organizational design: How words may inspire worlds. In M. Avital, R. J. Boland, & D. L. Cooperrider (Eds.), *Advances in appreciative inquiry: Designing information and organizations with a positive lens* (Vol. 2, pp. 131–146, kindle locations 1599–1807). Oxford, UK: Elsevier Science.

Zander, R., & Zander, B. (2000). *The art of possibility.* New York: Penguin Putnam.

Zeus, P., & Skiffington, S. (2000). *The complete guide to coaching at work.* New York: McGraw-Hill.

Zhang, P. (2007). Toward a positive design theory: Principles for designing motivating information and communicating technology. In M. Avital, R. J. Boland, & D. L. Cooperrider (Eds.), *Advances in appreciative inquiry: Designing information and organizations with a positive lens* (Vol. 2, pp. 45–74, kindle locations 619–1001). Oxford, UK: Elsevier Science.

RECOMMENDED READINGS AND RESOURCES

Coaching Presence

Gallwey, W. T. (2008). *The inner game of tennis: The classic guide to the mental side of peak performance.* New York: Random House.

Roberts, M. (2009). *The man who listens to horses: The story of a real-life horse whisperer.* New York: Ballantine Books.

Silsbee, D. (2008). *Presence-based coaching: Cultivating self-generative leaders through mind, body, and heart.* San Francisco: Jossey-Bass.

Tschannen-Moran, M. (2004). *Trust matters: leadership for successful schools.* San Francisco: Jossey-Bass.

Zander, R., & Zander, B. (2000). *The art of possibility.* New York: Penguin Putnam.

Story Listening

Drake, D. B. (2008). Thrice upon a time: Narrative structure and psychology as a platform for coaching. In: D. B. Drake, D. Brennan, & K. Gørtz, *The philosophy and practice of coaching: Insights and issues for a new era* (51–71). San Francisco: Jossey-Bass.

Gallwey, W. T. (2000). *The inner game of work.* New York: Random House.

Haven, K. F. (2007). *Story proof: The science behind the startling power of story.* Westport, CT: Libraries Unlimited.

Heath, C., & Heath, D. (2007). *Ideas that stick: Why some ideas survive and others die.* New York: Random House.

Expressing Empathy

De Waal, F. (2009). *The age of empathy: Nature's lessons for a kinder society*. New York: Harmony Books.

Hart, S., & Hodson, V. K. (2008). *The no-fault classroom: Tools to resolve conflict and foster relationship intelligence*. Encinitas, CA: PuddleDancer Press. To purchase the No Fault Game, go to: http://www.k-hcommunication.com/nofault.htm

Rosenberg, M. (2005). *Nonviolent communication: A language of life*. Encinitas, CA: PuddleDancer Press.

Rosenberg, M. (2006). *The nonviolent communication training course: Home study course*. Louisville, CO: Sounds True. To purchase the study course, a 9-CD set plus resource materials go to: http://www.amazon.com/exec/obidos/ASIN/1591794439/lifeinc

www.cnvc.org

www.nvcti.org

Appreciative Inquiry

Adams, M. G. (2004). *Change your questions, change your life: Seven powerful tools for life and work*. Mountain View, CA: Davies-Black.

Buckingham, M. (2007). *Go put your strengths to work: Six powerful steps to achieve outstanding performance*. New York: Free Press.

Cooperrider, D. L., & Whitney, D. (2005). *Appreciative inquiry: A positive revolution in change*. San Francisco: Berrett-Koehler.

Orem, S. L., Binkert, J., & Clancy, A. L. (2007). *Appreciative coaching: A positive process for change*. San Francisco: Jossey-Bass/Wiley.

VIA Signature Strengths Questionnaire. www.authentichappiness.sas.upenn.edu

Watkins, J. M., & Mohr, B. J. (2001). *Appreciative inquiry: Change at the speed of imagination*. San Francisco: Jossey-Bass/Pfeiffer.

www.celebrateschools.com

http://appreciativeinquiry.case.edu

Design Thinking

Brown, T. (2009). *Change by design: How design thinking transforms organizations and inspires innovation*. New York: HarperCollins.

Csikszentmihalyi, M. (1997). *Finding flow: The psychology of engagement with everyday life*. Cambridge, MA: Basic Books.

Kegan, R., & Lahey, L. L. (2009). *Immunity to change: How to overcome it and unlock the potential in yourself and your organization*. Boston: Harvard Business School Press.

Kelley, T. (2001). *The art of innovation*. New York: Doubleday.

Rock, D., & Page, L. J. (2009). *Coaching with the brain in mind: Foundations for practice*. Hoboken, NJ: Wiley.

Secretan, L. (2004). *Inspire! What great leaders do*. Hoboken, NJ: Wiley.

http://designthinking.ideo.com

The Reflective Coach

Fredrickson, B. L. (2009). *Positivity: Groundbreaking research reveals how to embrace the hidden strength of positive emotions, overcome negativity, and thrive*. New York: Crown.

International Association of Coaching. (2009). *IAC coaching masteries*® *overview*. Reprinted in Appendix D.

International Coach Federation. (2008b). *ICF professional coaching core competencies*. www.coach-federation.org/includes/media/docs/CoreCompEnglish.pdf (Retrieved on 7/6/2009)

Schön, D. A. (1983). *The reflective practitioner: How professionals think in action*. Cambridge, MA: Basic Books.

Weick, K. E. (1995). *Sensemaking in organizations*. Thousand Oaks, CA: Sage.

ABOUT THE AUTHORS

Bob and Megan Tschannen-Moran bring a unique combination of life experiences, training, and collaboration to the task of writing a book on the coach approach to instructional leadership and performance improvement in schools. Since 1974 they have successfully married their professional and personal lives to enhance and expand the contribution they make in the world.

Bob Tschannen-Moran, IAC-CC, is the president of LifeTrek Coaching International (www.LifeTrekCoaching.com) and president (2010–2011) of the International Association of Coaching (www.CertifiedCoach.org). Bob holds a master of divinity degree from Yale University and has received coach training from Coach U, CoachVille, FastTrack Coaching Academy, and Wellcoaches Coach Training School. Bob is certified as a coach by both the International Association of Coaching (IAC-CC) and Wellcoaches (CWC). He has served on the Wellcoaches faculty since 2004. Using a variety of strengths-based approaches, Bob has assisted many individuals and organizations, including schools, congregations, and corporations, to build positive relationships and achieve positive results. Bob writes and edits *LifeTrek Provisions*, a weekly electronic newsletter with some 20,000 subscribers in 152 countries, and is a sought-after public speaker and workshop facilitator. He coauthored a *Coaching Psychology Manual* with Margaret Moore (2010, Lippincott Williams & Wilkins) and contributed a book chapter on Skills and Performance Coaching to *The Complete Handbook of Coaching* (2010, Sage). Before founding LifeTrek

Coaching in 1998, Bob served as a United Church of Christ pastor for twenty years (coach@lifetrekcoaching.com).

Megan Tschannen-Moran, PhD, is a professor of educational leadership at the College of William & Mary in Williamsburg, Virginia. Her research interests focus on the social psychology of schools, examining the quality of interpersonal relationships and how these affect the outcomes a school can achieve. In this regard, she has studied the constructs of trust, collaboration, organizational citizenship, and school climate. Her book *Trust Matters: Leadership for Successful Schools* (2004, Jossey-Bass) reports the experience of three principals and the consequences of their successes and failures to build trust. In 2009, Megan served as the guest editor of a special issue of *Education Administration Quarterly* devoted to research on trust in schools. Megan's research interests also focus on the self-efficacy beliefs of teachers and principals as well as the collective beliefs of school faculties regarding their capability to foster the learning of all the school's students. Megan has published more than forty scholarly articles and book chapters, presents frequently at conferences, and consults regularly with school systems and leaders. She earned her doctorate in educational leadership at The Ohio State University and her bachelor's degree at Northwestern University (mxtsch@wm.edu).

Building on the research and method of this book, Bob and Megan oversee a coach-training program for instructional coaches, school leaders, and other educators tasked with the responsibility of improving teacher performance and school quality. The program utilizes advanced bridgeline and Internet technologies to create a virtual classroom that is easy for anyone to access with a telephone. Educators on three continents have experienced and helped to shape this dynamic training initiative. For more information or to sign up, write info@EvocativeCoaching.com or visit the Center for Evocative Coaching at www.EvocativeCoaching.com.

INDEX

Page references followed by *fig* indicate an illustration; followed by *t* indicate a table.